ENVIRONMENT AND SOCIETY

KIMBERLY K. SMITH, EDITOR

THE GREEN YEARS, 1964–1976

The Green Years, 1964–1976

When Democrats and Republicans United to Repair the Earth

Gregg Coodley and David Sarasohn

with a Foreword by Senator Ron Wyden

 UNIVERSITY PRESS OF KANSAS

Published by the University Press of Kansas (Lawrence, Kansas 66045), which was
organized by the Kansas Board of Regents and is operated and funded by Emporia State
University, Fort Hays State University, Kansas State University, Pittsburg State University,
the University of Kansas, and Wichita State University.

Library of Congress Cataloging-in-Publication Data

Names: Coodley, Gregg, author. | Sarasohn, David, author.
Title: The green years, 1964–1976 : when Democrats and Republicans united
  to repair the Earth / Gregg Coodley and David Sarasohn.
Description: Lawrence : University Press of Kansas, 2021. | Series:
  Environment and society | Includes bibliographical references and index.
Identifiers: LCCN 2020048513
  ISBN 9780700632343 (cloth)
  ISBN 9780700632350 (epub)
Subjects: LCSH: Environmental law—United States—History. | Environmental
  policy—United States—History. | United States. Wilderness Act. |
  United States. National Forest Management Act of 1976.
Classification: LCC KF3817 .C655 2021 | DDC 344.7304/609046—dc23
LC record available at https://lccn.loc.gov/2020048513.

British Library Cataloguing-in-Publication Data is available.

Printed in the United States of America
10 9 8 7 6 5 4 3 2 1

The paper used in this publication is acid free and meets the minimum requirements of
the American National Standard for Permanence of Paper for Printed Library Materials
Z39.48–1992.

Dedicated to Sam, Scout, Sarah, David, and Mimi
and
Alex and Peter

Contents

Foreword

Whenever David Sarasohn called to interview me for the *Oregonian*, I knew his head, heart, and hands would produce another powerful column. His head because David always asked thoughtful and incisive questions. His heart because David always brought his passion to reporting and spotlighting injustice. And his hands because David always wrote with the skills of a storytelling craftsman.

I'm thrilled that David again brings all those elements to team up with Gregg Coodley on this book immersing readers in an era when Americans of both political parties partnered to work on cleaning our air and water, preserving our natural treasures, and enhancing recreation opportunities to enjoy the outdoors.

Their book is timely, entertaining, and indispensable.

The Green Years, 1964–1976: When Democrats and Republicans United to Repair the Earth is timely because it clearly lays out for America now how earlier generations came together to pass landmark legislation—the Land and Water Conservation Fund, the Wild and Scenic Rivers Act, the Clean Water Act, the Clean Air Act, and more.

As America marks the fiftieth anniversary of Earth Day facing the urgent challenge of climate change, David and Gregg do not sanitize history by glossing over the extremist opposition that schemed to block environmental gains decades ago.

And in telling this story, David and Gregg give readers a clear blueprint of how to overcome current challenges by learning how these coalitions achieved so much in this significant window from 1964 to 1976.

Their book is entertaining because it brings to life the characters from the national stage like Senators Mark Hatfield, Warren Magnuson, and Henry "Scoop" Jackson, as well as Representatives Jim Weaver and Al Ullman. Any legislator reading about these legislative lions from the Northwest as well as elsewhere is reminded of the adage that our predecessors allow us—when we face the challenges of today—to stand on the shoulders of giants.

And anybody reading *The Green Years* will learn how the leaders from 1964 to 1976 themselves stood on the shoulders of giants in a long environmental history dating back to the state of Massachusetts enacting bird protections more than two centuries ago and the Antiquities Act more than a century ago.

At the same time, David and Gregg take great care to highlight a philosophy of political change that regularly comes up in conversations with Oregonians at my annual town halls in each one of the state's thirty-six counties—namely, that political change often does not start in Washington, DC.

And so their book reminds readers of the huge role played by high school and college students, such as Earth Day coordinator Denis Hayes, and also how even further back, Americans like Henry David Thoreau and John Muir laid the groundwork for the twentieth-century environmental movement by conveying to a larger audience in the nineteenth century their belief in the need to preserve nature.

Traveling around Oregon for my town halls and community meetings, I am eternally grateful whenever I see our state's unmatched rivers, mountains, and woods. And it's with the role models in mind whom David and Gregg have highlighted in their book that I used "river democracy" to collect more than fifteen thousand nominations for rivers and streams in my state that people believe should be added to the national Wild and Scenic Rivers designation list.

Protecting treasures in Oregon or anywhere else in America did not happen by osmosis. It happened because of the many people David and Gregg write about in this history detailing a remarkable era and telling the story of the many people with a purpose who helped to shape those times.

Finally, their book is indispensable because it shows how people and policy prevailed for the common good from 1964 to 1976. And it provides hope for how to replicate in the twenty-first century that twentieth-century world where red-state and blue-state Americans came together to produce a greener America.

The Green Years, 1964–1976: When Democrats and Republicans United to Repair the Earth will be on my bookshelf at home in Portland.

And it will be in my Senate office in Washington, DC, to serve as an essential resource for my staff and me to draw from as the work continues each day to fight climate change and build on the environmental achievements from the exceptional twelve-year era covered so comprehensively and accessibly in this book.

Senator Ron Wyden

Acknowledgments

We would like to thank James Stack, Anne Jenner, and Emily Hughes Dominick at the University of Washington Library Special Collections for their assistance in reviewing the papers of Senators Henry Jackson and Warren Magnuson.

We would like to thank the staff at the Hillsdale Library for their many efforts, as well as the interlibrary program of the Multnomah County Library. We would also like to thank the staff at the Denver Public Library. We also appreciate the assistance of the Lake Oswego Library in providing materials otherwise unavailable. We appreciate the assistance of Sam Coodley in obtaining some of the primary sources.

The technical assistance of Danny Henderson was essential to the production of the book. We want to thank Sarah Pendergraph for her detailed work getting the book into the proper style.

We appreciate the ongoing and extensive feedback as well as continuing encouragement from Lauren Coodley. We also appreciate the suggestions and analysis of Cheryl Coon. We appreciate the suggestions from Nora Coon and the attempts by Maggie Coon to get us access to further accounts of the period. We appreciate the valuable suggestions by Rick Seifert.

We appreciate Barbara Dudley and Michael McCloskey for generously sharing their time and insights. Michael McCloskey was also generous enough to provide additional material in terms of his unpublished writings and analysis.

We want to thank our agent Susan Schulman for all her efforts on our behalf. Our editor, David Congdon, has been a pleasure to work with. His suggestions have immeasurably improved the book. We also appreciate the assistance and creative problem-solving of Kelly Chrisman Jacques, the managing editor of the press, and the excellent work of our copyeditor, Amy Sherman. Once again, Nancy Gerth has created a superb index for our book.

We appreciate the support and encouragement of our wives, Karen Coodley and Lisa Sarasohn, during the many hours we worked on the book.

Major Environmental Advances of the Green Years

1964
Wilderness Act
Land and Water Conservation
    Fund Act
Classification and Multiple Use Act

1965
White House Conference on Natural
    Beauty
Highway Beautification Act
National Historic Preservation Act
Motor Vehicle Air Pollution
    Control Act
Water Quality Act
Solid Waste Disposal Act

1966
Clean Water Restoration Act
Endangered Species Preservation Act

1967
Air Quality Act

1968
Wild and Scenic Rivers Act
Redwood National Park
North Cascades National Park
National Trails System Act
Aircraft Noise Abatement Act

1969
Endangered Species Conservation Act
National Environmental Policy Act
    (signed January 1, 1970); with
    creation of Council on Environ-
    mental Quality

1970
Earth Day
Environmental Protection
    Agency created
Clean Air Act
Environmental Quality Education Act
Water Quality Improvement Act
Resource Recovery Act

1971
Lead Based Paint Poisoning Preven-
    tion Act
Alaska Native Claims Settlement Act

1972
Clean Water Act
Coastal Zone Management Act
Marine Mammal Protection Act
Marine Protection, Research and
    Sanctuaries Act
Environmental Pesticides Control Act
DDT banned in the United States

1973
Endangered Species Act
Environmental Protection Agency
    begins phase-out of leaded gas

1974
Safe Drinking Water Act

1975
Eastern Wilderness Act
Omnibus Wilderness Act

1976
Fisheries Management and Conserva-
    tion Act
Toxic Substances Control Act
Resource Conservation and
    Recovery Act
National Forestry Management Act
Federal Land Policy and
    Management Act

CHAPTER ONE

Earth Day, 1970

It was the largest organized demonstration in human history.

On April 22, 1970, an estimated twenty million Americans—one-tenth of the US population—participated in rallies, marches, teach-ins, and even some actual cleaning up of junk-polluted lands and rivers.[1] Two thousand community groups took part in the first Earth Day, with activities at two thousand colleges and ten thousand schools, and the National Education Association estimated that the festivities included ten million schoolchildren.

At Harris School in Chicago, students picked up litter along the streets and the Lincoln Park lagoon. Fourth grader Kurt Eckhardt told the *Chicago Tribune*, "We picked up cigarette tips, parts of old tires, empty whiskey bottles and beer cans. . . . By the time I am an adult and have to worry about these things, then it will be too late."[2] A high school in Oklahoma staged a mock funeral for a gasoline engine. Similarly, Grant High School students in Portland, Oregon, "beat an automobile to death" with an ax and buried it near the school.[3] Students from nearby John Adams High School scrubbed the Broadway Bridge. In Joliet, Illinois, high schoolers donned gauze masks to symbolize the pollution of the air they breathed. In Kentucky, 1,500 Louisville pupils crowded into the Atherton High School concourse to illustrate the problem of overpopulation. "Thousands of students throughout the Pacific Northwest," reported the *Oregonian*, "took to the woods to clean up hiking trails and pick up trash from river banks and lake shores."[4]

In Cape Girardeau, Missouri, local students scoured the highways picking up litter. Omaha students wore gas masks all day.[5] Sixty students in

Palos Verdes, California, observed Earth Day by riding horses to Miraleste High School.[6] Several hundred students from five Catholic high schools in Los Angeles marched to city hall.[7] Beverly Hills High School canceled classes for a speech by astronaut Scott Carpenter. Two hundred Gladstone High School students in Covina, California, were given the day off to pick up litter.[8] The *Des Moines Register* reported, "Virtually every school in the state celebrated Earth Day with either a clean-up campaign, specially prepared lessons or some other symbolic events."[9] Students at McKinley Junior High School in Cedar Rapids, Iowa, filled the school's trophy case with beer cans and other trash collected on the way to school.[10] Newspapers across the country reported the efforts of local residents.[11]

In New York, students at Pace College displayed three vials of water. The vial from far up the Hudson was clean, the one from the Hudson outside New York City was brown, and the vial from the East River "was a mess of filth."[12] At Trinity College in Connecticut, junior Joel Heriston took a bag of dirt from the campus and put it into a Connecticut Bank and Trust Company safe deposit box, "to dramatize the value of the earth."[13] Getting into the spirit, the bank offered him the safe deposit box for free for the year.

In California, students cut up their oil company credit cards, while Iowa State students set up barricades to keep cars out.[14] Appalachian students buried a trash-filled casket. Ohio University students marked cars with placards reading, THIS IS A POLLUTER.[15] A goat in Centralia, Washington, wore a sign reading, "I eat garbage. What are you doing for your community?"[16] In Tacoma, Washington, one hundred students rode down the freeway on horseback to protest auto pollution. Up the freeway at the University of Washington, "twenty-two-year-old naturalist Bob Pyle organized and directed a 'plant-in' at the Union Bay site of what had been a wetland biology preserve . . . until the University let it be filled as a dump."[17]

Environmental historian Victor B. Scheffer noted the range of events, which might include "a convocation, songfest, dance, and smorgasbord, along with panel discussions, symposiums, and talks by environmental evangelists."[18]

Congress adjourned, so that members could speak on Earth Day. At the University of Pennsylvania, Senator Edmund Muskie (D-ME) reminded listeners that the environmental issues connected to other issues, saying, "Those who believe that we are talking about the Grand Canyon and the Catskills, but not Harlem and Watts, are wrong."[19] Muskie added, "We are spending twenty times as much on Vietnam as we are to fight water pollution." Former vice-president Hubert Humphrey spoke at a Bloomington, Minnesota, high school, calling for the United Nations to establish a global agency to "strengthen, enforce and monitor pollution abatement throughout the world."[20] Senator Birch Bayh, speaking in Washington, DC, proposed the creation of a federal agency "to conquer pollution as we have conquered space." Washington governor Dan Evans suggested to students at Lewis and Clark High School in Spokane that Earth Day be made an annual event.[21] Legislatures from forty-two states passed resolutions to mark the day.

Politicians were not the only speakers. "Every leading environmentalist was booked to lecture long in advance," reported *Time* magazine. The ecologist Barry Commoner's schedule sent him dashing from Harvard and MIT to Rhode Island College, and finally to Brown University, with the antiwar pediatrician Dr. Benjamin Spock, the poet Allen Ginsberg, and various rock stars making appearances.[22] In Iowa, two educational TV stations ran hours of special Earth Day programming.

Cities competed to offer the biggest and most dramatic demonstrations. New York banned cars from Fifth Avenue and 14th Street, and a photo of the footloose crowds dominated the front page of the next day's *New York Times*.[23] "Huge light-hearted throngs ambled down autoless streets," reported the *Times*, "as the city heeded Earth Day for a regeneration of a polluted environment by celebrating an exuberant rite of spring. If the environment had any enemies, they did not make themselves known."[24] New York mayor John Lindsay said it was the first time he had paraded down Fifth Avenue without getting booed. An estimated 250,000 people came to Union Square to listen to speeches.[25] "Earth Day in Los Angeles Wednesday was marked by a host of antipollution programs and a notable absence of smog," reported the *Los Angeles Times*. "Thousands of Southland students and their elders heaped abuse upon all forms of environmental pollution. They deplored it in speeches, exhibits, demonstrations and students on high school and college campuses." In St. Louis, the United Auto Workers led a parade through downtown, featuring a smog-free propane-powered auto.[26] Earth Day in Birmingham, Alabama was part of the Right to Live Week; in Cleveland it was celebrated as part of the Crisis in the Environment Week.[27]

Judged the *Times*'s Philip Shabecoff, it was "the day environmentalism in the United States began to emerge as a mass social movement."[28]

In sparking the American environmental movement, Earth Day 1970 was a cause. But it was also an effect. Earth Day came in the middle of the greatest period of environmental progress in the United States. The groundswell of environmental victories began six years before, in 1964, and would continue six more years, until 1976. Nothing like it had happened previously, even under the two environmentally minded presidents Roosevelt. At least thirty-two major environmental bills were enacted during this period. These included a host of land measures governing wilderness, national trails, wild rivers, urban parks, Alaska, forests, and nonforested lands, not to mention the creation of multiple national parks, wilderness areas, national seashores, and national recreational areas. Three major bills attacked air pollution, while four aimed at clean water. Four major laws were passed governing use of the oceans. Multiple acts changed the way Americans disposed of garbage, and handled toxins and pesticides. Three acts protected endangered species. The Environmental Protection Agency (EPA) was created, while the National Environmental Policy Act mandated environmental impact statements for all government actions.

The legislation was created by politicians who were not generally lionized on Earth Day, and have been rarely remembered by environmental activists since. The bills were often years in the making, but frequently passed overwhelmingly, with a bipartisan consensus rarely seen since in environmental policy (or much else). Politicians who were never denounced as tree-huggers—and who probably never heard the term—left a legacy of support, if not affection, for nature.

Lyndon Johnson's historical reputation is shaped by Vietnam and civil rights, but his and Lady Bird Johnson's commitment to the land drove historic achievements in environmental legislation. Together with Stewart Udall, the secretary of the interior he inherited from John F. Kennedy, Johnson provided vital support for previously immobilized bills that became landmarks of environmental policy. Johnson would sign almost three hundred environmentally related bills in his five-year term.

It is harder to gauge the environmental legacy of Richard Nixon, the president who walked on the beach in wingtips but who signed some of the most important environmental legislation in history. With no particular interest in the subject, Nixon at first thought the bills were a cheap way of buying some support, then hoped they might provide a distraction from Watergate, and in his final days was simply too politically weak to stop them. But his administration included a bumper crop of environmental sympathizers, from EPA director William Ruckelshaus to White House advisor (and convicted Watergate conspirator) John Ehrlichman, with occasional surprise appearances by conservatives like Interior Secretary Wally Hickel.

In the Capitol, massive contributions were made by legislators now almost forgotten, such as the Pennsylvania Republican representative John Saylor, and by some remembered for very different things, like Henry Jackson and Howard Baker. In those years, the issue took root on both sides of the aisle, to a degree now unimaginable. Some legislators who were major forces in these achievements later saw their careers ended by the change in the issue's political environment.

Gaylord Nelson Has an Idea

Wisconsin senator Gaylord Nelson is given credit for creating Earth Day. "The objective," declared Nelson of his creation, "was to get a nationwide demonstration of concern for the environment so large that it will shake the political environment out of this lethargy and finally, force this issue on to the political agenda."[29] That was the goal that in 1970 took over college campuses and took cars off major cities' main streets.

In 1970, Nelson was a second-term senator who had been promoting the environment for much of his career. Born in Wisconsin to Progressive parents, who took him as a child to hear Senator Robert La Follette, he graduated from the University of Wisconsin Law School. He immediately joined the army in World War II, which he spent at Indiantown Gap in Pennsylvania as one of four white officers in a quartermaster company made up of two hundred black enlisted men. After returning to his hometown of Clear Lake, he ran unsuccessfully for the state legislature as a progressive Republican in 1946 but rebounded to win a state senate seat as a Democrat on the Truman tide in 1948. In 1958, again riding a national Democratic wave, he became only the second Democrat elected governor of Wisconsin in the twentieth century.

Despite Republican control over at least part of the state legislature, Nelson enacted an ambitious legislative program. Shortly after being reelected in 1960, Nelson surprised most of the state with his Outdoor Recreation Act Program, a one-cent cigarette tax to finance the state acquisition of land for recreation and conservation. Nelson won just enough Republican support to get the measure enacted. Later Republican governors would continue and expand the popular program. Udall called it "the boldest conservation step ever taken on a state level in the history of the United States."[30]

In 1962 Nelson toppled four-term senator Alexander Wiley, the senior Republican in the Senate. On taking office, Nelson told the *Christian Science Monitor*, "I think the most crucial domestic issues facing America, both on the national level and facing state governments, is the conservation of our natural resources. . . . They're being destroyed carelessly and criminally throughout the nation by the pollution of our waters, the drainage of wetlands, the rapid growth of our cities eating up land all around them."[31] "Nelson went to the U.S. Senate," his biographer Bill Christofferson wrote, "with a clear and ambitious agenda: to make environmental issues a part of the nation's public agenda."[32] Nelson repeatedly urged President Kennedy and his staff to focus on conservation as a popular and crucial issue, advising the president to declare that "there is no domestic issue more important to Americans in the long run than the conservation and proper uses of our natural resources."[33] In the same letter to Kennedy Nelson mused, "The question is how to maximize the effect—how to hit the issue hard enough to leave a permanent impression after the headlines have faded away—enough to shake people, organizations and legislators hard enough to gain support for a comprehensive national, state and local long range plan for our resources."[34]

Nelson and others persuaded Kennedy to undertake a five-day, eleven-state tour starting on September 24, 1963, to focus on conservation. Nelson later recalled, "I assumed if the president did a tour and said this was an important issue the press would believe him. . . . Every place we went, the press peppered the president with questions on foreign policy. They didn't really care what he had to say about the environment."[35] Nelson concluded that the trip "didn't do what I had hoped for. But it was the germ of the idea that ultimately became Earth Day . . . finding some event that would be big enough to bring this issue to the attention of the political establishment."[36] The next year, under President Johnson, Nelson was at the core of the group of senators successfully pushing the Wilderness Act. His cooperation with Johnson did not extend to all issues; Nelson was one of only three senators to vote against the initial $700 million appropriation for the Vietnam War.

Nelson conceived of Earth Day after speaking in California in 1969 following a massive oil spill fouling the coastline off Santa Barbara. Thinking of the college teach-ins on Vietnam, Nelson remembered, "It popped into my head. That's it! Why not have an environmental teach-in and get everyone involved?"[37] Nelson legislative assistant Dennis W. Brezina later recalled, "Nelson came up with this idea for establishing an Earth Day, a National Earth Day, a National Environmental Day. That started in '69, about the time I came on staff."[38] On September 20, 1969, Nelson announced the plan at a speech to the Washington Environmental Council, calling for a national teach-in on "The Crisis of the Environment" at every college on the same day in the spring. "I am convinced that the same concern the youth of this nation took in changing the nation's priorities on the war in Vietnam and on civil rights," he declared, "can be shown for the problems of the environment," which was "the most critical issue facing mankind."[39] The *Seattle Post-Intelligencer* reported on the address, noting, "Nelson [said], 'It will take the same kind of commitment that put men on the moon and built one of the most massive defense machines ever seen on Earth to solve the environmental crisis.'"[40]

Nelson's speech generated wide publicity and a massive volume of calls to his office. Brezina noted later of Nelson that "he had a down-to-earth kind of philosophical outlook on things, and he didn't use a lot of polysyllabic words. But he had a profound way of putting things. Simple, but with a context that gave it depth. He could speak very eloquently about the environment . . . he would inspire his staff."[41] Nelson would receive over one thousand requests to speak over the next few months. The *Des Moines Register* later reported that "if maybe 40 campuses held teach ins in the same day, he [Nelson] thought it would be a success."[42]

Back in Washington, Nelson set up a nonprofit organization, Environmental Teach-In, Inc., and persuaded moderate Republican representative Pete McCloskey of California to cochair it with him. Nelson raised seed money, with contributors including the Conservation Foundation, United Auto Workers (UAW) president Walter Reuther, and AFL-CIO president George Meany, while donating his own honoraria from environmental speeches. The eventual budget was less than $200,000.[43] When the organization was running out of money, Sydney Howe, the executive director of the Conservation Foundation, provided a $20,000 loan, eventually paid back with Nelson's speaking fees.

No union leader matched the environmental fervor of Reuther, who had persuaded the union to establish a UAW Department of Conservation and Resource Development in 1967. Reuther had earlier commented, "What good is another week's vacation if the lake you used to go to is polluted and you can't swim in it?"[44] Earth Day organizer Denis Hayes later commented, "Without UAW, the first Earth Day would have likely flopped. . . . [T]he UAW was by far the largest contributor to the first Earth Day. . . . It printed and mailed all our materials at its expense. . . . Its organizers turned out workers in every city where it has a presence."[45]

Brezina remembered, "Earth Day was an attempt to find a positive alternative to the disruptive tearing at the social fabric of America, particularly on college campuses . . . so there was a lot of planning."[46]

To coordinate the plan, Nelson hired Hayes, a former student body president at Stanford, who later recalled, "We consciously set out to build a movement to bring America back together. . . . But no one knew how gigantic it would be."[47] As a strategy, Hayes explained later, "We didn't want to alienate the middle class; we didn't want to lose the 'silent majority' just because of style issues."[48] Campus environmental groups began organizing in the fall, with Environmental Teach In, Inc. serving as a clearinghouse for information. "Earth Day worked because of the spontaneous response at the grassroots level," remembered Nelson later. "We had neither the time nor the resources to organize twenty million demonstrators and the thousands of schools and local communities that participated."[49] In fact, "if we had actually been responsible for making the event happen, it would have taken several years and millions of dollars to pull it off."[50]

On January 19, 1970, Nelson, along with Senators Alan Cranston (D-CA) and Claiborne Pell (D-RI), introduced a constitutional amendment stating, "Every person has the inalienable right to a decent environment. The United States and every State shall guarantee this right." Nelson argued, "In its degradation of the quality of American life—in its danger to the future of man himself, the environmental crisis has become a threat to the inalienable rights of life, liberty and the pursuit of happiness."[51] The *New York Times* commented, "As an 'environmental agenda' for the seventies, Senator Nelson proposes immediate action to rid the nation over the next decade of pollution from auto exhausts, jet aircraft emissions, hard pesticides, detergents that stimulate the growth of algae in lakes and streams, and solid waste such as containers that do not deteriorate for years."[52] The proposed amendment was a statement rather than a concerted attempt to amend the Constitution, but it helped publicize the gravity of the issue. Brezina later explained, "Nelson then came out with an environmental agenda, and to get press attention more than the feasibility of getting it passed, it led with a constitutional amendment that everybody had the right to a quality environment." Brezina added, "One of the functions of [Nelson's] office was essentially trying to legitimize the idea that environmental action might be appropriate at this point in time."[53]

In the two weeks before Earth Day, Nelson traveled the country promoting the event. On April 21, he told the UAW convention that the automobile was becoming a negative symbol, calling for development of pollution-free engines. The next day, Earth Day itself, Nelson spoke at teach-ins through the country. "Our goal is not just an environment of clean air and water and scenic beauty," he told a crowd. "The objective is an environment of decency, quality and mutual respect for all other human beings and all living creatures."[54]

Beyond the Enthusiasts

Earth Day appealed across the political spectrum. "Conservatives were for it. Liberals were for it. Democrats, Republicans and Independents were for it," reported the *New York Times*. "It was Earth Day, and like Mother's Day, no man in public office could be against it."[55]

Critics included right-wingers who saw it as a communist plot. Georgia comptroller general James L. Bentley sent out $1,600 worth of telegrams at taxpayer expense charging that Earth Day might be a communist plot because April 22 was Lenin's birthday, but later backed down and said he would cover the cost himself.[56] "The original conservationist, St. Francis of Assisi, was born on April 22"; retorted Nelson, "Queen Isabella was born April 22; and my Aunt Tillie was born on April 22."[57]

Critical of Earth Day, the two thousand delegates at the Daughters of the American Revolution convention passed a resolution stating, "The real problem of pollution of our environment is being distorted and exaggerated by emotional declarations and subversive propaganda."[58] A group calling itself the California Citizens Committee charged that the Earth Day movement was "part of the whole Marxist revolution now proceeding apace in America," but failed to persuade the Anaheim School Board to ban an Earth Day discussion of population control at a local high school.[59] Less stridently, Senator Gordon Allott (R-CO) warned, "Some extremists want to use the environment issue as one more club with which to beat America."[60] More darkly, according to West Virginia's *Dominion News*, "Oil man John Smith of Raceland, Louisiana, snorted at the proceedings, 'The kids campaigning for clean air are polluting their minds with marijuana.'"[61]

On the left, some saw an establishment plot to distract attention from Vietnam. "The very quiet tenor of the day, in contrast to the militancy of the antiwar movement," later complained environmentalist Mark Dowie, "suggested that environmentalism would remain genteel, white, and very polite."[62] The left-wing *Ramparts* magazine complained that any analogy between the Earth Day teach-ins and those protesting Vietnam was "obscene."[63] Yet at a Washington, DC, rally, Hayes called the Vietnam War "an ecological catastrophe," demonstrating that many did see a connection between the two issues.[64] Others on the left attacked Earth Day as a distraction from their causes. At the Earth Day rally at Indiana University, twenty students, members of the Women's Liberation Movement, dressed as witches and pelted participants with birth control pills.

The Nixon administration had mixed feelings.[65] "A number of environment-related government agencies, for example, were instructed to support Earth Day through office displays, press releases, and speeches at Earth Day events," explained historian Robert Gottlieb, "but then failed to address their own long-standing prodevelopment biases and actually increased security measures in anticipation of possible picketing."[66] Newspapers reported, "Although the President took no personal role in the observances, the White House sent word that he 'feels the activities show the concern of people of all walks of life over the dangers to our environment.'"[67] Nixon aide John C. Whitaker later wrote that Nixon "felt that his detailed thirty-seven-point environmental message to Congress a few months earlier had substantively dealt with the pollution problem. A proclamation on Earth Day could be seen as grandstanding. He also saw in the environment issue a potential backlash effect in fewer jobs, slower economic development and higher prices. He decided to remain quiet." In his memoir of the time, Whitaker noted that the White House had issued proclamations that week for National Archery Week and National Boating Week but had none for Earth Day.[68]

CBS correspondent Dan Rather characterized Nixon's attitude toward Earth Day as "benign neglect."[69] Myron Tubbs, assistant secretary of commerce for science and technology, suggested on a telephone conference call to an Indiana high school that "students monitor the noise pollution of rock n' roll music and hot rods."[70]

Somewhat cynically, the *New York Times* reported, "Vast numbers of United States Senators and Representatives, some Cabinet and sub-Cabinet members and everybody on the President's Environmental Quality

Council were spread out across the nation today, mostly on campuses, talking about how to improve a rapidly deteriorating environment. In their wake, they left quantities of litter, composed of speech texts and statements distributed across Washington."[71] At New York University, New York Republican senator Charles Goodell was greeted by a leaflet calling his speech "the biggest cause of air pollution." Newspapers noted the day's ironies; the *Robesonian* reported that "Maryland governor Marvin Mandel signed 21 bills and joint legislative resolutions dealing with the environment—but had to open his office windows when the room became hazy with tobacco smoke."[72] Rarely, even some environmentalists were critical. Calling Earth Day "a Hell of a waste of time," Ansel Adams told an audience that, more than rallies, conservation requires "a willingness to make sacrifices now in our way of living."[73]

A variety of businesses announced plans to reduce pollution. Gottlieb noted, "A number of companies and industry groups decided to embrace the event through advertisements, [and] displays at corporate headquarters.[74] The Reynolds Metal Company sent trucks to colleges to pick up aluminum cans collected in "trash-ins."[75] Scott Paper Company pledged $36 million to reduce the pollution it generated, while Sun Oil promised to conduct research to develop throwaway containers that could be easily destroyed.[76] Rex Chainbelt, Inc., of Milwaukee, announced the creation of a pollution control division, with the company's chairman, William Messinger, declaring, "In a short time, I believe, it will be considered a criminal act to pollute." Anheuser-Busch announced that it would develop equipment and systems to help dispose of the brewery's solid wastes. Texas Gulf Sulphur announced that it would work to reduce sulfur emissions from its natural gas processing.[77] Utilities tried to show off a benevolent image as well. Commonwealth Edison, based in Chicago, planned to send 175 speakers to different Earth Day events.[78] At the University of Illinois this backfired, when students disrupted a Commonwealth Edison speaker by throwing soot on each other and coughing loudly.[79]

Still, judged *Time* magazine, "Earth Day plans were largely calm and thoughtful."[80] The biggest disorder occurred when fifteen people were arrested at Logan Airport in Boston for blocking a corridor to protest the development of supersonic transport planes.[81] Student radicals stormed the stage when Michigan governor William G. Milliken tried to speak at Michigan State University, stopping the speech. Skeptical of any politicians, hecklers greeted Senators Edward Kennedy and Henry Jackson during speeches at Yale and in Seattle, respectively.[82] One man was arrested when demonstrators in Coral Gables, Florida, dumped twenty pounds of dead fish and a dead octopus in front of a local power plant.[83]

Earth Day Plants Seeds

Nelson received the lion's share of credit for making it happen. "And it all happened in the Northwest—and throughout the nation," concluded the *Oregonian*, "because a few months back Wisconsin Senator Gaylord Nelson expressed the conviction that clean water, air and land are the constitutional right of every citizen."[84] After the day's demonstrations, *Time* magazine observed, "Water, air and green space know no class or color distinctions."[85] Looking forward from Earth Day, Nelson predicted, "It could kick off one of the toughest—and most expensive—political fights this country has ever seen."[86] Brezina later recalled, "Earth Day turnout was in the tens of millions. I think twenty-two million or something like that. That has caught a lot of attention. Yes, and he [Nelson] became 'Mr. Earth Day.' Of course, there were thousands of people involved in it, but he was the political leader."[87] Historian Adam Rome wrote, "Earth Day was different because Gaylord Nelson made two inspired decisions . . . the teach-in model allowed Earth Day to be far more powerful than a traditional political demonstration. Nelson also decided not to be a micromanager. . . . Nelson's willingness to let others take ownership of the teach-ins made Earth Day even more powerful."[88]

The day demonstrated that the environment had become a major issue. Afterward, the Audubon Society declared, "Now, suddenly, everyone is a conservationist."[89] At the American Newspaper Publishers Association convention, it was the hot new topic of conversation. "'Everybody is against pollution now, instead of sin,'" one publisher told the *New York Times*, "suggesting that his cynical remark should remain anonymous. 'Of course, I'm against pollution too.'"[90] Brezina concluded that Earth Day "probably opened the door for legislating more definitively in the environment area. It wasn't predicted that it would be so profound. It struck a nerve in America."[91]

The day also showed a connection between activism and political action. New Jersey governor William T. Cahill signed a law creating a state environmental agency, while the Michigan House of Representatives passed a bill giving citizen groups legal standing in environmental cases.[92] There were more symbolic actions by politicians as well. The Buffalo City

Council paraded through the square at city hall, carrying shovels and brooms and a sanitation cart, symbolizing a commitment to clean up the city.[93] Rockefeller signed a law creating a Department of Environmental Conservation, then dedicated a bicycle rack under the steps of the New York capitol. The *New York Times* showed Rockefeller riding a bicycle with the caption, "A non-polluting vehicle."

Months later, President Richard M. Nixon established the Environmental Protection Agency. In the next years, Nelson was at the center of legislative activity producing the 1970 Clean Air Act, revisions in 1972 to the Clean Water Act, and passage of the Endangered Species Act. He was a sponsor of laws that preserved the two-thousand-mile Appalachian Trail, established fuel efficiency standards in automobiles, sought to control damage from strip mining, and led to a ban on the insecticide DDT. Pro-environmental views had not yet been effectively attacked as economic threats. In 1970, television, books, and magazines such as *Time, Life, Newsweek,* and *Look* took a friendly view of environmental issues.[94]

Earth Day accelerated the growth of environmental journalism. The first reporter with a focus on environmental issues was the *New York Times*'s Gladwin Hill, whose assignment started only in 1969. But by August 1970, the magazine *Editor and Publisher* reported that a hundred newspapers, citing strong public interest, had assigned reporters to the "ecology beat."[95] The moment also set off a groundswell of books on the subject, accelerating after Earth Day. In June 1971, with only slight exaggeration, a bibliographer at the Library of Congress said that more books about environmental issues had appeared in the year since Earth Day than in all the years before.[96] Educational programs about the environment also spurted in the late 1960s, jumpstarted by the Environmental Education Act of 1970.

For the first time, some environmental groups surrendered their tax-exempt status to enter politics. Hayes, the coordinator of Earth Day, founded Environmental Action, targeting the "Dirty Dozen" legislators with the worst environmental records. The League of Conservation Voters was founded to campaign for and against candidates on environmental issues. One of its first efforts unseated the anticonservation Maryland representative George Fallon, chairman of the Committee on Public Works, in the 1970 Democratic primary, sending a message to other politicians.[97] The 1970 midterms also saw victories for sixteen out of twenty pro-environmental measures on state ballots. The *New York Times* viewed the environment as a key issue in twenty-five states that year.[98]

The Roots of the Day

The first Earth Day was a moment in itself, and also a landmark of the most vital and productive decade of environmental protection in American history, from the long-deferred passage of the Wilderness Act in 1964 through the vast protective legal infrastructure assembled in the early 1970s. The seeming national consensus behind Earth Day illustrates several conditions that made the Green Years possible, conditions that have since faded like summer blossoms.

We think of the sixties and seventies as times of bitter national division, of battles in the streets, and furious language launched across political and generational lines. But partisan differences were less sharply drawn than the barbed-wire-and-broken-glass barriers of today when parties and party caucuses value both purity and purity tests. Congress featured, often in very prominent positions, Republican moderates and liberals, often from the Northeast and the West Coast, and Democratic conservatives and centrists, especially from the South and the mountain states; many of those figures will appear prominently in achieving legislation across the following chapters.

Throughout the Green Years, Democrats controlled both houses of Congress, often by heavy majorities, a key advantage for the movement. But there was still a vital Republican conservation tradition; in the 1960s Republicans were chronologically as close to Teddy Roosevelt as to Donald Trump. In both houses and in the Nixon and Ford administrations, Republicans played vital roles, a situation that would steadily decline over the following decades.

Americans also had a greater belief in government and its capacity to successfully address problems. In 1964 the American National Election Study found that 77 percent of Americans felt the federal government did the right thing most or nearly all of the time; by the end of the following decade the number was down to about a quarter of those sampled. Aside from a brief surge after 9/11, it has remained low since, limiting popular readiness to support government regulation of air, water, or anything else. Crucially, in the 1960s and the early 1970s America was in a steady state of economic growth, with no expectation that environmental legislation would interfere with it. Americans believed that they could afford everything—both a booming economy and a clean environment at the same time. Economic prosperity contributed to the growth and strengthening of established environmental groups, such as the Sierra Club and the Wilderness Society, and the rise of new ones, such as the League of Conservation Voters.

And opposition to pollution, the theme of the day, was a position difficult to oppose. In subsequent decades, a weaker political system would come up against tougher and more economically costly environmental challenges, notably energy choices and global warming. But as the centerpiece of the Green Years, Earth Day 1970 displayed emerging environmental values, the rising urgency of the movement and its supporters, and the politicians who translated the movement into legislation. "It did exactly what I was aiming for," Nelson said. "It was a big enough demonstration to get the attention of the political establishment and force the issue on to the political agenda . . . when the people demonstrated their interest, the politicians responded."[99]

From Nelson himself through all the officeholders who ventured out to speak—and sometimes get heckled—on the first Earth Day, the day provided a focus on the people who built the Green Years. Many who built the enduring American environmental framework are often remembered for other reasons. President Johnson may be most remembered for civil rights and Vietnam, President Nixon for openings to China and Watergate. Yet dramatic environmental advances occurred during their administrations.

Senator Henry "Scoop" Jackson's hawkish foreign policy views set him against the dovish Senator Frank Church of Idaho for more than a decade. Yet the two had an effective collaboration that helped enact major environmental laws. Representative John Dingell of Michigan is recalled largely as the DC champion of the auto industry, yet he had an impressive environmental record, particularly during the 1960s and 1970s. Senator Howard Baker is remembered as Senate majority leader and White House chief of staff, but at the end of his career he declared himself most proud of his role in the passage of the Clean Air Act.

Major legislation emerged from the fencing between two friendly adversaries, Representative Wayne Aspinall, a prodevelopment Democrat from Colorado who chaired the Interior Committee, and the strongly pro-environment John Saylor, the ranking Republican. Other major players included John Blatnik and Morris Udall in the House, and Clinton Anderson and Warren Magnuson in the Senate. Key figures in the executive branch included Stewart Udall under Johnson and Russell Train, John Whitaker, and William Ruckelshaus under Nixon and Gerald Ford. Just as in the civil rights movement, nonelected activists played a major role.

Environmentalists such as David Brower and Mike McCloskey of the Sierra Club and Howard Zahniser of the Wilderness Society all provided crucial pieces of the puzzle. Looming over the time was the legacy of Rachel Carson and her book *Silent Spring*.

The environmental victories of the Green Years did more than change the laws. They created entire new industries, such as technology to reduce air and water emissions. Backpacking and venturing into nature beyond the automobile became mass recreation. Revelations about chemical exposures created skepticism about some aspects of science and industry and spurred the natural food movement. Many products would be sold as "environmentally friendly" or "organic," often with wobbly evidence behind the claims.

The environmental fights also helped change the political landscape of the United States. The western states, largely dominated by Democrats in the 1960s, became Republican bastions, producing legislators determined to roll back environmental regulations—particularly those aimed at their states' resource extraction industries. Legendarily, as Johnson predicted, civil rights legislation cost the Democrats the South; in the same way, environmental legislation drove a political shift in the inland West.

The Green Years recast our planet and our politics. The magic of these successes would not continue. The following years did not bring even a fraction of such environmental victories. Indeed, most of the following decades saw more efforts to roll back environmental protections than to extend them, especially during the Reagan years and the Trump administration. Half a century later, the legislation from that time, although under attack, is still the basic structure of our environmental law, shaping our values and our thinking. It has provided the core of the protection of our land, water, air, and creatures. If some of it has proven less than needed, much of it might have been difficult to enact at all in today's politics. It is the legacy of a time, and of people, without much of our science or even our vocabulary. Many of its most crucial figures are rarely remembered as environmentalists, and in some cases barely remembered at all. In a country torn apart by war and Watergate, by race and rioting, they worked to preserve what was already endangered, sometimes crossing party lines, sometimes dragging reluctant allies.

This is the story of these years of environmental progress, of what happened and the people who made it happen, and what it can tell us as we go forward into the future.

CHAPTER TWO

Wilderness at Last

At an unsettled but hopeful time, it was a landmark American speech. On May 22, 1964, speaking at the University of Michigan commencement, President Lyndon Johnson spoke for the first time of "the Great Society." Written by Richard Goodwin, a star speechwriter for the murdered John F. Kennedy, the speech laid out priorities in education and battling poverty that marked the rest of Johnson's administration. Less noted in history is that it was also a major environmental moment, pointing toward years of monumental legislation. "The water we drink, the food we eat, the very air that we breathe, are threatened with pollution. Our parks are overcrowded, our seashores overburdened. Green fields and dense forests are disappearing," Johnson told the graduates.[1] Noting that the Great Society was "a place where the city of man serves not only the needs of the body and the demands of commerce but the desire for beauty and the hunger for community," Johnson made environmental concern an integral part of his reform program.[2]

Just a few months later, the speech would resonate in the passage of the Wilderness Act, landmark legislation that has shaped the preservation of American land ever since. It marked the start of a river of bills over a dozen years that redesigned the protection, and to a large degree the face, of natural America. Legislation protecting undeveloped public land, and expanding the territory that fit that description, had been bogged down in

Congress for seven years. And those years of endless hearings, rewriting, and futility were but a fraction of the time leading up to a federal wilderness policy. For decades, advocates had sought protection of the country's dramatic undeveloped territory, battling economic forces, regional pressures, and congressional roadblocks. When 1964 produced the Wilderness Act, the first major conservation legislation in memory, it indicated a new era and attitude, a signpost to a decade of historic new policy to follow. The path to cleaner air and waters, protected species, and a louder voice for nature ran through wilderness.

Wilderness in America

In the first years of America land seemed unlimited. "The great happiness of my country," proclaimed Albert Gallatin, Thomas Jefferson's secretary of the treasury, "arises from the great plenty of land."[3] Equally widespread was the belief that this land should be converted to productive use by taming its wildness. The vast wilderness that faced the early English settlers was viewed with fear and suspicion. William Bradford, author of the 1651 *Of the Plymouth Plantation: 1620–1647*, wrote that the Pilgrims encountered "a hideous and desolate wilderness, full of wild beasts and wild men."[4] Historian Roderick Nash, in his classic *Wilderness and the American Mind*, wrote, "Prejudice against wilderness had the strength of centuries behind it and continued to influence American opinion long after pioneering conditions disappeared."[5]

But the early 1800s heard the first voices calling for a reevaluation of the policy of unlimited exploitation of the earth. Painter George Catlin, who depicted the American frontier, wrote in 1832 that the primitive is "worthy of our preservation and protection. . . . [T]he further we become separated from that pristine wildness and beauty, the more pleasure does the mind of enlightened man feel in recurring to those scenes."[6] American transcendentalists, including Ralph Waldo Emerson and Henry David Thoreau, perceived the link between humans and the wild. Thoreau was not the first man to seek to live in the wilderness, but he was one of the first to write about it, saying, "I went to the woods deliberately because I wished to live deliberately, to front only the essential facts of life, and see if I could not learn what it had to teach."[7] Thoreau argued for protection of the wild areas and wildlife. "Why should not we . . . have our national preserves . . . in which the bear and panther, and some even of the hunter race, may still exist," he asked in the *Atlantic Monthly* in 1858, "not for food or sport, but for inspiration and our own true recreation?"[8]

In 1864 George Perkins Marsh, US ambassador to Italy after a term serving in Turkey, drew on his extensive travel to publish *Man and Nature, or Physical Geography as Modified by Human Action.*[9] He was worried that the United States was following the European path of deforestation, warning, "A desolation like that which has overwhelmed many once beautiful and fertile regions of Europe awaits an important part of the territory of the United States . . . unless prompt measures are taken."[10] Man's ability to change the earth, wrote Marsh, should include a sense of responsibility for the consequences of such actions.[11] He urged that the American settler in a region should "become a co-worker with nature in the reconstruction of the damaged fabric. . . . He must aid her in reclothing the mountain slopes with forests," so that "American soil . . . as far as possible, in its primitive condition . . . [will become] 'a garden for the recreation of the lover of nature.'"[12] Looking back at Marsh, the twenty-first-century environmentalist Bill McKibben praised his perception, noting, "The insight that humans could do damage to the natural world was novel and startling."[13]

Preservation into Policy

The same year that Marsh published *Man and Nature*, Abraham Lincoln authorized the first government attempt to protect wilderness, signing a law granting "to the State of California the 'Cleft' or 'Gorge' . . . known as the Yo-Semite valley . . . upon the express conditions that the premises shall be held for public use."[14] Yellowstone, the first national park in the world, was created in 1872 under President Ulysses Grant, who, according to biographer Ron Chernow, "had a complicated relationship with the American West," promoting railroads and granting huge tracts to settlers and miners even as he created the park.[15] The Northern Pacific Railroad supported the park as a way to build railroad ridership to it.[16]

Less than two decades later, another railroad issue in Yellowstone set off a very modern-sounding debate in Congress. In 1886, supporting a railroad crossing through the park, Representative Lewis Payson (R-IL) argued, "I can not understand the sentiment which favors the retention of a few buffaloes to the development of mining interests amounting to millions of dollars." William McAdoo (D-NJ) replied, "The glory of this area is its sublime solitude," and asked his colleagues to "prefer the beautiful and the sublime . . . to heartless mammon and the greed of capital."[17] The House rejected the railroad's application for a right of way, 107–65. It was a historic victory; in Nash's estimation: "Never before had wilderness values withstood such a direct confrontation with civilization."[18]

States also began to try to protect some of their land. In 1885 New York enacted the Adirondack Forest Preserve Act. An advocate for the land, Boston pastor William H. H. Murray, argued in 1869, "The wilderness provides that perfect relaxation which all jaded minds require."[19] In 1892, recognizing the benefits of the land beyond a source of timber, the state legislature created Adirondack Park, declaring it "ground open for the free use of all the people for their health and pleasure."[20]

A wandering Scottish immigrant, John Muir "was thirty when he first saw the Golden Gate and set eyes on the summits of the Sierra Nevada. It was the spring of 1868 and he knew at once that he had found his homeland," noted Stewart Udall in his book *The Quiet Crisis and the Next Generation*. As a result, "Muir, a city hater, came down from the mountains time after time to do battle for his wild lands."[21] Muir's battles led to the establishment of multiple national parks—Sequoia, Yosemite, Mount Rainier, Crater Lake, and Mesa Verde—and two others, Grand Canyon and Olympic, that began as national monuments and later became national parks. Muir's message echoed down centuries through the science of forestry and his legacy in advocacy, the Sierra Club. "People are beginning to find out that going to the mountains is going home; that wilderness is a necessity," proclaimed Muir, "and that mountain parks and reservations are useful not only as foundations of timber and irrigating rivers, but as foundations of life."[22] Developing the point, he wrote, "In God's wildness lies the hope of the world—the great fresh unblighted, unredeemed wilderness. The galling harness of civilization drops off, and wounds heal ere we are aware."[23]

Arguing that the wilderness was an important part of the American character, historian Frederick Jackson Turner wrote in the *Atlantic Monthly* in 1896, "Out of his wilderness experience, out of the freedom of his opportunities, [the American] fashioned a formula for social regeneration,—the freedom of the individual to seek his own."[24] The wilderness was becoming recognized as no longer an enemy but a source of American strength.

The new attitude resonated with President Theodore Roosevelt, who created both the National Forest Service and national wildlife refuges. Roosevelt had a personal appreciation for wilderness, although he also shared the utilitarian conservation view of his appointee Gifford Pinchot, noted conservationist and Pennsylvania governor. "There are no words that can tell of the hidden spirit of the wilderness," wrote Roosevelt, "that can reveal its mystery, its melancholy, and its charm." Wilderness fit Roosevelt's ideal of a "life of strenuous endeavor," and he argued in 1899, "As our civilization grows older and more complex, we need a greater and not a less development of the fundamental frontier virtues."[25]

Roosevelt seized a huge opportunity when Congress passed the Antiquities Act in 1906, intended to deal with scavengers savaging ancient American Indian structures in the West. The act specified that the size of the preserved areas should "be confined to the smallest area compatible with the proper care and management of the objects to be protected," but the exact size was left to the president.[26] "The Antiquities Act was a dangerous precedent to set with Roosevelt in the White House," observed historian Douglas Brinkley. "To think that Roosevelt wouldn't stretch his power to the extreme was naïve."[27]

Roosevelt benefited from the seemingly neutral words "objects of historic or scientific interest" inserted into the act by Representative Edward Lacey (R-IA). As journalist Irving Brant noted, Lacey had three goals: a Petrified Forest National Park; a Mount Olympic Range Elk Reserve (later to become Olympic National Park); and "to authorize the president, at his discretion, to establish national parks on the public domain by proclamation."[28] Roosevelt leaped at the language. From the passage of the bill in September 1906 until he left office in March 1909, Roosevelt created eighteen national monuments encompassing 1.2 million acres.[29]

Notably, in January 1908 Roosevelt declared a national monument of eight hundred thousand acres at the Grand Canyon. Speaking there, Roosevelt declared, "Leave it as it is. Man cannot improve on it; not a bit."[30] The Supreme Court would reject a legal challenge to Roosevelt's ability to declare the Grand Canyon a national monument, ruling that the canyon was "of scientific interest."[31] In addition to the national monuments and wildlife refuges Roosevelt created, the number of national parks existing in 1900—six—would be almost doubled by the end of Roosevelt's administration.[32] Most of Roosevelt's successors have created additional national monuments, protecting far more land and water than in the national parks.[33] Many monuments, such as Grand Canyon, Bryce Canyon, and Zion, subsequently became national parks.[34] Ironically, the Antiquities Act included no funding for its original purpose of protecting these areas from looters. Since the Forest Service lacked the resources or expertise to provide protection, the looting of artifacts continued unchecked.[35]

In 1916, under Woodrow Wilson, Congress created the National Park Service to manage the growing number of parks. In the bill, Representative William Kent (I-CA) declared the objective to be "to conserve the scenery and the natural and historic objects therein and to provide for the enjoyment of said scenery and objects by the public in any manner and by any means that will leave them unimpaired for future generations."[36] Led by its first administrator, Stephen Mather, a Sierra Club member inspired by Muir, the new service moved aggressively to manage the parks. Irritated by seeing cattle grazing in the national parks in 1914, Mather had written an irate letter to Secretary of the Interior Franklin Lane, who responded by naming Mather to his staff, and then to run the new Park Service.[37]

Mather and Lane set three clear priorities for the parks, stating, "The national parks must be maintained in absolutely unimpaired form for the use of future generations . . . they are set apart for the use, observation, health and pleasure of the people . . . the national interest must dictate all decisions affecting public or private enterprise in the parks."[38] "Unlike his Forest Service counterparts," judged Richard N. L. Andrews, "Mather successfully resisted the political pressures of most conflicting user constituencies, fending off proposals to open the parks for hydropower production, grazing, and other commodity uses."[39] Mather began educational and interpretive programs, used his own resources to supplement the service, and saw the rise of the automobile stimulate a tourism industry that bolstered the parks' economic appeal.[40]

Keeping Wilderness Wild

Still, many advocates became concerned that the existing federal policies did not guarantee the survival of wilderness. The automobile and its roads, which had spurred interest in the national lands, began to encroach on them. Roads in the national forests exploded from a few thousand miles in 1916 to ninety thousand by 1935.[41] "By 'wilderness' I mean a continuous stretch of country preserved in its natural state," declared a young forest ranger in New Mexico named Aldo Leopold, objecting to the development trends. "The majority undoubtedly want all the automobile roads, summer hotels, graded trails, and other modern conveniences that we can give them. . . . But a very substantial minority, I think, want just the opposite."[42] The idea of wilderness, he wrote, "is premised on the assumption that the rocks and rills and templed hills of this America are something more than economic materials." Wilderness, he declared, "is the very stuff America is made of."[43] Leopold noted that Americans "are so accustomed to a plentiful supply [of wilderness] that we are unconscious of what the disappearance of wild places would mean."[44]

In 1924 Leopold persuaded a regional Forest Service official to administratively protect half a million acres in the Gila National Forest as the Gila Wilderness Area. Influenced by Leopold, William B. Greeley, the head of the Forest Service, ordered an inventory of undeveloped areas in the national forests that might be considered wilderness. As a result, in 1929 the Forest Service issued the L-20 regulations, labeling certain wilderness as "primitive areas"; without banning road building or logging. The new rules aimed "to maintain primitive conditions of transportation, subsistence, habitation and environment to the fullest degree compatible with their highest public use."[45] In his later book *A Sand County Almanac*, Leopold, by then a professor at the University of Wisconsin, argued, "All available wild areas, large or small, are likely to have value as norms for land science. Recreation is not their only or even principal utility."[46] The case for keeping land open (and car-free) spread; forester Benton MacKaye declared, "The Appalachian Trail is a wilderness trail or it is nothing."[47]

Leopold's call was echoed by Bob Marshall, chief of the Division of Recreation and Lands for the Forest Service, who urged the creation of an organization "of spirited people who will fight for the freedom of the wilderness."[48] Historian Craig Sutter wrote, "Marshall's impulse was to explore, chart, and preserve. . . . As a result, he knew the nation's remaining wild lands better than anyone of his generation."[49] Marshall also wanted to make sure that the wilderness was not just for the elites. "After his return to the Forest Service in 1937 . . . Marshall laid out this combined social and environmentalist vision," wrote environmental historian Robert Gottlieb. "It included subsidizing transportation to public forests for low-income people, operating camps where groups of underprivileged people could enjoy the outdoors for a nominal cost, changing Forest Service practices that discriminated against blacks, Jews, and other minorities, and acquiring more recreational forest land near urban centers."[50] Marshall shared Leopold's concern that wilderness was fast disappearing, warning that it "is melting away like some last snowbank on some south-facing mountainside during a hot afternoon in July."[51] Asked how many wilderness areas were needed, Marshall responded, "How many Brahms symphonies do we need?"[52]

In 1934, Marshall, Leopold, and MacKaye, along with five others, formed the Wilderness Society to lobby for its protection.[53] The founding statement admitted, "We recognize frankly that the majority of Americans do not as yet care for these values of undisturbed nature. . . . All we desire to save from invasion is the extremely minor section of outdoor America which yet remains free from mechanical sights and sounds and smells."[54] The Wilderness Society also argued that since the wilderness lands were usually remote and of little economic value, their most valuable use was as wilderness.[55]

The advocates also warned that the existing protection was precarious. "Under the present system," warned Marshall in 1934, "a single unsympathetic administration could at any time wipe out our remaining primitive expanses. In order to escape the whim of politics . . . [wilderness areas] should be set aside by an Act of Congress, just as national parks are today set aside."[56] Influenced by Marshall, New Deal Secretary of the Interior Harold Ickes argued that the Park Service, part of his department, would protect wilderness better than the Forest Service. In a 1938 press release, Ickes stated, "Areas dedicated as wilderness national parks should be protected forever by provisions of law designed for that purpose. . . . I shall welcome it if the Congress of the United States will define and set standards for wilderness national parks, as well as provide for wilderness areas to be proclaimed and similarly protected by law in other national parks."[57]

Ickes had his staff draft a national park wilderness protection bill, introduced in February 1939. The bill proposed to preserve "perpetually for the benefit and inspiration of the people of the United States the primitive conditions existing within national parks and national monuments," and authorized the president to declare "wilderness areas when he determines that it would be to the public interest to do so."[58] The bill had a Senate hearing, but then got bogged down. Marshall did persuade the secretary of agriculture to tighten limits on federal primitive areas.[59]

Tragically, in November 1939 Marshall died unexpectedly in his sleep, at the age of thirty-eight. His financial legacy, including a bequest of some $400,000, kept the Wilderness Society going.[60] While World War II delayed his vision of a law permanently protecting wilderness, this idea endured. It would take almost twenty years before Congress considered legislation to give permanent protection to wilderness. By then, visitors to national parks had increased from 360,000 people in 1916 to more than 56 million, while the number visiting national forests had also skyrocketed.[61]

The dream was taken up by Howard Zahniser, executive secretary of the Wilderness Society, now formally supporting a law to protect wilderness. Zahniser drafted an initial wilderness bill in 1949 and persuaded a sympathetic congressman to request the Library of Congress to investigate "whether or not there is a need for a national wilderness policy; and, if so, what form it should take." The report endorsed the idea.[62] Zahniser's challenge, Udall would later explain, "was whether the nation's smallest conservation organization could persuade the Congress of the world's most development-oriented country to pass a law declaring that the resources in tens of millions of acres of its national lands were never to be developed."[63] After a director of the National Park Service urged more development to make the parks more accessible, Zahniser and David Brower of the Sierra Club worried that the federal primitive areas could be degraded.[64] "Hope in the United States for wilderness in the future," urged Zahniser, "depends on our success in developing a policy and program that provides for the preservation of wilderness as such, by the Federal government, with a presumption of perpetuity."[65]

The Wilderness Act Proposed

In 1956 Representative John Saylor (R-PA) and Senator Hubert Humphrey (D-MN) introduced a bill, revised multiple times by Zahniser, to create protection for wilderness areas. "We Americans are the people we are," declared Saylor, "largely because we have had the influence of wilderness in our lives."[66] Zahniser shipped Humphrey and Saylor's speeches, incorporating the text of the bill, to environmentalists across the country to win their support. Their proposal called for wilderness protection for 163 areas totaling 55 million acres, all already federally owned. Within these wilderness areas, commercial activity such as logging, as well as road and dam building, would be banned. Grazing, mining, and hunting would be permitted where they were already practiced.[67] Humphrey emphasized that the bill would provide congressional oversight of agency decisions to open primitive areas for development.[68] "Wilderness" would replace the earlier wording of "primitive areas," although wilderness advocates saw the two as essentially the same, except that wilderness would have statutory protection.

This Wilderness Act drew strong support from conservationists but vehement opposition from the timber, oil, grazing, and mining industries.

Udall, newly elected to the House from Arizona, avoided taking a firm position, since he believed the bill might threaten the existing concept of multiple use of the national forests.[69] The Eisenhower administration, the National Park Service, and the National Forest Service all opposed the bill. The agencies wanted to maintain their administrative authority over the primitive, or wilderness, areas. In vain did bill cosponsor Richard Neuberger (D-OR) insist, "This bill in no way reflects on the wonderful career services which now are in charge of wilderness areas and similar outdoor realms, but it actually seeks to safeguard these splendid men and women from undue political pressure, no matter what the source."[70] The proposal did not advance in Congress.

Perhaps no congressional figure, and certainly no Republican, was more vital to the eventual passage of the Wilderness Act than John Saylor. His father, a friend of Pinchot, was an attorney who shared his love of hunting and fishing with his son, along with the strong religious background that led Saylor to call America's natural wonders "special monuments to the Divine Being."[71] After graduating from Dickinson Law School, Saylor joined his father's law firm in Johnstown, and later succeeded him as city attorney. After serving in the navy during World War II, Saylor won a special election for a House seat. Speaking to a group of Republican congressional leaders, Saylor enraged them by calling them "snobs" who did not seek the support of ordinary workers. House minority leader Joseph Martin (R-MA) was so angry that he waited three weeks before giving Saylor a seat on the Committee on Public Lands, later renamed the Interior Committee.

Saylor, one of the committee's few nonwesterners, quickly opposed the massive public dam building in the West. By 1950 the Bureau of Reclamation had spent more than $2 billion constructing 175 dams.[72] Initially, Saylor's opposition was due to their cost, their competition with private companies, and the competition with other energy sources such as coal, a mainstay of Saylor's district. Coming from a working-class district, Saylor's fiscal conservatism was tempered by support for issues such as public housing and strengthening Social Security.[73]

Attacking a proposal for a dam that would submerge twenty thousand acres of Glacier National Park, Saylor argued that people expected the national parks "to be defended and protected against destruction by small groups of individuals who seek temporary or local gains."[74] In 1954 Saylor and Wayne Aspinall (D-CO) joined Joe Penfold, the western representative of the Izaak Walton League, to raft the Yampa and Green Rivers through

Dinosaur National Monument. "The two-day wilderness experience," wrote Saylor's biographer Thomas Smith, "proved a turning point in Saylor's evolution as a preservationist, heightening his appreciation for pristine lands and national parks and exposing him to an influential conservation leader."[75] Aspinall, who went on the trip despite not knowing how to swim, would not emerge with the same environmental commitment.[76]

In 1953, as part of the Colorado River Storage Project, Interior Secretary Douglas McKay announced a plan to build dams on the Colorado, including at Echo Park inside the Dinosaur National Monument, on the Colorado-Utah border. When the bill came before the Interior Subcommittee on Irrigation and Reclamation in 1954, Saylor was almost alone in fighting the proposal to build a dam that would damage the wilderness, and tried aggressively to remove the Echo Park dam from the bill. In contrast, Aspinall warned that if the dam were dropped, it would encourage conservationists for the next twenty-five years.[77] Testifying before Congress, Brant attacked the dams as "subordinating all values not measurable in dollars."[78]

Brower wrote Saylor, "I thank God for Pennsylvania which produced you (I assume) and which had the good sense (I know) to send you to Congress. I hope you know how widespread the admiration is felt for you all over the country owing to the magnificent fight you are playing in the battle."[79] The renowned novelist, conservationist, and historian Wallace Stegner edited *This is Dinosaur: Echo Park Country and Its Magic Rivers*, a book of essays and photographs supporting keeping the dam out of the monument.[80] General Ulysses S. Grant III, president of the American Planning and Civic Association and grandson of the US president who oversaw the first national park at Yellowstone, also defended keeping Dinosaur wild, stating, "Our industrial civilization is creating an ever greater need for the average man . . . to reestablish contact of nature." Grant added that it would be a shame to sacrifice Dinosaur for "a few acre feet of water and a few kilowatt hours."[81] House mail ran 80–1 against the dam. Unwilling to face a massive battle, Martin, now Speaker of the House, did not bring up the bill. When the Colorado River Storage Project came up again in the next Congress in 1956, Saylor was able to get the Echo dam removed. Conservationists then supported the bill, and the revised Colorado River Storage Project passed Congress. In Nash's view, "the American wilderness movement had its finest hour to that date."[82]

At a 1957 Sierra Club Conference on wilderness, Richard McArdle, chief of the United States Forest Service, commented, "Sportsmen know that some of the best hunting and fishing are in wilderness areas. . . . They may want better access to these areas." To deal with such pressures, McArdle called for Congress to "enunciate policy on wilderness."[83] That year, Saylor and Humphrey tried again. Their bill had hearings, but insufficient support. Instead, Senator Clinton Anderson (D-NM) suggested a national Outdoor Recreation Resources Review Commission, a proposal developed by Penfold, by this time conservation director of the Izaak Walton League. Anderson argued that the nation's natural resources "must be protected and developed only by sound planning intelligently based on the fullest understanding of all the pertinent facts and requirements,"[84] and the bill passed both houses.

When Humphrey tried again for a wilderness bill in 1959 public support had built, but despite long negotiations Humphrey failed to win Anderson's support. Anderson opposed the bill's proposal that the executive branch should designate wilderness and manage it through a National Wilderness Preservation Council. In the House, Aspinall, now chairing the Interior Committee, opposed the bill, warning Brower that "until the sponsors of the wilderness bill are able to get together with other users of public lands in the West and assure them that the Wilderness bill supporters are not endeavoring to destroy already established uses (which include water resource development, mining, grazing etc.), I shall continue to be opposed to the legislation."[85] Udall also opposed the bill, stating, "I will oppose any legislation that would disrupt our present forest management policies and practices."[86]

The battle over wilderness would turn on three pivotal questions. First, who would pick the initial land to be designated as wilderness? Second, who would decide on any additional wilderness? Would these decisions be made by the executive branch? Could it be by the executive, subject to congressional approval? What form would the congressional authorization take? Would it be solely up to Congress, requiring approval by both chambers? Third, would designated wilderness still be available for other "multiple use" activities, such as grazing, logging, and mining?

In the years to come, Wayne Aspinall would be a pivotal figure in the battle over the Wilderness Act and other public lands legislation. When he was a small boy, his parents, both troubled by lung ailments, moved the family from Ohio to the tiny town of Palisade, Colorado, on the western slope of the Rockies. In the arid region, the family prospered from their peach orchard, irrigated by water from the local Grand River. After serving in World War I, Aspinall returned to become a lawyer, and in 1930 rode the Depression's Democratic trend to the state legislature. In almost two decades there, he served as Speaker of the House and Senate majority and minority leader. Coming from his dry but irrigated family farm, Aspinall was absorbed in the issue of water. "In this semi-arid and arid state water is to be wisely husbanded with all the ingenuity and dedication that is possessed by man," he declared. "On this resource as on no other resource, the life and progress of the people of Colorado succeed or fail."[87]

After another stretch in the army during World War II, Aspinall toppled a Republican House incumbent in 1948, later admitting, "I was elected largely because Truman ran for the Presidency."[88] Reflecting his district, he secured a seat on the Interior and Insular Affairs Committee, which would be his focus during his entire time in Washington. "Aspinall represented an enormous district," noted his biographer Steve Schulte. "But for most of his congressional career, he could easily discern what his constituents believed: the land and the water that dissected it existed to be utilized for human benefit."[89]

In 1959, when Aspinall became chair of the Interior Committee, Saylor became ranking Republican. They would serve in those positions for the next fourteen years. While they often disagreed on environmental measures, they maintained good personal ties. Aspinall later said, "John Saylor was my friend in the highest meaning of such a relationship."[90] The committee was hugely important, handling about a fifth of all House bills and, under Aspinall, gaining a reputation for solid work. "Aspinall worked hard all day and cared little for Washington's social life," assessed Schulte. "The Interior Committee, it was said of him, constituted 'his whole life' after 1959."[91]

Wilderness Gains Western Advocates

A revised wilderness bill again failed in 1960, but Kennedy, who endorsed a wilderness bill during his presidential campaign, was elected. For secretary of the interior, he chose Udall, who would become a powerful environmental advocate over two administrations. Udall came from an unusual New Deal–backing Mormon family in the small town of Saint John's, Arizona. After fifty bombing missions in Europe as a gunner on a B-24 bomber, "Udall emerged from the war," his biographer Thomas Smith wrote, "a liberal idealist committed to international economic and social justice."[92] On his return to Arizona he opened a law practice with his younger brother

Morris and became active in Democratic politics, helped by his father's presence on the state supreme court. When the incumbent congressman retired in 1954, Udall won the seat. He joined the House Interior Committee, where he was a strong advocate of dams and other projects to bring water to Arizona.

During his three terms in Congress, Udall got to know Kennedy while they worked together on a labor reform bill. The relationship was bolstered by Udall's managing to deliver Arizona for Kennedy at the 1960 Democratic convention, despite the opposition of six-term Senator Carl Hayden (D-AZ) and other conservative Democrats. The job of Interior Secretary typically went to a westerner, Udall noted later, and "when Kennedy looked at the West, he didn't owe the West much and there was nobody he was particularly indebted to."[93] Udall's nomination won wide support, even from political opponents. Arizona's conservative Republican senator Barry Goldwater told him, "Regardless of our political differences, I feel you are most qualified to make an excellent Secretary of the Interior."[94] Aspinall was less enthusiastic. Udall later commented, "I think Wayne thought he was more experienced and wise, and that Kennedy had a made a mistake in picking a young squirt" as secretary.[95] Over time Udall gravitated more to protecting wilderness, in part due to feeling that he now represented the nation rather than a more conservative Arizona constituency. He hired Stegner as a special assistant.

Kennedy and Udall supported the wilderness bill reintroduced in 1961, which would set aside fourteen million acres, mainly the Forest Service's "primitive areas," for permanent protection. In May 1961 Udall told a reporter, "The glory of America has always been its green face . . . its spaciousness. . . . But our land is changing before our eyes. The bulldozers are eating away the last of the wild areas in the East and even in the west rapid population growth is exerting pressure on the open spaces."[96] Udall later recalled, "The Wilderness Bill had been before the Congress for three or four years. The question was: Was the Administration going to get aggressively behind it and push it? . . . I began moving in this direction. It was clear, too, that we needed some special funding vehicle if we were to have the money to buy park land and we began to work on the conservation fund."[97]

The 1961 wilderness bill was introduced in the House by Saylor and in the Senate by Anderson, now chair of the Committee on Interior and Insular Affairs. Born in South Dakota, Anderson was rejected by the army in

World War I because of tuberculosis. After spending nine months in a sanitarium in the drier climate of New Mexico, Anderson recovered enough to join the *Albuquerque Evening Herald* as a reporter. In 1923, he left journalism to open his own insurance agency. Anderson became wealthy and the head of the local Democratic Party. Early on, he met the local forester Aldo Leopold; Anderson later recalled that Leopold taught him "that the land cannot be exploited without regard for those who will inhabit it long after we depart."[98]

In 1932 Anderson became both the youngest national president of the Rotary Club and New Mexico state treasurer; eight years later he was elected to Congress, where he was named to head a House Committee investigating wartime food shortages. A month after succeeding FDR to the presidency in April 1945, Harry Truman named Anderson secretary of agriculture. In 1948, Anderson left to win a Senate seat, beginning a twenty-four-year tenure. Over time he became a skilled legislator. Biographer Richard Baker wrote of him, "A master legislative mechanic, he possessed an inner confidence and an understanding of his range of options that permitted him to use available power constructively."[99] On his election to the Senate, Anderson was named to the Senate Interior Committee, becoming chair of the Subcommittee on Irrigation and Reclamation in 1956. Among his first conservation measures was the Anderson-Mansfield Act in 1949, allocating money for reforestation of forest and range lands. Anderson, like many other western legislators, spent much of his first years in office fighting for water for his state, including passage of the Colorado River Storage Project in 1956, a bill he advanced by inserting language banning construction of dams within national parks or monuments. Anderson had opposed earlier drafts of the Wilderness Act, but now supported the idea of a wilderness bill, a position that he attributed to his contact with Leopold almost forty years earlier.[100]

Between the November 1960 election and the opening of the new Congress in January, Anderson's legislative assistant Claude Wood met several times with Zahniser and others to draft a bill that Anderson could support. On January 5, 1961, Anderson introduced S. 174, a new wilderness proposal. While previous proposals gave the president power to select both initial wilderness areas and any additions, Anderson's proposal required areas designated as wilderness to face congressional review before receiving permanent protection. In addition, Congress would decide on any subsequent additions to the wilderness system. The new Senate proposal had the backing of the Kennedy administration. Anderson persuaded Kennedy to send his message on natural resources to Congress a few days before the start of the Interior Committee hearings on the wilderness bill on February 27. Testifying, Brower also invoked Leopold, declaring, "No man who reads Leopold with an open mind will ever again, with clear conscience, be able to step up and testify against the wilderness bill."[101]

Once again, many people wrote in support to Congress. "Our mountains are so beautiful," one wrote, and another said, "and I would like to see them stay that way."[102] Opponents were also heard, one writing, "If you feel the Sporting Goods Business is far superior to the livestock, lumbering and mining business of the Western United States, then vote for wilderness bill 174."[103] Another charged, "S. 174 is as full of holes as a fishnet."[104] Ray Johnson from the West Tacoma Newsprint Company warned, "Establishment of a wilderness area under S. 174 would further remove more commercial timber from possible harvest."[105]

Deciding What's Wilderness

Senator Gordon Allott (R-CO) opposed the bill, which allowed the president to designate the initial areas of wilderness on the recommendation of either the secretary of interior or the secretary of agriculture. The Interior Committee compromised to allow mining surveys in wilderness areas "by means not incompatible with the preservation of the wilderness environment."[106] The biggest dispute was over review of areas for wilderness protection. The committee adopted a compromise that the Forest Service review each area within ten years. Anderson also agreed to a change, over the protests of wilderness advocates, allowing either chamber of Congress, as opposed to requiring both houses, to block presidential designation of a reviewed area as continued wilderness.

At the last moment, Allott offered another weakening amendment, requiring both houses of Congress to take affirmative action on each primitive area before it could be considered protected wilderness. Crucially, these areas would lack any protection until declared wilderness by both chambers.

Allott's amendment initially passed the committee 9–8 on July 13. Chairman Anderson then announced that as far as he was concerned, the wilderness bill was dead. But during the lunch break Anderson persuaded Utah Democrat Frank Moss to reconsider his support of the Allott amendment, while environmentalists contacted prominent contributors to Iowa

Republican Jack Miller, who urged him to change his vote. After the lunch break Moss called for reconsideration of the vote on the amendment, which was defeated 10–7, and the committee reported the bill out 11–4. Zahniser was euphoric, thanking Anderson for "a national contribution that will long be recognized in conservation history."[107]

The Senate debated the bill on September 5 and 6, rejecting other weakening amendments. Gallbladder surgery forced Anderson to return to New Mexico, but Frank Church (D-ID) stepped in to lead the floor fight, proclaiming, "The pending bill is of primary importance to westerners. . . . The vanishing wilderness is yet a part of our western heritage. We westerners have known the wilds during our lifetimes, and we must see to it that our grandchildren are not denied the same rich experience during theirs."[108] The Senate passed the wilderness bill 78–8. The bill allowed continuation of grazing "where it was already well established," while protecting six million additional acres.[109] Udall commented, "When Clinton Anderson of New Mexico became chairman of the Interior Committee in 1961, the Wilderness Bill had a tenacious advocate who would not be denied."[110]

Aspinall now told wilderness opponents that the support of Anderson, a well-respected westerner, "makes this rigid opposition that much more difficult."[111] On December 21, 1961, Aspinall pledged to try to harmonize the desires of wilderness supporters with "the basic multi-use principle of our federal land resources."[112] Among his other objections, Aspinall was sympathetic to the mining industry, which feared the bill's economic impact. Howard Gray, representing the American Mining Congress, testified, "The position of the mining industry is not arbitrary, nor does it stem from self-interest. It is based on the fact that our standard of living . . . demands adequate availability of mineral resources."[113]

The Outdoor Recreation Resources Review Commission (ORRRC), headed by moderate Republican Laurance Rockefeller and including both Saylor and Anderson, had been set up in 1958 to evaluate the public recreation resources. Stegner had written to the ORRRC in December 1960 supporting the idea of wilderness, stating, "We simply need that wild country available to us, even if we never do more than drive to its edge and look in. For it can be a means of reassuring ourselves of our sanity as creatures, a part of the geography of hope."[114] On January 31, 1962, the ORRRC issued its report, urging a major expansion of lands available for outdoor recreation and prompt action to protect wilderness.[115] Recreation was to be an important rationale for wilderness conservation. Writing the next year,

Udall called the report "a landmark analysis of our past failures and present opportunities in the use and protection of the environment."[116]

Udall, meanwhile, felt discouraged by the distance he felt from Kennedy, who rarely consulted his cabinet for advice and lacked much interest in the outdoors. Udall was heartened when President Kennedy sent a special message to Congress on March 1, 1962, urging Udall's priorities of new national parks, wilderness protection, and the Land and Water Conservation Fund. At Udall's suggestion, Kennedy hosted a White House conference on conservation in May 1962. Later that month, Udall wrote in the *New York Times Magazine* that wilderness reminds us that "we are not outside nature, but in it." America's "best thought has derived from our relationship with the land and its creatures."[117] A month earlier, Brower, speaking to the fourth Biennial Conference on Northwest Wilderness in Seattle, emphasized the urgency of the situation, warning, "This year may be the last chance we have to pass the bill."[118] But Aspinall still stood as a roadblock, attacking preservationists who wanted to establish "mausoleum-like museums in which people can go to see resources that cannot be utilized."[119]

In the spring of 1962 Udall and Zahniser both testified before Aspinall's committee in favor of a wilderness bill. Aspinall welcomed Zahniser, calling him "one of the most effective writers with regard to conservation values of the United States that we have."[120] Still, Aspinall pushed for continued resource use. Although Zahniser assured Aspinall that wilderness areas could still be places with traditional multiple uses if the wilderness nature of the areas were preserved, Aspinall would not support the bill.[121] "The autocratic Aspinall . . . had all the good and bad traits of an industrious hedgehog," Udall later wrote.

> Aspinall's hedgehog qualities came into play any time 'unreasonable outsiders' criticized his slow pace or intimated he was obstructing action on important legislation. He would roll himself into a self-righteous ball, flourish his spines, and complain that lazy senators saddled him with their detail work. Then, as he retreated into his burrow, he would make a mental note to shelve the legislation favored by members of Congress who had the temerity to criticize him.[122]

Aspinall said that the Kennedy administration would get a bill "even though you might not recognize it."[123] In the summer of 1962 he introduced his own bill, increasing lumbering, mining, and grazing in public lands, and shepherded it through the Interior Committee in place of

Saylor's proposal. His next step was unusual. On August 30, the full committee reported out the substitute bill, and then with the chairman's blessing, instructed the chairman to report it out "under suspension of the rules, which means that there could be no amendments from the floor," reported Paul Brooks in *Harper's*. "Aspinall explained this extraordinary move by saying it was to 'avoid having emotions take over and undo the work of the committee.'"[124] According to Brooks, Saylor charged that Aspinall was saying the House was "not competent or should be protected from making decisions in which emotions might be involved."[125] Saylor attacked Aspinall's proposal as "a bill to protect miners, lumbermen and other enterprising patriots against rampant conservationists trying to preserve two percent of the country as God has made it."[126] Udall told Kennedy that the bill contained "so many anti-conservation measures that it would have to be vetoed were it to pass."[127] Among other problems, it eliminated the president's longtime power to protect lands through the Antiquities Act or as national wildlife refuges.

Brooks reported further, "For only the sixth time in history, the Speaker of the House—under a deluge of telegrams from indignant citizens—denied a committee chairman's request. Now if the bill got to the floor, it could still be amended, perhaps even restored at zero hour to some semblance of its former self."[128] Lobbying from President Kennedy also helped persuade Speaker John McCormack (D-MA) to take this extraordinary step. Brooks wrote, "Aspinall's strategy was simple. He went home to Colorado. During the three remaining weeks before Congress adjourned, no one succeeded in getting any action and the bill was dead."[129]

Aspinall's maneuvers angered Saylor. Aspinall, noting "fundamental differences," urged Saylor not to "let them spoil a personal friendship which I value very much."[130] Aspinall pointed out that the Interior Committee had successfully passed bills creating three national seashores, "on par and having a status equal to that of the national park."[131] He promised Zahniser that he would work for a "fair and constructive bill" in the next year.[132] Publicly, Aspinall called himself a conservationist "with the same philosophy of Gifford Pinchot, Theodore Roosevelt and Franklin Roosevelt."[133]

Udall still felt that Kennedy's minimal interest in conservation hampered the push for the bill. Udall estimated Kennedy's ratio of involvement as "1% for conservation, 1% for agriculture, 3% for health and welfare, 5% for the economy, and 90% for defense and foreign relations,"[134] a formula that did not make the wilderness bill a priority. Udall said privately, "I long for a flicker of emotion, a response to the out of doors and the overwhelming majesty of the land."[135] President Kennedy gave rhetorical support to the environment, declaring, "Our common goal is an America of open spaces, of fresh water, of green country—a place where wildlife and natural beauty cannot be despoiled."[136] Yet the Kennedy administration was unable or unwilling to put its weight behind major significant programs to help achieve these ideals.

In January 1963 Anderson, with twenty-one cosponsors, introduced a wilderness bill identical to the one the Senate had passed, and the House had not considered, in 1962. Anderson had now given up the Interior chair to take over the Aeronautical and Space Committee, which carried more potential to bring federal funding back home. But Anderson was close to the new chairman, Henry "Scoop" Jackson (D-WA), and when Jackson was occupied with other issues, Anderson ran the Interior Committee hearings on the wilderness proposal.

On April 9, 1963, the Senate took up the Wilderness Act. With Allott absent due to the death of his mother, his junior colleague, Senator Peter Dominick (R-CO), offered multiple amendments on Allott's behalf to weaken the bill. First, he proposed that "the ordinary Mineral Leasing Acts and mineral laws remain in effect in the areas within the wilderness system until December 31, 1977."[137] Senator Alan Bible (D-NV) added, "I firmly believe there is nothing irreconcilable in having mining within a wilderness area." Church answered, "It is very difficult for me to speak against the amendment. I am mindful of the importance of the mining industry. It is one of the chief industries of my State. . . . I am opposed to the pending amendment. . . . If wilderness areas are to be established and preserved . . . then the bill must be strong enough to protect the integrity of the wilderness it embraces." Church added that the bill "makes clear that existing mines and valid, existing mining claims within the areas affected by the bill are to be preserved inviolate."[138] The amendment was defeated 56–26.

Again and again Dominick proposed amendments to weaken the act. Each time Church almost singlehandedly led the opposition to them. Responding to claims that the bill gave up too much congressional authority, Church retorted,

The present law delegates to the Secretary of Agriculture all the authority to create these primitive areas. . . . [W]hat sense does it make to indict the bill as some kind of abdication of congressional responsibility when years ago all the authority was transferred to the executive agencies? . . . [T]he areas that are presently being administered as wilderness . . . shall comprise the wilderness system. . . . [T]he bill specifically provides that not a single new acre may be added to the system without an affirmative act of Congress.[139]

Senator Maurine Neuberger (D-OR), one of only two other senators to speak in favor of the bill besides Church and Anderson, noted, "We have heard many statements to the effect that these primitive domains are amply protected under existing regulations. I disagree. . . . We must face the reality that if a miner wished to lop the top off Mount Hood, in Oregon, in order to get to minerals, he could do it. That is what the law says. It is legal. But is it necessary?"[140]

The Senate then passed the bill 73–12, with most Republicans and Democrats in favor and a handful of southern Democrats, some western Republicans, and a few other miscellaneous senators opposed. The yea votes included every western Democrat except Hayden, including more moderate to conservative senators such as Bible, Clair Engle (CA), and Gale McGee (WY). All but three eastern and midwestern senators— ranging in ideology from the very conservative Roman Hruska (R-NE) to the very liberal George McGovern (D-SD)—supported the bill.

The bill stated,

The wilderness system shall include all areas within the national forests classified on the effective date of this Act . . . as wilderness, wild, primitive, or canoe . . . the areas classified as primitive shall be subject to review . . . within ten years . . . the President shall advise . . . of his recommendations with respect to the continued inclusion with respect to continued inclusion within the wilderness system, or exclusion therefrom, of each area on which review has been completed in the preceding year. . . . [I]f Congress rejects a recommendation of the President . . . the land shall cease to be a part of the wilderness system. . . . Any primitive area, or portion thereof, on which a recommendation for continued inclusion in the wilderness system has not become effective within fourteen years following the enactment of this Act shall cease to be a part of the wilderness system.[141]

The bill also mandated that the interior secretary study any portion of the national parks, monuments, and wildlife refuges that "embraces a continuous area of five thousand acres or more without roads," for possible inclusion in the wilderness system. Another section read, "Any recommendation of the President . . . shall take effect . . . but only if . . . neither the Senate nor the House of Representatives shall have approved a resolution declaring itself opposed to such recommendation."[142]

Thus, the wilderness system comprised areas currently designated as wilderness, but all such areas had to be reviewed and recommended to be kept as wilderness, and not vetoed by either house of Congress, in order to remain protected. With regard to future additions, the bill said, "The addition of any area to, or the elimination of any area from, the wilderness system which is not specifically provided for under the provisions of this Act shall be made only after specific affirmative authorization by law."[143] "Wilderness is a demonstration by our people," later declared Anderson, "that we can take aside a portion of this which we have as a tribute to the Maker and say this we will leave as we found it."[144]

Saylor and others reintroduced the same bill in the House, where it once again ran into opposition from Aspinall. In a letter to President Kennedy in October 1962, Aspinall wrote that "in the interests of orderliness" wilderness preservation should be postponed until solution of the "broad question of the Executive-Legislative relationship in Federal Land use."[145] In 1963 Aspinall again tried to stall the bill. While claiming that he did not object to the preservation of some of the eight million acres designated as primitive by the Forest Service, Aspinall wanted to limit the possible land for wilderness. He also wanted an affirmative vote by Congress for any future wilderness designations.

Aspinall "resented being labelled anti-wilderness by the press."[146] He particularly resented Brooks's article in *Harper's*, carrying the title "Congressman Aspinall vs. The People of the United States," in which Brooks wrote,

> This spring Congressman Wayne Aspinall intends once more to use his position as Chairman of the Committee on Interior and Insular Affairs to frustrate the expressed will of the American people. Specifically, he is determined to block passage of the Wilderness Bill. . . . If you think that he can't get away with it—if you believe a single Congressman can't defy both his colleagues and the public at large, you underestimate Mr. Aspinall. Last summer he did exactly that."[147]

It looked like Aspinall would do it again. "The real fight," Jackson wrote a constituent, "is between conservationists' desire for a mechanism that will force Congress to act to keep an area out of the wilderness system and the efforts of opponents to require Congressional action before an area gets in."[148] Trying to win Aspinall's backing, Representative John Dingell (D-MI) introduced a bill requiring Congress to vote to give wilderness status to any future additions to the wilderness system.

In a further effort to win over Aspinall, Kennedy agreed to a public commission to review the management of the nation's 770 million acres of public lands,[149] but the commission proposal was stuck in the Senate Interior Committee, where Anderson would not commit to moving it forward. After talking with Aspinall's legislative counsel Milton Pearl, Senate Interior Committee land specialist Robert Wolf reported to Anderson, who asked him, "Do you think Aspinall really wants the commission?"[150] When Wolf answered yes, Anderson stated, "And I really want a Wilderness bill." Wolf recounted the exchange to another Senate Interior staffer, Ben Strong, who commented, "Clint's been waiting for something that Wayne really wants."[151]

Despite Aspinall's obstruction, Zahniser actively sought to work with him, writing to Wilderness Society president Harvey Broome when Aspinall became ill in May 1963, "I do hope that [Aspinall] is all right and will remain on the scene, for I have faith we going to be able to work things out with him. If so, our consensus will be broader and our prospects better."[152] Udall later commented, "Although Wayne Aspinall tried Zahnie's patience in a hundred different ways—and spent more than five years thwarting his hopes—like Job, Zahniser never responded with rancor."[153] Zahniser had reviewed a draft of the *Harper's* article, commenting that it was too bad that this "excellent interpretation" of the wilderness issue had dealt with Aspinall "in such a personal way."[154]

By the spring of 1963, Aspinall still had not scheduled hearings on the wilderness bill, telling administration officials that all he had received from wilderness advocates for his efforts in 1962 was "abuse, some of it unprintable." Aspinall's local paper, the Grand Junction *Daily Sentinel*, supported him, saying the attacks "prove to Westerners how vital to the west's very existence is the victory for which Aspinall is fighting."[155]

Wilderness advocates including the Wilderness Society and Saylor had decided to accede to Aspinall's demand that any further additions of wilderness would have to pass both chambers of Congress. As wilderness proponents made steps toward him, Aspinall told the press that a wilderness bill might be possible in the current Congress. Negotiations between Aspinall, Zahniser, and the White House continued into the fall of 1963.

After discussion with Aspinall, Saylor introduced a revised bill, which Aspinall called "an important step, very constructive," and promised hearings early in 1964. The bill would give wilderness status to some nine million acres, subject to review within five years and eventual congressional veto, and continue existing hunting, fishing, and grazing. The Saylor bill would terminate mining leases in the wilderness areas immediately. Aspinall continued to insist that existing mining in the proposed wilderness must be allowed to continue.

At the same time, Udall published his book *The Quiet Crisis*, warning, "America today stands poised on a pinnacle of wealth and power, yet we live in a land of vanishing beauty, of increasing ugliness, of shrinking open space, and of an overall environment that is diminished daily by pollution and noise and blight."[156] In a timely message to the Capitol, Udall wrote, "The status we give our wilderness and semi-wilderness areas will also measure the degree of our reverence for the land. . . . A wilderness system will offer man what many consider the supreme human experience."[157]

On November 21, 1963, just before flying to Texas, Kennedy urged Aspinall to pass a wilderness bill. Aspinall answered that while speedy passage was impossible in 1963, he planned to hold early hearings in 1964. Kennedy answered, "All right, you can't blame me for asking," seemingly expressing the casual attitude Udall bemoaned.[158]

It was his last environmental comment.

After Kennedy was assassinated on November 22, Aspinall said that the shock was "worse than the declaration of the three wars that I had witnessed." Biographer Steve Schulte wrote, "It is not an exaggeration to argue that Aspinall's certain and steady handling of the Wilderness legislation in 1964 relates to promises he made to the former president."[159]

The Arrival of Lyndon Baines Johnson

Udall did not know if the new president, Lyndon Baines Johnson—to whom he had denied the Arizona delegation at the 1960 Democratic convention—would retain him. Udall later recalled, "He called me in about the fifth of December. . . . It was plain that he hadn't forgotten the past, but he said, 'We've got a job to do and you can do your part.'"[160] Soon afterward, Udall sent Johnson a memo outlining his two biggest priorities, the wilderness bill and the Land and Conservation Fund.

Following Johnson's first meeting with his cabinet, Udall privately wrote, "He is really in the saddle now. Tough-minded, insistent on results, combines carrot and stick with [the] rare skill of a great Majority Leader in the White House." Udall continued that Johnson had high expectations and "will be merciless when we let him down, I predict."[161] In a later interview Aspinall commented, "It's my feeling that President Kennedy was not then as ambitious in his program as President Johnson was in his day. This had an effect on men like Secretary Udall, who was in the cabinet of each of them." Aspinall continued, "President Johnson came along. He took all that atmosphere of idealism . . . and he put into operation many of the things that I feel that Kennedy had merely wanted to talk about and perhaps didn't want specially to happen. So, Udall responded accordingly."[162]

Johnson's time in office was marked by Vietnam, civil rights, and his antipoverty efforts. Were it not for those issues, he would write in his memoirs, "I would have been content to be simply the conservation President. My deepest attitudes and beliefs were shaped by a closeness to the land, and it was only natural for me to think of preserving it. I wanted to continue the good work begun by Theodore Roosevelt."[163]

Six months in office, Johnson made his commitment public in his "Great Society" commencement speech at the University of Michigan, depicting the Great Society as "a place where man can renew contact with nature."[164] Two years later, political scientist Lynton Caldwell wrote of Johnson, "His espousal of natural beauty and environmental quality issues surprised and gratified conservationists who had not looked for this type of commitment from a professional politician from western Texas."[165] In his later memoir, Johnson wrote, "I have flown through the layers of filthy air above Los Angeles. I have seen the oily slime of the Hudson and Potomac Rivers. And I found such experiences repugnant, as perhaps only a man who grew up knowing nature at its cleanest could."[166]

The Senate had passed the wilderness bill in 1963. With proponents agreeing to accept a final product more akin to Aspinall's desires, the chances of a bill seemed higher. Aspinall had agreed to compromise, publicly announcing in January 1964 that he would try to pass a wilderness bill before Congress adjourned. Aspinall held hearings on several wilderness proposals early in 1964. Environmentalists favored the Saylor bill while Aspinall seemed to prefer a proposal by Dingell, which included a ten-year review period and allowed mining for ten years after passage. At the final hearings in late April 1964, Zahniser noted that he had attended eighteen prior House and Senate hearings on wilderness legislation. Testifying for a bill, Zahniser urged, "It may seem presumptuous for men and women who live only 40, 50, 60, 70, or 80 years, to dare to undertake a program for perpetuity, but that surely is our challenge."[167] Without legislative action, he warned, "we cannot expect to see wilderness endure in our country."[168] Dingell testified that Kennedy had said the bill would be "one of the most significant conservation landmarks in recent years."[169] Udall urged passage of a bill along the lines of the Saylor draft. Aspinall, arguing for allowing mining in wilderness areas, got Udall to admit that few such claims would likely be filed.

Prospects of the Saylor/Dingell proposals seemed promising when Aspinall became enraged by an April 30 *Washington Post* editorial. The *Post* commented that Aspinall was standing "like a Druid ready to resume a familiar ritual of delaying or killing wilderness legislation."[170] Aspinall stated that the editorial "was just about as dangerous, as far as killing wilderness legislation, as any article [could] be," threatening that further criticism would kill any bill.[171] To soothe the waters Public Lands Subcommittee chair Walter Baring (D-NV) and ranking Republican John Kyl (IA) went on the record to praise Aspinall's fairness in conducting the hearings. Kyl stated, "It has been my impression in the years we have debated this legislation that the chairman of the full committee has taken far too much personal abuse concerning this legislation."[172]

"We have some members of this Committee who are absolutely opposed to any wilderness legislation," Aspinall explained in an overview. "They have good reason; and we have some members of this Committee who are for any kind of wilderness legislation. They would lock up anybody's property. . . . Then we have great many moderates who would like to see some kind of decision arranged."[173] A few days later, in early May, Howard Zahniser died at the age of fifty-eight, from heart failure. Upset, Aspinall said that although "Howard did not live to see" the enactment of the Wilderness Bill, he knew "that the main battle had been won." Saylor pointedly added that there could not be any greater tribute to this "Apostle of the wilderness" than "to have Congress this year pass Howard Zahniser's dream legislation—a wilderness bill."[174]

In May, Anderson and Aspinall met in Anderson's Senate office and reached agreement on the details of the wilderness legislation. Anderson later recalled the moment when "Wayne smiled with pleasure, and somewhat to my surprise, took my offer; he seemed delighted that he could finally settle the dispute on terms favorable to himself and end the bitter antagonism of the conservationists."[175] The compromise allowed Aspinall's proposal for a commission to revise the laws governing public lands to move through the Senate Interior Committee. In addition, Aspinall got a wilderness bill that he could live with, allowing some commercial activities to continue in wilderness. Moreover, while the executive branch could suggest land for wilderness designation, the decision-making power would belong solely to Congress.

On June 10, the House Interior Subcommittee on Public Lands met in executive session. It amended Saylor's proposal and reported it to the full Interior Committee. The revision permitted mining for twenty-five years after wilderness status, changed the review period for lands to be considered for wilderness from five to ten years and removed the San Gorgonio Wild Area in Southern California from protection to allow construction of a ski resort.[176] The amendment also allowed the executive branch to remove primitive areas from protection, subject to a congressional veto. Existing primitive areas would be treated as wilderness until reviewed. On June 18 the House Interior Committee endorsed the bill unanimously and sent it to the House floor. Presenting the bill, Aspinall declared with "a deep sense of satisfaction" that the final language was "a compromise measure that I feel can be supported by everyone," adding, "The majority of members of the House Committee on Interior and Insular affairs continue to feel that preservation of areas for their wilderness values is a legitimate and worthwhile objective in the management of public lands."[177]

During the House debate, it became clear that Aspinall was not alone in wanting a weaker bill. Baring, the chair of the Interior Committee Subcommittee on Public Lands, which had held the hearings on the bill, snorted, "I never thought the bill was necessary in the first place." Baring continued, "I am personally strictly for multiple use of the public lands, but do recognize the need for the preservation of some primitive areas, however, not at the cost of the local economy, such as the cattle business, lumber and mining industries."[178] Nevertheless, Baring told the House he supported the bill. Saylor tried to reassure wavering representatives, pointing out that "the measure contains no authority for appropriations to acquire any land and waters that are not owned by the Federal government." More lyrically, he added, "Wilderness is not only fragile, but also perishable. . . . Once the stroke of the pen is made to change a wilderness area to one of development, the act has a finality that enables few comparisons."[179] Dingell, whose own bill was similar to the final product, told the House, "I shall not take time to emphasize the vital importance of this legislation which many of us regard, and as President Kennedy described so aptly, as one of the most significant conservation landmarks of recent years."[180]

Representative Morris Udall (D-AZ)—a member of the Interior Committee, a strong wilderness proponent, and now occupying his brother Stewart's former House seat—exulted, "Mr. Chairman, if the Congress keeps up the way we are going I think we are going to be known as the 'Conservation Congress.' In two weeks when this bill passes today . . . we will have enacted two landmark pieces of conservation legislation: the wilderness bill and the land and water conservation fund bill."[181] The Land and Water Conservation Fund was the vehicle providing the funding to acquire additional land for the future parks and wilderness.

On the House floor, Saylor introduced two amendments. The first restored protection for the San Gorgonio Wild Area and the second eliminated the executive branch's ability to open primitive areas to development, reserving the sole power to change their status to Congress. Over Aspinall's opposition, both amendments passed by an almost 2–1 margin, before the bill itself passed almost by acclamation.

The House bill differed in some major ways from the Senate version. The bill stated, "Each recommendation of the President for designation as wilderness shall become effective only if provided by an Act of Congress." Thus, permanent protection of an area would require the positive assent of both chambers. Another key clause read, "Areas classified as 'primitive' on the effective date of this Act shall continue to be administered under rules and recommendation affecting such areas . . . until Congress has determined otherwise."[182]

The ten House-Senate conferees who met to work out the differences between the two bills included Representatives Aspinall and Saylor, and Senators Jackson, Anderson, Church, Thomas Kuchel (R-CA), and Allott. Afterward, Anderson told the Senate, "In an age of automation, mechanization and exploitation of our vast natural resources, the amount of public lands shielded from the onslaught of man's ambition and genius becomes [ever] smaller. Our task in this age has been to stand off . . . that onslaught."[183] Aspinall thanked Saylor in presenting the conference report, saying, "There have been times when the gentleman from Pennsylvania and the Chairman of the committee have been so much in opposition to each other on this legislation that it looked as if it would be impossible for us ever to get together." Aspinall also mentioned Zahniser, whose name, he said, was one that "stands out like a beacon light to all of you," but who like the "patriarch of old was denied to experience his moment of victory."[184]

Aspinall commented, "The conference committee adopted the House version except for the following . . . " The biggest concession the House made was the amount of area needed to be considered wilderness. While the House had mandated a minimum of five thousand acres, the conference committee agreed to the Senate preference for wording of "at least five thousand acres or is of sufficient size as to make practicable its preservation and use in an unimpaired condition." Aspinall declared, "This legislation will be known as the Anderson-Saylor Act—named after two talented and able conservationists." Saylor hailed the final legislation, stating, "I think it is a tribute to the great system of American government that we can come to you today with a unanimous [conference committee] report."[185] With minor changes, the final bill indeed most closely resembled the House version, and passed both chambers overwhelmingly, 73–12 in the Senate and 373–1 in the House.

Passage and Implications of the Wilderness Act

Legislators had argued over what lands could qualify as wilderness. The act included several specific criteria. A wilderness area must be affected primarily by the forces of nature. It must have "outstanding opportunities" for solitude or primitive recreation. Finally, it should contain "ecological, geological or other features of scientific, educational, scenic or historical value."[186] While opponents hoped that these criteria would limit the lands that could be designated as wilderness, these secondary requirements were not mandatory. The conference committee eliminated a requirement in the House bill that the president must explain why an area should receive wilderness status.

The key distinction for what over time had been called variously primitive areas, wilderness national parks, wild areas, and finally wilderness was that they must be areas where nature was dominant, where human presence was ephemeral. Wilderness areas could not include significant roads or any commercial development. The only economic activities permitted would be those given to win passage of the bill, such as limited logging or mining for a time where such enterprises were present when the wilderness bill was passed.

Reflecting the utilitarian rationale behind the act, it stated, "Wilderness areas shall be devoted to the public purposes of recreational, scenic, scientific, educational, conservation and historical use."[187] In areas designated as wilderness, use of any motorized equipment was prohibited. Hunting, fishing, and existing levels of grazing were allowed. In a concession to Aspinall, mineral prospecting in wilderness areas would be allowed through 1983. The Wilderness Act did not add to the amount of public land but rather changed the level of protection provided for the designated land. Four federal agencies, the National Park Service, National Forest Service, Fish and Wildlife Service, and Bureau of Land Management, would each manage their own lands but treat wilderness areas under the rules of the Wilderness Act.[188]

Aspinall would enjoy new reviews vastly different from the *Harper's* article and the *Washington Post* editorial. The National Wildlife Federation honored Aspinall at the end of 1964 as Conservationist of the Year.[189] Aspinall later boasted, "I have three of the awards of the conservation groups. . . . These were in the years when the conservation organizations were paying more attention to the heart of conservation than either one of the extremes."[190] In a message significant for future arrangements, Aspinall now assured Stewart Udall, "I was 100% on your side. We may have our differences because of the differences of the executive and legislative operation, but, in my book, you have made a very effective, constructive and outstanding Secretary of the Interior."[191]

Shortly before Anderson's retirement, he commented about the Wilderness Act, "I felt a sense of positive achievement. It was the kind of imperfect compromise that often comes out of Congress, leaving a certain uneasiness in its trail, but it was important, nonetheless. I felt that we had done something significant for the generations of Americans who will follow us."[192] Udall later commented,

I often thought that had I had someone in the House as chairman of the [Interior] committee who was comparable to Senator Jackson, let's say, or Senator Anderson of New Mexico, that we might have gotten twice as much done. But he's [Aspinall] a very strong-minded, one-man committee, and very dominant and domineering, so you have to kowtow to him, work with him, get as much as you could, take your half a loaf and settle for that. And he was educable and flexible, to a degree.[193]

Doris Kearns Goodwin, who worked with Lyndon Johnson on his memoirs and then wrote her own book about him, reported, "Johnson orchestrated the signing ceremonies for each of his Great Society programs with the same concentrated care and intensity that he had bestowed upon every step of their march through the legislative process."[194] That sense of ceremony and history was vivid in the final step of the Wilderness Act.

On September 3, 1964, at a White House Rose Garden ceremony, President Johnson signed both the Wilderness Act and the Land and Water Conservation Fund Act. "This is a very happy and historic occasion for all who love the great outdoors, and that, needless, to say, includes me," declared the president. "The wilderness bill preserves for our posterity, for all time to come, 9 million acres of this vast continent in their original and unchanging beauty and wonder." Surrounding himself with Aspinall, Udall, Anderson, and Jackson, Johnson proclaimed in his most unifying mode, "I think it is significant that these steps have broad support, not just from the Democratic Party, but from the Republican Party, both parties in Congress."[195] Johnson, the master vote counter, saw the significance of the overwhelming endorsement from both sides of the aisle, and what it suggested about future possibilities.

For the next decade, through Democratic and Republican presidencies, protection of nature would be largely a bipartisan cause. Control of Congress would put Democrats in the lead, but Saylor's leadership on wilderness would point to crucial future Republican involvement, and to other Republicans playing key roles in the decade's environmental legislation. Wilderness proponents emphasized it as a resource for future Americans. Supreme Court Justice William O. Douglas wrote, "Today, we look backward to a time when there was more wilderness than the people of America needed. Today we look forward (and only a matter of few years) to a time when all of the wilderness now existing will not be enough."[196]

Notably, the Wilderness Act made no mention of protecting endangered species, ecosystems, or biodiversity. However, Dingell would note in 1970, "We should all recognize that many forms of wildlife found on the national wildlife refuges absolutely require a wilderness condition in order to survive."[197] Besides creating congressional coalitions, the Wilderness Act created a system that itself stimulated the country's environmental energies. It required the federal land agencies to review existing public lands that might qualify as wilderness and submit recommendations to Congress by 1974. This included 5.6 million acres of forest lands still protected as primitive, 22 million acres of national parks, and the 25 million acres of wildlife refuges. "The nation's most protective public land conservation law, the Wilderness Act of 1964, was a major compromise," noted the environmentalist Paul Hansen. "It protected only nine million acres. . . . But it did set up an inclusive and deliberate process for adding the highest level of protection to more areas of federal public lands."[198] The process would create a pressure for action.

Saylor commented in 1970, "It is widely recognized . . . that other areas beyond those specified for study by the parent [wilderness] act may warrant and, for wisest stewardship, require similar legal designation [as wilderness]."[199] Even prior to the passage of the Wilderness Act, Brower commented of these unprotected areas in 1962, "They are simply wilderness areas which have been set aside by God, but which have not yet been created by the Forest Service."[200] Adding new areas as wilderness required passage through both houses of Congress.

"The 1964 Anderson-Aspinall compromise was, in truth, a political wager," Udall would write, over two decades later.

> The concession the Colorado chairman demanded and got was an amendment that no lands could be added to the newly created Wilderness System unless both branches of Congress voted for such additions. Representative Aspinall was betting that this provision . . . would sap the strength of the wilderness movement. . . . A weary Senator Anderson had a contrary hunch that if his bill became law, wilderness activism was here to stay and flourish even in the West. Nearly a quarter of a century later, history tells us that Clinton Anderson . . . won his wager.[201]

In hindsight from another thirty years later, it is clear that wilderness activism has not disappeared, but that there has been a substantial backlash, particularly in some of the western states.

Conservationists quickly came to see Udall's point. Four years after the bill passed, Stewart Brandborg, Zahniser's successor at the Wilderness Society, told the society's board that Aspinall's "'blocking effort,' as we saw it at the time, has turned out to be a great liberating force in the conservation movement. . . . [T]he Wilderness Law, as it was passed, has opened the way for a far more effective conservation movement, in which people in local areas must be involved in a series of drives for preservation of the wilderness they know."[202]

Ironically, the Senate version had a provision that areas would lose protection as wilderness in the absence of a positive review within a set period. Since the Forest Service could not complete the bulk of its reviews within the ten years specified, these lands would have been opened to development. The House bill that largely became law, while requiring an Act of Congress for permanent protection, kept such existing protections in the absence of congressional action to remove them. As the result, much more of the originally specified wilderness remained protected than would have been the case had the Senate bill been enacted.

This organizing charge made the Wilderness Act more than a legal landmark, more than the first major environmental legislation in memory. Its galvanizing of conservation organizations made the act a spur for the legislation to follow, for the citizen pressure pushing all the sweeping congressional activity of the sixties and seventies. As much as providing stronger protections for federal primitive land, and increasing the acreage covered by the protection, the Wilderness Act helped plant the roots of the Green Years.

Udall won national acclaim for his role. In September President Johnson thanked him for the "leadership and the wisdom, the vitality and the vigorous approach . . . that he has provided from coast to coast in this field." *New York Times* columnist James Reston wrote that Udall "has done more to keep the problems of conservation before an increasingly urbanized country than any Secretary since Harold Ickes."[203] Saylor called Udall "the greatest secretary that ever held this office."[204]

That November Johnson won a sweeping victory over Goldwater, winning over 60 percent of the popular vote. Johnson's landslide also brought into office a host of liberal Democratic representatives and senators, creating a huge Democratic majority in Congress. Aspinall, whose district had been reapportioned by the Republican Colorado legislature, surprised many by winning a sweeping reelection victory. Beginning his own term, Johnson reappointed Udall as secretary of the interior. Later, he would tell his cabinet officer, "The Udall years are going to stand as a landmark in the history of your department and the history of the nation's conservation efforts—and for that, I am very proud."[205]

The Johnson administration would propose adding thirty more areas to the wilderness system, based on reviews completed by September 1967. The Senate agreed to twelve new areas, but opposition from Aspinall resulted in only four new areas being added.[206] But in the years since the passage of the Wilderness Act, wilderness protection has expanded tremendously. Through congressional action, the initial 54 wilderness areas comprising 9.1 million acres had increased by 2009 to encompass 757 wilderness areas and 109.5 million acres, 5 percent of the country's land area.[207]

Four years after the passage of the Wilderness Act, beset and battered by the deepening disaster of Vietnam and racial upheaval in the nation's cities, Johnson still returned to the issue of wilderness. In a letter to Congress March 28, 1968, two days before announcing that he would not run again, Johnson urged, "Inevitably, our work as public leaders affects not only us, but our posterity . . . our grandchildren and great-grandchildren will live in a different America from the one we knew, but it will be an America we have helped to build. They will . . . seek solace and recreation in parks and wilderness areas we preserve. So, we must build well now."[208]

In language originally written by Howard Zahniser, the Wilderness Act declared, "A wilderness, in contrast with those areas where man and his own works dominate the landscape, is hereby recognized as an area where the earth and the community of life are untrammeled by man, where man himself is a visitor who does not remain."[209] Decades of legislation and wilderness expansion later, Senator Jeff Bingaman (D-NM) observed, "Certain provisions of the Wilderness Act are unique among United States code because they read more like poetry than the fodder of legislatures and lawyers."[210]

CHAPTER THREE

Money, Beauty, and Recreation

KEY EVENTS:
The Land and Water Conservation Fund Act (1964)
Highway Beautification Act (1965)
Outdoor Recreation

Nobody, in his time or ours, has generally thought of Lyndon Johnson in terms of beauty. Besides his own jug-eared, big-nose, hangdog looks, he never appeared to be someone who savored the glories of the outdoors, always seeming more comfortable in a Capitol Hill caucus or working the phones with other politicians. But at the high point of his career, at the peak of his power and prospects, Johnson set out a clear vision and priorities about how he saw natural America. "Beauty is in danger," Johnson warned in 1964, as he sought a full term on his own and approached his time of greatest power. "And once man no longer walks with beauty or wonder at nature, his spirit will wither."[1]

Before the 1964 election, Johnson set up the Task Force on Natural Beauty, one of nine environmental task forces he would create. The motivation, explained Johnson's aide Richard Goodwin, was that "the Federal government has not developed comprehensive policies on preservation of the natural beauty of the nation."[2] Philanthropist Laurance Rockefeller, whom Johnson named to the task force, recalled Johnson's instructions: "You tell me what you think ought to be done; what needs to be done; and let me decide whether it can be done."[3]

Johnson would go into the 1964 election, less than a full year after taking office, with a broad record of environmental achievement. With the influence of Lady Bird Johnson and Secretary of the Interior Stewart Udall, it would remain a priority in his full term, as stronger Democratic majorities increased possibilities, and even after broader problems loomed over his White House. As costs from other ambitious programs and the Vietnam War pressured the national finances, Johnson would try to resist efforts by his budget office to trim spending on preservation and recreation. Johnson's assistant Joseph Califano Jr. told Udall, "Budget's trouble is that it consistently underestimates the way this man [Johnson] loves the land."[4]

The Land and Water Conservation Fund

Johnson's preelection achievements in 1964 included the Wilderness Act, a new national park and new national seashores, a new Bureau of Outdoor Recreation, and, crucially—after long efforts—funding to acquire new lands for recreation.[5] Udall had strongly pushed the idea of a Land and Water Conservation Fund to buy private property to expand protected public lands. "It would be like the highway trust funds, you know, where the funds would be earmarked," he recalled later. "The Bureau of the Budget was at first very reluctant about this. They went along with me in part finally because I agreed to go along with them with this system of charging fees at national park areas."[6]

Both ideas, funding for acquiring new areas and user fees, had been strongly backed by the Outdoor Recreation Resources Review Commission (ORRRC). President Kennedy had urged the idea on Congress both in 1962 and 1963, but action was slow. Unlike the Wilderness Act, the Land and Water Conservation Fund had the enthusiastic backing of Wayne Aspinall, who called the proposed fund "of greater significance to the whole of the American public . . . than any measure which our committee is likely to report to the House for a long time to come."[7] With the strong support of John Saylor, Aspinall introduced the administration bill in the House, and Interior Committee chairman Henry Jackson sponsored it in the Senate.

The Conservation Fund came before the House Interior Committee in 1963. The proposal called for raising $2 billion over the next twenty-five years to purchase private property for recreational uses. Revenue would be raised by selling surplus public property, taxing motorboat fuel, and charging admission and user fees at national parks, monuments, and recreation areas. Half or more of the money would be distributed to states to buy or improve recreation facilities.[8]

Opposition, especially in the Senate, focused on the user fees, the division of revenues between the states and the federal government, and how much of the money the states could use for developing facilities as opposed to buying land. Other objections were fundamental. "We do not believe it is the intent of the ORRRC . . . to have the Federal Government acquire lands," argued Donald Baldwin on behalf of the National Lumber Manufacturers Association. "The chief aim of Federal recreation activities should be the development of existing Federal recreation sites."[9] The National Association of Manufacturers and American Farm Bureau Federation also opposed federal purchase of additional lands. To pass the bill, its authors had to accept some limitations on land purchases.

Senate supporters agreed to defer to the House, where ultraconservative Rules Committee chairman Howard Smith (D-VA) refused to let the bill go to the floor. Smith had frequently blocked Kennedy administration measures, but with likely pressure from Johnson and House Speaker John McCormack, the bill was pried out of the committee and swiftly passed by both houses. In September 1964 Johnson signed the bill at the same time as the Wilderness Act.

Lady Bird and Beauty

The ORRRC report had urged a major expansion of lands available for outdoor recreation. With input from Senator Clinton Anderson (D-NM), the report was followed by the creation of the Bureau of Outdoor Recreation in the Department of the Interior, to coordinate recreation programs scattered through multiple federal agencies.[10] Edward C. Crafts, chosen to become director of this bureau, later recalled, "I think at the time the study was made there were about thirty-five federal agencies that in one way or another had something to do with outdoor recreation."[11]

With the bureau, the federal government began creating national recreation areas, where recreation was the top priority. Later, funding for states to expand their recreational facilities was added to the Land and Water Conservation Fund.[12] "We passed the Conservation Fund bill, we passed the Wilderness Bill, we had several new national parks bills—all of which were passed by Congress within a period of two weeks in September of 1964," noted Udall. "This, of course led on to a second phase in the president's new term because that gave us momentum," bolstered by Johnson's massive election victory.[13]

In February 1965 Johnson sent a special message to Congress calling for a "New Conservation" program. "Its concern is not with nature alone," he declared, "but with the total relation between man and the world around him."[14] Johnson noted that "for over three centuries the beauty of America has sustained our spirit and has enlarged our vision," and now the heritage had to be protected.[15] He proposed a campaign to clean up cities and blighted lands and using the new Land and Water Conservation Fund to add more national parks, seashores, recreation areas, wildlife refuges, and wilderness. The plan also called for improving air and water quality and preserving free-flowing scenic rivers.[16] "Environmental protection," noted Johnson biographer Robert Dallek, "commanded his attention and aroused his best instincts."[17] The message announced a White House Conference on National Beauty, which took place in May, attended by eight hundred people. At the conference, Johnson advocated beautifying cities and highways, noting, "Poison and chemicals pollute our air and water. Automobiles litter our countryside. These and other waste products are among the deadliest enemies that natural beauty has ever known . . . [Beauty should be brought] into the daily lives of all our citizens."[18]

Henry L. Diamond, then a young lawyer working on ORRRC, later recalled of the conference, "Once inside [the White House] cabinet members and Congressmen and concerned citizens sat around on the floor. The conferees told the president of the United States what ought to be done about natural beauty in America. They urged strong controls on strip mining. . . . [T]hey urged increased efforts at educating their fellow citizens so they could better understand the environment . . . [and] most important of all, the word went out from the White House that the president and First Lady cared."[19] Laurance Rockefeller said of the Johnsons, "This was the great thing that in both of their cases they inherited, as I did, the love of the land, the love of the soil, the respect for the outdoors, and the identity with it from childhood."[20]

As an infant, Claudia Alta Taylor was called Lady Bird, a nickname she could not shake. She said, "Nature is my first and most reliable companion."[21] Shortly after getting her second bachelor's degree from the University of Texas, she met Lyndon Johnson, and married him less than three months later. In 1936 he was elected to Congress, and she took over running his congressional office when he briefly went into the navy during

World War II. "When I think of Lyndon's being captured," she wrote a friend, "I think of O. Henry's 'Ransom of Red Chief,'" alluding to a story in which the kidnappers ultimately pay the hostage's family to take him back.[22] In 1943 the Johnsons bought a radio station, and Lyndon Johnson told Lady Bird, "You have to go down and take that place over."[23] The radio—later television—station would make them wealthy. Lady Bird, wrote Lewis Gould, "remained the one person in whom he [Lyndon Johnson] confided with complete trust."[24]

In the weeks after Johnson's 1964 election victory, Lady Bird decided to focus on "the whole field of conservation and beautification."[25] Crafts saw that the first lady's concern for natural beauty bolstered the president's environmental instincts. "She gave, in her quiet way, great support to our program," he wrote. "She stimulated his interest and, of course, this helped give us administration support."[26] Lady Bird viewed beautification in broad terms, considering it as the whole physical environment passed on to posterity.[27]

Lady Bird received so many requests for speeches on conservation and beautification that in March 1965 she set up a speakers' bureau made up of cabinet and Senate wives. "To the severest critics, the beautification projects of the First Lady were little more than aesthetic frivolities," wrote Martin Melosi. "This kind of criticism underestimates the influence that Lady Bird had on her husband and the catalytic role that she played in raising environmental issues to national attention."[28] Contemporaries recognized Lady Bird's impact. "I think she's had a terrific impact on people's awareness of natural beauty and the out of doors," concluded Edward P. Cliff, chief of the United States Forest Service at the time. "She's really been instrumental in getting the public to think about natural beauty and outdoor recreation in a way that they never have before."[29]

Starting with a campaign to clean up Washington, DC, Lady Bird told her staff to use the word *beautification* as little as possible, seeing it as sounding too superficial.[30] From 1965 to 1968 Lady Bird's campaign in Washington would landscape eighty parks, thirty-nine public schools, and eight playgrounds, improving both poorer neighborhoods and touristy official Washington.[31] Representative Julia Butler Hansen (D-WA), initially skeptical, later admitted that "the appearance of the city of Washington has improved a thousand percent within the 8 years I have been here."[32]

Following the White House Conference on Natural Beauty, President Johnson sent Congress a proposal to limit roadside signs and clutter.[33]

"[The] economy, and the roads that serve it, are not ends in themselves," he argued in the message. "They are meant to serve the real needs of the people of this country. And those needs include the opportunity to touch nature and see beauty."[34] Later, explained Lady Bird, "It became one of my hopes that potentially on scenic highways, which the federal government had helped fund, or had entirely funded, we could look at the country."[35] Roadside billboards had been controversial for years. Ogden Nash wrote about the issue in the 1930s, saying, "I think I shall never see a billboard lovely as a tree. Perhaps, unless the billboards fall, I'll never see a tree at all."[36] In 1958 Congress gave a 5 percent bonus in highway funding to states that controlled billboards, but fewer than two hundred miles of highway were affected.[37] In 1965 Secretary of Commerce John T. Conner admitted to a House committee that "the present law has definitely proved to be ineffective."[38]

The president's new proposal recognized the strength of the billboard and highway construction lobbies. The administration had reached an agreement with the powerful Outdoor Advertising Association of America (OAAA) to ban billboards along all interstates but allow them in commercial zones on other roads. However, the OAAA later turned against the bill. The proposal did not receive much support in Congress. Patrick McNamara (D-MI), chair of the Senate Public Works Committee, said flatly, "I'm not bothered by billboards."[39] The biggest obstacle was the funding for the proposed scenic improvements along the highways and to compensate owners who took down their billboards. The proposal also included the removal of roadside junkyards for the same purpose of scenic improvement. The administration's initial plan to finance the beautification program from the Highway Trust Fund engendered such strong opposition from groups that wanted the money solely for construction that the administration agreed to separate funding.[40]

Johnson now began to push harder for a bill, telling his cabinet, "You know I love that woman and she wants that Highway Beautification Act. . . . By God, we're going to get it for her."[41] The administration enlisted Walter Reuther, the powerful head of the United Auto Workers, to lobby for the bill, a useful move against McNamara. The result was a stronger bill—although it did compensate billboard owners. With that concession, the Senate passed the bill 63–14.

The House was less enthusiastic, and it took White House pressure on the roads subcommittee chairman John Kluczynski (D-IL) to get an acceptable product to the House floor. The bill barely escaped the Rules Committee, 7–6, and the billboard lobby launched a major effort against it. Massachusetts's Tip O'Neill, the future Speaker of the House, commented that "some billboards are more beautiful than old buildings."[42] George H. Mahon (D-TX) observed, "No one in the Texas delegation likes the bill, but no one wants to vote against Lady Bird."[43] With further weakening amendments, the House passed its bill 245–139 at 1 a.m. on October 8. Facing House defeat of a stronger bill, the Senate accepted the House version.

"This bill does more than control advertising and junkyards along the billions of dollars of highways that the people have built with their money—public money," Johnson said at the signing ceremony. "This bill will bring the wonders of nature back into our daily lives. This bill will enrich our spirits. . . . It does not represent what we need. . . . But it is a first step."[44] While the bill would be criticized as weak, clearly no stronger bill could have passed the Congress. The next year, when Senator Paul Douglas (D-IL) attempted to strengthen the law with a Junked Auto Disposal Act, it was killed by opposition led by scrap dealers and the steel industry.[45]

In 1967, Washington's senators, Warren Magnuson and Henry Jackson, cosponsored a bill to remove the federal mandate to pay for billboard removal. "The sole purpose of the bill," said Magnuson, "is to allow the states to decide whether or in what manner they will compensate for billboard removal or the screening or removal of junkyards."[46] Opponents rallied against the proposal. One wrote, "To force them [junkyards] to move without paying them a fair compensation would be to deprive them of their property unjustly."[47] The Highway Beautification Act had ordered states to remove billboards or face a reduction in federal funding. It was not until 1971 that any states, eleven in all, were notified that they would lose federal funding due to noncompliance.[48]

In 1968 the Federal Aid Highway Act would dramatically cut the money available for beautification, but advocates were able to beat off an amendment to eliminate it entirely. Over the next two decades more funding was restored, allowing for improvements with removal of roadside billboards and junkyards, but not elimination of the problem.[49] Lady Bird Johnson became both a force and a symbol. "By the end of her husband's presidency," her biographer Lewis Gould wrote, "the First Lady had established in the popular mind her identification with the environment, and she had transformed the term *beautification* into a word that connoted respect rather than triviality."[50]

The Conservation Effort Lands on the Beach

Beaches, where the sea crashes against the land, have long been classic recreation territory, and the United States has thousands of miles of dramatic shoreline along the Atlantic, the Pacific, and the Gulf of Mexico. But in 1963 Stewart Udall noted that only 7 percent of the shoreline in the lower forty-eight states had been preserved for recreation, calling for more space to meet a roaring need.[51] The government began establishing national seashore recreational areas within the National Park Service. President Kennedy's family compound at Hyannis Port on Cape Cod had become famous, and under the Kennedy administration the Cape Cod National Seashore became the first such recreation area. George Hartzog Jr., director of the Park Service, noted, "Our objective in the national seashore . . . is to provide a variety of recreational opportunities."[52] In his 1966 message to Congress, Johnson proposed establishing additional national seashores, lakeshores, and recreation areas.

"The President has got his heart in conservation," Udall told a reporter in the summer of 1965, "and is pushing it for all it's worth." Signing the Assateague Island National Seashore bill in September 1965, President Johnson said of future Americans, "We must leave them a glimpse of the world as God really made it, not just as it looked when we got through with it."[53] In 1965 the administration also proposed the National Historic Preservation Act, providing federal matching funds to cities for preserving historic places, and creating a committee to identify historic and archaeological properties to be administered by the National Park Service. With the support of Lady Bird and the National Trust for Historic Preservation, the bill passed in 1966.

The fall of 1965 also saw the passage of bills to regulate air and water quality, as well as major legislation such as the Voting Rights Act and Medicare. In 1965, the fabulous 89th Congress would pass 89 of 115 proposed laws from the Johnson administration.[54] Johnson noted, "My experience in the [National Youth Administration] taught me that when people have a hand in shaping projects, these projects are more likely to be successful than the ones simply handed down from the top. . . . [As president] I insisted on congressional consultation at every step, beginning with the process of deciding what problems and issues to consider for my task forces right up to the drafting of the bills."[55] Historian Doris Kearns Goodwin wrote, "Not only did Johnson put congressmen and senators onto his secret task forces, but he dispatched aides to the Hill for secret sessions with key members to determine what should be in both his messages and the drafts of his bills."[56] Henry Jackson later recalled of Johnson, "He understood fully, I think, the philosophy, the ideologies, of the senators. He was keenly aware of what would fly with them and what would not. He was very careful not to try to go over the line in that he would just push so hard it would get a reaction the other way. He measured his moves very carefully. . . . [H]e was always careful to make sure he had the votes."[57]

Besides the large Democratic majorities, Johnson's influence in Congress was greatly bolstered by his national popularity. During 1965, Johnson's approval rating ranged from 60 to 70 percent. Reporter Richard Strout wrote, "Rarely has one man dominated Washington as President Johnson does now."[58]

Udall felt that his relationship with Johnson helped make environmental legislation a priority for the president. Udall later recalled, "There was a rapport there that I'm sure other Cabinet members didn't have in that [Johnson] had a distinctive feeling—because of Johnson's rural background, his involvement in the New Deal Conservation programs—this was in his veins. He thought about the land the way Roosevelt did. . . . You could come up with a good idea and say, 'This is good for the land and good for the people' and he bought it."[59]

Finding Funding

During these years, in the face of the large number of proposed parks and other public lands, financial pressures built against new land acquisitions. Johnson was concerned about the increasing cost. "The spiraling cost of land acquisitions by the Federal Government, particularly for water resource and recreational purposes, is a matter of increasing concern," the president told Congress in 1966. "I have requested the Director of the Bureau of the Budget, together with the Attorney General, the Secretary of the Interior, and the heads of the other agencies principally concerned, to investigate procedures for protecting the government against such artificial price spirals."[60] Nevertheless Johnson did not shy away from supporting these new acquisitions.

The problem of the increasing cost of acquiring the land remained. "We would authorize a national park, national seashore and Congress would authorize as they did with Point Reyes, fourteen million dollars," Udall noted. "Then it turned out today, eight years later, that it is going to cost over seventy-five million."[61]

By 1968 the Land and Water Conservation Fund provided $88 million to purchase 313,000 acres for national projects and $128 million to fund state and local projects. But just to fund projects already authorized and proposed, Udall noted, the government would need $3.6 billion over ten years, while the fund—bringing in far less than anticipated—would yield less than $1 billion.[62]

In 1967 John Saylor proposed to increase the Conservation Fund with revenues from public land mineral-rights leases and offshore oil and gas leases on the continental shelf. Saylor estimated that this would produce $400 million to $500 million annually for the fund. Roy Taylor (D-NC), chair of the House Subcommittee on Public Lands, wanted to limit the revenues to oil and gas leases, and for only five years. Udall supported Taylor's plan, and it capped the revenue at $100 million annually. In early 1968 Aspinall scheduled hearings on the various proposals, calling it "one of the most important pieces of legislation that we have had for a long, long time." He warned Saylor, "If we ask for too much in this legislation we are not going to get anything."[63]

Congressmen from Texas and Louisiana, where the oil shelf drilling was located, led the opposition, demanding 37.5 percent of the offshore revenues for their states, despite a 1953 law giving resources from three to ten miles offshore to the federal government. Asked how Louisiana could then claim any share, Representative Hale Boggs (D-LA) answered, "I find myself, whenever the interests of my State conflict with the administration, supporting my State." Saylor replied, "I thought a hundred years ago, we settled that problem."[64]

The House Interior Committee settled on a bill limiting the fund's additional revenue from the offshore leases to $200 million. In May 1968 Aspinall and Saylor wrote to House members, calling the bill "one of the most important conservation measures to come before Congress."[65] Despite continued opposition from Texas and Louisiana, the bill passed easily in the House. Overcoming similar resistance from Louisiana's senators, the $200 million from the oil and gas leases became law.[66] "Congress has wisely fixed a new floor under the nation's conservation efforts," commented the *Washington Post.* "The bill is probably the most important conservation measure passed by the 90th Congress."[67] Without the bill, pointed out Crafts, "things like Cascades and Redwoods, and Padre Island, and Assateague and so on, they'd have been on the books, but there wouldn't have been the money to implement them."[68]

Before the 1960s the Department of the Interior was mainly concerned with the western United States. But in that decade, Crafts recalled,

> Udall conceived the department's functions as nationwide. . . . The Bureau of Outdoor Recreation really was the lead agency pushing Interior east of the Mississippi River, and in pushing Interior into the cities, because about 35 percent of the land and water money was spent inside metropolitan areas. For instance, we rehabilitated Prospect Park in Brooklyn; we bought a waterfront park in San Francisco. . . . This national function of Interior is one of the things that some people still don't understand.[69]

Together with new environmental rules, the Johnson administration's success in creating long-term funding for the expansion of national and local parks led to an unparalleled creation of new public spaces. From what may have been the country's broadest natural perspective, Melville Grosvenor, chairman of the National Geographic Society, called Lyndon Johnson "our greatest conservation president."[70]

CHAPTER FOUR

Lands, Rivers, and Trails

KEY EVENTS:
Wild and Scenic Rivers Act (1968)
National Trails Act (1968)
Redwood and North Cascades National Parks (1968)
The Battle over the Colorado River

In the fall of 1968 Lyndon Johnson seemed a completely isolated and abandoned president. Far from the huge domestic legislative accomplishments of 1965 and 1966, embattled by massive angry demonstrations against the Vietnam War that seemed to imprison him in the White House, driven from a possible reelection campaign by primary voters, and unwelcome at his party's convention and on the campaign trail, he appeared a symbol of political and national failure. For years, this image of Johnson has persisted through historic memory.

But those months, when Johnson's presidency seem hopelessly shattered, saw the achievement of major conservation advances, goals driven throughout his entire administration by Johnson and his secretary of the interior, Stewart Udall. The goals for Johnson's full term had been set out by Udall in a memorandum, "Where Do We Go from Here in Conservation," and they all became reality. In one week in the closing days of his administration,.Johnson signed legislation that would protect wild rivers, create major national parks on the West Coast, and envision a national trails system that would come to encompass eight scenic and nine historic trails hiked by millions every year. The signings marked a dramatic culmination of an environmental record amounting to more than three hundred measures, changing the face of the nation's land and water and the natural experience of Americans. "What he did," concluded environmental activist Laurance Rockefeller, "was get natural beauty, or environmental quality, established as a national goal . . . that it was something that was not a luxury; it wasn't something that was just for fun. It was a basic need of the American people."[1]

Johnson drove this objective with presidential statements and congressional encouragement, repeatedly making it clear that the goals were a personal priority. In a presidential message on the environment to Congress, Johnson offered a four-point conservation creed patterned on Franklin Delano Roosevelt's 1941 "Four Freedoms." Johnson pledged "the right to clean water," "the right to clean air," the "right to enjoy plants and animals in their natural habitats," and "the right to beautiful surroundings."[2] He concluded, "These rights assert that no person or company or government has a right in this day and age to pollute, to abuse resources or to waste our common heritage."[3]

Udall felt that he had several advantages in pushing his agenda. "In my department, I had a pretty free hand," he later recalled, "and with very few exceptions strong support [from Johnson]."[4] Floor votes tended to be overwhelming and bipartisan, pointing a way toward future legislation. Udall built close relations with Secretary of Agriculture Orville Freeman, who oversaw the Forest Service, and having come from Congress himself, "I rarely had to ask the White House to pass my bills. I passed them myself."[5] There was an exception: "I remember asking President Johnson to call Congressman Aspinall. . . . [H]e was always difficult, never easy to work with."[6]

Udall's influence was bolstered by an ally in the White House, Lady Bird Johnson, who joined him on trips to promote wilderness and protection. "Though you have abducted my wife on numerous occasions," Johnson wrote his secretary of the interior, "I am confronted by the sure knowledge that the two of you will be described in history's accounting as having changed, for the better, the visible face of America. Your energy and your undiminished zeal have been sources of great pleasure for me."[7]

The Rivers Begin to Flow Freely

Over the previous forty years more than seventy thousand sizable dams had been built on the nation's rivers, with only a few projects ever successfully blocked by local citizen objections.[8] The remaining rivers seemed at risk and the prospects of protecting them seemed remote. Two wildlife biologist brothers working on northwestern rivers, John and Frank Craighead, were early advocates of waterway protection. "As kids we canoed and swam in the Potomac," remembered John Craighead. "Years after we moved west, we went back and saw the Potomac. It wasn't anything like what we had known. I realized that we still had wild rivers in the west, but we wouldn't for long if we didn't do something to save them."[9] In 1955 the Craigheads wrote letters and articles, gave speeches, and lobbied to protect these wild rivers. Over time conservation groups and political figures began to embrace their idea.[10]

The Senate had created the Select Committee on National Water Resources to protect dam building from President Dwight Eisenhower's skepticism. Prior to 1960, opposition to western dams came largely from fiscal conservatives, concerned about the costs of the dams and the expanding role of the federal government. Opposition to dams because of their effects on fish and wilderness was something new. But the committee's staff director, Ted Schad, had absorbed some open-mindedness from the Wilderness Society's Howard Zahniser. Schad was even willing to listen when, at a Senate field hearing in 1959, the ruggedly built, sun- and wind-weathered Craighead brothers appeared out of nowhere, arguing for wild rivers unmarked by dams. Schad slipped into the Select Committee's 1961 report a recommendation that "certain streams be preserved in their free-flowing condition because their natural scenic, scientific, aesthetic, and recreational values outweigh their value for water development."[11] He later admitted that the senators on the committee may never have noticed this statement. In 1962 the Outdoor Recreation Resources Review Commission (ORRRC) report urged, "Certain rivers of unusual scientific, esthetic and recreation value should be allowed to remain in their free-flowing state and natural setting without man-made alterations."[12]

"As a congressman I was pro-dam," recalled Udall about the change in his thinking. "Suddenly I had the national responsibility and that put on my shoulders the burden of thinking for the nation."[13] Udall was also influenced by his raft trip through Glen Canyon before a dam submerged it, as well as trips on Maine's Allagash River, at the suggestion of Senator Edmund Muskie (D-ME), and Missouri's Current River with George Hartzog, whom Udall appointed director of the National Park Service. In *The Quiet Crisis*, Udall wrote in 1963, "Generations to follow will judge us by our success in preserving in their natural state certain rivers having superior outdoor recreation values."[14]

With Agriculture Secretary Freeman, Udall organized an interagency Wild and Scenic Rivers Study Team. It drew on unauthorized work led by Ted Swem, director of National Park Service planning, which produced a list of 650 possible rivers, cut down to 22 top candidates for protection.[15] In 1964 Senator Frank Church (D-ID) introduced the Wild Rivers Act drawing on the Interior Department's research. It began a process producing what Udall would call one of "the monumental pieces of conservation legislation of the 1960s," the Wilderness and Wild Rivers Act.[16]

Church, the son of middle-class Boise Republicans, recalled, "I learned all about the Democrats so I could argue with Dad. I ended up by converting myself."[17] In 1941 he won the American Legion National High School Oratorical Contest, and a scholarship, over 108,000 other contestants. After a semester at Stanford, he entered the army in 1943, serving in army intelligence in China. On his return, Church married his high school sweetheart, Bethine Clark, daughter of a former Democratic governor. After graduating Stanford Law School, he worked on building the Idaho Democratic party, and lost a state legislative contest. Against all odds, in 1956 the thirty-two-year-old Church ran for the US Senate, and defeated former senator Glen Taylor in the Democratic primary. Despite the Eisenhower reelection landslide victory for the Republicans, Church went on to topple GOP incumbent Herman Welker in November.

In 1961 Church reluctantly became involved in the fight over the Wilderness Act, despite Idaho resistance; one letter complained, "Timber is a crop and shouldn't be locked up to rot."[18] When Senator Clinton Anderson needed gallbladder surgery, Church agreed to serve as the floor manager of the proposed Wilderness Act, assuring Idahoans that the bill would not place any additional land under the federal government nor endanger existing grazing and mining. After the bill passed, Church overcame the anger of powerful mining and lumber companies to win reelection in 1962.

By 1965 President Johnson, at the urging of Secretary Udall, urged that portions of certain free flowing rivers should be identified and protected before they had been changed forever. In 1965 Church again introduced the Wild Rivers bill, protecting portions of six wild and undeveloped rivers and seeking further evaluation of nine others. Some senators wanted rivers in their states removed from the list, while others wanted some added, but the bill passed 71–1.[19]

But in the House, Interior Committee chairman Wayne Aspinall "considered unharnessed rivers a silly idea."[20] John Saylor assured Udall, "We'll just wear him down."[21] As early as 1958, Saylor had told a colleague, "I happen to be one of those folks that believe that there are certain advantages to keeping a little bit of the rivers that run this country as God made them."[22] He now introduced his own proposal, the Scenic Rivers Bill, named to include rivers not completely wild. His bill protected sixteen rivers while proposing study of sixty-five more. While the Senate bill had no deadline for deciding on the status of rivers, Saylor's bill called for a decision within three years for the protected rivers and within ten years for the studies. Construction of dams or other development would not be permitted during this evaluation period. Road building, grazing, and logging would be limited.[23]

But given Aspinall's opposition, the House took no action. "The chairman apparently didn't understand President Johnson's direct statement in his conservation message earlier this year," complained Saylor, "that the time had come to preserve free-flowing stretches of our rivers."[24] Still, the president told Congress on February 23, 1966, "I am encouraged by the response to my proposal for a national wild rivers system, and I urge Congress to complete this pioneering conservation legislation this year."[25]

During Johnson's full term in office, Senator Henry Jackson (D-WA) became prominent as an ardent supporter of the president's Vietnam policy, displaying a hawkishness that has marked his reputation, his presidential campaigns, and his place in history. But at the same time Jackson chaired the Senate Interior Committee, sending out a series of environmental measures for which, Vietnam critic Udall would admit, Jackson "deserved enormous credit."[26]

Growing up in Everett, Washington, a working-class mill town, Jackson's first job as a newspaper delivery boy saw him carrying 74,880 newspapers without a single complaint, winning him both a national award and the nickname "Scoop."[27] On his graduating from the University of Washington law school in 1935, Jackson's political views had been permanently shaped by the Great Depression. Three years out of school, Jackson toppled the county district attorney in a primary and two years later advanced to Congress, at the time its youngest member. Jackson built a reputation as a strong liberal at home and a foe of communism in the world, an image he used in 1952 to defeat conservative Republican senator Harry Cain. Named to the Interior Committee, Jackson cosponsored the

Wilderness Act bill in 1957, urging preservation of "our national wilderness system [while] meeting, outside the wilderness reserves, all our needs for commodities and for developed recreational areas."[28]

In January 1963 Jackson became committee chairman, and developed decisive control of the Interior Committee with what his biographer Robert G. Kaufman called one of the best staffs in Congress. "He had few peers in his capacity to master complex information and in his devotion to his job," Kaufman wrote of Jackson. "He also developed a clear and consistent agenda."[29] Jackson had another advantage, defined by his late-career colleague Daniel Patrick Moynihan (D-NY): "Scoop not only had unparalleled mastery of the issues, but could be trusted. If he said it was so, it was so."[30]

Despite their deepening differences on foreign policy, Jackson and Church maintained a close and productive relationship over two decades on the Interior Committee.[31] Still, despite the support Jackson was able to organize for the environmental proposals, the Congress deferred action in 1965 and 1966 on the Wild and Scenic Rivers Act, the National Trails System, and proposals for Redwood and North Cascades National Parks.

River Protection Treads Water on the Colorado

Complicating the Wild and Scenic Rivers issue was the dispute over western water, specifically the Colorado River. Arizona desperately wanted dams on the Colorado to provide more water to the state. California and other states feared Arizona grabbing too much water, while others, such as Colorado, wanted their own water projects. Arizona had won a Supreme Court case against California over the water, and now wanted additional dams or other facilities on the river—an idea strongly opposed by environmentalists, particularly near the Grand Canyon.

In 1963 the Interior Department proposed the Pacific Southwest Water Plan (PSWP), involving dams on the Colorado in the Grand Canyon and water development projects in other western states. The proposal incorporated the Central Arizona Project (CAP), supported by all Arizona legislators, to supply water to the state's swelling population. The new plan ran into opposition from both conservationists upset about the dams and water-hungry legislators from other western states. Aspinall favored the PSWP while many Arizona legislators wanted to focus on CAP. While the political clout of Arizona's powerful Democratic senator Carl Hayden, could get CAP through the Senate, it would be unlikely to pass the House.

In February 1964 a revised PSWP was introduced that included a large dam in the Grand Canyon. As a House member forty-five years before, Hayden pushed through a bill allowing for a dam in the national park. After some disputes with his fellow Arizonan Udall, Hayden now agreed to support the regional plan. The crowded legislative agenda, along with the need to get the support of California's legislators, led to the project not moving forward in 1964.

In January 1965 a revised plan, labeled the Lower Colorado River Basin Project, was introduced. Environmentalists again attacked the bill for proposing to build two dams that would affect the Grand Canyon stretch. Saylor attacked the plan as "one of the most unfortunate schemes ever to come out of the darkness of the Bureau of Reclamation."[32] The Budget Bureau supported the project, but without the dam nearest Grand Canyon National Park. Aspinall, wanting to make sure that the plan would not deprive Colorado and other upper Colorado basin states of their share of the water, now pushed a revised proposal that included five water projects in Colorado. The House Irrigation and Reclamation Subcommittee opened hearings on the bill on August 23, 1965, but the issue was deferred until 1966.

"I am convinced," the Sierra Club's David Brower wrote Udall, "that nothing you have done and nothing else you are hoping to do for conservation can offset the damage that will ensue if you let the Grand Canyon go down the drain."[33] But environmentalists could muster limited pressure; as Representative Morris Udall (D-AZ) later recalled, "At the time, the environmental movement consisted of a ragtag band of bird-watchers and backpackers and a handful of well-intentioned, relatively impoverished organizations whose grasp of lobbying and public relations skills was unremarkable and whose political clout was, with rare exceptions, negligible."[34]

When hearings resumed in May 1966 the bill remained hotly contested. Saylor attacked Secretary Udall's support of the proposal, asking, "How can he expect to be effective in the future pleading for the national park system and its expansion when he at this time appeals for an invasion of one of the Nation's oldest and best known parks?"[35] At the same time, Arizonans attacked Udall for being insufficiently supportive of the state's water needs. After rejecting a Saylor proposal to delete the Grand Canyon dam, the Interior Committee passed the bill 22–10.

On June 9, 1966, the Sierra Club unleashed a massive lobbying campaign against the dams, running full-page ads in a host of major newspapers.

Brower asked, "If we can't save the Grand Canyon, what the hell can we save?"[36] One ad asked, "Should we flood the Sistine Chapel so tourists can float nearer the ceiling?"[37] Morris Udall denounced the "inflammatory attacks" on the House floor, complaining, "I have seldom, if ever, seen a more distorted or flagrant hatchet job than this."[38] But the ads had an effect, spurring what Senator Thomas Kuchel (R-CA) called "one of the largest letter-writing campaigns which I have seen in my tenure in the Senate."[39]

Growing opposition kept the bill bottled in the House Rules Committee. When Aspinall ran into Brower in November at a conference, he refused a reporter's request for a joint photograph, saying, "You've been telling a bunch of a damn lies to the newspapers and now you want your picture taken with me?"[40] Reportedly at the urging of Morris Udall, the IRS revoked the Sierra Club's tax-exempt status.[41] The result was, as Roderick Nash wrote, "an explosion of protest . . . people who did not know or care about the threat to the Grand Canyon now rose in its behalf in the name of civil liberties."[42] Brower exulted that the American public "did not wish the tax man to jeopardize the world's only Grand Canyon."[43]

At the start of 1967 Udall announced a revised administration plan, replacing the dams on the Colorado with a coal plant in Page, Arizona, to provide power to pump the water to Arizona. The bill called for a National Water Commission to study the nation's water needs, instead of the prior bill's calls for studying sending water from the Columbia River in the Northwest to the Southwest, an idea that had riled Washington's Jackson.

The new proposal was hailed by Saylor and environmentalists, but faced opposition from Aspinall, who had developed his own new proposal including the five Colorado water projects and a Grand Canyon dam. He strongly attacked Udall's proposal both for dropping the Grand Canyon dam and for calling for further study on three of the Colorado state projects. "As far as I am concerned," he warned, "there won't be any legislation if we don't have Hualapai Dam [in the Grand Canyon] in the bill."[44] Udall's proposal did win support from Arizona's Hayden, chairman of the Senate Appropriations Committee, who had long pushed for dams on the Colorado. A bill akin to Udall's proposal passed the Senate 70–12. Aspinall called dropping the dam in the Grand Canyon "the death knell for the basin project,"[45] and adjourned the Interior Committee without taking up the Senate bill. Later in 1967, Stewart Udall took a raft trip down the Colorado near the Grand Canyon, further persuading him against a dam there. "I found myself as the decade wore on," he recalled later, "increasingly questioning some of [the] . . . major dam building projects that at the beginning of the 1960s had appeared to be sort of sacred cows."[46]

Aspinall's resistance infuriated Hayden and the rest of the Arizona delegation. In September 1967 Hayden attached the CAP proposal as an amendment to the Senate public works appropriations bill, which meant that it would avoid the House Interior Committee. Hastily returning to Washington, Aspinall met with Hayden and agreed to consider compromise legislation in early 1968, and Hayden withdrew his amendment.

While the controversy over the Colorado was in going on, in January 1967 Church, with thirty-eight cosponsors, reintroduced the administration's Wild Rivers bill. Saylor simultaneously reintroduced his bill in the House, and Aspinall surprised preservationists by introducing his own wild rivers in bill in April. Stewart Brandborg of the Wilderness Society commented, "He must have owed Saylor some really big favors."[47] In fact, Udall promised to support water development projects in Colorado in exchange for Aspinall supporting a rivers bill. Aspinall's bill protected fewer rivers, but also included strong measures against mining along the protected streams.

The Senate Interior Committee now amended the Church bill to include Saylor's classification scheme, and to protect segments of twelve rivers and study twenty-seven more. The revised Senate bill passed in August 1967, 84–0.[48] But Aspinall, claiming that the Interior Committee had too much other business, did not schedule hearings in 1967. Aspinall and Saylor now reached a compromise, agreeing that in 1968 the Interior Committee would consider a western water bill and a Wild and Scenic Rivers bill, as well as national park status for the redwoods and the North Cascades.

Early in 1968 Aspinall introduced a new western water bill, providing for a Central Arizona Project, powered by a coal-fired steam plant, to bring water to Arizona with no dams near the Grand Canyon. The bill also included five water projects for Colorado, guaranteed California's share of the river, and created a national water study excluding any mention of the Columbia. The House passed it on a voice vote. Differences with a similar Senate bill were resolved in one-on-one meetings between Aspinall and Jackson. Johnson signed the resulting bill on September 30, 1968.

Having achieved his longtime goal of getting more water for Arizona, the eighty-nine-year-old Hayden retired. But Stewart Udall's support of a bill that did not have all that Arizonans wanted ended any future political prospects he might have in the state. The coal plant in Page would spread air pollution across the region. The Central Arizona Project ended up costing almost $3.5 billion more than had been estimated, while fueling rapid and massive growth in Phoenix and Tucson.[49]

Twenty years later, Morris Udall mused, "In hindsight, what amazes me most about the dams we nearly built on the Grand Canyon (and the one we did build at Glen Canyon) was how cavalier the process was. Here were congressmen nonchalantly contemplating the drowning of hundreds of miles of free-flowing rivers—rivers that most of us had never seen."[50] In 1975 Congress passed a bill sponsored by Udall and Senator Barry Goldwater (R-AZ) that expanded Grand Canyon National Park to include the sites of the dams proposed in the prior decade.[51]

The Wild Ride of a Wild Rivers Bill

In 1967 Church had reintroduced the National Wild and Scenic Rivers bill in the Senate. "It is the policy of Congress to preserve, develop, reclaim, and make accessible for the benefit of all of the American people," declared the bill, "selected parts of the Nation's diminishing resource of free-flowing rivers."[52] The bill would protect six rivers, all in the West, from human development, including stretches of the Salmon and Clearwater in Idaho. In addition, the bill directed the secretaries of the interior and agriculture to consult on eight other river systems, including some in the East, with the governors involved.

To meet objections, the bill promised compensation to water users who suffered economic damage as a result of limits on development. Legislators found that most of those who wrote to Congress on the subject, perhaps most notably fishermen, were supportive of the bill.[53] "As vice president of the four-state Association of Northwest Steelheaders," Hal Bacon wrote Jackson, "I convey to you the extreme interest our conservation dedicated group has in wild rivers legislation."[54] Letters against the bill stressed economics, such as a warning against "poor development of water resources."[55] The Senate passed the bill 84–0.

On March 8, 1968, Johnson sent his last conservation message to Congress, appealing for further legislative action. "A clear stream, a long horizon, a forest wilderness and open sky—these are man's most ancient possessions," argued the embattled president. "In a modern society, they are the most priceless."[56] The same month, Aspinall scheduled four days of subcommittee hearings for the various river protection bills, attending all hearings himself. To opposition from property owners and development advocates, Saylor argued, "The fact is that you and I have seen such law-less and irresponsible treatment of our streams and their environs that only through Federal law will we be able to protect the aesthetic values and other natural benefits which God bequeathed when he formed these magnificent waterways."[57]

The Johnson administration wanted to protect twelve rivers while Saylor wanted stretches of sixteen, but Aspinall stuck at four, telling Charles Callison of the National Audubon Society, "I can tell you very frankly you are not going to get all 16."[58] The final committee bill protected six rivers, agreed to study twenty-eight others, and kept Saylor's classification system. At an Interior Committee hearing in June, Representative Sam Steiger (R-AZ) wailed, "Under the guise of protecting scenic values, this legislation will stifle progress, inhibit economic development and incur a staggering expenditure."[59] In spite of such diehard opposition, the Interior Committee approved the bill on July 1, 1968.

To ensure passage before the end of the session in October, the committee sought suspension of the rules, which would block amendments. Saylor was surprised when other representatives from Pennsylvania opposed this, wanting to remove two rivers in the state from the list. The vote to suspend the rules failed to get the necessary two-thirds majority. When Stewart Udall suggested submitting the bill under the usual rules, Saylor answered that the bill "is defeated for this Congress in my opinion, and I have no intention of seeking a rule to have its further consideration."[60]

Yet when Congress returned from August recess, Aspinall and Saylor requested reconsideration of the bill. The Rules Committee scheduled the bill for debate with amendments allowed. Edward Crafts assured legislators that the bill wouldn't affect any "water rights protected under state law."[61] Saylor couldn't stop an amendment removing Pennsylvania's Susquehanna River, which he called "one of the few scenic rivers left in the East," from the bill's protection.[62] The bill then passed the House 265–7. Congressional colleagues praised Saylor as "Mr. Conservation" for pushing though a rivers measure that would "mark a place in the history of conservation for all time to come."[63]

In the Senate, Church was equally important, even though in Secretary Udall's estimation, Idaho was "considered pretty much in the grip of the user interests . . . the timber, mining and other interests."[64] Idaho journalist Bill Hall noted that while there were only a few hundred environmentalists in Idaho, "Everybody is a hunter or fisherman. . . . At one time we had 700,000 people in the state and something like 450,000 hunting and fishing licenses."[65] Church appealed to these outdoor enthusiasts to build support for the Wild Rivers legislation. LeRoy Ashby and Rod Gramer wrote, "Church himself believed that most of his constituents were sympathetic to conservation as long as they did not view it as a threat to their livelihood."[66] Church also emphasized the economic benefits of protecting the environment, reminding one constituent that "tourism is Idaho's fastest growing industry."[67]

The final House-Senate bill protected parts of eight rivers and four tributaries, and designated portions of twenty-seven others for future consideration. It simplified the classifications to wild, scenic, and recreational, with different protections for each. Congress would decide on future inclusions. Dam building and mining were prohibited. The *New York Times* called the final product "a bill of far reaching importance to establish for the first time a national program to protect scenic and wild rivers. . . . This bill [is] an admirable companion to the Wilderness Act of 1964."[68] The act also authorized the secretary of the interior to acquire land along the designated rivers either through purchase or condemnation in areas where less than 50 percent of the land is public. Property owners could also agree to conservation easements, maintaining ownership on condition of avoiding development.

"We finally got the Scenic and Wild Rivers Bill, as it became known, in the last year of President Johnson's administration," Udall recalled in 1969. "It took four years to break [Aspinall] down. You did this by, number one, passing a Senate bill, a good Senate bill, and that put some pressure on. The conservation organizations indicated they wanted it and they kept pushing it. The president kept it high up on his agenda of needed conservation legislation. You just had to wear him down."[69]

The act would gain popularity over the years. Two years after passage, under President Nixon, Secretary of the Interior Walter Hickel and Secretary of Agriculture Clifford M. Hardin designated "all or portions of 47 rivers in 24 states as potential additions to the National Wild and Scenic Rivers System."[70] By the early twenty-first century the Wild and Scenic Rivers System encompassed parts of over two hundred rivers covering some twelve thousand square miles.

A Long Fight over Long-Lived Trees
Three days before signing the Wild and Scenic Rivers bill on October 5, 1968, Lyndon Johnson signed the bill creating Redwood National Park.

The struggle had been similarly long and bitter. Huge stands of redwoods once ran nearly hundreds of miles along the northern California coast, encompassing an estimated two million acres. Widespread logging had destroyed most of the redwoods when some were protected in a California state park in 1901, others in the Muir Woods National Monument in 1908. By the 1960s California had preserved some fifty thousand acres of virgin redwoods in twenty-eight state parks, most small and not near each other. In the 1960s the Sierra Club, the Save-the-Redwoods League, and others called for protecting much of the remaining territory, estimated to be 10 percent of the original acreage, as a single national park.[71]

"The redwoods are one of nature's masterpieces in America and the world. Yet, at the present rate of logging and with destruction resulting from inadequate conservation practices, the future of the redwoods is in doubt," Johnson declared at a White House ceremony in June 1964. "I have directed Secretary Udall to prepare a plan for a Redwoods National Park and to have it ready for presentation to Congress next January."[72] Johnson repeated his request for a Redwood National Park in his 1966 congressional message, noting, "We cannot restore—once it is lost—the majesty of a forest whose trees soared upward 2000 years ago."[73] Johnson's commitment was bolstered by the First Lady, who made a trip with Udall to redwoods territory to promote the park.

Conflict between logging companies and environmentalists had delayed the establishment of the park. Trying to protect some of the redwoods, Udall proposed a thirty-nine-thousand-acre park in early 1966, with the bill introduced by Kuchel and Representative Philip Burton (D-CA). The Sierra Club held out for ninety thousand acres, a bill introduced by Representative Jeffrey Cohelan (D-CA) and Senator Lee Metcalf (D-MT), while another proposal would have largely limited the new park to already existing state parklands. With a crowded committee schedule, Aspinall refused to hold hearings without a compromise.[74]

The redwoods issue saw the national emergence of Michael McCloskey, who became the executive director of the Sierra Club in 1969. After graduating from Harvard and the University of Oregon law school, McCloskey was hired by Brower as the club's first field organizer, and began pushing for the wilderness bill, building pressure on Aspinall in his district and at field hearings. In 1965, McCloskey moved to San Francisco, first as assistant to the club's president and then as conservation director. The club's board, McCloskey wrote, "had decided to assign priority to three campaigns: establishment of a Redwood National Park, establishment of a North Cascades National Park and keeping the Grand Canyon free of dams."[75]

The campaign was hampered by disagreement between the Sierra Club and the Save-the-Redwoods League over the park's location, and by 1967 more than fifty different Redwood Park proposals, with different sizes and locations, had been introduced in the House. Aspinall began hearings in the Subcommittee on National Parks and Recreation in June 1967 but refused to promise fast action. Writing to Richard Lamm, then a young Democratic activist who would later become governor of Colorado, Aspinall snapped that environmentalists "did not seem to realize or will not accept the fact that the Treasury just doesn't have unlimited funds for these purposes."[76] In July 1967 the president wrote Aspinall that while he understood the committee's "substantial workload," he considered the Redwood bill to be "of first and highest priority."[77] Aspinall responded that the issue was more complex than he had thought, but that the National Parks Subcommittee would schedule hearings and tour the site of the park during the 1968 spring recess.

In 1966 the Sierra Club had worked with Interior Committee chairman Jackson and ranking Republican member Kuchel on a new bill. By trading some Forest Service land to private owners in exchange for land for the park, the new bill created a park of over sixty thousand acres and passed the committee. But when the bill reached the Senate floor on November 1, 1967, Allen Ellender (D-LA), chair of the Senate Agriculture and Forestry Committee, opened the debate with an amendment to eliminate the land trade, arguing, "The Weeks Act, enacted in 1911 . . . contains a prohibition against [this land trade]. . . . [W]hen Mr. Udall sent to Congress his proposed bill, there was no provision in it which would have permitted the exchange of federally owned forest lands for privately owned lands."[78] Frank Moss (D-UT) responded that the trade would put lands on the local tax rolls, benefiting especially the smaller counties and saving the federal government money.[79] Still, Ellender pressed his amendment, saying he wanted to prevent a new precedent.

Kuchel appealed to the Senate, saying, "It has been a long tortuous trail for people to try to put together a bill that can become law. There is no use kidding ourselves. The hour is late. If the Senate refuses to go along with a bill that is feasible and realistic, and which is endorsed by conservation groups concerned with redwood preservation, we might just as well forget about it and let the redwoods be chopped down," adding later, "The committee does not want this exchange to be a precedent, but there is only one place in all of God's globe where we have these trees which were living at the time when Christ died."[80]

Jackson interposed that the real issue was that the Forest Service in the Agriculture Department would be giving up land while the Park Service in the Interior Department gained. "This is an ancient fight between the Department of Agriculture and the Department of the Interior," he noted, "which goes back to 1908." He then read a letter he had received from Secretary Udall two days earlier, promising, "If the creation of the Redwood Park hinges on this kind of compromise, I can only express my personal view that such a compromise would be acceptable only if everybody concerned pledged firm adherence in the future to the existing policy of protecting the Federally owned lands in our National forests against land exchange."[81] Ellender sniffed, "That is the personal view of Secretary Udall and not the view of the Department nor the administration." John Stennis (D-MS) agreed, "I would like to see California and the Nation have the park, but I think it is a bad mistake . . . to throw aside, now, or bypass, this firmly established and proven policy."[82] Ernest Gruening (D-AK), who had proposed a stronger Redwood bill, argued, "The establishment of an adequate national park for the preservation of the notable redwood trees of California is one of the worthiest objectives ever sought. . . . [T]he bill agreed upon . . . is the proposal on which it has been possible to obtain agreement. . . . The important thing is to act now to preserve the redwoods still in existence."[83]

George Murphy (R-CA) challenged the whole idea, saying, "There has been some question . . . whether there is, indeed, a strong and definite need at this particular time for the establishment of such a Federal forest enclave. . . . [T]he finest stands of the towering, majestic redwoods which we all seek to preserve are already protected by existing State parks." He went on to conclude, "[T]his bill, S. 2515, would have a needlessly troublesome effect on private industry, on the economy of the proposed park area, and on the Federal budget itself."[84]

After rejecting the Ellender amendment 51–30, the Senate passed the Redwood National Park bill 77–6, providing for a two-part park of sixty-two thousand acres at a cost of $100 million. Conservationists appreciated Jackson's efforts, one writing, "Thank you for reporting out and fighting for a good bill creating a Redwoods National Park."[85]

House Interior Committee members, including Aspinall, Saylor, and Morris Udall, toured the proposed park area in April 1968 and conducted hearings. Udall reported that after Aspinall woke them at 6 a.m., "We go to breakfast and then we have a meeting and then we dash out in the field and tramp through the Redwoods. We go back to several hundred witnesses until 6:30, then the Chamber of Commerce has a dinner to make some points with us. If there is time between 12 and 1 AM, it's all our own."[86]

In the committee hearings in Washington the next month, Udall spoke for the Senate bill. Aspinall wanted a smaller park, while Saylor favored enlarging it. Saylor and Aspinall now came to a secret arrangement. If Saylor would agree to the committee bill for a smaller park, Aspinall promised not to resist a bigger park in the House-Senate conference committee. The committee then passed out a bill for a park of twenty-eight thousand acres. Aspinall sought suspension of the rules and a ban on amendments. To get the needed two-thirds for suspension, Aspinall promised "to try to find in conference the answers by which the acreage can be increased to a reasonable and logical amount."[87] Environmentalists were shocked by the proposal, and Aspinall reported more hate mail for the Redwood bill than for any other legislation.[88] In the floor debate, he declared, "This is the only sure way we have of getting a redwoods bill passed this Congress."[89] The small park proposal let Aspinall get a bill through the committee and House while keeping his standing as a friend of the timber industry.

The House-Senate conference conferees included Aspinall, Saylor, Jackson, and Kuchel. The committee agreed on fifty-eight thousand acres, about half land taken from the timber companies and half from state parks. Environmentalists were pleasantly surprised by the outcome. Aspinall said happily that he "would rather be an individual's target at the beginning of the game and his darling at the end, rather than vice versa."[90] The House approved the revised bill 329–1, and the president signed the Redwood National Park bill on October 2, 1968.[91] "In the last supplementary budget that went through, we had $55 million right in there [for the Redwood National Park] with the Defense Department and their emergency appropriations. This is an emergency," remembered Udall. "You know, I said to myself, we're making some headway; we're getting the right kind of priorities where something like this is considered as important as more money for the military."[92]

The Sierra Club's McCloskey commented later about the politics of the park, saying that Saylor "was our hero. . . . On many issues when we wanted help, we began with him. . . . People like Aspinall stood in our way." McCloskey noted that the final bill contained a big economic subsidy for retraining loggers, stating that this and the land costs meant that "Redwood was the most expensive national park in the world."[93]

Jewel of the North

The same day Johnson signed Redwood National Park into existence saw the creation of another national park up the coast. For years, Jackson had worked for a North Cascades National Park in his home state of Washington. While much of the land was already national forest, conservationists feared that that the Forest Service planned additional road building and other development in the region. Local preservationists began to push to create a national park in the areas. Proposals to create studies were introduced in Congress in 1959, 1960, and 1961 by Representative Thomas Pelly (D-WA), but did not advance. There was opposition to even studying the area. One constituent wrote to Jackson in 1961, "A brief exam of the Olympic peninsula reveals the best reason for no more national park areas. . . . [W]hy force the Cascade area into a dead and static facsimile?"[94]

In 1963 McCloskey produced a 130-page report, "Prospectus for a North Cascades National Park." McCloskey remembered, "Senator Henry Jackson of Washington responded with interest and induced the administration of President John F. Kennedy to set up a process to study the idea."[95] Interdepartmental cooperation led to a five-member study team, two members from the Department of Agriculture, two from Interior, and the head of the Bureau of Outdoor Recreation as chair. In December 1965, by a 3–2 vote with the Agriculture representatives dissenting, the team recommended converting some national forest land into a North Cascades National Park.[96]

Jackson then spent a year and a half resolving disagreements between the Interior and Agriculture Departments over boundaries. In February 1966 he held public hearings on the proposal in Seattle. He received multiple letters about the proposal, one supporter writing, "I hope there will be something left to experience."[97] Nancy Riddell wrote, "I am writing to you at the urging of my science teacher. Our class feels that it is necessary to pass the bill involving the North Cascades National Park and Ross Lake Recreation Area."[98] Opponents also made their voices heard, one insisting, "Multiple use of the land areas considered for a national park will be more beneficial."[99] In an institutional blast, "the Omak Chamber of Commerce go[es] on record as opposing the enactment of any legislation establishing a National Park in the North Cascades . . . [and urges] that management be continued under the administration of the Forest Service."[100]

Jackson negotiated compromises between timber and mining interests, averse to any limits on their operations, and environmentalists who wanted the maximum area free of commercial development. "Jackson also managed his local constituency beautifully," noted Udall. "Jackson balanced things well. His colleagues and his constituents trusted him."[101] Jackson arranged a compromise that maintained the timber available for cutting while protecting a large area of wilderness. Good relations between Secretary of Agriculture Freeman and Udall were helpful, for although Freeman opposed creating the national park largely out of Forest Service land, he did not resist enough to sink the bill. Jackson agreed to make the Lake Chelan area a recreation area to accommodate hunters, since hunting was forbidden in a national park. "The Senate approved this bill on November 2, 1967," Jackson triumphantly wrote a constituent. "The bill provides for a North Cascades National Park of 504,500 acres, a Ross Lake National Recreation Area of 105,000, a Lake Chelan National Recreation Area of 62,000, a Pasaytan Wilderness of 520,000 acres and addition to Glacier Park Wilderness totaling 10,000 acres."[102]

Taking up a parallel bill, the House Subcommittee on Parks and Recreation held hearings in April 1968 in Seattle. Some eight hundred people asked to testify. "I don't know who these people are," complained Aspinall. "Are they hippies[?] . . . Of course they have the right to testify, but they will repeat the same thing over and over again."[103] Aspinall received major criticism for his handling of the hearings. Following the hearings, subcommittee chairman Roy Taylor (D-NC) said that he was "giving low priority to a North Cascades National Park because he had received so much mail in opposition to it." Aspinall agreed: "There is too little time in this congressional session to resolve the continuing controversy over the project."[104]

Yet in July the House Interior Committee held additional hearings. Aspinall was very concerned with the Colorado River Basin Project. Taylor was interested in a proposal for a Blue Ridge Parkway that extended into North Carolina. Both were before Jackson's Senate Interior Committee. Following the additional hearings, the House Interior Committee unanimously passed the bill on September 4, 1968, followed shortly thereafter by the full House.

Stewart Udall called the North Cascades National Park "a monument to Henry Jackson, which never would have been done unless he wanted it to be done."[105] Udall also admitted, "Without presidential interest it never would have been done."[106] On October 2, 1968, Johnson signed the bill, along with Redwood National Park, and the National Trails System Act, providing $6.5 million for land acquisition while protecting the 3,100-mile Pacific Coast Trail and the 2,000-mile Appalachian Trail.

Trails across the Nation

The Appalachian Trail was the brainchild of Benton MacKaye, a New England forester and one of the eight founders of the Wilderness Society, who proposed the trail in an article in 1921.[107] The Appalachian Trail Conference, a coalition of hiking clubs formed in 1925, built one segment of the trail after another, with help from volunteers and later from the Civilian Conservation Corps. The trail was completed in 1937. The National Forest and Park Services signed a 1938 agreement to protect the 875 miles of trail on federal lands.

In May 1964, after learning that private landowners were increasingly closing down the segments of the trail on their property, Senator Gaylord Nelson (D-WI) unsuccessfully introduced a bill to protect the Appalachian Trail. The next year he introduced a new bill to establish a national system of hiking trails. The idea was supported by Saylor in the House and by conservation groups. The bill picked up a powerful advocate in President Johnson, who in his 1965 message on natural beauty called for a system of trails around the nation, both near cities and farther away. "In the back country," declared Johnson, "we need to copy the great Appalachian Trail in all parts of America."[108] In 1966 Johnson told Congress, "I am submitting legislation to foster the development by Federal, state and local agencies of a nationwide system of trails and give special emphasis to the location of trails near metropolitan areas."[109] Udall stated in a 1969 interview, "This was really a Johnson administration initiative. . . . He was very receptive on this."[110]

On April 1, 1966, Nelson and Jackson introduced Johnson's national hiking trails bill, which would protect the Appalachian Trail and study nine other trails for possible inclusion in a national network. "Hiking trails . . . represent perhaps the most economical form of public investment in outdoor recreation," argued Nelson. "There ought to be a place to hike within an hour's reach of every American."[111] The bill did not pass the

Senate Interior Committee. Meanwhile, Johnson had commissioned trail studies by the executive branch. Completed in 1967 by the Departments of Agriculture, the home of the Forest Service, and Interior, the report urged the establishment of different trail categories similar to the classification of different rivers in the Wild Rivers bill. The combined report recommended four trails for initial inclusion in a national system.

The administration prepared a bill introduced by Saylor and others proposing four classifications: national scenic trails; national park, forest, and recreational trails; state park, forest, and recreational trails; and metropolitan trails. The initial four trails were all national scenic trails: the Appalachian Trail, stretching 2,000 miles from Georgia to Maine; the Pacific Crest Trail, traveling 3,100 miles from the Mexican to Canadian border; the Continental Divide Trail, 2,300 miles long from Canada to New Mexico; and the Potomac Heritage Trail, 825 miles from Pennsylvania to the Atlantic Ocean. The estimated cost for acquisition and development of the four trails was $30 million.[112]

The bill went to the House Interior Committee's Subcommittee on Public Lands. Aspinall was reluctant to allocate such a large sum, noting that three previously authorized projects, Cape Cod National Seashore, Point Reyes National Seashore, and the Delaware Water Gap National Recreation Area, had not been fully funded. As a result, the Interior Committee, with Saylor and Aspinall in agreement, approved a bill setting up a national trails system, but recommended only the Appalachian Trail for initial inclusion. The committee allocated $5 million for land acquisition and $1 million for development. Pushing the trails and rivers proposals, Saylor stated that both "could very well become the most popular conservation measures ever passed by the Congress of the United States."[113] The House passed the trails bill 376–18.

In the Senate, the administration bill establishing four trails and allocating $30 million had already been passed. Jackson wrote a supporter of the trails, "If you and your friends wish to write to Congressman Aspinall, I am sure it would help in indicating how widespread is the support for a National Trails System."[114] Another supporter applauded, "I heartily commend your [Senate Interior] committee for its work on the newly approved National Trails bill. . . . In the face of accelerating land costs, the establishment of National Parks and Trails . . . are of top priority."[115] The House-Senate conference committee now compromised, recommending the Pacific Crest and Appalachian trails for initial designation, listing fourteen other trails for study for possible later addition and allocating $6.5 million for land acquisition and trail development.

By the end of the twentieth century the national trail system had expanded to include eight scenic and nine historic trails. By 2001 less than 25 miles of the 2,144-mile Appalachian Trail remained in private hands while an estimated three to four million people hiked some portion of the trail each year. Of the seventeen trails, the Park Service is responsible for twelve, the Forest Service for four, and the Bureau of Land Management for one.

End of a Presidency

Udall pushed Johnson to make a dramatic grand gesture of protecting more land before leaving office. In a memo to the president on July 26, 1968, Udall suggested a "parting gift to future generations" by using the Antiquities Act to set aside a large amount of land in national monuments. Udall remembered, "The President said, 'Go ahead . . . make a review and in the fall . . . you can spread out your proposals to me.'"[116]

Bureau of Recreation chief Edward Crafts later recounted what happened:

> Udall had done, with the help of the president, a great many things in conservation. Udall visualized that it would be wonderful thing if the administration could go out with a great big last splash—a big bang. A last big conservation step. And he had the Park Service and some of the other agencies working for at least six months on a program proposal for additional lands. . . . We had a rehearsal in Interior before the meeting with the president. We met with the president about noon the same day. Udall presented the proposals and it was a tremendous package. . . . Mrs. Johnson joined the group about the middle of it, listened to it. She was obviously enthusiastic, and I think the president was enthusiastic.[117]

Udall proposed preserving seven million acres, including six million in Alaska, which would have increased the size of the National Park Service holdings by 25 percent. Udall argued, "Well, Mr. President . . . if Herbert Hoover could put in 4 million acres, I think 7 million is about right for Lyndon Johnson."[118]

Crafts continued, "Johnson asked how the Hill would react to this. And Udall said he had checked with Jackson and John Saylor and their general reaction was favorable. The president asked about Wayne Aspinall and

Udall ducked responding."[119] Johnson was concerned about leaving office with a final controversy. He subsequently learned that Udall had not discussed the plan with Aspinall. Udall later admitted, "I didn't talk to people like Congressman Aspinall . . . because I knew they would be negative."[120] When the President had his staff brief Aspinall on the proposal, Aspinall exploded, saying, "If the President took this action . . . I would see that it never had a penny for maintenance of those lands. . . . I'll introduce legislation to repeal the Antiquities Act."[121] Johnson called Aspinall, who told him, "Mr. President, Secretary Udall has never spoken to me about this particular matter." Johnson asked, "Wayne, what if I cut it down to 345,000 rather than 7 million [acres]?"[122] Aspinall still opposed the idea but said it he would not make a big fuss at that level.

As the last week of the presidency finished, Johnson continued to ponder how much land to protect. He was further irritated when the news leaked to the press from the Interior Department about the action before he had made any decision. Udall noted that Johnson "called up and raised hell with me, that we had put out the announcement that this had been approved."[123] Finally, Johnson told an aide, "These are just too big. . . . [A] president shouldn't take this much land without approval of Congress. . . . We'll settle on these."[124] In the end he set aside only 384,000 more acres as national monuments, including the new Marble Canyon National Monument in Arizona, on his last day in office on January 20. Crafts commented, "In my view it's a shame that the whole thing wasn't done . . . it's a shame from the standpoint that it was good for the country, and it's a shame from the standpoint that I think Udall and Johnson ended on an awkward note."[125]

Udall tried to repair the rift with Johnson, writing to Johnson shortly after he left office, "I'm painfully sorry—that our last two days ended in discord and disarray."[126] Johnson never communicated again with Udall before dying of a heart attack in January 1973. Lady Bird Johnson did stay in touch, writing to Udall,

> Like you, I will look back on the last five years full of achievements made together with satisfaction and pride and I know Lyndon does also—and it's that big backlog of satisfaction and building-for-the-future contained therein that I see rather than the disarray of the last few days. The country was lucky to have you as Secretary of Interior and I shall always appreciate your making me feel I could play a role and have at least a bit of influence in a field I deeply love.[127]

Johnson aide Joseph A. Califano Jr., wrote, "Johnson particularly prided himself on two achievements. For the first time in generations, in his last two years in office a President had preserved more land for conservation than the nation had bulldozed and paved over for industrial and urban development; and of the 35 National Park areas he pushed through Congress, 32 were within easy driving distance of large cities."[128] The total included the five national seashores, six national recreation areas, the first national lakeshore as well as additional national monuments, national historic parks and sites and national memorials that were established.[129]

Johnson's environmental role has been overshadowed over time by his other victories and defeats. Laurance Rockefeller concluded about the Johnsons, "It seems to me that they both inherited and passed on to the American people a legacy of love of the land and the soil and the awareness that God, man and nature are all one; and that if you lost sight of one, you might easily lose sight of the others."[130] Udall wrote in a 1968 memo, "A general conclusion—quite inescapable—is that Presidential leadership has changed the outlook of the nation with regard to conservation . . . the total environment is now the concern . . . the quality of life is now the perspective and purpose of the new conservation."[131]

In his memoir *The Vantage Point*, Johnson wrote,

If we are serious about making our country habitable for the generation that will come after us, we can no longer tolerate the abuse of the air, the water and the land as places to dump the waste products of our affluence. We must begin to devote a proportionate amount of our resources and our ingenuity to reversing the tide of pollution we have created . . . we must be prepared to shoulder the enormous costs this will entail, and we will have to demand that industry bear a fair share of the burden of doing business.[132]

When history looks at Lyndon Johnson and land, the first view is devastated, defoliated, and bomb-cratered stretches of Vietnam. But vast American wilderness areas, beautified roadways, recreational lands, wild rivers, and trails across the country also bear the mark of his presidency. It is the image and result that will endure the longest, a legacy celebrated, generally unknowingly, by millions of Americans in every season.

CHAPTER FIVE

Tackling Pollution in the Johnson Years

KEY EVENTS:
Motor Vehicle Pollution Control Act (1965)
Water Quality Act (1965)
Clean Water Restoration Act (1966)
Air Quality Act (1967)

Dirty air had seemed an inescapable aspect of the Industrial Revolution. Senator Edmund Muskie (D-ME), deeply involved in attacking this problem, wrote, "The notion that you could somehow prevent the escape of gases into the atmosphere and yet continue the functions that produced them had been inconceivable. . . . Most of us had accepted the idea that if we wanted civilization and its technological wonders air pollution was a by-product, something that went with progress, and not something we could really prevent."[1]

The widespread use of coal for heating and industry made the air of many cities perpetually hazy. Cities producing steel, such as Pittsburgh, were legendary for smoke-filled atmospheres. The automobile also spewed into the toxic brew that was much of America's urban air. "By a coincidence of geography, meteorology, and history," noted Muskie, "Los Angeles became the early warning signal for automotive pollution in the United States."[2] In fact, pointed out Supreme Court Justice William O. Douglas in 1972, "Los Angeles smog is killing pines in the San Bernardino Mountains far to the east of the city. By 1970 it had killed 40% of them."[3]

Regulation Takes to the Air

Before World War I, the only steps to limit pollution came when some cities passed ineffectual smoke abatement ordinances. The International Association for the Prevention of Smoke was formed in 1907, aimed at "pollution control."[4] In 1908 Frederick Law Olmsted Jr. observed, "The dweller in a town burning bituminous coal needs no definition of the smoke nuisance. The great cloud that hangs over the city like a pall can be seen from any neighboring hilltop," adding, "The first step in abating smoke is to pass a law or ordinance, making the emission of black or dark gray smoke an unlawful act."[5]

The first acute air pollution catastrophes erupted after World War II. On October 25, 1948, Donora, Pennsylvania, endured a cloud of noxious air, a mixture of sulfur dioxide, nitrogen oxides, and metal dust from a local steel plant, that killed twenty people and sickened six thousand others, including 88 percent of the town's asthmatics.[6] When a cloud of sulfur-laden smog paralyzed London for a week in December 1952, resulting in some four thousand deaths, the usually conservative *Times* of London warned that "even under less abnormal conditions the noxious matter in polluted air must have a detrimental effect on human and animal health."[7] The poor air was linked to the city's widespread use of coal. A similar episode in New York City in 1953 resulted in some two hundred fatalities in a short period.[8]

By 1968 an estimated one hundred million cars and trucks were shooting some 180 billion pounds of contaminants into the air in the United States, adding to industrial pollution.[9] In 1966 the Public Health Service reported, "Motor vehicles emit carbon monoxide, which reduces man's ability to transplant oxygen to his tissues; lead, which increases man's body burden of this toxic metal; carcinogenic hydrocarbons and reactive hydrocarbons and nitrogen oxides, which combine with sunlight to produce eye-irritating, plant-damaging, and visibility-obscuring photochemical smog."[10] Air pollution was known to damage hearts, lungs, and fetal development, while greatly exacerbating asthma, the leading chronic disease among children.

Still, pollution control efforts were halting. In 1963 only fourteen states had statewide air pollution laws of any kind.[11] "If it hadn't been for the question of air pollution, I doubt that there would be the heightened general concern about pollution," noted Muskie. "You cannot escape air pollution . . . in too many cities and towns you can taste it and almost feel its deposits in your lungs."[12] Muskie would be a key figure in the environmental advances of both the Johnson and Nixon administrations. Born to immigrant parents in 1914 in the polluted timber town of Rumsford, Maine, Muskie's close-up experience—from boy to politician—of the poisoned Androscoggin River shaped his environmental outlook. He attended Bates College on a scholarship and then Cornell Law School. After joining the navy in World War II, Muskie practiced law in Waterville and became active in Democratic politics. In 1954, after three terms in the state legislature and serving as chairman of the Democratic State Committee, Muskie ran for governor. In one of the nation's poorest states, he ran on economic development and resisting the dominance of big business and became Maine's first Democratic governor in the twentieth century. Four years later he defeated a three-term Republican incumbent to reach the Senate.

Muskie, as chair of the Subcommittee on Air and Water Pollution, pushed through the Clean Air Act of 1963, which increased funding for air quality research, encouraged the development of exhaust control devices for automobiles, and gave the federal government the authority to regulate major sources of air pollution.[13] The act also gave states grants to cover up to two-thirds of the cost of creating state air pollution programs. However, neither the Department of Health, Education and Welfare (HEW) nor the states followed through with public hearings on air pollution, let alone injunctions to restrain polluters.

In 1964 Muskie held additional congressional hearings on air pollution in six cities, noting that "our war on air pollution was in its infancy."[14] Muskie recalled, "Representatives of the automobile manufacturers testified that they did not believe automotive pollution was a national problem, but that if the Congress insisted on the deadline contained in the Senate bill, the manufacturers had the capacity to meet it."[15] Muskie's campaign brought him an unexpected endorsement when a housewife in Cicero, Illinois, outraged at the dirty air, mailed him an envelope of soot.[16]

LBJ Steps In

President Johnson was determined to attack the problem. "In a series of speeches and messages during 1965," wrote biographer Robert Dallek, Johnson "declared his determination to reduce air and water pollution not only by cleaning up the country's atmosphere and waterways but by setting air and water quality standards that would prevent pollution before it occurred."[17] From the perspectives of both Larry O'Brien, a Johnson political aide, and Donald Hornig, his science advisor, the pollution issue was personally important to Johnson.[18] From a policy standpoint,

Martin Melosi wrote, "Antipollution was an integral part of the Great Society."[19]

In November 1965 Johnson declared, "The technology that had permitted our affluence spews out vast quantities of wastes and spent products that pollute our air, [and] poison our waters. . . . Pollution now is one of the most pervasive problems of our society."[20] At Johnson's urging, Congress passed the Motor Vehicle Air Pollution Control Act of 1965. The act authorized HEW to establish emission levels for new motor vehicles, which accounted for 52 percent of the nation's air pollution. However, the deadline for compliance was left to the discretion of HEW, which was slow to produce the standards.[21] Automakers could be covered by meeting the standards on one prototype engine, leaving their mass-produced cars essentially outside the regulations.

Another air pollution catastrophe occurred in 1966 in New York City, killing an estimated eighty people and sickening many more.[22] The *Saturday Evening Post* noted the poor quality of the city's air in general, saying that breathing it was the equivalent of "smoking two packs of cigarettes a day."[23] Amendments to the Clean Air Act in 1966 provided states with federal subsidies to cover the operation of state and local air pollution programs.[24] The need to go beyond the 1965 act was clear, because the air wasn't. In January 1967 Johnson proposed strengthening the law, saying, "The situation does not exist because it was inevitable nor because it cannot be controlled. Air pollution is the inevitable consequence of neglect."[25] The resulting Air Quality Act of 1967 set standards for air quality rather than specific emissions requirements, and created an explicit national goal "to protect and enhance the quality of the Nation's air resources so as to promote the public health and welfare and productive capacity of its population."[26] Muskie won a unanimous vote in his committee and in the Senate for the measure, leading Senator John Sherman Cooper to proclaim, "I have never seen in my service in the Senate a better demonstration of the committee legislative process."[27]

The act gave the federal government authority over ambient air quality standards, as well as some authority over industrial and motor vehicle emissions. The federal government would undertake research and fund states to help them set their rules. If states failed to act, HEW could set the standards for them, and could sue states if air pollution posed "an imminent and substantial endangerment" to public health. At the signing ceremony in November, Johnson said, "I would like to begin this morning by reading you a little weather report. . . . '[D]irty water and black snow pour from dismal air . . . to the partial slush that waits for them below.' Now that is not a description of Boston, Chicago, New York or even Washington D.C. It is from Dante's 'Inferno'. . . . But doesn't it sound familiar? Isn't a forecast that fits almost any large American city today?"[28] He continued, "Either we stop poisoning the air or we become a nation in gas masks."[29]

Johnson admitted that the law was not as strong as he wanted, and that "additional, bolder legislation will be needed in the years ahead."[30] Significant weaknesses in the law soon became apparent. By 1968 less than a quarter of the ninety-one air quality regions had firm standards of any sort and many of these were quite weak.[31] By 1970 no state had even completed a full set of standards for any pollutant.[32] "I think the Public Works Committee has been sort of leading the charge on this," commented Birch Bayh (D-IN), "and Senator Muskie was interested in this problem."[33] Muskie's prominence on pollution contributed to his being named the Democratic candidate for vice-president in 1968. Despite Nixon's victory, Muskie's strong performance in the campaign made him the frontrunner for the Democratic nomination for president in 1972.

Water Pollution Bubbling Up

Water pollution had been recognized as an issue even before the formation of the United States. In 1647 the colony of Massachusetts passed regulations against pollution of Boston Harbor, while in 1726 South Carolina enacted a statute to limit pollution harmful to fish.[34] The increasing urbanization of the American population created the need to assure drinkable water and the elimination of waste. Many cities built waterworks to supply their residents with water, often from great distances, and sewer systems to dispose of the wastes, but the incoming water was not always pure, while the sewage flowed untreated into nearby rivers, leading to recurrent outbreaks of cholera and other illnesses in downstream towns. The Massachusetts Sanitary Commission's Report of 1850 was one of the first analyses of the sanitation problems of the city. Among its many recommendations were statements such as, "We recommend that, before erecting any new dwelling house . . . the owner or builder be required to give notice . . . of the sanitary measures he proposes to adopt."[35]

While water treatment would eventually eliminate most waterborne infections, industry increasingly dumped nonbacterial toxins into the water, the easiest route to dispose of waste products from manufacturing.

Historian Robert Gottlieb wrote, "By World War I, heavy metals such as lead, organic chemicals such as benzene and naphtha, and a variety of other toxic substances . . . were being discharged in significant amounts into the air, water, and land."[36] After World War II these were joined by petrochemicals, detergents, pesticides, and herbicides. The dominant approach to wastes was hoping that larger volumes of waters would diffuse them. The years from 1900 to 1950 saw a doubling of the American population and a 700 percent increase in industrial capacity.[37] By midcentury, few rivers or lakes were not at least somewhat polluted.

Sewage, mainly fecal wastes, caused other problems. The organisms needed to break them down required so much oxygen in this process that many waters became oxygen-starved, particularly in the Northeast and Midwest with their high concentrations of people and industry. These oxygen-deficient waters became known for, in the words of historian Paul Milazzo, "frequent fish kills, putrid odors, and zones practically devoid of life—except for eels, suckers, and an overabundance of algae that thrived in waters with excessive amounts of nitrogen and phosphorus."[38]

Since the growth of population and industry outpaced control efforts, the nation's water quality declined.[39] Historian Richard Andrews wrote, "Construction of municipal sewers and wastewater treatment plants was perennially underfunded, . . . due to competing local priorities and resistance to urban needs by rural-dominated state legislatures. Only during the 1930s did construction of municipal wastewater plants keep pace with urban growth, aided by Depression-era federal public-works programs which financed over five hundred wastewater treatment plants."[40] Historian Philip K. Micklin wrote of the 1940s and 1950s, "Only a few states developed comprehensive pollution control programs and those that had water-quality standards failed to enforce them."[41]

The problem of wastes and water pollution peaked in the 1950s and 1960s. In 1955, of the 165 million people in the United States, only 55 million had adequate sewage treatment.[42] Nationwide Public Health Service studies in the early 1950s documented more than twenty-two thousand sources of water pollution.[43] In 1963 nationwide pollution from municipalities, industry, and agriculture killed 7.8 million fish. Lake Erie was so polluted with coliform bacteria, phenols, iron, ammonia, chlorides, and phosphates from industrial processes and municipal sewage that it was deemed "ecologically dead."[44] In the middle 1960s one-third of Americans were not served by any sewage system, while 60 percent of those two-thirds who were had their sewage inadequately treated.[45]

The first federal action was the Water Pollution Control Act of 1948. In this act and in further amendments in 1953 Congress authorized limited loans and technical assistance to states for the construction of municipal waste treatment facilities, yet did not actually appropriate any money for this purpose.[46] The act also stated that primary responsibility for water pollution belonged to states and local authorities.

In 1955 the Eisenhower administration proposed that the federal government create voluntary clean water standards for interstate waterways. A Senate bill to this effect moved to the House Rivers and Harbors Subcommittee of the House Committee on Public Works, chaired by Congressman John Blatnik (D-MN). Representative Iris Blitch (D-GA), motivated by opposition by industries in Georgia, objected to and blocked what was expected to be an uncontroversial bill. Angered by the industry opposition, Blatnik told his aide Jerry Sonosky in August 1955, "If they don't like S. 890, give them one they really won't like."[47]

John Blatnik was born on August 17, 1911, in northern Minnesota. Blatnik served as an educational advisor to the local Civilian Conservation Corps, then taught chemistry and became an assistant superintendent of schools before winning a state senate seat in 1940. After wartime service in the Office of Strategic Services, often behind enemy lines in Italy and Yugoslavia, he beat a Republican incumbent to enter Congress in 1946. A New Deal Democrat, Blatnik supported job-creating government projects. He became chairman of the House Public Works Committee Subcommittee on Rivers and Harbors in 1955.[48] Blatnik succeeded in defining water pollution as a threat to the nation's water supply and hence a threat to economic growth. Blatnik stated, "Pollution is a waste of water. . . . Pollution can be just as effective in reducing a water resource for use as is a period of drought."[49]

In 1956 Blatnik reintroduced the water pollution bill, selling it as a jobs program to labor and a source of economic growth to municipalities while legislators could appreciate the good created by projects in their district. To Sonosky, Blatnik "made pollution controllers out of every member of Congress who had a channel to dig, a harbor to deepen, a bridge to build, [or] a post office to name."[50] The successful legislation, the Water Pollution Control Act of 1956, authorized $50 million annually in grants to municipalities, while expanding technical assistance for ten years for the construction of waste treatment facilities. The US Public Health Service was to assist the states in developing comprehensive plans for eliminating water pollution in interstate waterways, and within states when requested.[51] The act also established the Water Pollution Control Advisory Board and expanded research on the issue.[52]

Yet the cost of waste treatment facilities so dwarfed the assistance offered that few states developed extensive treatment programs or created strong or enforceable water pollution control programs.[53] Blatnik succeeded in passing a successor bill in 1958 increasing annual expenditures for treatment facilities from $50 million to $90 million. However, the bill was vetoed by President Eisenhower, who referred to water pollution as something to be solved by state and local governments.[54] Lyndon Johnson later recalled, "One of the real disappointments of my last year as Majority Leader was that President Eisenhower did not see the necessity of taking forceful action at the national level."[55]

Other legislators began to realize how pollution affected water supplies. In 1959 the Senate created the Select Committee on National Water Resources, chaired by Senator Robert Kerr (D-OK), to look at programs to increase water resources. Milazzo wrote that in analyzing water issues, "the preeminence of pollution over all other water resource issues took the committee staff by surprise."[56] Instead of just recommending more dams, the committee urged "a program of reservoirs and waste treatment plants."[57] The new president, John F. Kennedy, welcomed the report, stating, "To meet all needs . . . we shall have to use and re-use the same water, maintaining quality as well as quantity."[58]

Under Kennedy, Blatnik pushed through the 1961 Water Pollution Control Act amendments, increasing spending for waste treatment and giving the federal government authority over both interstate and navigable waters. Theoretically, the secretary of health, education and welfare could sue polluters when states failed to act. Congressman John Dingell (D-MI) stressed the importance of controlling water pollution, stating, "These substances which are inserted into the waters of our land today are not the substances which we know or understand or, indeed, of which we have any understanding. . . . Rather these substances are not only often in their own right toxic but they may even permit the waters to harbor other toxic matters."[59] In practice federal authority was limited, as the government would have to prove interstate damage to health and welfare to get an abatement order against a polluter.[60]

Elected to the Senate in 1962, Gaylord Nelson (D-WI) brought up the effects of the new synthetic detergents that had been developed during the 1940s, which were resistant to breakdown. One component, alkyl benzene sulfonate, produced persistent foam on the water.[61] The phosphates in the detergents caused algae blooms that covered miles of lakes. In 1963 Nelson persuaded Congress to pass a bill to ban nonbiodegradable detergents by mid-1965, eliminating alkyl benzene sulfonate. After claiming that this would be practically and financially impossible, detergent manufacturers agreed to make the change by the proposed deadline. Nelson introduced a new bill in 1965 phasing out phosphates in detergents and requiring that detergents be tested for environmental and health effects before being used, but this proposal was blocked by the powerful detergent industry.

Johnson Turns to Water Pollution

The next step to control water pollution occurred under President Johnson, after his 1964 electoral landslide swept in the most liberal Congress since 1936.[62] During the first session of this Congress in 1965, Johnson was able to get a host of legislation passed, including antipollution measures. Johnson proposed to "provide, through the setting of effective water quality standards, combined with a swift and effective enforcement procedure, a national program to prevent water pollution at its source rather than attempting to cure pollution after it occurs."[63]

Muskie later wrote, "When I was a boy, we didn't think about 'pollution'. . . . Yet, it was our river, the Androscoggin, that stirred public concern and indignation even before World War II. . . . [T]he mill wastes were visible . . . there was a tremendous stench and the paint on houses began to peel."[64] As the first Democratic governor of Maine in the twentieth century, Muskie recognized water pollution as a problem, saying in 1955 that it had "serious economic implications for existing industries," especially recreation and tourism. As governor he tried to lure a manufacturer to the town of Bedford, only to have the company choose to locate out of state due to the pollution in the Saco River.[65] Governor Muskie called for legislation to address water pollution, particularly to access funds available under the 1956 Water Pollution Control Act.[66]

Muskie's proposals to improve water quality faced pushback from industry and from unions afraid that further regulations would make business leave the state.[67] Muskie later wrote, "In January of 1957, I proposed to the legislature that we create a state program to match the federal grants to build treatment facilities. I also suggested . . . to set classifications [of stream quality] for what ought to be, not just what existed. There was resistance and a fight on the floor of the Maine House."[68]

When Muskie won election to the Senate in 1958, he got off on the wrong foot with majority leader Lyndon Johnson (D-TX). Johnson met with Muskie soon after his election. Wanting control of his vote, Johnson told Muskie, "Many times, Ed, you won't know how you are going to vote until the clerk calling the roll gets to the M's." When the issue of changing the filibuster rules came up, Johnson asked Muskie how he was going to vote. Muskie answered, "The clerk hasn't gotten to the M's yet."[69] Johnson punished Muskie by rejecting Muskie's preferred committee choices, instead putting him on Banking, Government Affairs, and Public Works. Milazzo noted, "Johnson used the Public Works Committee as a repository for incoming members with a penchant for independence and an inclination toward liberal activism."[70] Lady Bird Johnson later noted Johnson's closeness with the chair of the Senate Public Works Committee, Senator Robert Kerr (D-OK), saying, "Kerr soon became one of our great favorites. Big, tough."[71] Johnson relied on Kerr's domination of the committee, but in December 1962 Kerr suffered a heart attack and was replaced by Patrick McNamara (D-MI), who made Muskie the chair of the relatively new Subcommittee on Air and Water Pollution. When Muskie heard the assignment from the staff director, Ron Linton, he cut him off after the word *air*, saying, "Air? What the hell do I care about air coming from Maine?" Yet Muskie soon transformed himself into the Senate's leading expert on both air and water pollution. Linton explained that Muskie "spent lots of time mastering arcane issues you would normally leave to staff and staff would leave to technical consultants."[72]

Muskie became skilled at building consensus within his subcommittee, encouraging discussion and the participation of minority members, as well as in managing bills on the Senate floor. Muskie persuaded the Senate to pass water pollution legislation in 1963, but the bill died in the House when Congress adjourned. Joel K. Goldstein wrote, "In 1963 fighting pollution brought little political payoff."[73] Muskie worked to build up national support for water pollution control by holding subcommittee hearings in multiple cities, thus highlighting local water pollution issues.

The subcommittee also produced the first Senate documentary, *Troubled Waters*, a short film showing how the issue of water pollution affected Americans. Narrator Henry Fonda ended the film with the words, "To live, man must use and pollute the water. But if he abuses it [and] fails to do his best to restore its natural purity, then water will no longer be able to serve him. And factories will close, farms dry up, people disappear."[74]

A severe drought in the northeastern United States from 1963 to 1967 increased support for water pollution control. One congressional aide remarked, "When all is said and done, our best friend on the water pollution bill was the Northeastern drought. If anything gives a guy courage to thumb his nose at a lobbyist, it's 400 housewives screaming about watering their lawns."[75]

Now Johnson put aside any residual animosity to work with Muskie to try again. The result was Senate passage of the Water Quality Act of 1965 by a 68–6 vote in January. The Senate bill required states to develop quality standards for interstate waterways and their tributaries within two years, and to develop implementation plans to achieve these standards. The bill created the Federal Water Pollution Control Administration (FWPCA) in HEW to monitor the results.[76] HEW could issue water quality standards for interstate waterways if states failed to set adequate regulations. Muskie believed that water quality standards, rather than being totally uniform, had to reflect "the differences in water uses, the intensity of water uses, and the availability of water, river by river and portion of river by portion of river."[77] The act also expanded funding for the construction of wastewater facilities. In March 1965 the majority of the House Public Works Committee passed a bill that did not include federal water quality standards. While Blatnik favored the standards, opposition from industry and agriculture kept them out of the House bill, which passed unanimously on April 28, 1965. The final House-Senate conference committee bill gave states until June 30, 1967, to establish water quality standards for interstate streams. Otherwise, they faced a byzantine combination of state and federal standard setting.

When Johnson signed the bill, he commented, "Today we begin to be masters of our environment. . . . Additional bolder measures will be needed in the years ahead. But we have begun."[78] Johnson later wrote in his memoir about the signing ceremony for the bill, saying, "I asked Robert L. Hardesty of my staff to draft a signing statement for the occasion and to 'make it tough.' 'Find out which industries are the guiltiest,' I said,

'I want the stockholders to know what their companies are doing to our environment.'" At the ceremony, Johnson said, "There is no excuse for a river flowing red with blood from slaughterhouses. There is no excuse for papermills pouring tons of sulfuric acid into the lakes and streams."[79] In his memoir, Johnson wrote, "That evening I watched reports of the speech on the television news shows with considerable satisfaction. I thought to myself: 'That should make them stop, look and listen.'" He continued, "I received angry telegrams from the presidents of almost every papermill company . . . denying that one single ounce of sulfuric acid was poured into the water from their plants."[80] Johnson went on to say, "I asked Hardesty for an explanation, and he immediately called HEW. 'Well,' came the reply, 'it's not really sulfuric acid. It's sulphites . . . we just thought sulfuric acid sounded better.' They were just trying to help the President, they insisted, but the President had to make numerous apologies as a result. Still, I believed the point was valid."[81]

When the US Chamber of Commerce pushed back against the regulations, James Quigley, the acting commissioner of the Water Pollution Control Administration told them, "You must accept the principle that the cost of pollution control from now on is part of the cost of doing business."[82] In his 1966 State of the Union address, Johnson called for stronger water pollution laws "to clean completely entire large river basins."[83] In his 1966 message to Congress, Johnson stated, "I seek to make [this] . . . that point in time when Americans determined to resist the flow of poison in their rivers and streams. I seek to make them ancient history for the next generation. . . . I propose that we begin now to clean and preserve entire river basins from their sources to their mouths."[84] Muskie worked closely with the subcommittee's ranking Republican, J. Caleb Boggs (R-DE), in drafting a bill to help cities build improved water treatment facilities. The final bill, the 1966 Clean Water Restoration Act, authorizing up to $6 billion for waste treatment facilities, passed in the Senate 90–0 and in the House 313–0. Historian David Goldfield wrote, "the marriage of large public works projects with environmental protection proved a good union for bipartisan support."[85]

Nelson felt that even this funding for waste management facilities was clearly inadequate, estimating that $50 billion to $100 billion would be needed. Nelson proposed increasing funding while raising the federal share for local sewage treatment facilities to 90 percent. Nelson argued, "Cleaning up the waters of America is even more important than the building of the interstate highway system," which was built with a 90 percent federal share.[86] Congress would only agree to a 30 percent federal share, with just a few billion dollars for building treatment plants.

While water quality standards were controversial, there was widespread support for funding for waste treatment facilities in the 1966 Act.[87] California governor Ronald Reagan, later famous for his disparagement of government, wrote Johnson in June 1967 asking for more federal funding for waste treatment. He "reminded the president that his objective was not merely to prevent pollution but also to preserve and enhance the quality of California's waters."[88]

Johnson, as well as Muskie, was key to the passage of the clean water legislation. Historian Julian Zelizer wrote, "Johnson's insights and actions, his legislative experience, and his tactics had been crucial in getting the legislation passed. . . . It [also] took the huge House and Senate majorities the recent election had created."[89] Johnson later talked about the opposition that had limited the strength of the air and water pollution laws, saying, "These measures met with considerable resistance. Powerful special interests, particularly in industry, foresaw that it would be expensive to change their methods of operation in order to meet strict new federal pollution standards."[90]

As the decade proceeded, the evident pollution of rivers and lakes increased public support for cleanup efforts. In a widely read article published in the *Saturday Evening Post* in April 1966 titled "Our Dying Waters," environmentalist John Bird began, "We have filled our streams with raw excrement and garbage, laden with disease. We have stained them with oil, coal, dust, tar dyes and chemical 'liquors' discharged by industries."[91] The Hudson River was so polluted that Senator Robert Kennedy (D-NY) quipped, "If you fall in here, you don't drown—you decay."[92] *Newsweek* commented on the Hudson, "The desecration of one of the nation's scenic resources is bad enough . . . but the destruction of the river as a water resource is criminal."[93] Nearly ten thousand lakes were affected by phosphate-induced eutrophication, where algae growth lowered the oxygen in the water, leading to the death of other plants and fish.[94]

Johnson followed up the legislation with an executive order mandating secondary wastewater treatment at all federal facilities and ordering pollution to be minimized by all federal grantees and contractors.[95] Muskie successfully opposed an administration proposal for regional water agencies, preferring to keep control at the state level.[96] The Senate passed measures to deal with oil pollution and acid mine drainage in 1967 and ship and thermal pollution in 1968, but the House failed to act. Muskie's 1968 proposal that oil companies should be liable for the costs of discharges from offshore oil drilling did not advance through Congress either.

The water acts under Johnson did not achieve as much as hoped. While some 9,400 water treatment plants were built from 1957 to 1969, this remained inadequate.[97] The funding for waste treatment facilities, as Nelson predicted, was insufficient to meet the need. Facing opposition from local industries and a host of competing priorities, many states created either no water quality standards or weak standards. By late 1971 fewer than thirty states had plans that met minimum standards, while federal enforcement under the 1965 act was limited to interstate waterways.[98]

Interior Secretary Stewart Udall attempted to protect streams with quality already exceeding state standards by an explicit "nondegradation" directive, which would force new sources of pollution to provide the "highest and best degree of waste treatment available under existing technology."[99] Udall's proposal elicited a tornado of opposition. The Western Governors Conference unanimously condemned the plan as an intrusion into state and local decision making, while the US Chamber of Commerce challenged Udall's authority to set effluent limits.[100] Ironically, despite the opposition to Udall's proposal, almost all states incorporated nondegradation into their eventual water standards.[101]

While the clean air and water acts of the Johnson administration did not solve either problem, they were a solid recognition of air and water pollution as major problems demanding national action. That action would happen in the next four years.

CHAPTER SIX

The Green Nixon

KEY EVENTS:
National Environmental Policy Act (1969)
Council on Environmental Quality (1969)
Environmental Protection Agency (1970)
Environmental Quality Education Act (1970)
Clean Air Act (1970)

Nothing in Richard Nixon's entire previous political career would have suggested that his presidency would produce the basic structure of American environmental protection. Yet during Nixon's cut-short time in office, often while the attention of the nation—and sometimes the attention of the president—was focused elsewhere, the United States installed its fundamental laws attacking pollution and directing conservation planning. Nixon's first two years in office saw the passage of the National Environmental Policy Act, the creation of the Council on Environmental Quality and the Environmental Protection Agency, and the passage of a strong Clean Air Act, among other accomplishments.

From the time he returned to southern California from World War II, to be recruited to run against an incumbent Democratic congressman, Nixon's political life was marked by strident anticommunism and sharp partisan attacks. The tactics brought him to the House, a swift elevation to the Senate, and election as vice-president before he turned forty. Set back by a narrow defeat for the White House in 1960, and a solid loss running for governor of California in 1962, Nixon rebounded to win the presidency in 1968, running mostly on street crime and a secret plan to end the Vietnam War.[1] The environment played a minimal role in his campaign. According to Nixon advisor John C. Whitaker, only one of eighteen radio addresses that Nixon recorded was about natural resources or the environment. Whitaker noted, "Campaign staff couldn't remember fielding a single question touching on the issue."[2] But if Nixon—who would become known for walking on the beach in wingtips—had little affinity for the natural world, he clearly saw it as a potential political opportunity, a way to attract voters through a policy that would take little of his time or attention. As a result, major environmental advances came under a president who took limited interest.

Other conservatives and Republicans were more interested. "One of the most serious problems in American society goes to the quality of life in the world around us," warned columnist James J. Kilpatrick in 1969. "The problem essentially is a problem of conservation—of conserving some of the great values of America—and conservatives, of all people, ought to be in the vanguard of the fight."[3] In the House, John Saylor argued, "The American people are light years ahead of Members of Congress as to awareness of our environmental decline. . . . The public support is out there for a massive drive against further erosion in the quality of our lives if only all of us in Congress will bite the hot bullet and respond."[4]

Support for the environment was bipartisan—and strong. "When President Nixon and staff walked into the White House on January 20, 1969," recalled Whitaker, "we were totally unprepared for the tidal wave of public opinion in favor of cleaning up the environment that was about to engulf us."[5] Since a key segment of Nixon's supporters, prosperous suburbanites, increasingly supported environmental protection, Nixon decided that an increased role for the federal government in protecting the environment would be popular.[6] Championing this viewpoint was Nixon's senior aide John Ehrlichman, who in 1969 was named by Nixon to lead the Domestic Affairs Council, a policymaking group, to make recommendations to Nixon. Ehrlichman's "own politics were moderate to liberal," explained Nixon biographer Evan Thomas, "especially on the environment, which he had learned to cherish living in the Pacific Northwest."[7] Whitaker, who assumed significant responsibility for environmental issues in the administration, commented later, "Ehrlichman sold him [Nixon] on the environment. He made Nixon see it was politically dangerous if he didn't get on board. He [Ehrlichman] brought in pollsters to say, 'This thing is catching fire.'"8 Nixon's younger brother Ed, who also lived in the Pacific Northwest, was also a strong environmentalist and may have had some influence over the president. Ed Nixon later recalled, "My interest was, when I talked to my brother about issues, issues about the environment that had been going from when he was in Congress."9

In addition, President Nixon believed in the power of government. "[Nixon's] approach to governance was essentially positive," wrote Thomas. "He believed that he could get things done—and that it was his duty to try. . . . [H]e embraced the mid-twentieth-century ethos that government existed to solve problems."10 In his memoirs, Nixon would write, "I wanted to be an activist president for domestic policy, but I wanted to be certain that the things we did had a chance of working."11 Nixon advisor Roy Ash insisted, "We didn't have an antigovernment attitude."12

Building a National Environmental Policy

The first major environmental legislation passed under Nixon's administration, the National Environmental Policy Act, took environmental policy in a radical new direction. Crucially, the act, signed by Nixon on January 1, 1970, required that "for any action that is going to affect the quality of the human environment, it is necessary to make a federal impact statement."13 The newly formed Council on Environmental Quality would evaluate government actions in terms of their environmental impact. As first chairman of the council, Nixon named Russell Train.

Born to a prominent Republican family, Train went to Princeton and Columbia law school. While serving on the US Tax Court, his interest in African wildlife led him to found and become chairman of the African Wildlife Federation in 1961. In 1964 Train resigned his judgeship to become the full-time chief executive officer of the Conservation Foundation. President Lyndon Johnson responded, "I am grateful to learn that you will be applying your great gifts to the conservation effort—an endeavor which, more than ever, is crucial to the future of our nation."14 Johnson later appointed Train vice-chairman of the National Water Commission, where Train became friendly with Senate Interior Committee chairman Henry Jackson. Looking for a way to make federal decisions take the environment into account, Jackson asked Train if the Conservation Foundation could deploy Lynton Caldwell, an expert in the area, to serve as a consultant to Jackson's committee. Train agreed.

In 1963 Caldwell, a professor at Indiana University, published "Environment: A New Focus for Public Policy?" in the journal *Public Administration Review*. Caldwell emphasized how environmental responsibilities were divided among different government agencies. "There appears to be no clear doctrine of public responsibility for the human environment as such," complained Caldwell. "It therefore follows that concern for the environment is the business of *almost* no one in our public life."[15] To fix this, he urged, "Some new facility at the highest levels of policy formulation will be needed to provide a point at which environmental policy issues cutting across the jurisdictional lines of existing agencies can be identified."[16] As a result, J. Brooks Flippen wrote, "Caldwell proved to be the key architect of the environmental impact statement process so critical to the National Environmental Policy Act."[17]

Caldwell, of course, would not be the only architect of incorporating environmental issues into government decision making. Many environmental activists, drawing on lessons from legal battles particularly over the Hudson River, stressed the importance of considering the environmental consequences before government decisions were made. Another source for this concept was the landscape architect Ian McHarg, who developed a popular course at the University of Pennsylvania, Man and the Environment, starting in 1957. In his 1969 book *Design with Nature*, McHarg argued that developers had to justify the effects of their actions on the natural world.[18]

Existing coordination, provided by the Office of Science and Technology, set up under John F. Kennedy and expanded under Johnson, was initially limited. Under director Donald F. Hornig, the Office of Science and Technology broadened its responsibilities to include most major environmental issues faced by the Johnson administration.[19] Still, coordination was often missing. In 1967 and 1968 Jackson held hearings on Everglades National Park to demonstrate the conflicts between government agencies and the lack of consideration of environmental impact. The Department of the Interior was trying to acquire more land for the park. The Army Corps of Engineers proposed a series of dams and canals that would drain water from the park, endangering its wildlife. The Department of Transportation proposed a huge airport close by, further curtailing water flow as well as creating massive airplane noise.[20] Jackson summoned the three agency heads to appear together. "It was obvious," recalled his aide Bill van Ness, "that they had little or no recognition that their programs were in conflict with each other."[21] As National Park director George Hartzog Jr. put it, "When I came in as director [in 1964], we were at the point where the two bureaus [Corps of Engineers and Park Service] were hardly speaking on the issues."[22]

Seeing the situation, explained historian Robert Kaufman, "[Jackson] wanted a mechanism to force federal decision makers at the lowest possible levels to identify objectives and conflicts before they committed funds and undertook irreversible actions."[23] In addition, Jackson wanted the process to consider the environmental effects of each proposal. Jackson's Interior Committee staff director, Dan Dreyfus, suggested that the proposed environmental impact statements "be modelled on a synthesis of the Fair Employment Act of 1946 and the interagency review process for the Bureau of Reclamation."[24]

In 1968 the Senate Interior Committee and the House Subcommittee on Science, Research and Development, chaired by Emilio Daddario (D-CT), held joint hearings on creating a national policy on the environment and institutions to coordinate it. While Daddario was particularly interested in increasing environmental research, Caldwell argued, "Of equal and perhaps greater importance at this time is the establishment of a system to insure [sic] that existing knowledge and new findings will be organized in a manner suitable for review and decision as matters of public policy."[25] Action would have to await a new administration and new Congress in 1969.

After Nixon was elected, he set up several transitional task forces. Train was appointed to chair a task force on environmental issues. "We recommend," began their report, "that improved environmental management be made a principal objective of the new Administration."[26] The four-page report made specific recommendations, among them that Johnson's Council on Recreation and Natural Beauty be transformed into a Council on the Environment, to be chaired by the vice-president.[27] The report emphasized wide voter support for environmental protection, calling it a "unity issue" that could rally support.[28] Parts of the Train report resonated with Nixon. He declared in his inaugural address, "In rebuilding our cities and improving our rural areas; in protecting our environment and enhancing the quality of life—in all these and more, we will and must press urgently forward."[29] Assessed Flippen, "Nixon did not personally give the environment a great deal of thought relative to other issues, but his administration could still use it to his political advantage."[30]

In Train's view, "The emphasis the White House was giving to the environment was led by John Ehrlichman. . . . There can be little doubt that Ehrlichman was responding to clear signals from Nixon and that Nixon was determined to get out in front of the Democratic Congress on the issue. . . . There is no evidence of which I am aware that Nixon had any real personal interest in environmental matters. I certainly never heard him express any." Instead, "[Nixon's] reaction to these issues was that of a highly political animal. He read the polls and he had to be aware that concern for the environment was rapidly rising among the American people. His political instincts told him that he and the Republican Party could not afford to be seen as anti-environment. . . . [H]e would want to seize the environmental high ground from the Democrats, particularly from . . . Ed Muskie."[31] Nixon's choice as secretary of the interior, Alaska governor Wally Hickel, was initially seen as antienvironmental. But before his Senate hearing, Hickel told Muskie, "Senator, when you get to know me, you and I are going to be on the same side on this whole fight over the environment and pollution."[32] Nixon appointed Train as Hickel's undersecretary.

Little noticed by the public, the pumping of crude oil from offshore wells had increased from 7 million barrels in 1955 to 222 million barrels in 1967.[33] One week after Nixon's inauguration, crude oil began to leak from a well off the coast of Santa Barbara, California. The massive spill washed ashore, coating the beaches and killing birds and seals. Public outrage over the spill helped raise support for more protection of the environment. Stewart Udall, the preceding secretary of the interior, took responsibility for allowing the drilling, calling it "the conservation Bay of Pigs."[34] Hickel later recalled, "The White House didn't want to make it look like too big an event, you know, and I said, 'Just tell the truth about that.' That's the biggest disaster I've ever seen happen by the public sector."[35] In one of the first of several actions that would irritate the White House and please environmentalists, Hickel added, "I demanded that all companies who hold drilling leases in the outer Continental Shelf accept liability for cleanup even before the course of the spill is determined."[36]

The Council on Environmental Quality would later say of the spill, "No one was killed . . . no one suffered permanent health damage . . . no large numbers of people were threatened. . . . Yet the event dramatized what many people saw as thoughtless insensitivity and lack of concern on the part of government and business to an issue that had become very important to them. It brought home to a great many Americans a feeling that protection of their environment would not simply happen but required their active support and involvement."[37] Hickel would agree: "That Santa Barbara thing changed the whole image [in] the United States on the environment. It changed a lot."[38]

Seizing the moment, Jackson told the biennial Wilderness Conference in March, "While we have completed an enviable, even unprecedented record of legislative awareness of the value of wilderness, conservation, recreation . . . we have not constructed a philosophy for future guidance. . . . I have introduced legislation which has as its purpose the establishment of a national strategy for management of the human environment."[39] Jackson scheduled hearings on his proposal in April. He viewed the Nixon task force's proposed Environmental Quality Council (EQC), a cabinet-level coordinating committee, as "a highly visible but ineffectual gesture," since cabinet members were unlikely to criticize programs in other departments. Jackson persuaded the administration to delay its creation until after the hearings.[40] Nixon's science advisor, Lee DuBridge, who had earlier "dismissed peremptorily the need for" the National Environmental Policy Act (NEPA),[41] now announced the administration's willingness to work with Jackson on a national environmental policy.[42] Jackson's NEPA would create a council of environmental experts to assess public policies, but the initial draft provided no formal process for considering environmental impact. At Caldwell's urging, Jackson revised the bill, mandating that all proposed federal actions include "a finding" by a "responsible official" that all potential environmental effects had been properly assessed. With that requirement, Jackson stated, "No agency will . . . be able to maintain that it has no mandate or no requirement to consider the environmental consequences of its actions."[43]

Still, on May 29, 1969, Nixon issued an executive order creating his proposed EQC, chaired by DuBridge and made up of several cabinet members, to coordinate environmental policy. It quickly proved of little use. "Cabinet officers are likely to be ineffective because they lack time to do creative homework," judged Whitaker. "With a broad issue like the environment, no one is in charge. . . . Most importantly, the federal establishment had to have a signal that the environment issues were a concern of the President—that a maximum effort was needed."[44]

In August, recognizing the failure of the EQC, Nixon decided to set up an environmental task force, initially under his aide Egil Krogh, to make further recommendations. He soon replaced Krogh with Whitaker. The task force worked better, explained Whitaker, "because it had access to the

President through Ehrlichman and, when necessary, directly to the President."[45] By Thanksgiving weekend, the task force supplied Nixon with a sixty-five-page outline of preliminary recommendations. The report covered five major areas, including a proposed Department of Environment and Natural Resources, air pollution, water pollution, cleaning up federal facilities, and outdoor recreation. "Mr. Nixon studied the recommendations over the weekend at Key Biscayne," related Whitaker, "scribbled marginal notes and gave the task force its first guidance."[46]

Meanwhile, Jackson's Interior Committee devised its own approach. "It sounded like a definition of an environmental ethic," reported journalist Robert Cahn, who attended the committee hearing. "The bill proposed a council of three members whose principal duties would be to analyze environmental trends, advise the president on national environmental policy, and periodically appraise federal environmental programs."[47] Caldwell, testifying again, warned that the process needed an enforcement provision. He argued for "measures to require the federal agencies, in submitting proposals, to contain . . . an evaluation of the effect . . . upon the state of the environment."[48] Jackson agreed, calling for "an action-forcing mechanism" that departments must comply with.[49] Accordingly, the bill required that government proposals include an environmental impact statement, and created a Council on Environmental Quality (CEQ) to advise the president and oversee the environmental impact statement process. Jackson had gotten implicit White House agreement not to oppose the legislation too strongly.

"The public sense of priorities and those of government are poles apart with respect to the importance of environmental matters," Jackson had told the National Audubon Society that spring.[50] The few constituents who wrote on the issue tended to confirm his feeling. "We were pleased to learn that you have introduced a bill on environmental policy," wrote one. "We are particularly interested in part 6 regarding the necessity of Federal agencies spelling out and justifying the environmental impact of proposed activities."[51]

On White House orders, Train wrote, he and Hickel testified against the bill, defending the EQC, but "Jackson and his staff and, I suspect, every other member of the committee were well aware that this position was directly contrary to my personal convictions. . . . The EQC had met several times but had proven ineffectual."[52] Train successfully lobbied to change the administration's position, arguing that support "would identify the Republican Party with concern for environmental quality."[53] Train won approval to testify for the bill in the House.[54]

To pass the NEPA, Jackson had to accommodate Senator Edmund Muskie (D-ME), whose water pollution proposal included a different environmental council. Eventually, Muskie agreed to support Jackson's bill, meaning Muskie's subcommittee would give up jurisdiction.[55] In exchange, Jackson changed the bill's original requirement that the environmental impact statement be "a formal finding."[56] Muskie's concern, explained Paul Milazzo, was that "the bill's vague 'finding' provision offered an escape hatch, immune to judicial review, for developmentally minded departments to pay lip service to environmental values while advancing their own priorities." Jackson conceded, wrote Milazzo, although he "viewed federal administrators as reasonable men who could be conditioned to solicit new information and consider policy alternatives."[57]

In the final bill, agencies had only to issue a "detailed statement" about environmental impact, but, crucially, it would be subject to judicial review. In addition, federal agencies were required to consult with environmental agencies in preparing their statements, which had to include alternatives to the proposed actions. All statements, along with the commentary from the environmental agencies, had to be available to the president, his environmental advisors, and the public. Jackson also included a proposal for a citizens group to advise the council. Laurance Rockefeller, an obvious choice to chair the group, wrote "to express my appreciation for your help in connection with appropriations for the Citizens Advisory Committee on Environmental Quality."[58] Finally, Jackson agreed to new language ensuring that the environmental impact statements did not "in any way affect the specific statutory obligation of federal agencies to comply with environmental standards."[59] Muskie was particularly worried that the bill might constrain the agencies regulating water pollution.[60] Muskie's efforts strengthened the effect of the environmental impact statements.

With Muskie's support, the bill passed the full Senate with little opposition. In the House, the chair of the House Interior Committee, Wayne Aspinall, was not interested in the issue. Jackson instead joined with John Dingell (D-MI), chairman of the Fish and Wildlife Subcommittee of the House Merchant Marine and Fisheries Committee, a long-time environmental advocate. Dingell led the campaign in the House for the bill.[61] The House debate focused on the Council on Environmental Quality. Sidney Yates (D-IL) argued that the council "will give Mr. Nixon the opportunity to seize the initiative in restoring the quality of our environment. He must not fail."[62] But one letter writer complained to Jackson that the council members had "no real power to oppose any Federal project they felt would endanger the natural surroundings."[63] By contrast, the environmental impact statement was largely ignored. Few legislators, noted Flippen, saw its significance.[64] Some political scientists doubted its practical impact, and even environmentalists missed its meaning.

Around this time David Brower, the longtime executive director of the Sierra Club, was forced to resign by the board of directors for alleged financial mismanagement. Brower had been a loud, prickly force in the movement; Train had observed, "Thank God for David Brower. He makes it so easy for the rest of us to be reasonable."[65] Brower's replacement, Michael McCloskey, said of Jackson's bill, "Even though I gave the lead testimony for the supporting groups before the Senate Interior Committee, I did not foresee the importance of this requirement that agencies document the impact of their proposals on the environment and inform the public of their findings."[66]

Following the Santa Barbara oil spill, Hickel and Train focused heavily on preventing further spills, especially in gulf drilling and the proposed Alaska oil pipeline. "I organized an Interior-wide task force to help deal with the complex issues presented by the pipeline project," recalled Train. "All of the environmental analyses that were to prove so critical to the ultimate resolution of the pipeline issue were initiated and organized prior to the enactment of the National Environmental Policy Act of 1969. We were, in fact, pioneering the entire environmental impact process."[67] Resistance came from the oil companies, who wanted pipeline construction approval before the environmental issues were resolved.[68]

The Department of the Interior also successfully opposed the new airport endangering the Everglades, invoking a key ally. "I developed an excellent working relationship with John Ehrlichman . . . who was interested . . . and supportive," explained Train. "It was Ehrlichman's clout, pure and simple, that ultimately resolved the issue in Interior's favor."[69] Initially counsel to the president, Ehrlichman was swiftly elevated to a lead role on domestic issues. Nixon's chief of staff, H. R. Haldeman, commented, "John's a very intelligent guy, and he tracked well with Nixon . . . John Ehrlichman was not an advocate, he was a broker. He was brought in to broker [other aides] . . . not to have a view of his own."[70] Together, Ehrlichman and Haldeman became known in Washington as "the Germans" or "the Berlin Wall." Nixon, explained Haldeman, looked to

> the two of us because we were the two within that whole apparatus that basically functioned the way we saw a staff ought to be functioning: as internal operatives, honest brokers; no agenda of our own to forward . . . the objective there was to get down to the essence of the issue before the President. . . . [I]t was not just a matter of presenting him with the alternatives; it was the alternatives with a recommendation.[71]

Ehrlichman's crucial environmental role has been largely overlooked. "Ehrlichman saw the President regularly . . . equally important, Ehrlichman was 'pro environment,'" wrote Whitaker. "A land use lawyer in Seattle before joining the administration, he understood the complexities of the environmental issue and the various regulatory strategies that could be employed. . . . Whatever else history may say about John Ehrlichman, those who worked closest to the Oval Office on the environment issue know that he was a staunch advocate of environmental quality and that a great deal was accomplished by his effective advocacy."[72]

Driven by the environmental mood in Congress, the Senate-House conference committee produced a strong bill close to Jackson's proposal. Two minor concessions to the House were a small loophole requiring that environmental impact statements be made "to the fullest extent possible" and a requirement that federal agencies had to consult with the CEQ but were not required to obtain its approval for their actions.[73]

By this point, Train's prominence led to problems with Hickel. "While it was easy to blame Hickel's considerable ego, the fault was not all on one side," conceded Train. "He was not the only one with an ego."[74] Train now lobbied hard to become chairman of the new CEQ. He sought the support of Ehrlichman, who "suggested that I leave the matter to him to run down."[75] Nixon eventually agreed, announcing Train's appointment on January 29, 1970.

In signing the NEPA, Nixon proclaimed that the new decade must be "the years when America pays its debt to the past by reclaiming the purity of its air, its waters, and our living environment."[76] Flippen noted, "Nixon said nothing of his earlier opposition, but rather portrayed himself as the ultimate champion of environmental quality."[77] He mentioned Jackson only briefly, while Dingell smarted under the lack of credit. "With his informal comments bordering on self-congratulation," judged Flippen, "the law appeared as much a victory for the administration as one for the nation."[78] Privately, Nixon wrote in a memo about environmentalism, "I think interest in this will recede."[79] Outside the White House, Jackson was widely praised, with one constituent writing, "Your support of conservation causes is a point of pride of the people of Washington."[80] The director of the King County Building Department called the bill "a milestone in the legislative responsibilities of our Federal government."[81]

The Council on Environmental Quality Kicks In

Against some expectations that he would appoint weak figures or those opposed to regulation, Nixon chose a strong environmentally minded trio to serve on the CEQ. Train was, Whitaker later recalled, "for the environment first, Nixon second."[82] Joining Train would be Gordon MacDonald, a geophysicist and vice-chancellor of the University of California at Santa Barbara, and Robert Cahn, a *Christian Science Monitor* writer who had won a Pulitzer Prize for a 1968 series about public attitudes toward the national parks.[83] Cahn was surprised by the offer since, in his words, "I was not a Republican and had, in fact, been critical of President Nixon's environmental efforts—or lack of them."[84] The trio worked well together, but Train was clearly the dominant voice.[85]

In an executive order, Nixon required each executive branch agency to review its own regulations and eliminate those "that prohibit or limit full compliance with the purposes and provisions of [the NEPA]."[86] Nixon's order went beyond the legislative requirement for consultation with the CEQ, ordering compliance with CEQ guidelines in preparing environmental impact statements and holding public hearings. "The initial reaction to this requirement within the executive branch," reported Train, "was, to say the least, confused."[87] CEQ was to coordinate all federal environmental programs and monitor agency compliance. Nixon's order gave the CEQ the explicit backing of the White House in its relations with other government agencies. Still, Train acknowledged, "Implicit in our situation at CEQ was an understanding that our recommendations to the president were for him (and his staff) only. . . . [I]f we had disagreements with White House policy, we would not normally go public with them."[88]

Powerful executive bodies, Train understood, resented "the very idea that one small agency of the government could have the authority . . . to monitor, review, and comment on the projects of all other executive agencies."[89] The Water Quality Improvement Act, signed by Nixon in April 1970, established an Office of Environmental Quality as support staff for the CEQ.

Nixon had pledged that the CEQ "will occupy the same close advisory relation to the president as the Council of Economic Advisers does in fiscal monetary matters."[90] But, Cahn noted, the CEQ had very little interaction with Nixon:

> We . . . hoped to be able to argue face-to-face with the president for positions favorable to the environment. But that was wishful thinking. . . . Every proposal or suggestion had to be presented on paper, to the Domestic Council or designated presidential assistant—Whitaker, in our case. The proposal then went to the budget officials. Finally it would go to John Ehrlichman, who, if he saw fit, would reduce the proposal to a short position paper to the president, stating the pros and cons.[91]

Train recalled, "I had practically no substantive meeting with Nixon while I was head of CEQ."[92]

Train felt that the CEQ, with a staff of fifty-four people, was too small to conduct studies and long-term analysis of environmental policies. In the spring of 1970 Train proposed a quasi-independent Environmental Policy Institute, jointly funded by the federal government and private institutions, to perform analysis. The proposal was supported by Whitaker and Ehrlichman, as well as Office of Management and Budget chief George Schultz. Nixon endorsed the concept in his 1971 message on the environment. In 1971 Jackson introduced a bill for a National Environmental Policy Institute, but Nixon vetoed the proposed candidate to head the institute, economist Alain Enthoven, as too liberal. The issue was postponed until after the 1972 election and then indefinitely. The problem, Train concluded, was Nixon's "concern over the directorship and nervousness about an independent, freestanding institution that might not prove controllable."[93]

Still, the CEQ could have a strong policy impact, notably on the Cross Florida Barge Canal issue. "In addition to being a multi-million-dollar boondoggle offering little real benefit, the canal would ruin the scenically wild Oklawaha River," recalled Cahn. "The White House really didn't want a study [of the canal's costs and benefits] done because of the canal's inflammatory political status in Florida."[94] Then Jackson, a potential 1972 candidate against Nixon, attacked the White House indecision in a Florida speech in January 1971. Train urged the president to halt the project, seeing "probably more political advantages than disadvantages in stopping the project," and Nixon quickly announced, "The Council on Environmental Quality has recommended to me that the project be halted, and I have accepted its advice."[95]

Explained Cahn,

> Long afterward, John Ehrlichman told me that he himself had made the Cross Florida Barge decision without clearing it beforehand with the president. . . . After the president's next trip to Key Biscayne, and after hearing from some Florida interests, he told Ehrlichman that the decision to stop the Cross Florida Barge Canal had been a mistake. "No, it was a good decision," Ehrlichman replied, and he told the president that thousands of favorable letters and telegrams had been sent to the White House congratulating the president for his bold action.[96]

But the kind of input Nixon heard in Florida could have an outsized impact. Cahn concluded, "At CEQ, we found all too often that political considerations unnecessarily became the deciding factor in decisions affecting the environment."[97]

By January 1970 Nixon was ready to act on the Whitaker task force recommendations. Seizing the issue in his 1970 State of the Union speech, Nixon declared,

> Restoring nature to its natural state is a cause beyond party and beyond factions. . . . Clean air, clean water, open spaces—these should once again be the birthright of every American. If we act now, they can be. . . . The program I shall propose to Congress will be the most comprehensive and costly program in this field in America's history. . . . We can no longer afford to consider air and water common property, free to be abused by anyone without regard to the consequences. . . . This requires comprehensive new regulations.[98]

Nixon emphasized the need for more parks, saying, "As our cities and suburbs relentlessly expand, those priceless open spaces needed for recreation accessible to their people are swallowed up—often forever. . . . Therefore,

I shall propose new financing methods for purchasing open space and parklands now, before they are lost to us."[99] Letters and editorials praised Nixon's stance.

A few days later, before presenting his environmental message to Congress, Nixon signed an executive order requiring all federal agencies and their facilities to comply with air and water quality standards by December 31, 1972. "Such compliance was notoriously lacking, particularly on the part of defense agencies," mused Train long afterward. "Almost three decades later. the task is still ongoing."[100]

The NEPA required the president to submit an annual environmental quality report or message to Congress. Train and the CEQ assumed responsibility for writing the message. "We started work and asked for a meeting with the president," recounted Cahn. "Five months later we were still trying to meet with him."[101] When the CEQ staff finally made it to the Oval Office,

> We left the meeting vaguely frustrated, feeling like outside visitors as the president handed each of us souvenir paperweights, pens, cufflinks, and golf balls. The president had done most of the talking. He had not sought our advice on anything. . . . I think the meeting clinched for us the feeling that had been growing over the months that whatever we hoped to accomplish as a council, we would have to do without the president's personal support.[102]

The CEQ tried to push several proposals into the message, notably on land use and toxic substances. "The Office of Management and Budget vigorously opposed our land use proposals, partly because of the $100 million we proposed giving states . . . to prepare statewide land use controls," wrote Cahn. "We appealed to Ehrlichman and our proposals stayed in the package."[103] Before his firing, Hickel had joined the CEQ in supporting a land use policy.[104] But proposals for premarket testing of toxic substances and a tax on sulfur oxide pollution were rejected.

In his 1971 State of the Union speech Nixon proclaimed, "Building on the foundation laid in the 37-point program that I submitted to Congress last year, I will propose a strong new set of initiatives to clean up our air and water."[105] William Ruckelshaus, first administrator of the EPA, later explained the relationship between the CEQ and the EPA, recalling "A lot of the Presidential initiatives really came out of CEQ. . . . [Train and I] both decided they should keep that sort of substantive development role of legislation. . . . [W]e had a very good relationship. It wasn't as though the administration had too many people concerned about the environment."[106]

Train noted that the report emphasized the economic costs of pollution, warning, "'Our price system fails to take into account the environmental damage that the polluter inflicts on others.'"[107] Cahn admitted, "The final product emerging in the February 10, 1971, environmental message to Congress presented some significant legislative concepts. And most remarkable . . . was the proposed entry of the Federal government for the first time into such matters as land-use planning, control of toxic substances, strip mining, ocean dumping and power plant siting."[108]

The Environmental Movement Goes to Court

Environmental law had been in upheaval well before the NEPA. One pioneer was attorney Victor Yannacone, who sued county officials in New York over the spraying of DDT in 1966. He followed this in 1968 with a suit against the Hoerner Waldorf pulp mill in Missoula, Montana, arguing, "The people of the valley live at the bottom of a veritable sewer of bad air . . . the issue is, whether the right to breathe clean air is a constitutionally protected right."[109] Yannacone's brash urban litigation ethic troubled some established conservationists, more used to sedate Ivy League types than to a lawyer from Brooklyn Law. Uncharacteristically, Brower, who would later come to symbolize an aggressive approach, sniffed that the Environmental Defense Fund, a new legal group, needed "some people who are older and stuffier."[110] But many lawyers would be inspired and influenced by Yannacone's argument that "industry owes the American people the cleanest air and the cleanest water that the existing state of the art in pollution control can secure."[111]

Advocacy groups quickly learned the power of the environmental impact statement, bolstered by the Freedom of Information Act, a Johnson-era innovation providing public access to a much wider range of government documents.[112] Environmental groups began to sue government agencies for failure to comply with the statute. In *Calvert Cliffs Coordinating Committee, Inc. v. Atomic Energy Commission*, three environmental groups challenged the commission's proposal for a nuclear power plant in Maryland. Appeals Court judge J. Skelly Wright rejected the AEC's position, writing, "NEPA imposes a substantive duty upon every Federal agency to consider the effects of each decision upon the environment and to use all practicable means, consistent with other essential considerations of national policy, to avoid environmental degradation."[113] As part of an agency backlash, Randolph Trower, commissioner of the Internal Revenue Service, announced that the IRS was formally reviewing the tax-exempt status of organizations that sued polluters. Train told Thrower, "'Litigation brought by private groups that rely on contributions for their support [has] strengthened the process of enforcement of antipollution laws.'"[114] The IRS decided to drop the investigation. Many in Congress were taken aback by the NEPA's impact. Senator James Eastland (D-MS) complained, "Everybody is in favor of protecting the environment, but this business of yelling 'ecology' every time we get ready for a new project has got to stop."[115]

A transformation in administrative law also empowered the environmentalists' legal strategy. "Starting in the mid-sixties," wrote Paul Milazzo, "federal courts began to revise the legal definition of 'standing,' which allowed broader classes of interests to sue private concerns or the government without having to demonstrate actual economic or physical injury."[116] In 1970 law professor Joseph Sax argued that citizens had a legal right to a clean environment, but since administrative agencies often failed to provide it, citizen groups could sue to enforce the "public trust" created by environmental laws.[117] The courts largely accepted the idea, and the corollary that citizens had standing to sue. Many of the major environmental laws, including the Clean Air and Water Acts, explicitly gave citizens the right to sue to force compliance.

The founding of the Environmental Defense Fund (EDF) in 1967 was followed by the formation of two other environmental legal groups, the Natural Resources Defense Council (NRDC) and the Sierra Club Legal Defense Fund. The EDF and NRDC enlisted scientists and economists to help with prospective lawsuits. Swiftly, these groups began to sue both government agencies and industries for noncompliance with environmental laws. Other attorneys worked at the local level to fight environmentally unsound land development. One observer concluded, "Environmentalism used litigation as no other social movement has before or since."[118] Even defeats provided progress. In 1969 the Sierra Club sued to stop construction of a ski resort in an area largely surrounded by Sequoia National Park. When the case finally reached the Supreme Court, the court ruled that the Sierra Club had not shown harm and therefore lacked standing to sue, but Justice William Douglas dissented.

Appointed to the court at age forty by Franklin Delano Roosevelt,

Douglas brought an environmental consciousness to the court from his long youthful walks in Pacific Northwest forests and his adult summers in a remote Cascades cabin. During his nearly thirty-seven years on the court—the record tenure—Douglas not only argued for conservation in his judicial rulings, he urged protection of nature on elected officials and cabinet departments and led protest hikes—including one, ultimately successful, to prevent a highway on Washington's Olympic Peninsula Coast that was joined by Howard Zahniser and supported by the Wilderness Society. Margaret McKeown, a judge on the Ninth Circuit Court of Appeals, later called Douglas "a one-man lobby shop for the environment."[119]

In the Sequoia case, Douglas argued, "The critical question of standing would be simplified and also put neatly in focus if we fashioned a federal rule that allowed environmental issues to be litigated before federal agencies or federal courts in the name of the inanimate object about to be despoiled, defaced or invaded."[120] Douglas pointed out that other inanimate objects—ships in maritime cases, corporations—were granted standing. In his own dissent, Justice Harry A. Blackmun asked, "Must our law be so rigid and procedural concepts so inflexible that we render ourselves helpless when the existing methods and traditional concepts do not quite fit?"[121] Revising its pleadings to show harm, the Sierra Club was able to block the resort.

In defining an adequate environmental impact statement, courts described the NEPA as an "environmental full disclosure law," ruling that an environmental impact statement must include opinions from experts, concerned private or public organizations, and even ordinary citizens. The definition, explained Milazzo, "extended the planning process beyond the bounds of an agency's conventional expertise to ensure a multidisciplinary review."[122] Even so, wrote Cahn, "I felt disappointed that so many agency heads fought, ignored or delayed compliance. Practically all of the impact statements we received clearly had been prepared after the decision was made . . . the 'post-facto' approach became standard."[123] Cahn added, "Being in the Executive Office of the President, the Council of Environmental Quality could take no public position. . . . [T]he environmental organizations and legal groups . . . more than made up for our official silence. . . . What CEQ was unable to do in bringing executive agencies into line—especially without support from the White House or the Office of Management and Budget—environmental groups accomplished through the courts."[124]

In a 1974 case, Justice Douglas warned, "The tendency has been to downgrade this mandate of Congress [the NEPA], to use shortcuts to the desired end, and to present impact statements after a project has been started, when there is already such momentum that it is difficult to stop. . . . One hesitates to interfere once a project is started, but if the congressional mandate is to be meaningful it must be done here."[125] The National Environmental Policy Act was to grow in importance over the years, spurring many states to pass similar environmental impact laws. Environmentalists learned that the environmental impact statement could be a powerful weapon to block or change projects. Kaufman wrote, "The National Environmental Policy Act stands as Jackson's crowning achievement in the area of environmental policy."[126] Ironically, Jackson's vision of the environmental impact statement was, as Kaufman writes, "a short document laying out the costs and benefits of a given project, rather than a labyrinthian process involving mountains of detail, which environmentalists used to block key projects such as the Alaska pipeline for years."[127] Supreme Court decisions had helped increase the detail required. Whatever the details required, Jackson still believed in the benefits of assessing the environmental consequences, telling a business group that the country must insist "on the kind of investment in public and private sectors that achieves our social and economic goals of clean water, clean air and clean land."[128]

The Council on Environmental Quality was to have its greatest importance during the Nixon years, playing a leading role in developing legislation on control of pesticides, toxic substances, land use, noise control, and ocean dumping.[129] On September 12, 1972, the *Washington Post* commented, "The remarkable achievement of the CEQ during the past three years has been the extent to which, despite political pressures, it has managed to impose upon the federal establishment a decent regard for environmental concerns."[130] Yet the NEPA only applied to new proposed federal government actions, having no impact on existing policies, such as subsidies for agriculture, mining, or logging.[131] In addition, specific energy-related legislation, such as the Alaska pipeline, could win exemption from the law. The NEPA would remain unchanged by any significant amendment and would be copied by more than half of US state governments, as well as over eighty other nations and multinational institutions such as the European Union and World Bank.

By 1980 agencies had filed over eleven thousand environmental impact statements. Of these, 10 percent provoked litigation, and courts blocked action in about 20 percent of these cases.[132] Thus, while environmental impact statements effectively blocked only 2 percent of proposed projects, the need to consider the environmental impact stopped many more actions from even being considered. Justice Douglas wrote in 1972, "NEPA has paid great dividends. The bureaucrats are forced to think in ecological terms; and the long-suppressed naturalist or biologist in the bureau is at last allowed to educate his superiors . . . and the public at large."[133] Without the power to mandate the most environmentally healthy choices, the NEPA became most effective in delaying damaging projects as well as dissuading consideration of some of the most blatantly environmentally destructive initiatives. Its very effectiveness led President Donald Trump to call for a weakening of the law in July 2020.

The Environmental Protection Agency Finds Success and Enemies

Beyond the NEPA, Nixon had his own plans for environmental action. On February 10, 1970, Nixon sent Congress a message with thirty-seven proposals for environmental action, twenty-three for legislation and fourteen through administrative action, calling for "fundamentally new philosophies of land, air and water use, for stricter regulation, for expanded government action."[134] The White House proclaimed, "This is the most far-reaching and comprehensive message on conservation and restoration of natural resources ever submitted to Congress by a President of the United States."[135] Nixon was lauded for his proposals. "President Nixon deserves praise for giving an unprecedented emphasis to the environmental needs of the country," commented the *New York Times*. "But if the country is really to make peace with nature . . . [it will demand] the chlorophyll of good green cash."[136]

One recommendation of the Whitaker task force was for governmental reorganization. Noting that some eighty agencies dealt with different aspects of pollution, the task force recommended creation of a Department of Environmental and Natural Resources. Secretaries of the interior from Harold Ickes to Stewart Udall had championed variations of this idea, to expand the role and size of the Interior Department. Conversely, they were resisted by departments, such as agriculture, that would shrink or have a reduced role.[137] In 1969, to address management in government, Nixon created the President's Advisory Council on Executive Reorganization, chaired by Litton Industries CEO Roy Ash. Ash's group initially also recommended expanding the Interior Department into a Department of Natural Resources, encompassing most of the existing department while drawing agencies from other federal departments. This department would also oversee an agency to oversee marine policy, the National Oceanic and Atmospheric Administration (NOAA). Robert Finch, the secretary of health, education and welfare, recalled, "our first proposal, as you may recall, had to do with simplifying government by function . . . you would have human resources . . . and natural resources."[138] The final reorganization was not decided in time to be included in the president's February 1970 message.

While Hickel supported the proposal, Train argued against a Department of Natural Resources, feeling that combining resource management and environmental protection in one agency would create inter-agency conflict. Train wrote to Ehrlichman, "I believe such a department would be excessively unwieldy and exceedingly difficult to administer."[139] Train admitted in 2006, "There was some logic [to the idea], but I testified against it, against building a bigger bureaucracy. I was opposed to burying environmental responsibility in a big conglomeration with everything from Indian affairs to reclamation. The environment would have been submerged."[140] He later concluded that his most persuasive argument may have been when he warned, "I believe the present proposal would simply add Muskie to the opposition and give him an issue. Proposal of a separate environmental protection agency would neutralize his position in this regard.'"[141] Given the opposition from other cabinet departments, particularly agriculture and commerce, the Nixon administration decided to hold off a Department of Natural Resources, but the idea would not be completely dropped until the end of the Ford administration.[142]

Train instead successfully advocated a separate Environmental Protection Agency, the final recommendation of the Ash committee, made on April 29, 1970. Finch recalled, "I took the lead as a member of the Ash commission in testifying so that we at least got a separate agency for the environmental protection, EPA, and more importantly, or just as importantly, to get the standard setting in another agency, CEQ, so that [we] weren't having the enforcement people trying to deal with the setting of standards."[143] The Ash proposal for the EPA took components from other cabinet departments. Interior would give up the Federal Water Quality Administration while the Department of Health, Education, and Welfare would lose the Bureau of Water Hygiene, the National Air Pollution

Control Administration, the Bureau of Solid Waste Management, and the Bureau of Radiological Health.[144] Pesticide regulation and research was transferred from the Agriculture and Interior Departments, respectively, and radiation regulation from the AEC. "Probably President Nixon's main reason for favoring EPA," concluded Whitaker, "was that he did not want to undertake major departmental reorganization, including that entailed in the DNR [Department of Natural Resources], until an overall plan was perfected."[145]

Nixon created the NOAA, installed in the Commerce Department, and the EPA with an executive order in July 1970. The EPA took over the environmental responsibilities of some 63 existing agencies, from 10 cabinet departments, as well as 16 independent agencies.[146] It also took 5,650 employees and a $1.4 billion budget from these agencies.[147] Congress offered minimal resistance, as Muskie and most Democrats supported an independent environmental agency. Whitaker told Ash, "I think we can all look back with justifiable pride and tell our grandchildren about EPA."[148] Initially, the EPA did not cast a giant shadow. Jackson wrote one constituent, "Thank you for your recent suggestion concerning the possibility of using NASA as a pollution control agency. As you may know, the recently established EPA will consolidate programs . . . in the field of pollution abatement and control."[149]

When Nixon's first choice to head the EPA, Wisconsin governor Warren Knowles, declined on the grounds of ill health, Nixon chose assistant attorney general William Ruckelshaus. During his confirmation hearing, Muskie warned of the pressures that would be exerted on Ruckelshaus to delay or weaken environmental regulations for financial reasons. Ruckelshaus, hoped Muskie, would become known as "Mr. Clean."[150]

A graduate of Princeton and Harvard Law School, the thirty-eight-year-old Ruckelshaus had worked for many years with the Indiana Board of Health on air and water pollution control. At the time, Ruckelshaus later remembered, "The environment was really seen as a health issue."[151] He had been a state legislator and deputy state attorney general, and an unsuccessful Republican nominee for the Senate. "My Republican roots are from my heritage," he explained later. "My grandfather was chairman of the Republican party in Indiana. . . . And so my allegiance to the party was really more through my association with my family and their Republican roots than it was philosophical. But still, there were parts of the party in those days that I really felt strongly about and wasn't uncomfortable as a Republican."[152] Ruckelshaus's nomination was strongly supported by his boss, attorney general John Mitchell, as well as by environmentalists.

The EPA opened on December 2, 1970, its goal being "the protection, development and enhancement of the total environment."[153] Five days later, Ruckelshaus declared that the EPA had "no obligation to promote commerce or agriculture," its sole mission being the "development of an environmental ethic."[154] To environmental expert Robert Collin, "The first and most important mission was to establish the credibility of the EPA, so as to ensure that the public and the regulated community realized that the government was serious about its charge to protect the environment. One way to do that was through enforcement."[155] Shortly after its creation, the EPA filed lawsuits against the cities of Detroit, Cleveland, and Atlanta for polluting their rivers with sewage. Similar actions against industry followed.[156] In its first year, EPA would refer 152 industrial pollution cases for prosecution. Its beginning, Ruckelshaus wrote, "was like trying to perform an appendectomy while running the 100-yard dash."[157] Train later concluded of Ruckelshaus, "As I got to know him over time, I learned to appreciate his keen intelligence, practical approach, good judgment, and fine sense of humor, the latter being an invaluable asset in government."[158]

The Environmental Protection Agency may have been Nixon's most substantial environmental accomplishment. "In just one quick maneuver, Nixon had unraveled the jurisdictional quagmire that characterized the federal government's pollution-fighting bureaucracy," judged Flippen. "He had established an agency with enough independence and enforcement power to answer the clarion call of the day, a legacy that remains today."[159] Ruckelshaus later commented that Nixon created the EPA "because of public outrage about what was happening in the environment. Not because Nixon shared that concern. . . . That's the way democracy is supposed to work. The President feels he's got to respond to something the American people feel is very important."[160] The success of the EPA was not assured at its inception. Ruckelshaus later admitted, "If I had known what I was getting into, I probably wouldn't have accepted."[161] Milton Russell, who served as an assistant administrator at the EPA later in the decade, wrote, "Within days and weeks, Ruckelshaus and his then tiny staff issued a series of far-reaching orders and regulations that transformed the way our environmental commons were to be treated."[162]

As a result of these policy measures, progress in cleaning the air and water, as well as in reducing the harm from pesticides and chemicals and in protecting wetlands and other ecological resources, did occur in the succeeding decade, first under Ruckelshaus and then under his successors, Republican Russell Train and Democrat Doug Costle. . . . This remarkable trio of leaders was able to infuse the political appointees who served under them with that vision, which then enabled them to recruit and maintain an exemplary civil service staff that was not only skilled and resourceful, but also imbued with the mission of the agency.[163]

Ruckelshaus later recalled, "I not only found it exciting and interesting and challenging, which are three things I think you should look for in a job, I also found it very fulfilling because you were really trying to work on something which was beyond your immediate concerns . . . and knowing that you tried as hard as you could and made some progress at it is a very fulfilling exercise."[164]

With little direct contact with Nixon, Ruckelshaus dealt with other administration figures, recalling, "Russell Train was the head of the Council of Environmental Quality, which was part of the White House. We worked together almost—at least weekly, if not daily. John Ehrlichman was a very important contact at the White House," and John Whitaker, too, "was a very important person at the White House."[165] Ehrlichman, Ruckelshaus noted, had been "a lawyer in Seattle who had specialized in land use kind of issues . . . and was basically sympathetic to the need to do something about the environment."[166] Of Nixon, Ruckelshaus recalled, "Every time I'd meet with him he would just lecture me about the 'crazies' in the agency and advise me not to be pushed around by them."[167]

As EPA head, Ruckelshaus moved aggressively during 1971. The EPA won a court order against Armco Steel, a chronic polluter and major donor to President Nixon. Publicity about its contributions caused the White House to ignore Armco's request to rein in the EPA.[168] Later that year, with the air in Birmingham, Alabama, exceeding emergency particulate levels, the EPA secured an injunction forcing local industries, most notably U.S. Steel, to shut down their production until the air quality improved. Improving weather allowed the order to be lifted a day later, but it was an important demonstration that a major industry could be shut down to control unacceptable levels of pollution. "The independent adversarial position of EPA as a national environmental protection regulator agency was a phenomenon which had no parallel in other industrial democracies and none in American history," judged Andrews. "It also represented a sudden and extraordinary reversal of the long-standing primacy of business interests in American governance."[169]

By 1980 the EPA had grown to a staff of thirteen thousand, with a budget of $5.6 billion plus authority over another $1.6 billion for toxic waste cleanup.[170] It has survived in the almost forty years since then, despite increasingly vehement attacks from archconservatives—perhaps the best testament to its effectiveness.

A Bipartisan Change in the Air

With the new administration and new Congress, the air pollution issue surfaced on several fronts in 1969. In May, Warren Magnuson (D-WA), chair of the Senate Commerce Committee, introduced the Federal Low Emission Vehicle Procurement Act, explaining that it "requires the Federal government to direct its purchasing power toward cars, trucks and buses which produce little or no pollutants."[171] In December, the House Interstate and Foreign Commerce Committee's Subcommittee on Public Health and Welfare, chaired by Paul Rogers (D-FL), held hearings on the weaknesses of the 1967 Air Quality Act. Meanwhile, Nixon's environmental task force, directed by Whitaker, was developing a plan to address the deficiencies of the earlier acts.

Acting on these recommendations, President Nixon in early 1970 proposed a new Clean Air Act, including national ambient air quality standards. Driven both by a desire to undercut Muskie and by the increasing political pressures for environmental action, Nixon urged "comprehensive new regulations." In his 1970 State of the Union address, he declared, "The great question of the seventies is, shall we surrender to our surroundings, or shall we make our peace with nature and begin to make reparations for the damage we have done to our air, to our land, and to our water?"[172] The 1967 law, said the president, was a "useful beginning, but had a number of shortcomings."[173] He proposed national minimum air quality standards, with states allowed to enact stronger standards. To reach these levels, states could set specific emissions limits for all stationary sources of pollution.

The administration proposal raised emission standards for 1973–1975 model year cars. The federal government would have authority to regulate fuel contents, including the lead added to gasoline to make engines runs more smoothly. "The automobile has become our number-one environmental problem," warned Hickel. "The automobile has simply too high a priority in this country."[174] The secretary unsuccessfully argued for including mass transit in the highway trust fund. Finally, the plan would create a five-year research plan on how to achieve further advances.[175] "These new standards," promised Nixon in his environmental message, "represent the best present estimate of the lowest emission levels obtainable by those years."[176] In his message Nixon also borrowed from Magnuson, pledging "to marshal both government and private research with the goal of producing an unconventionally powered, virtually pollution-free automobile within five years."[177]

The CEQ created an eight-member advisory committee on using the funds allocated to develop low emissions engines, drawing limited Detroit enthusiasm. "I got the impression that while the auto makers publicly espoused the goal of a new cleaner and more energy-efficient automobile," related Robert Cahn, "it was not a very high priority with them. . . . [T]he American automakers all took the position that any change away from the internal combustion engine was a decision to be made at some time in the distant future."[178]

The Rogers subcommittee held hearings on Nixon's proposal in March 1970, and three months later reported out an almost identical bill, which passed the House 375–1. While this proposal was moving forward, Ralph Nader's Center for the Study of Responsive Law harshly attacked Muskie, blaming him for the weaknesses of the 1967 act.[179] Environmentalists were unhappy that the House bill wasn't stronger, with Udall commenting, "Environmentalists have muffed their first big legislative test since Earth Day spotlighted them on the side of the angels. If they want to get results from now on, they'll have to swap their halos for a lot more political savvy."[180] The newly formed Clean Air Coalition, which included environmentalists and the auto and steel workers' unions, lobbied for a stronger Senate bill. The coalition had been organized by Environmental Action, a new group formed by Denis Hayes and the other organizers of Earth Day.[181]

Muskie now introduced tougher legislation in the Senate, saying, "Here is a chance for [Nixon] to put his support where his words are."[182] Compared to the administration's proposal, the Muskie bill proposed standards both stronger and more specific. It authorized the newly formed EPA to set national ambient air quality standards, based solely on human risk, for the six most common air pollutants. It regulated emissions from motor vehicles, stationary sources of pollution, and other polluters. It required states to develop implementation plans to meet these standards, subject to EPA approval.[183] The standards mandated a 90 percent reduction in hydrocarbons and carbon monoxide by 1975 and a 90 percent reduction in nitrogen oxide by 1976.[184] The proposal also empowered citizens to sue private companies and government agencies that violated air quality standards.[185] Every new "point source" of air pollution would need a federal permit and to adopt the best available pollution-control technology. Finally, the bill increased federal subsidies for state air pollution control programs.[186]

A crucial component in creating and pushing through this stronger bill was the partnership between Muskie and the subcommittee's new ranking Republican, Tennessee's Howard Baker Jr. Baker studied engineering at Tulane University, but after navy service in World War II decided to go to the University of Tennessee law school. Baker's father served in the United States House of Representatives from 1951 to 1964. The younger Baker married Joy Dirksen, daughter of Senate minority leader Everett Dirksen, further cementing his political ties. When his father died in 1964, Baker ran for an open Senate seat. After a narrow loss, Baker won a Senate race in 1966.

On the Subcommittee on Air and Water Pollution, Baker proved indispensable in the quest for stronger air pollution legislation. "If Ed Muskie was the master of the environmental ship before anyone even thought about the environment in terms of public policy," wrote Leon Billings, Muskie's executive assistant at the time, "Baker quickly became his first mate and later his co-captain. . . . Within a year of Baker's arrival they'd worked together to write the Clean Air Act and, within three years, the Clean Water Act."[187] Baker's biographer J. Lee Annis Jr. explained, "Contrary to [Baker's] generally conservative instincts, he concluded that maintaining any standard [of air quality] would require stringent federal regulations. . . . Muskie soon was describing Baker's work as indispensable, recognizing, like other less mechanically inclined members, that Baker had studied engineering, continued to skim scientific journals and understood far better than they the technological complexities of pollution control."[188]

Muskie commented that Baker was "a great believer in the potential of American technology" and in the need to establish "standards that would force industry to expand the potential of technology for dealing with environmental problems."[189] Together, recalled Billings, Muskie and Baker "drafted such innovative concepts as 'the polluter pays.' . . . Among their other innovations were joint and several liability, statutory standards and deadlines, citizen participation and citizen suits, timely judicial review, health and welfare based standards, funded mandates, and an enforceable legal mandate that pollution be reduced to the maximum extent possible."[190]

In 1980, when Baker was the Senate Republican leader, he wrote, "I've seen [Muskie] withstand the most extraordinary type of pressure and abuse in public hearings and in private, over the developing [of] new air and water pollution legislation. . . . I recall the acute harassment that came from the automotive industry about the necessity to do these things; and whether smog was hurtful at all."[191] Muskie, Baker explained, gave each subcommittee member a fair hearing, and the group usually made decisions by consensus. Muskie "believed that we could compromise without surrendering principles"; Baker noted, "he knew that compromise—he called it, by the way, comity—was the essence of a workable legislative process."[192] Muskie would comment, "If you've got both the chairman and the ranking member, a Republican, both supporting a committee position, then that's a very powerful influence in the Senate."[193]

One factor that made Clean Air Act passage possible, recalled Baker later, was that television was less important than it would become. Since political campaigns were less expensive in 1970, senators didn't have to spend as much time raising money or feel as beholden to their donors. There was less single-issue lobbying, especially by constituents, thus making it "easier to be a leader and less essential to be a follower."[194] Additionally, at the time, senators and representatives wrote legislation themselves. One more advantage, he remembered, was that committee members enjoyed working on an issue like clean air, instead of always talking about Vietnam.

While Muskie emphasized standards based on science, another subcommittee member, Thomas Eagleton (D-MO), successfully argued for specific statutory deadlines to convince the public that progress would occur. Muskie would comment in 1975, "We made a calculated decision in 1970 to challenge the [auto] industry to produce things that were not then in existence as essential to cleaning up the environment . . . that's the only way—the forced technology concept—the only way you are going to prod this technology. We understood the risks fully."[195]

The Senate Clean Air bill gave the EPA the ability to make limited extensions to the deadlines when warranted by technological problems in achieving them. Requests from polluters for further delays would require congressional approval.[196] The act identified 189 pollutants that contributed to smog, established standards to regulate their emissions, and required factories and power plants to install special smokestack filters, called scrubbers, to reduce the discharge of ash and other pollutants into the air.[197]

"Members [of the subcommittee] . . . searched for months for a way to reduce automotive pollution," wrote Annis. "Some were intrigued by the possibility that the auto industry might develop a pollution-free steam engine that someday might rival the internal combustion engine. But such zeal subsided once car makers detailed the structural and environmental deficiencies of steam-powered vehicles."[198] Edward Cole, president of General Motors, persuaded the senators that the answer was the catalytic converter. "I'm convinced that without the catalytic converter we never would approach the air quality standards that we knew we needed then," recalled Baker about the decision, "and certainly know that we need now."[199] To win support for the proposal, Baker and John Sherman Cooper (R-KY) successfully pushed to exempt dealers and distributors from liability for defective converters. Annis pointed out, "Chrysler and Ford, whose research and development programs were not as advanced at GM's, were placated by another Baker-Cooper measure establishing a review procedure if their 1975 models did not meet the bill's standards."[200] When Gaylord Nelson (D-WI) proposed banning the internal combustion engine by January 1, 1975, Muskie used the threat to persuade the committee to accept the more moderate goal of a 90 percent reduction in emissions.[201]

Environmentalists endorsed Muskie's tougher bill. Train urged Nixon to support it, while Commerce Secretary Maurice Stans opposed it.[202] Whitaker felt that Nixon could not afford politically to oppose the bill. Backing the stronger bill, Train wrote to Ehrlichman, "gives [Nixon] visibility on the air pollution issue."[203] In late September the Senate passed Muskie's bill unanimously. "People have all sorts of conspiratorial theories on what constitutes power in the Senate," observed Muskie. "Real power up there comes from doing your work and knowing what you are talking about. . . . The most important thing in the Senate is credibility. Credibility! That is power."[204] Ehrlichman suggested trying to stall the bill until after the election in hopes of then getting a weaker version, but Muskie's superior knowledge and prestige allowed him to push through a conference committee bill. Vital in the writing of the final bill, recalled subcommittee staffer Karl Braithwaite, was Muskie's approach of "searching out the secure middle and pushing through the best bill he can get that will be carried by a substantial secure majority."[205]

In December 1970 bipartisan majorities in both houses passed a Clean Air Act closer to Muskie's Senate version than the House's Nixon version. It included Muskie's auto emission standards and deadlines for emission reductions. The only concessions to Nixon's bill were a provision that the National Academy of Sciences should study the feasibility of meeting the various deadlines, and another allowing the EPA to grant an extension if a company had made a good faith effort to comply. Urging Nixon to sign the bill, Train argued, "The basic features of the Senate bill were derived from the Clean Air Act amendments you proposed to the Congress in your Message on the Environment."[206] Whitaker urged an elaborate signing ceremony that would gain credit for the bill for the White House. Cooper personally appealed to the president to sign the bill. Finally, Nixon signed on December 31, 1970.

The Clean Air Act retained a major role for states, giving them nine months to present plans for complying with the standards within three years. Governors could apply for extensions. States were to establish emissions standards for existing factories, subject to federal oversight, as well as over used cars.[207] Aside from new autos, gasoline additives, and airplanes, states were free to legislate tougher standards.[208] Crucially, the bill put the burden of proof on the polluter to demonstrate that its output was not dangerous, as well as establishing new enforcement mechanisms and penalties. The EPA was also given the power to regulate fuel, an authority it would later use to eliminate lead from gasoline.[209]

To celebrate passage, the administration held a ceremony and press conference, to which Muskie was not invited. At the press conference, Ruckelshaus described how the White House welcomed the act.[210] The White House press release claimed credit without mentioning Muskie.[211] Nevertheless, noted Flippen, "Congress and the Democrats still held the political momentum. During 1970 they, more than the administration, saw their bills through to fruition and received the lion's share of the credit."[212] Muskie felt vindicated that the competition for political credit resulted in stronger legislation. "You take a look at the Clean Air Act and the Water Pollution Control Act. Those are two of the most detailed statutes ever written by Congress," recalled Muskie aide Eliot Cutler. "The reason is because Muskie insists on it. Writing detailed statues—and getting broad political agreement on them—is much tougher than writing broad statutes and saying to some agency administrator, 'You take care of the problem'. . . . What Congress is doing now, by deciding the numbers and decimal points, is taking responsibility for the political heat."[213]

The act's impact would still largely depend on the standards produced by the EPA. Automobile standards, Ruckelshaus later explained, "took up a very large part of my time in the first years that I was there."[214] He recalled his good relations with Muskie and Baker and their strong belief in action, and that, "I think they believed I was trying as best I could to implement these laws that they had passed."[215] Asked when the honeymoon with Nixon ended, Ruckelshaus replied, "Pretty quick, pretty quick . . . after the announcement of the air pollution standards that I mentioned, it was very apparent that the actions this agency would take would have a significant impact on—could have on—the economy of the country . . . the fact that the White House was agitated when we announced these standards and a lot of people erupted, isn't surprising to me."[216]

After the EPA announced rigorous auto emissions standards for 1975 and 1976, Nixon, infuriated at being caught in the middle between environmental advocates and business, told Ford executives Henry Ford II and Lee Iacocca, "Environmentalists are a group of people that really are not a damn bit interested in safety or clean air," and promised to protect the auto industry from these "enemies of the system."[217] But as Ruckelshaus, Train, and Whitaker urged, Nixon did not follow Stans's advice to publicly attack environmentalists.[218]

Noting the attacks on the Clean Air Act, Muskie wrote in 1972, "We are hearing the same old complaints that the problem is not as serious as we have claimed, and the cost of compliance may ruin the [auto] industry."[219] Muskie, in fact, was not yet satisfied, writing, "I think we have written some good legislation. But it has not yet made a sufficient impact. . . . We have produced pollution at a faster rate than we have moved."[220] Ruckelshaus recalled, "The scientific uncertainty with which we're dealing . . . surprised me. . . . By no means are we certain at what levels [pollutants] cause what kinds of effects, either environmental or in public health."[221] Ruckelshaus noted the need for national standards since state efforts varied widely: "Some were quite good, like California, who had been trying to regulate pollution for longer than the Federal government . . . and others were not."[222]

Nixon, Parks, and the Environmental Quality Education Act

Nixon had a particular interest in one environmental issue—parks—and Jackson had a bill on the subject. "The purpose of this measure," Jackson told the Senate, "is to make surplus Federal property available to State and local governments for park and recreational purposes."[223] After Jackson accepted an amendment from William Proxmire (D-WI) adjusting the price the federal government would charge, the Senate passed the bill without opposition.[224]

In his 1970 message Nixon endorsed the idea, urging, "I propose full funding in fiscal 1971 of the $327 million available through the Land and Water Conservation Fund for additional park and recreational facilities, with increased emphasis on locations that can be easily reached by the people in crowded urban areas."[225] In his environmental message, Nixon added, "By Executive Order, I am directing the heads of all Federal Agencies and the Administrator of General Services to institute a review of all Federally owned properties that should be considered for other uses. . . . I am establishing a Property Review Board to recommend to me what properties should be converted or sold . . . the net effect would be to increase our capacity to add new park and recreational facilities."[226] Nixon told Whitaker, "When in doubt, make a park of it." Whitaker believed it was one of the few environmental issues that Nixon really cared about. "He felt very strongly about parks," explained Whitaker, "particularly because he'd been brought up in a reasonably poor environment and he realized that the folks in his area couldn't afford a trip to Yellowstone or the great pristine parks, so somehow we had to bring the parks to them."[227]

Nixon's proposal to fund the plan with a 50 percent increase in funding for the Land and Water Conservation Fund, to be used for matching grants to communities to create parks, passed Congress with large bipartisan majorities.[228] "Special emphasis," the president promised, "will be placed on identifying properties that could appropriately be converted to parks and recreation areas."[229] By September 1976 the Nixon and Ford administrations had converted 82,232 acres across every state and many US territories, valued at nearly $241 million, into 642 parks, most in or close to cities—despite frequent strong opposition from federal departments, notably defense, that had owned the land.[230]

Donation of federal land would be central to another administration initiative. After flying over New York harbor in May 1971, Nixon said, "What we need to do is to bring to the 20 million people who live in this area those recreational opportunities that they otherwise could not have."[231] In following years, Nixon signed acts creating the Gateway National Recreation Area around New York City and the Golden Gate National Recreation Area around San Francisco. Three new national seashore areas were designated in 1970, along with one new national park (Voyageurs) and one new national monument and three new wilderness areas. Four more national recreation areas were created in 1972.[232] "With the creative, cooperative effort of local government and private individuals it was not necessary for the federal government to buy all lands within recreation areas," explained Hartzog. "With our society moving as rapidly as it is toward an urban situation, I think the need for national recreation areas—well, let me say for outdoor recreation areas—is going to continue to accelerate."[233]

In August 1970 Nixon told Congress, "It is vital that our entire society develop a new understanding and a new awareness of man's relations to his environment. . . . [T]his will require the development and teaching of environmental concepts at every point in the educational process."[234] The Environmental Quality Education Act, working its way through Congress at the time, expanded environmental education in colleges and public schools, and was signed in October. But afterward, reported Dennis Brezina, aide to the bill's sponsor, Gaylord Nelson, "it looked like the management people [in the administration] did not want the Environmental Education Act to really happen, which meant they weren't going to create an Office of Environmental Education."[235] Supporters pushed back. In hearings in 1971, Representative John Brademas (D-IN) called in Commissioner of Education Sidney P. Maitland. "The opening salvo from Brademas is, 'When are you going to start obeying the law?'" reported Brezina. "It ended with Maitland apologizing and saying he would create the office."[236] The program, Brezina explained, "was the educational side of the environmental movement. It was small, but it had potency, and it's an established phase now, 'environmental education.'"[237]

The act, whose funding would be supplemented with money from the Elementary and Secondary Education Act of 1965, won the support of the National Education Association, the biggest teachers' union. By the mid-1970s almost all states had an environmental education program, with at least a state specialist responsible for drafting an environmental curriculum for high schools.[238] The Environmental Quality Education Act would be repealed under Ronald Reagan in 1981, but by that time environmental studies had grown rapidly at all levels from grade schools to postgraduate education.[239]

The first two years of the presidency of Richard Nixon, who saw himself as a world statesman with a grand geostrategic vision, produced dramatic domestic environmental advances, with new structures and standards that reshaped America's policies, America's land, and America's air. Yet despite the considerable amount of legislation and activity, and the number of people in his administration who were involved and deeply committed, Nixon was never concerned about the details of environmental policy. As Flippen noted, "Nixon wanted to win the environmental vote, but cared little for the issue itself."[240] Nixon's indifference, or at least his preoccupation with other issues, actually opened up possibilities, Train concluded: "The very fact that Nixon delegated almost complete responsibility for dealing with environmental policy to his staff may well explain how we were able to put together such a comprehensive and far-reaching set of environmental initiatives."[241] As Nixon wrote in a domestic issues memo to his staff in March 1970, "I consider [the environment] to be important [but] I don't want to be bothered with the details. Just see that the job is done."[242]

CHAPTER SEVEN

High Tide on Nixon Water Policy

When Richard Nixon was elected president in November 1968, one-third of the nation's sewage went untreated and half of water treatment plants were overloaded.[1] In 1969, the year he became president, water pollution was estimated to kill as many as forty-one million fish in forty-five states, with chemical poisons and thermal pollution considered the leading killers.[2] Beginning with the Santa Barbara oil spill immediately after Nixon's inauguration, a series of stunning events dramatized the problem. While only 17 percent of Americans considered pollution an important issue in a 1965 Gallup poll, the percentage had risen to more than half in 1970.[3] In June, Americans saw the Cuyahoga River, running through Cleveland, literally catch fire, an intense inferno that damaged two bridges. The image, including a *Time* magazine cover showing the burning river, imprinted the vision of poisoned water on the national consciousness.

Congress Dives into Water Quality

The Santa Barbara spill led Congress to pass the Water Quality Improvement Act of 1970, making oil companies and tankers financially liable for spills. It created criminal penalties for failing to report spills and ordered the secretary of the interior to regulate the discharge of human waste from vessels. The bill also provided $412.5 million to study and clean up polluted waters.[4]

While the public's anger over pollution rose in 1969, Nixon's task force had been drafting proposals for the president, and some administration officials had surprising sympathies. In 1969 Secretary of the Interior Wally Hickel irritated administration budget officials when testifying before

Muskie's pollution subcommittee. Instead of defending the budgeted $214 million annually for secondary sewage treatment, Hickel declared, "We need a minimum of $600 million or perhaps $800 million a year."[5]

Nixon presented his plan for controlling water pollution in his February 10, 1970, environmental message. "To clean up our nation's waters," he told Congress, "I am proposing a five-year, $10 billion Clean Water Act to provide the municipal treatment plants needed to meet our water quality standards nationwide, and I am proposing a comprehensive enforcement plan with strong new legal weapons to insure [sic] that no city and no industry is allowed to continue polluting lakes and rivers."[6] Nixon proposed precise federal effluent standards controlling what could be dumped into the waters. In his message, Nixon called for expanded authority: "I propose that the Federal pollution control program be extended to include all navigable waters, both inter- and intra-state."[7]

To help pay for waste treatment, Nixon proposed creating an Environmental Financing Authority (EFA). If a city could not market its own bonds for waste treatment facilities, the EFA would buy the bonds and sell them itself, thus making the EFA the entity of last resort. The law also increased penalties for noncompliance, up to $10,000 a day, with the Department of the Interior having subpoena and discovery power for full and quick investigations into violations. Nixon noted that the program illustrated "a simple but profoundly significant principle: that the nation's waterways belong to us all, and that neither a municipality nor an industry should be allowed to discharge wastes into those waterways beyond their capacity to absorb the wastes without becoming polluted."[8]

Another portion of Nixon's message received less attention. "Water pollution has three principal sources," he noted: "municipal, industrial, and agricultural wastes. . . . Of these three, the most troublesome to control are those from agricultural sources, animal wastes, eroded soil, fertilizers and pesticides. . . . Effective control will take time, and will require action on many fronts: modified agricultural practices, greater care in the disposal of animal wastes, better soil conservation methods," and more.[9] Nixon urged more research into ways to control these "non-point source" causes of water pollution.

Even with broad proposals, Nixon complained that the program was not striking enough. After visiting a sewage treatment facility in February 1970, Nixon griped to his staff, "Lyndon Johnson will be remembered for [saving] the Redwoods. I will be remembered for sewage treatment plants."[10] Later, of course, he might have settled for that. On the issue, there was a strong consensus that state efforts had been insufficient. "Since the passage of the Water Quality Act of 1965, the States have taken many different approaches in developing water quality standards," Environmental Protection Agency (EPA) administrator William Ruckelshaus told the Senate Subcommittee on Air and Water Pollution in March 1971. "The uncertainty and confusion resulting from this diversity of approach have often delayed the establishment of enforceable standards."[11]

Some in the administration advocated a system of permits and fees for effluents, creating financial incentives for reducing pollution, but environmental groups, with public support, favored direct regulation. Nixon aide John C. Whitaker also noted that since the fees were a type of tax, they would have to pass the congressional finance committees, which seemed unlikely.[12] Nixon's eventual proposal advocated a strong and direct regulatory approach. Nixon told Ehrlichman that the administration's "slow start might allow the opposition [the Democrats] to seize the initiative."[13] Yet Nixon's proposal barely increased funding beyond prior appropriations. Nixon thought that higher funding would either cause a budget deficit or require higher taxes.[14]

Edmund Muskie—the Democratic presidential prospect whose craggy image seemed to loom over the Nixon administration's environmental thinking—proposed a similar bill, but with double the funding. His bill also proposed water quality standards for all navigable waters and required state and federal enforcement on limits of effluent discharges. Besides the differences in funding, Muskie's bill also had stricter statutory deadlines and allowed citizens to file suit against violators.[15] Given the divergence between the two proposals, Congress could not reach agreement before the end of the 1970 session.

Muskie had been expanding the subcommittee's professional staff, bringing in more ecological experts, including Leon Billings, named subcommittee staff director in 1966. He would work closely with Thomas Jorling, an environmental specialist who became the subcommittee's minority counsel in 1969. The Senate Public Works Committee added an Environmental Advisory Panel in January 1970, consisting of chemists, geologists, sanitary engineers, lawyers, regional planners, and ecologists, who would contribute greatly to the writing of the committee's proposal.

Through 1970–1971, the subcommittee struggled to write water quality standards. John Tunney (D-CA) proposed a "national target water quality standard" with the objective that all American waters be clean enough to swim in, without health risk, by the end of 1980. Tunney argued that this would "focus national effort, provide an easily understandable measure of commitment, and encourage rational cost-effective program decisions."[16] While Tunney's standard would distinguish the bill from past and other proposals and was simple to understand, Muskie doubted its economic and practical feasibility. The subcommittee staff substituted language that the national minimum water quality standard be sufficient to protect "a balanced population of naturally recurring shellfish, fish and wildlife."[17] Muskie remained doubtful, cautioning, "When you talk about setting a standard against which you can prosecute people . . . as well as give plant managers and engineers some standard by which to design their pollution control equipment, you have to have something that is pretty precise."[18]

The committee staff, exploring how to get to Tunney's standard, realized that its implementation would require control of non-point source pollution. Billings wrote to Muskie to say that implementation "would require a major investment in such problems as combined sewer overflow, urban surface runoff, . . . agriculture waste management, waste control, controls over forest cutting and a host of land use measures."[19] Billings and Jorling instead proposed trying to control pollution by more stringent regulation of point source effluents, with softer measures to start to control the non-point sources of water pollution. In addition, they proposed to use ideas recently tested by the Corps of Engineers for land-based "living filters" as a place to divert water pollution rather than the traditional approach of trying to dilute the pollution.[20]

Senator Howard Baker (R-TN) now proposed another approach, incorporating Billings and Jorling's ideas, emphasizing setting and enforcing limits on effluents. Water quality standards would be secondary or even omitted entirely. The subcommittee struggled to achieve consensus. The August 6, 1971, working draft retained water quality standards and required states to devise plans to achieve swimmable/fishable waters by 1980 unless they could show the cost was prohibitive, but also included a no-discharge provision that made effluent limits the key variable. Attempts by the Nixon administration, proposed by John Sherman Cooper (R-KY), to reduce the budgeted funding for water pollution control were narrowly defeated in the subcommittee. Based on its 1971 hearing, the Senate Public Works Committee concluded that the "pollution problem is more severe, more pervasive, and growing at a more rapid rate than was generally believed."[21]

The Nixon administration attacked the subcommittee proposal as unrealistic. Both the EPA and the Council on Environmental Quality (CEQ) thought the goals to meet the proposed water standards by 1976 and swimmable/fishable waters by 1980 were "unachievable and irrational."[22] The EPA noted the problem of knowing the level of effluent control needed to achieve the specified water quality, and the difficulty of setting a single national standard given the variations across the nation. Years later, Ruckelshaus noted, "It was not possible to make every waterway in the country fishable by 1980 or 1983, the date they finally adopted. . . . [W]hat we did achieve over that ten-year period was appreciable advances in making places fishable and swimmable."[23]

The subcommittee staff realized that the proposed water standards were not viable, since they required pollution control officials to predict the effect of effluents on the complex ecosystems of every river or lake. Instead they turned to Baker's proposal to focus on effluent controls. Muskie commented, "If you gear your process to increasing control over effluent discharges, you will have a direct benefit on water quality, 'but working backward from water standards to determine limits for effluents' was like trying to unscramble an egg."[24] The revised bill now proposed eliminating all industrial discharges, unless sanctioned by permits, by 1985.

Everyone agreed on the complexity of the legislation. "In my thirteen years of experience in the Senate," said Muskie, "no bill has consumed so much time, demanded so much attention to detail and required such arduous efforts to reach final agreement as did this act."[25] The Public Works Committee held 33 days of public hearings, heard 170 witnesses producing 6,400 pages of testimony, and collected another 470 written statements. The committee held another 45 executive sessions on the bill.[26]

The Nixon administration did not like the revised bill, attacking the idea of deadlines and trying to retain state ambient standards. CEQ director Russell Train warned that ending discharges by 1981 "would be very costly compared to the benefits or ineffective."[27] The administration was frustrated that subcommittee Republicans so often defended the proposal.[28] Muskie did agree to convert the 1985 no-discharge target into a statement of policy rather than a hard deadline.

Given the apparent impasse, Train looked for other ways to address water pollution. He persuaded Nixon to sign Muskie's 1970 legislation, passed in the wake of the Santa Barbara oil spill, to make oil companies liable for spills. After the spill, the administration had suspended but not canceled drilling leases in the area. In the summer of 1970 Congress appeared ready to cancel them. Trying to win political credit and head off Congress, Nixon announced his own decision to rescind the leases, saying it "illustrates our commitment to use off-shore lands in a balanced and responsible manner."[29]

In 1965 Gaylord Nelson had warned, "A dull gray tide of pollution is moving through our Great Lakes, following the path of human progress," but had been unable to get action during the Johnson administration.[30] Now, Train's leadership spurred the creation of the United States–Canada Joint Working Group to address the problem. The working group issued a report in June 1971, pledging both countries to build treatment plants as well as eliminate the release of mercury and other toxic substances into the Great Lakes.[31] The Great Lakes Water Quality Agreement in 1972 weakened specific requirements for reduction in certain wastes, but by 1976 Train could boast that the cleanup was "one of the greatest success stories in American history."[32]

In 1969 US detergents contained two billion pounds of phosphates, all eventually ending up in the water.[33] The CEQ proposed legislation to limit their release into the Great Lakes, which had led to eutrophication creating, according to one report, "a mat of algae two feet thick and a few hundred miles in extent."[34] Resistance from detergent manufacturers blocked any administration proposal, leading Representative Henry Reuss (D-WI) to comment, "the Interior Department is a branch office of Procter & Gamble."[35]

While the CEQ continued to urge the eventual elimination of phosphates from detergents, initial industry alternatives were found to be possible carcinogens or caustic. Although the EPA supported labeling detergents' contents, the Federal Trade Commission refused to require listing of ingredients. Nelson quipped, "If the right hand washes the left hand in this Administration, it apparently does not do so with detergents."[36] Then, on September 15, 1971, in a joint news conference, the EPA, CEQ, and surgeon general endorsed phosphates as less harmful than alternatives, a position Reuss called "a capitulation to soap and detergent makers."[37] Critics noted that the president of Procter & Gamble, the biggest detergent maker, chaired the Detergent Sub-council of President Nixon's National Industrial Pollution Control Council, created in 1970 to reassure the corporate community regarding impending waves of environmental regulation. The EPA argued that waste treatment facilities could remove the phosphates. In 1972 congressional hearings recommended a reduction of phosphate content. But while the industry now supported this to pre-empt stronger state and local limits, no bill emerged.[38]

Digging Up the Refuse Act of 1899

With the administration and Congress now appearing deadlocked, attention turned to an ancient statute, the Refuse Act of 1899, originally seen as blocking only dumping large materials that would interfere with shipping. But section 13 of the act had made it illegal to "throw, discharge or deposit . . . any refuse matter of any kind or description whatever, other than that flowing from streets and sewers and passing therefrom in a liquid state, into any navigable water of the United States." The law imposed fines for each violation "up to $2500 and/or imprisonment and entitled citizens who reported the violations to collect up to half the fine."[39]

Starting in 1960 the Supreme Court had broadened the act's practical impact. In *United States v. Republic Steel*, the court ruled that industrial effluents fit the definition of refuse and that their discharge could be restricted. In 1966, the court went further, in *United States v. Standard Oil*, to define refuse as "all foreign substances and pollutants."[40] The court, led by Justice William O. Douglas, made the old statute a mechanism to address water pollution. Hickel saw the act's potential, first using it in March 1970 to limit large discharges of heated water into Florida waters. He used it again that summer against mercury contamination.[41] "We dusted off the 1899 Refuse Act for the teeth we needed to straighten out the nation's water problems," Hickel would explain. "That was law enough. All that was lacking was guys with guts [to use it]."[42]

Reuss, chairman of the House Government Operations Subcommittee, also saw the possibilities of the Refuse Act. In March 1970 Reuss's subcommittee released and publicized a report calling on the Corps of Engineers, Federal Water Pollution Control Administration, and Justice Department to "institute injunction suits against all persons whose discharges or deposits . . . violate the Refuse Act."[43] Reuss released a guide for citizen activists on suing polluters under section 13 and collecting their share of the fines. Soon the Justice Department was flooded with calls reporting violations of the act.

While the Justice Department for the most part tried to defer to state or federal water pollution officials, it did create a pollution control section to deal specifically with Refuse Act prosecutions. Such prosecutions were easier than under the water quality acts; settlements often mandated stricter restrictions and cases could apply to both intrastate and interstate waters. By December 1970 the CEQ urged using the Refuse Act as a major tool against pollution. The Corps of Engineers had previously resisted the new interpretation of the law, arguing that the act's force "lies in the effect [that such effluents] have on the navigable capacity of the waterway" and not with "minor illegal discharges of industrial wastes having no perceptible effect" on navigability.[44]

However, many administration officials saw a permitting program under the act as a good way to impose stronger limits on the discharge of industrial pollution. Even conservatives usually opposed to regulation felt that the approach was better than ongoing litigation. On December 23, 1970, Nixon issued Executive Order 11574, the Refuse Act Permit Program, requiring all dischargers of pollution to have a valid federal permit, issued by the Corps of Engineers, by July 1, 1971. Polluters had to identify the type and volume of their discharges and certify compliance with water quality standards. The EPA would review the permits and issue regulations on the type and quantity of allowable effluents.[45]

Environmentalists had misgivings about the plan, noting that it was more complicated than the simple language of the Refuse Act. Since EPA would have to review over forty thousand permits and give recommendations to the Corps, the EPA allowed states to review permit applications on its behalf, often only requiring dischargers to meet weak state standards.[46] EPA program administrator John Quarles confessed that the situation's technical complexity, the limited manpower available to the EPA, and the July 1 deadline limited the EPA to setting standards for only the most flagrant polluters.[47] For its part, industry didn't want to apply for permits that would force companies to disclose their wastes and possibly put them in legal jeopardy.[48]

But federal officials as well as private citizens initiated many successful actions under the Refuse Act, resulting in significant changes.[49] The threat was, Ruckelshaus later recalled, "You shut them down it they didn't comply. . . . It was an imaginative interpretation of the law and we used it for a couple of years until the Clean Water Act passed in 1972, and I think after that we essentially stopped using it."[50] In fact, the mandatory limits of the Refuse Act would be replaced by limitations, but not an absolute ban, found in the Clean Water Act. But by that time the atmosphere—and the attitude of the Nixon administration—had changed dramatically.

CHAPTER EIGHT

The Atmosphere Changes

KEY EVENTS:
Clean Water Act (1972)

Around the middle of 1971, Richard Nixon began to feel doubts about the environmental agenda. Perhaps more importantly, he began to feel that he didn't need it. The antiregulation pushback that he was getting from his core conservative supporters came to be bolstered, especially in 1972, by increasing public support for his foreign policy outreach to the Soviet Union and China. Gradually, Nixon came to believe that his reelection would not depend on environmental advances, and that such policies were upsetting his most crucial supporters. Over time he would transform from the president with a powerful environmental record in early 1970 to one who spent much of 1971 complaining about the rulings of his own Environmental Protection Agency to the president who, just before the 1972 election, vetoed the Clean Water Act—and saw his veto thunderously overridden. He spent the rest of his time in the White House resisting environmental progress—with steadily less ability to stop it. Sometimes, the moment is more powerful than the president.

Nixon Takes a Tactical Turn

The changes began to surface in White House conversations. In private, Nixon began to gripe that the environment "was no sacred cow,"[1] and increasingly associated environmentalism with a hostile Left. He told H. R. Haldeman, his chief of staff, "The environment is not a good political issue. I have an uneasy feeling that perhaps we are doing too much."[2] Still, the administration tried to make enough environmental concessions to avoid political criticism. "In a flat choice between smoke and jobs, we're for jobs," Nixon told aide John Ehrlichman, his domestic policy counselor. "But just keep me out of trouble on environmental issues."[3]

The Southeast Asia–driven upheavals of 1970 and 1971 caused Nixon to realize, J. Brooks Flippen noted, "that while environmental quality was important politically, his fate ultimately lay with other issues."[4] After writing to Nixon criticizing the administration for not reaching out to protesting students, Secretary of the Interior Wally Hickel would be fired after twenty-two months in office.

The Council on Environmental Quality (CEQ) also faced pushback from other agencies, resenting its oversight and the need to write environmental impact statements. "Although agency performance has been improving," Russell Train wrote later about compliance with environmental requirements, "it is still not satisfactory."[5] In 1971, trying to sharpen the environmental impact process as a tool, the CEQ issued new guidelines requiring federal agencies to wait at least ninety days after issuing the first draft of an environmental impact statement, and at least thirty days after issuing the final draft, before moving ahead on projects. Henry Jackson called it "a step in the right direction."[6] As the White House withdrew from environmental advocacy, environmentalists seized on the environmental impact statement as a weapon to slow or stop projects. Jackson commented that the National Environmental Policy Act (NEPA) would remain "one bright spot" if the administration continued to swing further against environmentalism.[7]

By late 1971 it was harder for environmental advocates in the administration to convince the president to invest political capital in further reforms. EPA Administrator William Ruckelshaus admitted that the environment might not be a great issue for Nixon, but argued that being against the environment would result in severe criticism.[8] The environmentalists' sin, Flippen wrote, "was political opposition more than actual inordinacy. It was for Nixon, nevertheless, a mortal sin, just cause for a detour on the road to reelection."[9]

Industry complained about the cost of pollution controls, with the Chamber of Commerce warning, "All existing firms will be adversely affected, but in some cases the economic impact will be severe."[10] Responding, the EPA cited air pollution's estimated $25 billion annual damages.[11] A proposal by Train and the CEQ to limit sulfur oxides, generated by electrical power plants, mining, and smelting, fell victim to the administration's waning interest. Secretary of Commerce Maurice Stans, before leaving to raise money for Nixon's reelection campaign, complained that business had become "a whipping boy for the environment."[12] An executive at the timber company Weyerhaeuser groused, "This uninformed environmentalist phenomenon . . . has the potential to destroy much of the social and economic progress made in the past few decades."[13] The administration tried to weaken the EPA's role under the Clean Air Act in setting air quality standards, ordering it to consider economic impact. The White House also ordered the EPA to appoint more Republicans. White House aide John C.Whitaker rejoined that partisan EPA appointments would cause "a negative public reaction that the choices were made on political grounds."[14]

By the end of 1971 Nixon had gained immense political capital with announcements of negotiations with both the People's Republic of China and the Soviet Union, strengthening his view that foreign policy and the economy would be much more important issues than the environment. Early in Nixon's administration, Ruckelshaus observed, he wasn't comfortable resisting a popular issue such as protecting the environment, but as he became more popular and it was clear that environmental advocacy wasn't helping him much, he became more hostile. Ruckelshaus privately shared the opinion that Nixon didn't care about the environment except as a political issue. Ruckelshaus later commented that Nixon "never once asked me if there were a problem with the environment the whole time I was there."[15] Speaking to businessmen at the Economic Club of Detroit in September, Nixon proclaimed, "We are not going to allow the environmental issue to be used sometimes falsely and sometimes in a demagogic way basically to destroy the system."[16]

Ruckelshaus continued to fight. In 1971 the EPA initiated Operation 5000, a program to replace five thousand open waste dumps with covered sanitary landfills.[17] In 1971 the EPA issued the first permits allowing the discharge of treated wastewater back into navigable water. Just before the 1972 Republican convention, Ruckelshaus announced a ban on the interstate shipment of pesticides to control predatory animals. The EPA staff spent much of its first five years trying to finalize national air quality standards, write the technology-based requirements for pollution control in each industry, and approve the required permits.[18] In 1972 five auto companies asked the EPA for a one-year suspension of the 1975 hydrocarbon and carbon monoxide standards. "I thought I was going to have to give them a variance when we started the hearing," recalled Ruckelshaus later. "At the end of the hearing, I didn't think I could give them a variance."[19] During testimony, "the automobile companies' testimony was very weak. The Japanese automobile companies not only said that they could meet the standard but they would be happy to show the American companies how to meet it."[20] Ruckelshaus denied the suspension, ruling, "Emission reduction required to meet the 1975 standards can probably be achieved in a number of current engines."[21] When the auto companies' legal appeal got the Supreme Court to send the issue back to the EPA for reconsideration, Ruckelshaus compromised, slightly easing the standard outside California.[22]

Whitaker concluded about the Clean Air Act,

Congress gave Nixon much of what he asked for [in terms of air pollution] in his first environmental message to Congress. . . . By trying to legislate technologies that were not yet perfected and arbitrarily fixing deadlines for control of auto emissions . . . Congress started a process that led in the ensuing years to costly solutions for cleaning our air. On the other hand, there is no doubt that the pace of improvement in air pollution abatement technology increased because of this legislation.[23]

Environmentalists applauded Ruckelshaus's efforts, especially compared with the rest of the administration. The Sierra Club's director Philip Berry later recalled him as "a gutsy guy."[24] In 1973 political scientist Walter Rosenbaum wrote, "To date the agency has been considerably more dedicated to its mission than many veteran observers could have predicted."[25]

But the 1971 creation of the Office of Management and Budget (OMB), recommended in the Ash government reorganization report, contributed to the antienvironmental backlash. Ash himself would become OMB head in 1973 and he related, "When John Ehrlichman left the government [in April 1973] there was a void. . . . I largely took over many domestic policy matters."[26] The OMB now moved into the White House, reporting directly to the president. "OMB tends to have an institutional skepticism, a 'show me why' sort of view," Ash later admitted. "It's so easy to see the downside of everything, prospectively, and to conjure up more downsides that are there than to think on the upsides that go with them."[27] He added,

"OMB's institutional view is to be challenging, if not skeptical, of all department money proposals."[28]

In 1972, reflecting the president's changing attitudes, Ehrlichman had initiated what he called quality of life reviews to evaluate proposed regulations to find what the White House felt was the proper balance between economic and environmental concerns. These new guidelines mandated that the EPA submit any proposed regulation to other agencies for their input before the White House, in the form of the OMB, would decide whether to approve it.[29] The White House intended this process to limit further environmental proposals. Train called it "a troublesome process," complaining, "I spent a great deal of time disputing claims that cleaning up the environment was unacceptably costly."[30]

Energy Enters the Equation

One factor in Nixon's growing opposition to environmental regulations lay in his concerns about American energy production, as an energy shortage began to loom.[31] Lawsuits challenging the construction of the Alaskan oil pipeline angered him, and he persuaded Congress to exempt nuclear power from the environmental impact statement requirement. Train publicly decried "the current tendency to make the environment the whipping boy of our energy problems."[32]

When Ruckelshaus announced on June 14, 1972, a ban of almost all uses of DDT by the end of the year, Nixon was furious, writing, "I completely disagree with this decision. . . . I want plenty of effort to get it reversed."[33]

The Clean Water Wars

By then, Nixon's active opposition to the clean water proposal from Senator Edmund Muskie (D-ME) made his environmental reversal clear. Muskie's bill called for $25 billion for waste treatment centers, half from the federal government, half from the states. The Nixon administration countered with a proposal of $12 billion in funding for waste treatment. The Muskie proposal required "the best available technology" by companies to reduce their discharge into water, while the Nixon plan required the more relaxed "best practical technology." Both bills gave the federal government jurisdiction over water quality standards.[34]

Trying to derail Muskie's proposal, Nixon ordered the Department of Commerce to study the economic impact of environmental regulations, specifically Muskie's bill. Ehrlichman told the staff, "Make sure [it] isn't biased toward the environment."[35] Environmentalists argued for the stronger Muskie proposal. The National League of Cities and the US Conference of Mayors argued for more funding for the building of municipal facilities. By the end of the Nixon administration the estimated cost to implement water treatment would rise to $60 billion.[36] Testifying against the Muskie bill, Train argued that too-stringent standards might cause industries to move to foreign countries. He also stated that the higher costs required to achieve greater pollution requirements could cause inflation as well as a backlash, warning that "public acceptance for environmental programs" might diminish.[37]

In private Nixon was far more critical. He criticized the CEQ's 1971 annual report, warning against "ecological perfection at the cost of bankruptcy."[38] Whitaker later argued, "The cost of achieving the last 3% reduction, that is, to reach zero discharge, would require approximately $200 billion more."[39] By this time Nixon was telling staff, "We are doing too much, catering to the left in all of this." Especially since, as Nixon commented, "You can't out-Muskie Muskie."[40]

But the Senate Public Works Committee unanimously reported out the bill on October 19, 1971. Muskie later noted, "I like to bridge the party gap and concentrate on the issues. . . . [A]s you move forward in bringing a program to life, making it work, you've got to have consensus."[41] Muskie stated that strong legislation was needed because otherwise "the quality of our environment will continue to deteriorate."[42] William Proxmire (D-WI) proposed forcing polluters to pay for their discharges, but Muskie successfully argued, "We cannot give anyone the option of polluting for a fee."[43] A proposal by Gaylord Nelson (D-WI) to establish an $800 million fund for low-interest loans to small businesses for pollution control passed unanimously.[44]

In November 1971, the Senate passed, 86–0, a clean water bill that had become even stronger, with funding of $28 billion and Muskie's "best available technology" language. The bill called for water quality that would sustain fish and wildlife by 1981 and a goal of zero discharge of pollutants by 1985.[45] The bill created a National Pollutant Discharge Elimination System, banning discharges of effluents without a permit. This was a major change from the Clean Air Act two years earlier, which required permits only for new sources of air pollution. Although the states could create their own permit process, they would have to secure and maintain EPA approval. Lloyd Bentsen (D-TX) commented, "While some states have very good programs, the pressures on them to develop their resources and attract industry—often in direct competition with other states—are too great for them to withstand the debilitation of their regulatory programs. For this reason alone, EPA ought to establish a close and continuing oversight."[46] The bill gave the EPA administrator power to order compliance or sue when he found violations of the statute.

The Nixon administration moved to weaken the bill in the House. Launching a massive lobbying campaign, the administration argued that the Senate bill gave too little weight to the cost of compliance. "Unfortunately, it appears that the Administration has undergone an environmental metamorphosis," observed Muskie, "emerging from the cocoon not as a butterfly, but as a moth."[47] John Blatnik (D-MN), chairman of the House Public Works Committee, hoped to avoid further House hearings, instead pushing through the Senate bill. The ranking Republican, William Harsha, of Ohio, and other members objected to the bill's cost. The first markup session, on November 16, featured heated argument, and later that day Blatnik suffered a mild heart attack. The same day White House officials, including Ehrlichman, Whitaker, and Ruckelshaus, met with the Republican members of the committee.[48] With Blatnik in the hospital, the committee, now led by Robert E. Jones (D-AL), was persuaded by the administration to hold more hearings in hopes of weakening the bill.

The administration claimed that the bill would cost $316.5 billion over twenty-five years, much of it spent to clean up the last 10 percent of pollution.[49] Muskie and environmentalists rejected the figures; Friends of the Earth estimated the cost as $50–55 billion.[50]

The administration also enlisted business to attack the Senate bill. The National Association of Manufacturers director of environmental affairs declared, "Blind pursuit of pure water is a form of economic brinkmanship."[51] The administration put together a panel of sanitary engineers and economists under the president's science advisor, Edward E. David Jr., who stated, "Much of the professional community is extremely critical of the approach to water quality embodied in the proposed [Senate] legislation."[52] Testifying at the House hearings, Ruckelshaus indicated his preference for water quality standards over the Senate's effluent limitations as the primary mechanism. He also argued that the EPA should delegate permitting to states with a good water pollution control program in place, and step in only if the states failed.[53]

The House Public Works Committee reported out its proposed bill just before Christmas, with a proviso that the National Academy of Sciences would ascertain the deadlines' economic implications within three years. In the interim the deadlines for "zero discharge" stood as "national goals" rather than "national policy." The deadline for industries to use the best available technology was pushed back from 1981 to 1983, and the phrase "not to exceed" was added before the funding provisions. The bill reduced the emphasis on effluent limits and downgraded the idea of no discharge. However, the federal funding was increased by $4 billion more than in the Senate bill, triple Nixon's original proposal.[54]

The bill was initially enmeshed in presidential politics, as Muskie was the frontrunner for the Democratic nomination through the winter of 1972. But his position faded with attacks by Nixon campaign tricksters, and by April 27 he had dropped out of the race. One observer noted that Muskie's intellectual integrity, which served him well in the Senate, was a liability in the campaign, judging that there was "not enough demagoguery in Muskie to be a good campaigner."[55] The presidential aspirations of another environmental champion, Senator Scoop Jackson, would be doomed by his hawkish positions on Vietnam. Muskie and Jackson's elimination meant the environment would not be the focus of the 1972 election, although both parties' platforms supported environmental regulation.

Efforts to strengthen the water pollution bill on the House floor failed, and on March 29, 1972, the full House passed what was essentially the House bill by a vote of 380–14. Nixon now tried to deadlock the House-Senate conference committee, telling Republicans in private, "The environmentalists are going crazy. The trouble with environmentalists is that everything they do is for the rich."[56] He was tapping into a frequent criticism made by environmental opponents, often covertly backed by large industry, that environmental concerns were a concern only to upscale urbanites.

In July Nixon told Senator Howard Baker (R-TN), a member of the conference committee, that he planned to veto any bill that emerged from the conference committee. Baker urged the president against a veto, arguing that the increased money was necessary given the scale of the problem.[57] The conference committee met some forty times from May to September 1972 to try to reach agreement.

The conference committee's final bill, in September 1972, kept the House's larger funding of $18 billion for waste treatment facilities for the next three years. It kept the strongest features of the Senate bill, including mandating the "best available technology," water quality that would sustain fish and wildlife by 1981, and zero emissions by 1985. It retained strong federal jurisdiction over water quality standards. The bill was weakened only by referring to the deadlines as goals rather than policy and mandating that the funding "was not to exceed" the specified amounts.[58] The bill allowed pollution reduction by "best practical technology" by 1977, but tightened standards in the second phase, requiring use of the "best available technology" by 1981.[59] Polluters had to show that they had used "the maximum use of technology with economic capability and [that this] will result in reasonable further progress toward the elimination of the discharge of pollutants."[60] The Clean Water Act went further in making limits on discharges of pollutants the key feature.

The final bill required an EPA permit for any discharge of pollutants into US waters, and granted citizens standing to sue polluters if the citizen had an interest in swimming, fishing, or other activities on the involved waterway.[61] The Clean Water Act also authorized the EPA to set standards for "toxic water pollutants," as the Clean Air Act did for toxic air pollutants. "Obviously, no one expects every industry in America to go to zero pollution overnight," Blatnik told a radio audience. "However, the national interest demands that every industry in America start moving now in that direction. Our national goal should be a massive and continuing restoration of our rivers and lakes, our harbors and our coastal waters to the end that they once again be clean enough to swim in and pure enough to drink from, and there is no reason we cannot accomplish that by the mid-1980s."[62]

On December 21, 1971, federal Judge Aubrey Robinson had ruled that the Corps of Engineers permit program required filing of environmental impact statements, declaring, "Obedience to water quality certifications under the Water Quality Improvement Act is not mutually exclusive with the NEPA procedures."[63] The ruling suggested that the EPA would have to file an environmental impact statement for every discharge permit. In conference committee, Muskie and Baker proposed an amendment explicitly exempting the EPA from filing environmental impact statements for most Clean Water–related actions, except for new pollution sources and construction plans for treatment works. In early October the Senate passed the final bill 74–0, the House passing it 366–11.

Ruckelshaus sent Nixon a thirty-three-page summary of the bill, writing that he would "strongly recommend" the president sign it. Ruckelshaus pointed out that the sums allocated were in line with EPA and CEQ estimates of construction needs. Ruckelshaus also argued that the president could "impound funds," that "through these administrative mechanisms, storm and combined sewer projects could largely be deferred."[64] Other prominent Republicans argued against a veto. Representative John Anderson (R-IL) warned Nixon that a veto "would endanger the sense of national purpose which has surrounded consensus pollution control."[65] Whitaker called the bill the "most important piece of environmental legislation before Congress this year, symbolically and politically," and argued that the conference committee had heard the administration's arguments and made the bill more realistic.[66]

Events dramatized the problem of water pollution. Contamination forced Massachusetts to ban the sale of shellfish, and the governor asked Nixon to declare a state of emergency. Six weeks before the election, New Jersey ordered that drinking water be boiled in some areas. The New York City water commissioners estimated the cost of clean drinking water at almost a billion dollars for the city alone.[67]

The administration was split. The Office of Management and Budget, Council of Economic Advisors, and the Department of the Treasury urged a veto, while the EPA, CEQ, and the Departments of the Interior and State urged Nixon to sign the bill. Nixon had hoped to pocket veto the bill, letting it die while Congress was out of session, which would be less politically damaging. Blatnik persuaded congressional leaders to stay in session specifically to force Nixon to act on the bill.[68] For Nixon the final straw for a veto was an otherwise unrelated Senate rejection of a debt ceiling conference report that would have allowed the president to limit spending for fiscal year 1973. Nixon vetoed the bill on October 17, arguing that while the goal was "laudable" the expenditure was "unconscionable."[69] He insisted that "environmental protection has been one of my highest priorities as President," but that he saw as *the highest national priority the need to protect the working men and women of America against tax increases and renewed inflation."*[70]

Congress moved to override the veto the next day, with the White House making only a minimal effort to sustain it. Not a single House member spoke to defend the veto and the override passed overwhelmingly, 247–23. The Senate agreed, overriding by 52–12. Three weeks before a Republican president would be reelected in a landslide, congressional Republicans joined to rebuke him. The stronger Clean Water Act had become law.

The *New York Times* hailed the act as a "critical step towards improving our environment."[71] Much of the credit went to Muskie for holding together a bipartisan coalition. "It is the national goal that the discharge of pollutants into the navigable waters be eliminated by 1985," proclaimed the act. "It is the national policy that the discharge of toxic pollutants in toxic amounts be prohibited. . . . It is the national policy that Federal financial assistance be provided to construct publicly owned waste treatment works."[72]

Nixon's opposition persisted. Before passage, he had ordered his legal counsel John Dean and Justice Department staff to advise him whether the phrase "not to exceed" allowed the president to spend less than was ordered in the bill. They reported that the phrase would indeed allow this. Impoundment—the decision not to spend allocated funds—had occurred rarely, usually during wartime. In 1950 Congress had authorized impoundments when expenditures became unnecessary due to "change in requirements" or "other developments subsequent" to a bill's passage. "Before Nixon, presidents were careful to use this power only when they could anticipate the support, or acquiescence, of the majority of the legislators," explained James Sundquist. "President Nixon brought the impoundment issue to a climax by asserting his power to withhold appropriated funds, derived from whatever constitutional and statutory sources, was without limit."[73]

After the election, Nixon ordered that spending on water waste treatment facilities be limited to $9 billion, half the $18 billion budgeted in the act. "I stated that even if Congress were to default its obligation to the taxpayers through enactment of this legislation," he declared, "I would not default mine." Muskie charged "a flagrant disregard of congressional intent."[74] Governors, mayors, and others protested loudly.

The Nixon Administration Runs Dry

In May 1973 the US District Court for the District of Columbia ruled that the impoundment was illegal.[75] On February 18, 1975, a unanimous Supreme Court agreed. By then, Richard Nixon was no longer president.

Train had loyally supported Nixon's reelection and defended the administration's environmental accomplishments. In March 1972 Whitaker urged Train "to devote substantial portions of your calendar to increasing public awareness of what the administration has accomplished in the environmental area. . . . [W]e must capitalize on your position as his chief environmental advocate to be his public surrogate on the issue."[76] During the campaign, the other two members of the CEQ, Robert Cahn and Gordon MacDonald, had resigned. "The bureaucracy," explained Cahn, "has grown slow in giving weight to environmental factors in decision making."[77] Nixon replaced them with weaker advocates.

Although Nixon won reelection in a landslide, 1972 also saw sweeping victories for environmentalists in congressional elections. Multiple states passed large environmental bond issues, with North Carolina enacting an "environmental bill of rights."[78] The day after the election Nixon demanded the resignations of his cabinet and staff. He named four domestic super-"counselors" to oversee human resources, community development, economic affairs, and natural resources. Running the last area was Secretary of Agriculture Earl Butz, who had declared, "There are many more important things than the environment."[79] Whitaker was shifted from the White House to the Interior Department, ending any direct line of environmental advocates to Nixon. Nixon now proposed dramatic spending cuts, such as an 80 percent slash for solid waste disposal and hacks at the CEQ budget and staff. Congress resisted many of these cuts.

"Once the Muskie candidacy was destroyed and the 1972 election was won overwhelmingly," explained Train, "Nixon's interest in the environment would begin to wane."[80] Still, Nixon sought to portray himself as an environmental warrior. In his annual environmental address in early 1973, he boasted, "We are well on the way to winning the war against environmental degradation," although he did seek a balance between economic growth and environmental protection.[81]

In early 1973 the US Court of Appeals for the District of Columbia rejected the auto companies' suit to delay the Clean Air Act's standards. The court sent the issue back to the EPA for technical analysis. Nixon now insisted that Ruckelshaus accept a proposal by General Motors. Nixon told an aide, "Pull Ruckelshaus in when he goes too far. I want sympathetic consideration of this request."[82] Faced with strong pressure from the administration and an auto industry threat that the new standards would dramatically raise car prices, Ruckelshaus had to agree.[83]

Rapidly, the Watergate scandal came to absorb Nixon, driving him ever closer to conservatives. As Flippen noted, this meant "denouncing the environmentalists he had earlier courted."[84] In 1973, when the CEQ strengthened its standards for agency compliance with the NEPA, the White House ordered most of the new regulations dropped.[85] Nixon saw an opportunity when Watergate forced out FBI director L. Patrick Gray. In April 1973 Nixon filled the slot with Ruckelshaus—whom he sarcastically called "Our old friend, Mr. Clean"—largely to remove him from the EPA.[86] Train moved over to take his place, explaining, "The action had really moved from CEQ and its policy focus to EPA and implementation."[87] Nixon emphasized that Train was not to act independently of the administration, that his job was to "balance environmental protection with other pressing needs."[88] The message was clear. "What I did not see clearly at the time, however," Train later admitted, "was the extent to which the environmental honeymoon had come to an end and how much the conflict between environmental and energy objectives would characterize the years immediately ahead at EPA. . . . As the economy soured during the Gerald Ford administration, environmental programs also became the whipping boy for inflation and job losses."[89]

In 1973 concern arose over the small amounts of sulfuric acid vapor produced by catalytic converters. Before the Senate Public Works Committee, Train testified that the risks "were sufficiently uncertain not to justify the abandonment of the catalytic converter."[90] By January 1975 research had disproved the device's health threat, but in March Train acceded to the auto companies' request for a one-year suspension of the 1977 emission standards.[91]

The CEQ, without Train and with a greatly reduced budget, became much less important. In June 1973, when courts blocked the Alaska pipeline for not satisfying the NEPA, Nixon proposed an exemption for the pipeline. Train and the EPA would soon have their hands full trying to protect existing laws. The Yom Kippur War of October 1973 between Israel and an Arab coalition set off an Arab oil embargo, creating shortages, long lines at gas stations, and a huge spike in US gasoline prices. The Nixon administration announced Project Independence to make the United States energy self-sufficient by 1980. Congress swiftly passed the Federal Right of Way Act of 1973, explicitly authorizing the Alaska pipeline and blocking further environmental challenges.

Attacking the Clean Air Act as hampering energy independence, Nixon proposed weakening the standards to allow increased use of sulfur-oxide-producing coal and ordered executive agencies to craft proposals to weaken the act. Train resisted, warning, "I don't think we can achieve full energy independence of all external sources by 1980 without substantial damage to the nation's environment."[92] But the oil crisis, he later recalled, "left little support for new environmental initiatives and much pressure for rolling back environmental standards."[93] When environmental advocates were battling pollution, they could count on being the hometown favorite. A struggle seemingly against energy supplies would be a different ballgame.

In 1974, for the first time in four years, Nixon did not send an environmental message to Congress. Instead, he pushed to increase offshore oil drilling. One aide wrote that Nixon had given orders "to prepare as soon as possible legislation that would remove all environmental roadblocks to energy production and supply by cancelling environmental inhibitions."[94] Nixon proposed putting off Clean Air Act deadlines, allowing a deterioration in air quality if necessary. Train refused to testify before Congress in support of this bill, earning a rebuke from the president.

The Clean Air Act had mandated a 90 percent reduction in carbon monoxide and hydrocarbon levels by 1975 and a 90 percent reduction in nitrogen oxide by 1976, and set limits on sulfur oxide emissions. The act allowed the EPA to grant temporary extensions and variances, but the courts would rule that the EPA could not let air quality deteriorate in states already meeting the federal requirement. The administration now called for permanently weakening the standards and extending the time for compliance. The existing regulations required industry to install scrubbers on smokestacks to reduce emissions. The proposal would allow industry to permanently substitute cheaper tall smokestacks, which would simply disperse air pollution rather than reduce it. Finally, all energy-related activities would be exempted from the NEPA. The EPA would be mandated to consider economic costs as well as health and environmental issues.

Train persuaded the administration to drop the exemptions from NEPA and the requirement that the EPA consider economic costs in its regulations, noting that the effect of Watergate helped limit the damage. "Nixon was deep in the Watergate morass," he explained, "and, at the time of my fight over the effort to gut the Clean Air Act for energy reasons in March 1974, his resignation was a scant five months away."[95] The situation strengthened Train's bargaining position but hardly his popularity: "I seldom went to a meeting on energy and the environment without feeling like the proverbial bastard at a family reunion."[96]

In June Congress passed the Energy Supply and Environmental Coordination Act, giving auto makers two more years to implement the standards, while allowing the EPA to suspend sulfur oxide emission limits to encourage conversion of power plants from oil to coal. However, the law did not permanently weaken the standards or allow tall smokestacks as an alternative to reducing sulfur oxide pollution. The act did not, Muskie rejoiced, "do the damage that some in the administration had proposed."[97] Still, Train could not get the administration to focus more on conservation, despite arguing that "America held 6% of the world's population, but constituted more than a third of its energy demand."[98] He did have the EPA ask auto manufacturers to post fuel economy information on new cars, which the EPA then publicized.

Train's disagreement with the rest of the Nixon administration did not go unnoticed. But Nixon, in the final throes of Watergate, could not afford to dismiss the popular EPA chief, especially since Train "paid close attention to [his] congressional relationships. With the exception of Senator Scott [R-VA]," he said, "I had unfailing support from the Republican minority on the key Senate Committee on Public Works . . . 'during my tenure at EPA, it would have been impossible to have had a more supportive relationship than I had with this committee on a bipartisan basis.'"[99] After Nixon was forced to turn over secret White House tapes showing his complicity in the coverup of the scandal, he resigned on August 9, 1974. One of his last official acts was vetoing the budget for the EPA as excessive.

Over the subsequent thirty years, the Clean Water Act resulted in a noticeable improvement in the quality of the nation's water with less negative impact on the economy than its critics had predicted. Between 1972 and 1990 the United States spent roughly $50 billion on sewage treatment facilities, roughly what Nelson had estimated would be needed.

American waters remain a regulatory battlefield, with the Obama administration expanding areas covered by the Clean Water Act, while the Trump administration, backed by a Republican party now largely devoid of environmental advocates, pushed to limit the act's effects. The Biden administration is likely to resume the efforts to achieve cleaner waters.

The EPA's 2000 Water Quality Inventory estimated that 61 percent of rivers and streams, 54 percent of lakes, 49 percent of estuarine square miles, and 22 percent of assessed Great Lakes shoreline miles completely met the water quality standards. Even so, this left 300,000 river and shore miles and five million lake acres still polluted.[100] America's waters are much cleaner than they have been, but the goal of zero discharge and universal swimmable waters is still an ocean away.

CHAPTER NINE

Saving the Oceans

KEY EVENTS:
Marine Mammal Protection Act (1972)
Coastal Zone Management Act (1972)
Fishery Conservation and Management Act (1976)

Eight days after Richard Nixon became president, America's thinking about its oceans was suddenly upended. Just offshore from the lovely California coastal city of Santa Barbara, sometimes called "America's Riviera," a Union Oil drilling platform had a blowout. Before it was capped, a hundred thousand barrels of crude oil would gush into the sea, fouling hundreds of square miles of the Pacific Ocean and scores of miles of postcard-class coastline. It covered the nation's breakfast tables with wrenching images of oil-soaked seabirds, many of them dead. "My God, that was, I didn't realize how massive an oil spill that was until I went out there and took a look," said the stunned new secretary of the interior, Wally Hickel. "My God, that was a disaster."[1]

Public outrage wasn't helped on February 5 when Union Oil's president, Fred Hartley, told Edmund Muskie's Senate Subcommittee on Air and Water Pollution, "I think we have to look at these problems relatively. I am always tremendously impressed at the publicity that death of birds receives versus the loss of people in our country in this day and age."[2] Two days later, after consulting with the president, Hickel stopped all oil operations in the Santa Barbara Channel, an order that held until April.

A Different Ocean View

Throughout its history, the United States had seen its oceans as moats against the rest of the world and rich grounds for fishing (often overfishing), rather than resources needing protection. The arrival of offshore oil drilling moved Congress not so much to safeguard the seas as to apportion them between the states and the federal government. Little attention was paid to warnings from the deep, such as from oceanographer Jacques Cousteau, who warned that human dumping of toxins and wastes could poison seas and even oceans, leading to decreasing production of seafood and oxygen. "Public opinion can save our dying oceans," forecast Cousteau, "but I believe the oceans will have a narrow escape."[3] Even ten thousand oil spills a year, spitting into the seas anywhere from one to ten million barrels of oil, failed to rouse alarm.[4] Although the Johnson administration got Congress to pass a bill for studies and inventories of the coastal areas, it failed to provide any funding.[5]

But by the late 1960s damage to coastal regions was becoming inescapable. Through dredging and filling, the country's total wetlands had been cut by 60 percent.[6] While estuaries were estimated to produce up to two-thirds of seafood consumed by Americans—with some yielding more food per acre than the richest farmland—pollution, dredging, and filling had taken a massive toll. San Francisco Bay had lost all of its oyster production by 1930 and all of its clams by 1948, and its shrimp harvesting had collapsed from more than sixty million pounds annually to a minuscule ten thousand pounds.[7] Damage was also clear throughout the Pacific, Atlantic, and Gulf coastal regions.

Plans Land on the Coasts

After the Santa Barbara oil spill, with a request from Hickel for new project ideas, Russell Train decided to look at protecting the nation's coastal regions, with three-quarters of the nation's population residing nearby. Train established an interagency task force with the Interior Department to draft a proposal, telling the members, "I do not want word out to the Congressional Committees or other agencies that we are drafting legislation."[8] Seeing an opportunity on the coasts, Train knew that Senator Ernest Hollings (D-SC) was working on his own bill, and might try to preempt the administration.[9] "The clamor for protection of coastal zones was at the time much greater than demand for national land use regulation," wrote

John Whitaker. "Both population and industry were highly concentrated in coastal zones and recreational needs were expanding more rapidly in coastal areas."[10]

The Train committee's eventual proposal encouraged states to draft coastal management plans. The Department of the Interior would pay half the cost of developing the plan and then half the plan's operational costs. Plans would have to protect ecologically fragile areas, override local zoning laws, and follow federal regulations.[11] Hickel, Train, and Whitaker saw a political advantage in focusing on the coasts. The Interior Committees in both chambers of Congress were dominated by members from western, largely inland states, and they would be less likely to oppose something that did not affect their states. Hickel's support for environmental measures won him support from the press. The *Christian Science Monitor* commented, "Events so far indicate that Hickel is a very good secretary."[12] Hickel's praise from the media and environmentalists alarmed Nixon, who wrote to Ehrlichman, "This worries me. He may be caving in too much to his critics."[13]

Action on coastal zone management was delayed in part by jurisdictional disputes. The administration's original bill put the program in the Interior Department, but the House Merchant Marine and Fisheries Committee had insisted on it going to Commerce. The final language gave primary jurisdiction to Commerce, but with Interior having veto power. Congress finally passed the Coastal Zone Management Act in 1972, one of three major bills addressing the nation's oceans: one addressing the quality of the waters connecting the land to the sea, one focusing on the survival of the marine mammals—whales, dolphins, porpoises, seals—that carried much of the excitement and drama of the sea, and one seeking the preservation of the great ocean fisheries that supported both coastal economies and the oceanic ecosystem. Richard Nixon would not last his two terms, but legislation during that eight-year period would contribute dramatically to the health of both the nation's oceans and the creatures living in them.

The Coastal Zone Management Act aimed "to preserve, protect, develop, and where possible, to restore or enhance the resources of the Nation's coastal zone for this and succeeding generations."[14] State participation in coastal zone management planning would be completely voluntary, with no federal standards or management imposed on states not developing a plan. Grants would cover two-thirds of state costs of developing coastal management plans, and half the costs of creating new estuarine sanctuaries. This National Estuarine Sanctuaries Program eventually became the National Estuarine Research Reserve Program.

The administration was divided on the bill, with the EPA and the Department of the Interior opposed while the Council on Environmental Quality (CEQ) and Office of Management and Budget (OMB) favored it. Opponents argued that the bill might preempt a larger land use bill, already passed by the Senate and then before the House. Critics also argued that the bill gave the federal government too much power in the mandated review of state plans, while others bemoaned the lack of penalties for states not developing plans.

Nixon thought the bill's funding excessive. But, Whitaker wrote, "Nixon concluded that the overriding need to control land use planning in ecologically fragile coastal zones should not be delayed even though he preferred a national land use approach. . . . Because there was such strong public support for protection and control of the coastal zone, a presidential veto would undoubtedly be misunderstood—and it was just a week before the presidential election."[15] Nixon signed the act just before the 1972 election. To reduce cost, no funding was budgeted by the administration for two years. For the second year, Whitaker and Hollings managed to get $5 million, later increased by Congress to $12 million. Whitaker saw the joint effort as a strategy to win Hollings's support for other administration proposals.[16]

Unusually, the act required that federal actions in coastal zones must conform to state plans, giving states an additional incentive to develop a plan. The act gave states tremendous flexibility in management and in what areas were covered. It defined the coastal zone broadly as the sea and adjacent lands, to the extent that the shorelines have a direct and significant impact on the coastal waters. Washington state's plan won the first approval in 1976. Washington senators Henry Jackson and Warren Magnuson praised their state's plan as "a comprehensive and innovative method for management of its coastal zone."[17] All thirty-five eligible states, as well as territories, would participate in the program during the 1970s. By 2006 over 99 percent of the nation's shoreline was under the management of the act.[18]

In 1976 Congress returned to the issue. The Senate Commerce and Interior Committees, chaired by Magnuson and Jackson respectively, reported out similar bills giving money to coastal states to deal with coastal energy activity, including the impact of energy facilities and fixing related environmental damage. It also increased the federal share of the cost of coastal zone programs from 66 percent to 80 percent, plus $50 million annually for land acquisition to protect public beach access. "The Coastal Zone Management Act was designed to bring order to the planning process at the local level," declared Magnuson. "The bill the Senate has now passed will enable states to develop an adequate capability."[19] After the House reduced the spending, President Gerald Ford signed the bill in July.

Estuaries had gained protection from the 1972 Clean Water Act, whose National Estuary Programs allowed governors to nominate estuaries of national significance for the development of nonbinding management plans. Congress specified sixteen priority estuaries, including Chesapeake and San Francisco Bays.[20] Additional protection was given to wetlands, which were vital for fish and wildlife protection, among other benefits. Landowners needed to get permits from the Army Corps of Engineers for dredging or filling in wetlands linked to navigable waters. Resistance from landowners who argued that this was a "taking" reducing the value of their property would lead to significant litigation.[21]

In 1972 Nixon proposed special tax incentives to protect coastal wetlands. Wetlands "contain some of the most beautiful areas left on this continent," he declared. "These same lands, however, are often some of the most sought-after for development. As a consequence, wetland acreage has been declining as more and more areas are drained and filled for residential, commercial, and industrial projects."[22] Nixon's proposal, which limited tax depreciation for new structures and limited agricultural assistance for farming in wetlands, did not advance in Congress.

Keeping Marine Mammals Afloat

Controversy moved offshore with the drive to protect marine mammals—whales, dolphins, porpoises, and seals. Whales "are supposed to be under the protection of the International Whaling Commission," complained Supreme Court Justice William O. Douglas. "But it is almost wholly dominated by the commercial whaling interests. . . . [T]he killings since the 1920s now exceed all whale killings over the prior four-hundred-year period." Douglas concluded, "The whales have few friends in court."[23]

The slaughter had lowered many whale populations to critically low levels. The public was also upset about the slaughter of dolphins and porpoises caught in fishermen's nets, as well as the clubbing of seals. "The shifting fashions were not kind to another marine mammal, the fur seal of the North Pacific Ocean," Stewart Udall pointed out. "In its first twenty years of operation the Alaska company took enough sealskins to repay the entire cost of the Alaska purchase . . . by 1911 . . . only 5% of the original seal population remained."[24] Despite some international treaty limitations, the hunting of seals continued for the next sixty years. "Each spring some 250,000 harp seals are clubbed to death," wrote Douglas, "so that their pelts can be made into coats, handbags and luggage."[25]

In 1971, Senator Fred Harris (D-OK) and Representative David Pryor (D-AR) introduced a bill to ban the killing and importation of all marine mammals. Critics argued that not all these mammals were endangered, that some were crucial to the diets of Alaskan natives, and that the bill would require the United States to terminate an agreement with Canada and Japan that banned the killing of seals at sea and managed hunting elsewhere. Still, horror at pictures of seal hunting produced wide public support for this proposal. The administration countered with a bill to set up a commission to study the issue as well as a permit system for culling of the animals.

The House Merchant Marine and Fisheries Committee settled on a bill that would ban killing marine mammals but allow exceptions. Committee chairman Edward Garmatz (D-MD) sent the bill to the House floor on March 9, 1972. Opposition primarily came from those who thought the bill too weak. Garmatz attacked its opponents, calling them "not really conservationists—they are more properly referred to as preservationists—and their basic position seems to be that man should leave all animals alone. They blindly oppose all forms of wildlife management, disregarding the cold reality that the balance of nature has already been disrupted." John Dingell (D-MI), chairman of the relevant subcommittee, agreed: "It is not at all a weak bill. It is a strong bill, providing extensive and ample protection for marine mammals," adding, "The criticism of the preservationists . . . turns on the discretion which Congress vests in the secretaries [of interior and commerce]. . . . Before issuing any permit for the taking of marine mammals, the Secretary must first have it proven to his satisfaction that any taking is consistent with the purposes and policies of this act."[26] Mario Biaggi (D-NY) objected, "The Committee bill does not provide sufficient support and pressure for finding ways to catch tuna without killing porpoises and dolphins." But Biaggi's amendment to prohibit fishermen's incidental killing of these animals was rejected as too sweeping. Morris

Udall (D-AZ) argued that the bill's sixty-day moratorium on takings was insufficient, and Dingell and the House accepted his amendment for a five-year ban on killings of marine mammals. In March, the House passed the bill 362–10.[27]

The Senate passed its bill four months later. After the bills went through conference committee, President Nixon signed the bill on October 21, 1972, two weeks before election day. The month of October 1972, amid a presidential campaign with minimal mention of the environment, saw the Coastal Zone Management Act, the Marine Mammal Protection Act, and the Clean Water Act all become law—a high tide of water-based environmentalism.

The Marine Mammal Protection Act (MMPA) prohibited "the act of hunting, killing, capture and or harassment of any marine mammal; or, the attempt at such," and created a five-year moratorium on the import, export, or sale of any marine mammal or marine mammal part in the United States.[28] Authority to enforce the act was divided between the US Fish and Wildlife Service, under the Department of the Interior, and the National Marine Fisheries Service, under the Department of Commerce. The secretary of commerce had responsibility for whales, porpoises, dolphins, seals, and other sea lions. The secretary of the interior had responsibility for the other marine mammals, including walruses, polar bears, manatees, and sea otters.[29] The MMPA specifically preempted state laws, although it exempted Alaska natives.

In the early 1970s incidental dolphin deaths were running at over three hundred thousand a year, caused particularly by tuna fishermen in the Pacific.[30] To deal with the situation, the act directed the secretary of commerce, through the National Oceanic and Atmospheric Administration, "to immediately undertake a program of research and development for the purpose of devising improved fishing methods and gear so as to reduce to the maximum extent practicable the incidental taking of marine mammals in connection with commercial fishing."[31] The act granted the commercial fishing industry a two-year grace period, after which permits would be required for incidental deaths of marine mammals.[32] The act resulted in major changes in fishing techniques. Over the 1970s and early 1980s, after numerous court cases and quotas, incidental deaths had fallen to twenty thousand a year. Additional 1988 amendments to the MMPA, including requiring all US fishing boats to carry an official observer, produced the almost complete elimination of incidental deaths by the mid-1990s.[33]

The Commerce and Interior Departments could grant exceptions, but economic reasons alone would not qualify. To issue a waiver, the relevant secretary generally had to determine that a species was at its optimum sustainable population, and that the waiver would not reduce its population below that level.[34] The act also established the Marine Mammal Commission, a three-member panel appointed by the president to "conduct a continuing review" of the status of marine mammals and make recommendations on further measures.[35]

The act directed the secretary of state to try to negotiate international agreements to protect marine mammals.[36] Although the United States had persuaded most of the member nations in the International Whaling Commission to put a moratorium on whaling in 1972, it lacked the required two-thirds of nations to go into effect. The moratorium, albeit with loopholes, finally received the necessary support in 1982.[37] A 1979 Packwood-Magnuson Amendment threatened economic sanctions on any nation whose fishery operations diminished the implementation of a marine mammal treaty signed by the United States.[38] The combination of the Marine Mammal Act and the international moratorium on whaling has resulted in recovery of many mammal species.

Warren Magnuson Looks to the Sea

In the Senate, the bill had been managed by Magnuson, who over five decades would become a major force in protecting the health of the seas. After graduating from the University of Washington law school in 1929, he won a seat as a Democrat in the state House of Representatives in 1932. Two years later he became the King County prosecutor, and two years afterward was elected to Congress. In the House, Magnuson became close with another freshman, Lyndon Johnson. House Speaker Sam Rayburn brought the two to the attention of President Franklin Delano Roosevelt. Magnuson later said of Roosevelt, "He was very, very good to me . . . I played poker with Roosevelt in the White House."[39] Magnuson combined being a very hardworking congressman with the life of a Hollywood playboy and movie studio ally.[40]

After Pearl Harbor, Magnuson joined the navy, serving on the carrier *Enterprise* in the Pacific while remaining in Congress, until Roosevelt ordered all congressmen in service to return to Washington. In 1944 he advanced to the Senate. When Truman replaced Roosevelt, Magnuson continued to play poker at the White House with the new president, and played a powerful role in bringing jobs, military bases, and public power to his state. In 1955 Magnuson became chair of the Senate Commerce Committee, a position he would hold for the next twenty-three years.[41]

As chairman, Magnuson became deeply involved with ocean legislation, helping to push through a proposal from Hubert Humphrey (D-MN) to support ocean research. In pushing the bill, Magnuson used Cold War arguments, saying, "We're competing with the Soviets in the oceans as well as in space."[42] Magnuson also was instrumental in creating the National Oceanic and Atmospheric Administration. His aide Warren Featherstone Reid called him a "romantic" about the ocean.[43]

Johnson, who would be best man at Magnuson's second marriage, remarked, "Maggie can smile though more legislation than any other senator can get through by wheeling and dealing. Most legislators are burdened by 100 pounds of hate on their backs. Maggie doesn't hate anyone."[44] As Magnuson put it, "I had no trouble explaining my case to other senators. I didn't have any feuds. It was never a matter of wheeling and dealing. When you are through with an issue you don't hold a grudge."[45] Eugene McCarthy (D-MN) declared that "Maggie is the most loved man in the Senate."[46] Lady Bird Johnson later recalled, "We used to have a few vacation weekends with him and his lady love of the current time."[47] Magnuson was also close to John F. Kennedy, spending the day before Kennedy's inauguration at Kennedy's home. He stayed good friends with Johnson, recalling, "After the election, he [Johnson] would come around and grumble [about his job as vice-president]. I'd say, 'You asked for it and we [Rayburn and Magnuson] told you not to do it.'"[48]

After a surprisingly close reelection win in 1962, Magnuson added consumer protection to his legislative interests. Biographer Shelby Scates wrote, "By 1968 . . . nine major pieces of consumer protection bore the name Magnuson."[49] Ralph Nader said, "[Magnuson] would go on to become the greatest legislative consumer advocate of the century."[50] After Johnson became president, Magnuson worked closely with him on legislation, including the civil rights bills. Magnuson aide Jerry Grinstein commented that the different approaches of the men complemented each other in passing laws, noting, "Johnson used force to get his way. Magnuson engendered trust among his colleagues."[51] To Magnuson, "Lyndon was a good listener."[52] In contrast, "Nixon was a loner. He never had any particular contact with anybody except minions he'd have around him."[53]

Casting for a Fisheries Fix

Magnuson would bring considerable institutional clout and personal connection to his drive for the 1976 Fisheries Management and Conservation Act, commonly called the Magnuson Act. Advances in commercial fishing technology threatened to wipe out entire fisheries. Huge foreign factory fishing ships devastated vast stretches of the ocean, severely damaging fish habitat and frequently grossly overfishing an area.

Management of fisheries was not a new idea. Even in the laissez-faire 1920s, the decline of the Alaskan salmon fisheries spurred the Alaskan Fisheries Act of 1924, authorizing sufficient federal control over fishing seasons and methods to quickly revive the state's salmon fishery.[54] Magnuson became aware of the issue in 1966, when a supporter showed him the lights of Russian factory ships off the Washington coast. He contacted the president, demanding action. Johnson aide Joseph Califano told the president that Magnuson reported "a tremendous furor over the Soviet fleet. That commercial and sport fishermen in Washington were up in arms. The State Department isn't moving fast enough—he wants your personal attention."[55]

With diplomacy unsuccessful, Magnuson drafted a bill banning foreign fishing boats within two hundred miles of the American coast and reintroduced it for years. In December 1974 the Senate passed it 68–29, but the House took no action. The following March, Magnuson reintroduced the bill in the new Congress, promising "a much stronger bargaining position" for the United States in dealing with foreign fishing fleets.[56]

This time the House acted first, passing a similar bill that summer. The Senate took it up in January 1976. Opponents argued that such unilateral action was dangerous at a time when the United Nations was trying to reach an international agreement on the law of the sea. Mike Gravel (D-AK) warned, "If it sets up a whole host of potential areas of conflict, we have not addressed ourselves to the conservation problems with regard to fisheries.[57] Muskie (D-ME) responded, "I remind the Senator of our conversation we had with one of the Russian delegates at the [Law of the Sea] conference in Caracas. He had taken vigorous exception to our support of this 200-mile legislation. I suggested to him, 'You can take the step to avoid our taking unilateral action of this kind by simply voluntarily restricting your activities in our waters.'"[58] Added Ted Stevens (R-AK), the Russians "have admitted 100% overfishing in one year alone. One or two more years like that, and if those Soviet computers get screwed up again, we will really be in trouble."[59]

Muskie noted his own long advocacy for international arrangements, but "the Senator cannot promise there will be an agreement . . . so I am not content to wait, and I do not think we are going to jeopardize the Law of the Sea Conference."[60] Magnuson himself argued, "If we went fishing off the Japanese coast . . . early enough in the morning, the Japanese Diet would meet in the afternoon and throw us out. That is also true for all the countries that are fishing off our coast."[61]

Divisions did not follow either partisan or ideological lines. Joining the liberal Gravel in opposition, conservative Strom Thurmond (R-SC) insisted, "It is my belief US fishing rights are being and can be advanced through bilateral and multinational negotiations . . . the legislation would end a long-standing U.S. policy of not recognizing unilateral claims of oceans' jurisdiction."[62] Thurmond also emphasized the military's objections, quoting Chief of Naval Operations James L. Holloway's testimony, "The effect of a 200-mile territorial sea extending off the coasts of many countries would be detrimental to military mobility."[63] Magnuson answered that the bill's "provisions expressly disclaim any Congressional intent to affect navigation rights . . . the bill does not create any territorial sea."[64] John Durkin (D-NH) warned, "Large foreign fishing fleets have robbed coastal fishery resources . . . at least 14 species of fish have been endangered."[65]

Alan Cranston (D-CA), with Robert Griffin (R-MI), offered an amendment "to negotiate a compromise between the proponents of the bill's purposes, which is to protect our fisheries from depletion, and opponents of unilateral action by the United States."[66] Muskie retorted that the amendment "offers nothing . . . we are asked to go to a 1958 treaty, which has never protected anybody, as the source of relief to those people [fishermen] and their injured rights. . . . [W]hy do Senators think this measure is before the Senate today? Because nothing else has ever worked."[67] Magnuson added, "The 1958 convention, of course, is only binding on the ratifying nations, none of whom fish over our coast."

Commenting on lack of progress at the Law of the Sea Conference, Lee Metcalf (D-MT) noted, "So far the United Nations have been able to agree only on where to meet next." Edward Brooke (R-MA) agreed, "I also believe we must act now so our endangered fishing stocks can be protected by 1977. If we fail, fish life on our continental shelves may not survive the years of negotiation that will surely follow."[68] John Pastore (D-RI) put in, "We want an international agreement. We've been trying to get an international agreement. But the trouble is that those who are invading our waters, destroying our [lobster] pots, cleaning up our fishes, do not want agreement. . . . We are not saying that this become effective the minute it is enacted. We are saying it becomes effective in July of 1977. Why? Because we want the parties to work out an international agreement."[69] Bob Packwood (R-OR) chimed in, "We have waited 10 years. All we are asking in this bill, and we don't want it gutted with this [Cranston] amendment, is to give us a chance to protect our own fishing industry . . . we are going to have to set some standards so our fishermen do not overfish. . . . [A]s far as morality is concerned, the most moral people in the world are the fishermen, who have waited and waited."[70]

A test vote on the Cranston amendment showed it losing 64–31. Cranston told the Senate, "Having recognized defeat when it was sustained, having learned anew of the great strength of the Senator from Washington, the Senator from Maine, and their allies . . . I ask unanimous consent that I may withdraw my amendment."[71] The Senate passed the Fisheries Management and Conservation Act 77–19 on January 28, 1976.

The act banned foreign fishing fleets within two hundred miles of the US coast. Foreign fishing would be banned unless countries extended "substantially the same fishing privileges to vessels of the United States with respect to an equivalent fishery."[72] The act created eight regional fishery management councils, made up of American fishermen, aided by expertise from the National Marine Fisheries Service. For each fishery, the councils were to determine the maximum sustained yield to resist depletion, limiting overfishing to allow recovery of damaged fisheries.[73]

The Fisheries Act resulted in the major recovery of many American fisheries. The act originally exempted highly migratory species such as tuna, but this loophole was closed by a 1990 amendment.[74] To reduce overfishing by US fishermen, a further 1996 amendment cut allowable catch limits and reduced the number of boats with government buybacks.[75]

The Santa Barbara oil spill took a long time to clean up, and much longer to have its effect on American legislation. But after eight years, coastal zones, marine mammals, and crucial offshore fisheries had gained major protections, reversing dangerous threats that seemed on track to blight American coasts and the creatures defining the world's oceans. The Green Years extended far out into the deep blue.

CHAPTER TEN

Protecting Endangered Species

KEY EVENTS:
Endangered Species Preservation Act (1966)
Endangered Species Conservation Act (1969)
Endangered Species Act (1973)

"In New England they once thought blackbirds useless, and mischievous to the corn," observed Benjamin Franklin. "They made efforts to destroy them. The consequence was, the blackbirds were diminished; but a kind of worm, which devoured their grass, and which the blackbirds used to feed on, increased prodigiously; then, finding their loss in grass much greater than their saving in corn, they wished again for their blackbirds."[1] Possibly following Franklin's insight, in 1818 Massachusetts passed the earliest American action to protect wild animals: "An Act to prevent the destruction of certain useful birds." It noted that these birds "were instruments in the hands of Providence to destroy various noxious insects, grubs and caterpillars." The ranks of these favored birds included quail, partridge, woodcocks, snipes, larks, and robins, and a two-dollar fine would be assessed should bodies of these birds be found in a hunter's possession.[2]

It was a long flight path from Franklin's perception, and Massachusetts's second thoughts about killing particular species, to what would become one of the most striking achievements of the Green Years: the Endangered Species Act of 1973. For centuries, Americans were largely indifferent to the decimation and even elimination of animals, killing great numbers for economic and entertainment reasons. Awareness of the value of species preservation built slowly, but in the atmosphere of 1973 the Endangered Species Act passed overwhelmingly, with Republicans joining Democrats in speaking for the bill, finding arrangements to make it work, and defeating efforts to weaken it. Over the following decades, as lawsuits supporting tiny creatures stymied large projects, some of the act's original supporters were taken aback. But if they didn't always see the value of warding off extinction, Benjamin Franklin might have.

For centuries the concept of endangered animals would not have occurred to most Americans. The slaughter of individual animal species was sometimes part of a deliberate policy. In the 1630s the colonies of Virginia and Massachusetts Bay began paying bounties for the scalps of wolves. The statutes of Rhode Island Colony in 1639 and 1646 read, "All such who shall kill a Fox shall have six shillings and eight pence," and, "Newport shall pay four pounds for the killinge of a wolfe, and Portsmouth twentie shillings."[3] Laws giving payments for the slaughter of wolves and other large predators would continue through most of the twentieth century.[4]

The bison, or buffalo, of the American plains were slaughtered to deprive the Plains Indians of the animal that supplied most of their needs. An estimated one million bison were killed each year from 1872 to 1875. Although General Philip Sheridan reportedly had told the Texas legislature that buffalo should be exterminated to defeat the Indians, historian Dan Flores argued that this account is a false myth."[5] In 1874, President Ulysses Grant did veto a law to protect the buffalo to aid in the war on the Plains Indians. Two years later the House passed another protective bill, but it died in the Senate when news arrived of Custer's destruction at Little Bighorn, strengthening the argument for any tactic to weaken the Indians.[6]

Even after the defeat of the Plains tribes, the killing continued. The painter George Catlin lamented the species' disappearance, writing, "It is a melancholy contemplation for one who has travelled as I have, through these realms, and seen this noble animal in all its pride and glory, to contemplate it so rapidly wasting from the world."[7] Theodore Roosevelt wrote in 1885, "Gone forever are the mighty herds of the lordly buffalo . . . [T]he extermination of the buffalo has been [a] veritable tragedy of the animal world."[8] It took the near-extinction of the bison, down from plains-covering millions to a few hundred survivors, before many even grasped the concept of extinction. Bison were wiped out east of the Mississippi by 1800, and from most of the West by the 1880s. Yellowstone National Park was created in part to preserve the bison, estimated by 1900 to have dwindled to twenty-five.[9] Contrary to his reputation as favoring elimination of the buffalo, Sheridan urged expansion of Yellowstone to provide greater protection to buffalo and elk, successfully urged limitations on development there, and sent in the US Cavalry to run the park until the National Park Service was established in 1916.[10]

The passenger pigeon missed even the bison's narrow survival. From an estimated five billion in 1800—about a third of the total number of birds in the United States—passenger pigeons went totally extinct.[11] Other species, such as the eastern elk, expired without much notice. Other nineteenth-century casualties included the Steller's sea cow, the sea mink, the great auk, and the Labrador duck, not to mention various plants. Since the British first landed, an estimated five hundred North American species have been erased.[12] Zoologist Vincenz Zisweiler listed multiple ways humans wipe out other species, including (1) destruction of habitats, (2) introduction of foreign species, (3) overhunting, for food, other body parts, or sport, (4) elimination as alleged pests, (5) capture for live animal trade, (6) destruction by introduced diseases, and (7) overcollecting eggs.[13]

The Beginnings of Animal Protection

Dissent built slowly. As early as 1789 the English philosopher Jeremy Bentham, talking about the treatment of both slaves and animals, proposed, "The question is not, Can they talk? But, Can they suffer?"[14] In 1796 Reverend Nicholas Collins argued at the American Philosophical Society that birds should be protected from extinction until people better understood their role in nature.[15] Darwin's *Origin of Species* further challenged the idea of absolute differences between animals and humans. Stories featuring animals as central characters became popular in the 1890s. Ernest Seton's *Wild Animals I Have Known*, published in 1898, went through nine printings in eighteen months.[16]

The end of the nineteenth century saw more organized efforts to protect selected animals. George Bird Grinnell, editor of *Forest and Stream*, campaigned to end the hunting of bison in Yellowstone, while William Hornaday, head of the New York Zoo, organized the Bison Society to create a refuge. America also imported the idea of hunting not for meat but as a sport, particularly for gentlemen. Sportsmen's clubs began to proliferate after the Civil War, guided by "the unalterable love of fair play, the first thought of genuine sportsman."[17] The most notable was the Boone and Crockett Club, formed in 1887 by Grinnell and Roosevelt.[18]

Sportsmen encountered a problem. "The supply of game was declining rapidly," noted Thomas Dunlap. "To save their sport, hunters had to create a mass movement and call in the government to save the animals."[19] Sportsmen's clubs and magazines, such as the *American Sportsman, Forest and Stream, Field and Stream,* and the *American Angler,* launched toward the end of the nineteenth century, drove the creation of refuges and limits on hunting to prevent extinctions. By the 1920s most states imposed rules on hunting. Aldo Leopold of the University of Wisconsin, who taught the first course on wildlife management and wrote the first textbook on the subject, noted in 1933, "The history of American management [of animals was] until recently almost wholly a history of hunting controls."[20] Predators remained harshly regarded. Under the Animal Damage Control Act of 1931, the US Biological Survey paid bounties for killing wolves. The efforts were so successful that in all but the most remote locations wolf populations dropped sharply. Predators and prey both suffered from loss of habitat.

Wild animals initially fell under the jurisdiction of state governments. The Supreme Court, in *Martin v. Waddell,* ruled in 1842 that New Jersey had jurisdiction over the oysters in a privately owned mudflat. Subsequent cases expanded state authority. The first federal action came in 1868 when Congress banned killing certain fur-bearing animals in newly acquired Alaska.[21] The United States Fish Commission was created in 1871 to try to revive the nation's fisheries. In 1884 Congress created the Office of Economic Ornithology and Mammalogy, later renamed the Biological Survey, to research animals and, later, plants. However, the Biological Survey also increased the federal government's involvement in the killing of predators, particularly wolves, largely driven by the livestock industry. In the mid-1920s the survey added a Division of Predator and Rodent Control, using livestock industry funding to hire hunters to kill predators.[22]

Representative John F. Lacey (R-IA) grew up on a remote Iowa farm, feeling a closeness to nature that lasted his entire life, including a membership in the Boone and Crockett Club. He returned from the Civil War to become a lawyer and win election to Congress, eventually chairing the House Committee on Public Lands. The Lacey Act of 1894 gave the Department of the Interior power to arrest poachers and lawbreakers in the national parks. It was followed by the broader Lacey Act of 1900, driven by the extinction of the passenger pigeon, banning the transportation of illegally taken birds or bird parts across state lines—almost a forerunner of the later Endangered Species Act. At least as significantly, Lacey was an author of the Antiquities Act of 1906.

In 1903 Roosevelt established the first official wildlife refuge at Pelican Island, Florida. In 1899, before becoming president, Roosevelt had written, "I would like to see all harmless wild things, but especially all birds, protected in every way. . . . When I hear of the destruction of a species I feel just as if all the works of some great writer had perished; as if we had lost all instead of only part of Polybius or Livy."[23] Under Roosevelt, Congress created fifty-one national wildlife refuges. In the West, these were designed to preserve land for large mammals like elk and bighorn sheep. Elsewhere the emphasis was on wetlands that hosted migratory birds, along the nation's four north-south flyways.[24] Local Audubon Societies to protect birds grew into the National Association of Audubon Societies in 1905. In 1913 the Weeks-McLean Act gave the secretary of agriculture power to regulate duck and goose hunting, holding that migration classified waterfowl as interstate commerce.[25] The Migratory Bird Treaty Act of 1918 ratified a 1916 protective treaty with Canada. The Supreme Court rejected a challenge by Missouri, enforcing significant federal jurisdiction over wildlife.

The federal government now began to employ professionals in wildlife protection, first in the Biological Survey and then in the Migratory Bird Conservation Commission, established in 1929, charged with identifying lands for purchase to protect critical bird habitat. In *Hunt v. United States* in 1928, the Supreme Court gave the federal government authority over deer in an Arizona national park, ruling, "The power of the United States to thus protect its lands and property does not admit of doubt."[26] In 1931 the National Park Service banned poisoning predators in the national parks, with the new Park Service director Horace Albright pledging "total protection to animal life."[27] In his 1933 book *Game Management*, Leopold made cogent arguments against killing predators.

The Franklin D. Roosevelt administration created a New Deal for wildlife. The 1934 Fish and Wildlife Coordination Act required water development agencies to consult with wildlife agencies in planning projects, foreshadowing the National Environmental Policy Act in 1969. Other legislation assessed a fee on hunting licenses and taxed guns and ammunition, using the revenues to protect wildlife and acquire habitat.[28] The Biological Survey became the Fish and Wildlife Service (FWS) in the Department of the Interior, managing the nation's wildlife reserves under respected conservationist Jay N. Darling. By 1940, 160 new wildlife refuges had been established.[29] Support for wildlife started at the top. Informed that a proposed army artillery range at Henry Lake, Utah, might cause the extinction of the trumpeter swan, Roosevelt told the Secretary of War, "Henry Lake, Utah, must immediately be struck from the Army planning list for any purpose. The verdict is for the Trumpeter Swan and against the Army. The army must find a different nesting place."[30] The 1940 Bald Eagle Protection Act was later amended to include golden eagles as well as the endangered whooping crane. The Dingell-Johnson Act of 1950 taxed fishing equipment to support wildlife refuges.[31]

By the 1960s Americans understood more about the interrelationship of species.[32] "Cattlemen, whose herds had devastated so much of the original range, looked upon the prairie dog as a competitor for what was left," reported scientist Franklin Graham. "They induced the government to initiate their vast poisoning programs."[33] The billions of prairie dogs of the mid-1800s were reduced to less than 1 percent—also endangering the black-footed ferret, which fed on prairie dogs.[34] In 1965 the Interior Department limited the poisoning of prairie dogs to try to save the ferrets.[35] In 1962 Secretary of the Interior Stewart Udall appointed a committee led by Starker Leopold, the eldest son of Aldo Leopold, to investigate predator control. Its report strongly argued for protecting predators, stating, "Many animals which have never offended private property owners or public resource values are being killed unnecessarily," far more than necessary to protect people and livestock. The report suggested that predator control be limited, ideally only to individual animals that had killed livestock.[36]

Protecting Endangered Species: A Beginning

The same year, the FWS created an endangered species committee, later the Office of Endangered Species, which published the first list of sixty-three species facing extinction and was charged with devising plans to protect them. "Who are we to say that those who come after us may never see some of today's rare and endangered species?" asked Rachel Carson in *Audubon Magazine* in 1962. "What right do we have to destroy the scientific record contained in a living species? How do we know that we may not have great need of what it has to tell?"[37]

In 1964 the Land and Water Conservation Fund Act authorized the secretary of the interior to purchase land for the preservation of wildlife. When some in Congress complained that such powers should be explicitly conferred by Congress, the administration decided to prepare further legislation. The path went through the House Subcommittee on Fisheries and Wildlife Conservation, chaired by John Dingell Jr. (D-MI). When Dingell was six, his father, John D. Dingell Sr., was elected to the House from Detroit. As a congressional page, Dingell Jr. was present when Roosevelt asked Congress for a declaration of war after the bombing of Pearl Harbor. After service in World War II, the younger Dingell became an attorney, and met his first wife during a summer as a park ranger in Colorado. When his father died in 1955 the twenty-nine-year-old Dingell won the seat, beginning a six-decade career strongly supporting healthcare and civil rights. And although he was considered the House voice for the automobile industry, he also began his crusade to protect the environment. He later recalled, "[Dad] would always see to it that my brother and I had the means of hunting and fishing and enjoying the out-of-doors. . . . Made a conservationist of me."[38] In 1963 Dingell sponsored bills to establish federal clean water standards and allowing government to sue businesses for destroying fish and waterfowl. Three years later he proposed national air quality standards. Dingell would coauthor the National Environmental Policy Act (NEPA) in 1969 and play a large role in enacting the Clean Water Act.[39]

In January 1966 the *New York Times* reported, "A fight by conservationists to save certain species of American fish and wildlife from extinction is rapidly losing ground to bulldozers, pesticides, explosives and apathy."[40] Interior Secretary Udall warned that if humans continued to "encroach on priceless habitat, we run the risk of damaging these and other forms of life as well."[41] That spring, Dingell held hearings before his fisheries subcommittee to evaluate federal efforts "to properly manage all wildlife resources." Dingell attacked "indiscriminate trapping, shooting, and poisoning programs."[42] Dingell's hearings, and complaints about the government's limited and ill-defined authority, led the Johnson administration to propose and Congress to pass the Endangered Species Preservation Act of 1966, aimed at protecting native endangered species.[43] It established the National Wildlife Refuge System, consolidating management of more than two hundred refuges. The act directed government agencies to protect threatened species in consultation with FWS, but only to a "practicable" extent and when consistent with that agency's missions. Protection of endangered species was ironclad only in the refuges, and the act did not address trade in the body parts of endangered species.[44]

The act gave the secretary of the interior $5 million a year to purchase land for additional refuges and empowered him to list endangered fish and wildlife facing extinction and protect habitat. The first list included the timber wolf, grizzly bear, Florida panther, Florida manatee, whooping crane, and more than seventy other species.[45] In 1967 Dingell sought to strengthen the act, forbidding the importing of pelts from endangered animals, with wide public support. "The wild creatures that are man's companions on the earth are rapidly disappearing," warned the *New York Times*. "There are 250 species—the blue whale, the polar bear and the leopard, the fearsome tiger and humble alligator—now facing extinction. Man, the great predator, preys upon these animals, recklessly and relentlessly in pursuit of money."[46] Wayne Aspinall assured a constituent urging his support, "You are quite right in stating that I am interested in and in favor of intelligent conservation legislation.[47]

In August 1968 Dingell's bill passed the House without opposition, but opposition from furriers stalled the bill in the Senate. The *New York Times* objected, "The fur trade's publicity campaign to promote a fashion for exotic spotted cats . . . is hastening to extinction some of the rarest and most beautiful mammals on the face of the earth."[48] Still, the congressional session concluded without a new law. Although furriers continued their opposition in the next session, environmental support was enough to overcome it. The Endangered Species Conservation Act of 1969 passed Congress almost unanimously.[49] Signing it, President Richard Nixon called the bill "the most significant action this nation has ever taken in an international effort to preserve the world's wildlife."[50]

The act extended protection to invertebrates, amphibians, and reptiles, and expanded the Lacey Act to prohibit interstate trade in illegally taken reptiles, amphibians, and crustaceans. Species outside the United States now qualified for the endangered species list. Still, domestic and foreign species received different levels of protection. The act directed the secretary of the interior to facilitate an international conference on the protection of threatened species. In 1973 the resulting Convention on International Trade in Endangered Species of Wild Fauna and Flora banned international trade in endangered species. The 1969 act also gave the secretary the authority to list species threatened with extinction and control their import and export. Additional money from the Land and Conservation Fund could be spent on each project to buy land for species protection. However, the act did not allow the secretary to restrict trade in a species until it was threatened with worldwide extinction.[51]

In 1970 Interior Secretary Wally Hickel used his new authority to list eight species of whales as endangered. He also banned the import of whale products and effectively ended American whaling by the end of 1971. Hickel later recalled, "I said, 'What's going to happen when there's no whales left?' 'Well, we'll have to find a replacement.' I said, 'Find the replacement now. I'm going to put those whales on the endangered species list.'"[52] The earlier endangered species acts allowed for hardship exemptions. Hickel's successor, Rogers Morton, granted the first exemption in late 1971, lifting the ban on hunting endangered whales. By the end of the year thirty-seven exemptions had been granted, and thirty thousand tons of oil from endangered sperm whales was imported.[53]

In 1970, after an NBC documentary showed wolves being hunted from a helicopter, Representatives John Saylor (R-PA) and David Obey (D-WI) introduced legislation to ban hunting from aircraft. Saylor, a lifetime hunter, denounced the "low breed" of people who used aircraft to hunt. He noted that only five thousand wolves remained in North America, with four thousand killed in the previous four years. The bill passed the House but not the Senate. Saylor and Obey reintroduced the bill in 1971, following another NBC documentary showing hunters in helicopters chasing polar bears. They gained support by pointing out that in just the previous year, seven hundred eagles had also been killed. With support from Gaylord Nelson in the Senate, the Airborne Hunting Act passed both houses and was signed by President Nixon.

Saylor then attacked the Interior Department's predator control program, which poisoned wolves, coyotes, mountain lions, and other predators. "The war on predators has been waged with little scientific knowledge of their beneficial roles," he charged, "with little moral or ethical consideration for man's responsibility in conserving natural life as an integral part of the environment."[54] In 1971, the Council on Environmental Quality and the Interior Department studied predator control and concluded, "Not only are many of the several hundred field agents the same former 'trappers,' but . . . [t]he substantial monetary contribution by the livestock industry serves as a gyroscope to keep the bureaucratic machinery pointed towards the familiar goal of general reduction of predator populations."[55] Responding unhappily to the study's recommendations to eliminate most use of poison, House Agriculture Committee chairman William Poage (D-TX) accused Russell Train and an Interior Department official, "You love coyotes more than sheep."[56]

In his 1972 environmental message, Nixon rejected "the old notion that 'the only good predator is a dead one,'" and shortly issued an executive order prohibiting agencies from poisoning predators on federal lands.[57] A month later the EPA banned the interstate shipment of several poisons for use in predator control. The 1972 Federal Environmental Pesticide Control Act then required states to follow federal rules on poisoning predators.[58] In March 1974 Nixon met with Poage and agricultural leaders who claimed that the poison ban was ruining the sheep industry, but refused to rescind the order.[59] Interior Department statistics showed few requests for exemptions from the ban and minimal loss of animals. But in 1976 President Gerald Ford weakened the ban, approving the use of sodium cyanide on federal lands.[60]

Wild burros and horses had been killed for decades, initially to deprive American Indians of their use. The Wild Horses and Burro Act of 1959 and then the Wild and Free-Roaming Horses and Burros Act of 1971 moved against the practice, ultimately banning the taking of the animals on federal lands. A supporter wrote Senator Henry Jackson, a cosponsor of the bill, "I never expected to write you about anything as I'm very strongly opposed to your pro-Vietnam views. . . . You must be a good and kind man to defend the wild horses."[61]

Environmentalists still felt that the endangered species laws were too weak and limited. Supreme Court Justice William O. Douglas, a fervent environmentalist, wrote in 1972, "The killing of alligators had greatly increased; some 127,000 were killed in 1968, 1969 and 1970. . . . Most of the hides went to an Atlanta middleman who sold the hides to Japan."[62] The growth of environmental consciousness after 1969 built momentum for a stronger law. Protecting animals, advocates realized, required protection of their habitats. In 1968, on his way out, Udall wrote, "If we do our work well, and capitalize on the insights science gives us into habitat maintenance, within a decade there should be no more endangered species of fish or wildlife."[63]

Endangered Species Find Refuge in Law

In 1972 Dingell introduced the bill that would become the Endangered Species Act, supporting all threatened or endangered species, and closing the exemptions loophole in the 1969 act. The bill was attacked, Dingell noted, "by belittling the species it seeks to protect. How easy is it to dismiss the protection of a fish, a mollusk or even a plant?"[64] President Nixon also called for "a stronger law to protect endangered species of wildlife."[65] The proposal, introduced by Dingell in the House and Mark Hatfield (R-OR) in the Senate, did not pass in 1972. When Dingell reintroduced his bill in 1973, the Nixon administration supported a similar Senate proposal. Before the Senate Commerce Committee, Samuel R. Pierce, general counsel for the treasury, cited Nixon's position that "the limited scope of existing laws requires new authority to identify and protect endangered species before they are so depleted that it is too late."[66]

When the Senate Subcommittee on the Environment held hearings on the bill on June 18 and 21, 1973, Ted Stevens (R-AK) declared, "The Subcommittee should be ready following these hearings to once again report to the Senate a strong and sufficient species protection bill."[67] E. U. Curtis Bohlen, the deputy assistant secretary of the interior for fish and wildlife and parks, testified,

Our bill follows closely the precedent established by the Congress in 1966 and 1969, when it enacted the first legislation to protect fish and wildlife endangered in the United States and abroad. . . . Even though we may not be able to save all endangered species, we must make an effort. One way to accommodate that effort is to act before a species reaches the level of being in imminent danger of extinction.[68]

Harrison Williams (D-NJ) argued for his even stronger bill, telling the subcommittee that it would "provide increased protection by the Federal Government for endangered species of fish and wildlife. In addition, it would initiate a program of protection for endangered flora."[69] Environmentalists preferred Williams's bill. Tom Garrett, wildlife director for Friends of the Earth, testified,

Senator Williams's bill has one monumental improvement over any other bill. The definition of "taking" in his bill has been widened to include degradation of habitat. . . . We are pleased with the inclusion of plants in the protection in Senator Williams's bill and Congressman Dingell's bill. . . . We particularly welcome the emphasis on land acquisition in these bills . . . if we do not preserve the habitat of species . . . whether or not plants or animals are protected from deliberate molestation becomes, eventually, academic.[70]

Witness after witness testified for the bill. Maxwell E. Rich, executive vice-president of the National Rifle Association, stated, "We are in full accord with the purpose of the act."[71] Again, the main objections came from the fur industry, whose spokesmen objected to some environmentalists' flat condemnation of hunting animals for fur. The biggest concern, raised by Stevens, was over preempting state regulation. Williams responded that the bill "in no way limits the power of any state to enact legislation or regulations more restrictive than the provisions of the act."[72] On July 24, 1973, the Senate passed the bill 92–0. "While the bill was not perfect," declared Stevens, "I believe it takes a major step in the protection of American endangered and threatened species."[73]

The atmosphere in the House had become more responsive. In 1972 environmentalists and other liberals successfully challenged Aspinall in the Democratic primary for his House seat, opening up the Interior Committee chair for the more sympathetic James Haley (D-FL). As the committee hearings opened, the Convention on International Trade in Endangered Species of Wild Fauna and Flora (CITES) opened for nations to sign in Washington. CITES set up separate classifications for endangered and threatened species, requiring import and export permits for trade in each species, and regular meetings to discuss enforcement and modifications to the agreement.

On September 18, 1973, the House took up the act, H.R. 37. Leonor Sullivan (D-MO), chair of the Committee on Merchant Marine and Fisheries, opened debate by declaring, "H.R. 37 should be enacted at the earliest possible moment. . . . [T]hat additional protection for endangered species and plants is necessary is indisputable . . . for the most part, the principal threat to animals stems from destruction of their habitat. . . . H.R. 37 will meet this problem with funds for acquisition of critical habitat through the use of the land and water conservation fund."[74] Dingell stated, "H.R. 37 amends and extends laws now on the books . . . [First,] it extends protection to animals which may become endangered, as well as those which are now endangered. . . . Second, it extends protection to animals which are in trouble in any significant part of their range. . . . Third, it makes taking of such animals a Federal offense."[75] William F. Goodling, of Pennsylvania, the committee's ranking Republican, assured his party members, "H.R. 37, as reported out by the committee unanimously, embodied the vast majority of proposals of the [Nixon] administration."[76]

In response to questions from Don Young (R-AK) on whether the bill would interfere with Alaskan natives' hunting rights under the Marine Mammal Protection Act, Dingell assured him that "the Secretaries of Commerce and Interior clearly have adequate authority to regulate subsistence hunters."[77] James R. Grover (R-NY) noted, "I know of no opposition to H.R. 37."[78] Frank Annunzio (D-IL) appealed, "Passage of this measure today will be one more step toward righting a serious wrong. Simply stated—many of the thousands of animal species which have disappeared from the face of the Earth have gone because of the interference of mankind."[79] Don Clausen (R-CA), a once and future opponent of environmentalists on many bills, urged, "The need for this legislation is overwhelming."[80] In the face of widespread public support, last-ditch efforts to weaken the bill failed.

Dingell downplayed his role as floor manager—and noted the sweeping support for the measure—by saying, "A reasonably bright herding dog could have run the floor on the Endangered Species Act without any change in result."[81] No member spoke against the bill, which passed 391–12. "Passing the Endangered Species Act . . . was not a partisan process. It was a genuine meeting of the minds," Dingell observed much later. "We liberals came together with conservatives who understood that 'conserve' is the core concept of both conservation and conservatism. Today, small 'c' conservatives are not even on the Endangered Species List; they're extinct."[82]

The conference committee followed the Senate language defining "taking" as actions that might harm a listed species, rather than the House version banning only directly injuring or killing a listed animal.[83] The reconciled bill passed the Senate unanimously and the House 345–4.[84] President Nixon signed the bill on December 28, 1973, declaring, "Nothing is more priceless and more worthy of preservation than the rich array of animal life with which our country has been blessed."[85] Although Nixon worried about the costs of the bill, he signed it after the Office of Management and Budget assured him that "Interior and Commerce might implement strict management guidelines to hold down costs."[86]

The act sought to "provide a means whereby the ecosystems upon which endangered species and threatened species depend may be conserved, to provide a program for the conservation of such endangered species and threatened species, and to take such steps as may be appropriate to achieve the purposes of the treaties and conventions set forth."[87] Now, killing—or even harassing—endangered species was prohibited throughout the nation rather than just in certain refuges. The final act incorporated Williams's concept of protecting the habitat of endangered species. The act enjoined all federal agencies to take responsibility for protecting endangered or threatened species on lands under their jurisdiction. The Endangered Species Act also protected threatened species, defined as "any species which is likely to become an endangered species with the foreseeable future throughout all or a significant portion of its range."[88] Threatened species received a lower level of protection, which required the assent of the state involved. The Endangered Species Act was originally authorized for five years, to be reauthorized every five years for the first two decades.[89] The act allowed private citizens to petition the secretary to list a species and receive a formal hearing.[90]

Although the act was notable for expanding endangered species protection to plants and many tiny animal species, most of the debate focused on protecting large animals. Dingell talked of protecting American animals such as the timber wolf and wolverine and nonnative species such as elephants and kangaroos.[91] Williams observed, "Most animals are worth very little in terms of dollars and cents . . . the pleasure of simply observing them . . . is unmeasurable."[92] In signing the bill, Nixon made no mention of protecting plants, celebrating "the needed authority to protect an irreplaceable part of our national heritage—threatened wildlife."[93]

The near-unanimous support for the act would not last. Historian Shannon Petersen noted, "To many politicians, the ESA must have appeared to be a win-win situation, which seemed especially true because no significant special interest group came forward to oppose it. . . . Few at the time opposed the ESA because no one anticipated how it might interfere significantly with economic development or personal property interests."[94] Petersen noted that no one in Congress, in all the committee and floor discussion, anticipated that the ban of taking an endangered species might lead to regulation of activities on private property. Even most of the environmental community did not envision the act creating land use regulations.[95]

When the act started having an economic impact, or interfering with public or private projects, it drew a strong backlash. Conservatives attacked the Endangered Species Act for hurting land values when it blocked development. Ranchers criticized the protection of wolves, which would occasionally kill livestock. Yet the first major legal case involving the act, the 1975–1976 delay in constructing an interstate highway that would threaten the habitat of the Mississippi sandhill crane, did not harm the popularity of the act. The crane was the kind of animal people and politicians expected to protect, and the interstate was easily rerouted. But when construction of Tellico Dam on the Little Tennessee River was halted by the 1973 discovery of the snail darter—a small fish thought to live only in this river—the situation was different. The snail darter was listed as an endangered species in 1975 and a portion of the river was deemed a critical habitat. Legal action halted the dam while the case was appealed to the Supreme Court. The Supreme Court, finding in 1978 that "the value of endangered species is incalculable," ruled for the darter and against the dam.[96]

But as the litigation was proceeding, the Senate acted to amend the law. On April 12, 1978, John Culver (D-IA) and Howard Baker (R-TN), now minority leader, introduced a bill to create a seven-member cabinet-level committee, nicknamed the "God Squad," with the authority to exempt federal agencies from the requirements of the Endangered Species Act. The bill passed the Senate 94–3 and the House 384–12, and was signed by President Jimmy Carter. The "God Squad" exemption has been granted only twice, for the whooping crane in 1978 and the northern spotted owl in 1991. To Baker's dismay, the committee refused to exempt protection of the snail darter. Baker eventually persuaded Congress to pass an exemption allowing completion of the dam. Ironically, snail darters were also discovered in nearby streams, while the dam failed to live up to its promised benefits.

In the coming years, a widening gap would emerge between those believing that all species had a right to exist and those believing that only popular or monetarily valuable animals deserved protection. As a freshman, Young voted for the Endangered Species Act. Much later, when he became chairman of the House Resources Committee, Young asserted—contrary to much of the public record—that Congress "envisioned trying to protect, you know, pigeons and things like that. We never thought about mussels and ferns and flowers and all those subspecies of squirrels and birds."[97]

But while there has been strong pressure to amend or repeal it, the Endangered Species Act remains the law of the land. The Sierra Club's Michael McCloskey wrote in 2019 that the act "remains the first and most far-reaching federal law imposing controls over large areas of private land. . . . Efforts to repeal and fatally wound it have never made it through."[98] In the face of an unprecedented wave of species extinctions, the Endangered Species Act may seem ineffective.[99] Yet experience shows that listing a species often can aid its recovery. Half of the species listed appear to have benefited from the act's protection. By the end of the 1990s twenty-nine species—including the gray wolf and the bald eagle—had improved their status, either upgrading from endangered to threatened or escaping the Fish and Wildlife list entirely.[100] Half a century later, the living landscape of America is steadily shaped and protected by a law that could not be passed today.

CHAPTER ELEVEN

Tracking Toxins across Land and Sea

KEY EVENTS:
Resource Recovery Act (1970)
Environmental Pesticide Control Act (1972)
Marine Protection, Research and Sanctuaries Act (1972)
Resources Conservation and Recovery Act (1976)
Toxic Substances Control Act (1976)

One of the most influential figures of the Green Years died just as the moment was getting under way, before she could see any of the historic legislation that reshaped America's lands and waters. But Rachel Carson's voice, warning of the lethal threat of chemicals and evoking humanity's deep connections to and dependence on the sea, echoed through the public debate of the following decade. For a century, the American conservation movement had focused on preserving places and inviting people to visit them. Only relatively late, after chemicals, old car bodies, and what was delicately called solid waste had been strewn thickly onto land and in water, did the understanding arise among Americans of the need to address not only the preservation of the natural world but also its poisoning.

The increasing, and increasingly wealthy, American population created a massive growth in waste products from industry and consumer goods, often littering the countryside. "As the number of factories and the size and scale of their production increased, so did their impact on the environment," noted historian Samuel Hays. "Persistent growth in both consumption and production led to the persistent growth in waste."[1] Annually,

Americans threw away 80 million tons of paper products, 100 million tires, 60 billion cans, and 30 billion glass bottles. In 1969 the estimated solid waste produced in the United States equaled 4.3 billion tons.[2] Surprisingly, half was agricultural wastes, notably manure and animal products. Whereas the average American in 1920 tossed 2.75 pounds of garbage daily, by 1970 the average daily refuse pile had reached 5 pounds.[3]

And much of it was toxic.

The postwar years saw a massive explosion in the use of chemicals, which became an increasing part of the American experience. The 127 million pounds of pesticides produced in the United States in 1947 had almost quintupled by 1960. Herbicides, used to kill weeds and other unwanted growth, also proliferated, covering over a hundred million acres by 1959.[4] When it was introduced during World War II, DDT was the most effective insecticide ever seen. For the next twenty years, DDT and its derivatives were almost universally applied, earning Swiss chemist Paul Mueller the 1948 Nobel Prize in Medicine. Yet even during the war there was concern about its toxicity. In 1945 Clarence Cottam, a scientist at the Interior Department, warned that DDT "will kill a lot of things we don't want killed. It kills beneficial insects as well as obnoxious insects."[5] Evidence of its harm continued to mount as tree-spraying campaigns resulted in dramatic drops in songbird populations. DDT residue was found everywhere, including in penguins and fish in Antarctica, where it had never been used.

In 1962, the crisis found its chronicler.

Rachel Carson Shows Man's Impact on the World

Born on a farm in Pennsylvania, Carson earned a master's degree from Johns Hopkins in 1932, but her family's finances kept her from going further. She started working at the US Bureau of Fisheries, later to become the US Fish and Wildlife Service, as an aquatic biologist. Carson later commented, "Eventually it dawned on me that by becoming a biologist I had given myself something to write about."[6] She published her first book, *Under the Sea-Wind*, in 1941. The *New York Times* called it "skillfully written as to read like fiction but is in fact a scientifically accurate account of life in the ocean."[7] Carson became editor-in-chief of publications for the Fish and Wildlife Service. Her book *The Sea Around Us*, published in 1951, became a bestseller—and reawakened sales of *Under the Sea-Wind*. The *Times* commented, "Once or twice in a generation does the world get a physical scientist with literary genius."[8]

The Sea Around Us was an immediate sensation. It spent eighty-six weeks on the *Times* bestseller list, nine of its fourteen chapters ran in the *New Yorker*, and it won the National Book Award for Nonfiction. It also made points about the sea, and humanity's connection to it, that resonated in later debates on ocean protection. "It is a curious situation that the sea, from which life first arose, should now be threatened by the activities of one form of that life," wrote Carson. "But the sea, though changed in a sinister way, will continue to exist; the threat is rather to life itself."[9] The success of *The Sea Around Us* enabled Carson to write full-time and gave her credibility when something else came up.

In 1957 a friend wrote to Carson describing the effect that DDT had on a nearby bird sanctuary. Carson began researching the issue, but in early 1960 she learned she had metastatic breast cancer. Despite side effects from radiation therapy, she kept writing, spending four years reviewing hundreds of existing studies showing the damages from chemicals. "I guess that all that sustains me," she wrote, "is a serene inner conviction that when, at last, the book is done, it is going to be built on an unshakeable foundation."[10]

Excerpts from *Silent Spring* appeared first in the *New Yorker* in June 1962. The chemical industry quickly counterattacked, labeling Carson a communist or an environmental extremist. One company tried to get the publisher to withdraw the book.[11] "Perhaps not since the classic controversy over Darwin's *The Origin of Species*," wrote her biographer Paul Brooks, "has a single book been more bitterly attacked by those who felt their interests threatened."[12]

In *Silent Spring*, Carson warned, "As man proceeds toward his announced goal of the conquest of nature, he has written a depressing record of destruction, directed not only against the earth he inhabits but against the life that shares it with him."[13] She declared, "It is not my contention that chemical insecticides must never be used. I do contend that we have put poisonous and biologically potent chemicals indiscriminately into the hands of persons largely or wholly ignorant of their potentials for harm."[14] In a statement with a deeply personal resonance, she argued, "Man, alone of all forms of life, can *create* cancer-producing substances," and warned, "We tolerate cancer-causing agents in our environment at our peril."[15] Anticipating critics, the book included a fifty-five-page appendix citing six hundred principal sources. "This appendix," wrote Stewart Udall, "was Rachel Carson's way of saying to her critics, 'Here is your substantiation. Tear it apart if you can.'"[16]

Carson's environmental impact was dramatic. When she testified in a Senate Commerce Committee hearing on pesticides in 1963, largely driven by a CBS Reports special, "The Silent Spring of Rachel Carson," Abraham Ribicoff (D-CT) told her, "You are the lady who started all this." Ernest Gruening (D-AK) said that *Silent Spring* would change the course of history the way *Uncle Tom's Cabin* had changed attitudes before the Civil War.[17] After reading the *New Yorker* excerpts, President John F. Kennedy ordered his Presidential Science Advisory Committee to study the issue. In its report, issued in May 1963, the committee concluded, "The accretion of residues in the environment [can] be controlled by orderly reduction in the use of persistent pesticides. As a first step, the various agencies of the Federal Government might restrict wide-scale use of persistent insecticides except for necessary control of disease vectors. . . . Elimination of the use of persistent toxic pesticides should be the goal."[18] The *Christian Science Monitor* headline read, "Rachel Carson Stands Vindicated."[19]

Before the Senate Committee on Commerce, Carson urged "an independent commission . . . made up of citizens of high professional competence . . . with the power to resolve conflicts [about pesticides] and make decisions on the basis of what the public interest as a whole demands."[20] No such action was taken at the time. Then, in November 1963, five million dead fish were found floating on the surface of the Mississippi River, victims of the pesticide endrin, which Carson had called "the most toxic of all chlorinated hydrocarbons," making DDT "seem by comparison almost harmless."[21] This new disaster gave powerful support to Carson's arguments, and in December 1963 she received the Audubon and Cullum Medals and election to the American Academy of Arts and Letters.[22] Yet her cancer was progressing, and she died on April 14, 1964, at the age of fifty-six. "What made *Silent Spring* an ecology primer for millions," assessed Udall, "was Carson's skill as a simplifier, her uncanny ability to use science as a mirror, reflecting its subtleties in the materials of life itself . . . 'Silent Spring' was, in effect, the first global environmental impact statement prepared by a scientist."[23] At Carson's funeral, Udall served as an honorary pallbearer.

Pesticides Start to Stir Policy

As secretary of the interior, Udall ordered, "It is essential that all pesticides, herbicides, and related chemicals be applied in a manner fully consistent with the protection of the environment . . . the guiding rule for the Department shall be that when there is a reasonable doubt regarding the environmental effects of the use of a given pesticide, no use should be made."[24] His position set off a conflict with the Forest Service, which was carrying out widespread spraying, a dispute that Udall called "essentially kind of a little cold war between Interior and Agriculture."[25]

Theoretically, the Department of Agriculture regulated pesticides under the Federal Insecticide, Fungicide and Rodenticide Act (FIFRA), but over two decades the department had initiated criminal proceedings only twice and investigated fewer than sixty out of an estimated fifty thousand annual pesticide accidents. It had not even set up a procedure to ban unsafe pesticides.[26] Oversight was by the department's Pesticide Regulation Division, which mainly responded to farmers and other pesticide users. Appropriations for FIFRA were controlled by the House Appropriations Committee's agriculture subcommittee, dominated by Chairman Jamie Whitten (D-MS). Whitten was so pro-pesticide that he wrote a book, *That We May Live*, rebutting *Silent Spring*, which he called "not a balanced account of the place of pesticides in the world. [Americans] must know that its conclusions are not endorsed by the vast majority of scientists and physicians."[27]

In 1964 Congress acted to strengthen FIFRA, shifting the burden of determining a chemical's safety from the government to the manufacturer. When President Lyndon Johnson signed the bill, he declared, "By closing loopholes which permitted pesticides to be sold before they were fully tested, this bill safeguards the health and the lives of all of our fellow Americans. I am sorry that one voice which spoke so often and so eloquently for measures like this—the voice of Rachel Carson—is still today. She would have been proud of this bill and of this moment."[28] Describing the change, the *New York Times* said approvingly, "Under the new amendment to the law, the department would have the authority to prevent the sale of pesticides until their safety had been established."[29] But the Agriculture Department, seeing its mandate as increasing farm productivity, did little.

In 1968 the General Accounting Office, the congressional watchdog agency, attacked the Department of Agriculture for not acting to protect the public from "misbranded, adulterated or unregistered pesticides," noting that the department had neither removed potentially dangerous pesticides from the market nor reported the violations of FIFRA it had discovered.[30] The next year, a House investigation found that from 1964 to 1969 the Department of Health, Education and Welfare had objected to the registration of some 1,600 pesticide products, yet the Pesticides Regulation Division of the Agriculture Department had registered "many, if not most" of them.[31]

Strengthening the Resistance to DDT

Every year beginning in 1966, Senator Gaylord Nelson regularly introduced a bill to ban DDT due to "overwhelming evidence of damage to the environment," but it went nowhere.[32] In 1969, responding to public concern, the Nixon administration limited DDT's use in residential areas. The next year, the Interior Department moved to ban sixteen pesticides, including DDT, on lands under its jurisdiction. But industry appeals blocked the ban while the legal process unfolded. At the same time, the Agriculture Department proposed phasing out DDT use for fruits and vegetables, except when "essential," but this too was appealed by the chemical companies. Moreover, use of DDT for cotton fields, 75 percent of DDT use, was untouched.[33] Nelson complained angrily, "No single use of DDT in the United States has been stopped." Although Nelson urged an immediate halt to DDT's use and manufacture as "an imminent hazard to the public," Secretary of Agriculture Clifford Hardin denied imminent danger.[34] Facing environmentalist attacks on the administration's position, Nixon's science advisor Lee DuBridge warned, "Pesticides are straining our image on the whole environmental issues."[35]

As soon as the Environmental Protection Agency (EPA) was created in late 1970, it began the process of banning DDT. However, not until June 14, 1972, would EPA administrator William Ruckelshaus announce the end of almost all further use of DDT in the United States, effective at the end of the year. Ruckelshaus explained, "Man may be exposing himself to a substance that may ultimately have serious effects on his health."[36] Besides, he commented later, "You put more and more of it into the environment and it was having less and less effect on the target species because they were building up resistance to it."[37] Environmentalists sued to make the ban immediate, while pesticide manufacturers challenged it. The ban was finally upheld by a federal appeals court on December 13, 1973. "There is no question that it was politically charged, and I was accused of making a political decision," Ruckelshaus recalled later. "I talked to [John] Ehrlichman about it. He said that the president would not be happy with that decision. . . . The president never called me about it."[38]

Although DDT use had been declining, use of other pesticides had been growing. In 1969 the president's environmental task force reported that eight thousand manufacturers were mixing nine hundred basic chemicals into sixty thousand registered pesticides, producing about eight hundred million pounds annually. John Whitaker noted that the complicated regulation of pesticides under many agencies had prevented the task force from placing a proposal about pesticide regulation in the 1970 presidential environmental message.[39] Nelson now unsuccessfully proposed banning several of these pesticides, such as aldrin and dieldrin, as carcinogens, as well the herbicide 2,3,5-T, the major component of Agent Orange, which was used in Vietnam as a defoliant. Nelson also unsuccessfully called for a national pesticide commission and creating uniform standards for pesticides.

Legislating against Poison

In Nixon's second environmental message to Congress, on February 8, 1971, he proposed a Federal Environmental Pesticides Control Act, replacing FIFRA. It would give the EPA power to classify pesticides by risk, removing jurisdiction from the Agriculture Department, and from Whitten. The EPA could reject "any pesticide that posed an imminent threat to human health."[40] Only "approved pesticide applicators" would qualify to administer more hazardous substances, reducing their casual use. The new law would also create the authority to register and inspect pesticide factories and to conduct research into pesticides.[41]

Farm state legislators blocked the plan. Ehrlichman and Whitaker, over Russell Train's objections, now proposed amending instead of replacing FIFRA, keeping pesticides under the jurisdiction of the congressional Agriculture Committees in each chamber. That would avoid the more environmentally minded Commerce committees, which Whitaker feared would "increase the cost of legislation so much or make its provisions so unbalanced in favor of environmental concerns that the bill would be a likely candidate for veto." Whitaker admitted that the subsequent bill might be too weak, but "Representative Page Belcher (R-OK) convinced [me] he could guide a bill through that committee that would be tough enough to prevail on the floor, even after some planned (and modest) concessions to environmentalists following Senate Commerce Committee hearings."[42]

The Agriculture Committees in both chambers passed almost identical bills. On June 15, 1972, the Senate Subcommittee on the Environment opened a hearing on the bill with chairman Philip Hart (D-MI) declaring, "The proposed legislation contained several weaknesses that Senator

Nelson and I hope to remedy by amendments we have introduced."[43] Nelson added, "It is important that any bill to reform pesticide regulation . . . contain provisions for informed public decisionmaking on pesticides before the public health, the environment, or the commerce of this Nation are threatened or actually injured." He noted that pesticides banned in the United States could still be exported, and proposed that exporters should at least have to disclose hazards to foreign customers. William Futrell of the Sierra Club sought "a provision allowing citizen suits," and Gerald Butler of the Environmental Defense Fund objected that while "much of the proposed new bill is a substantial improvement . . . the bill is not nearly so effective as it could be."[44]

On the second day of hearings, the chemical industry stressed the "vital role of pesticides in promoting public health and in producing an adequate supply of food and fiber."[45] The National Agricultural Chemicals Association supported the bill with reservations, particularly about states enacting their own regulations. Hart and Nelson had proposed that the data behind each product be available to other manufacturers, to avoid monopolies. The industry representatives supported the Agriculture Committee bill protecting the data as trade secrets. The Commerce Committee adopted some of the Hart-Nelson amendments strengthening the bill, which then passed the Senate 71–0.

In the House, proenvironmental forces supported the bill as written, fearing that a stronger version would fail, and it passed 288–91. President Nixon signed it on October 21, 1972, shortly before the 1972 election, declaring, "We will now be able to ensure that we can continue to reap the benefits which these substances can contribute . . . without risking unwanted hazards to our environment."[46] EPA permits were now required for use of pesticides, which had to be registered and classified for general use or use only in restricted situations. Pesticides posing a high risk to humans or the environment could be limited or banned.[47] The bill required industry to conduct studies to prove safety. Unlike the Clean Air Act, which considered only human health, the new legislation balanced risks against economic benefits. The act created a new EPA Scientific Advisory Panel to review all pesticide decisions, giving pesticide supporters a voice.[48] The act grandfathered in all pesticides sold before 1970 pending EPA review. "Industry thus bore the burden of proof for justifying new pesticides even if they might be safer than existing ones," noted Andrews, "while the EPA bore the burden for banning existing ones: new pesticides were guilty until proven innocent, while old ones were innocent until proven guilty."[49] The same year the Senate passed Nelson's bill for a federal pilot program to study integrated pest control, minimizing pesticide use in favor of natural solutions. To Nelson's disappointment, the bill did not pass the House.

The Environmental Pesticides Control Act gave the EPA the task of reviewing the thirty-five thousand pesticides in use by 1976. In 1975 the act was amended to weaken it, requiring the EPA to notify the Agriculture Department about any proposed cancelations of pesticides and to assess the economic impact before changing the status of any pesticide.[50] In 1978 Congress would eliminate the deadline for pesticide review by the EPA, requiring assessment only "as expeditiously as possible."[51] The 1978 amendment allowed the EPA to study the 600 basic pesticide components, rather than every product. By 1986, the EPA hadn't completed final assessments on any of the 600 ingredients, but had produced preliminary assessments on 124, implementing at least partial use restrictions on 60 percent of these. The EPA had completed another 32 special reviews on particularly dangerous ingredients, banning 5 and restricting another 26.[52] Critics blamed the lack of resources for the slow pace. They also objected that a chemical banned in the United States could still be manufactured and sold abroad. While DDT was largely eliminated in the United States by 1972, Whitaker noted, fifty-six million pounds of it were manufactured for export in 1974.[53]

The EPA had acted against the worst chemicals, limiting the use of the herbicide 2,4,5-T in April 1970. On October 1, 1974, Train, by this time EPA administrator, halted the production of the pesticides aldrin and dieldrin, having concluded that they were carcinogenic and widespread in the American population. Train followed on December 24, 1975, by suspending most uses of the pesticides heptachlor and chlordane. Whitaker concluded that limiting the use of five of the twenty most widely used pesticides was an important step, which many farmers felt went too far.[54]

Lead and the Safe Drinking Water Act

Pesticides were not the only toxins used in America. Lead had long been known to have major toxicity, causing anemia, neuropathy, and abdominal pain and other disorders, particularly in children. Yet in the United States the use of lead had increased significantly, doubling from 1940 to 1977 mainly due to the use of leaded gasoline.[55] In the late 1960s many community groups, particularly in large cities, had begun programs to screen for lead in children. These found higher-than-expected lead levels. In 1971 Congress responded with the Lead Based Paint Poisoning Prevention Act, limiting lead in paint and creating paint removal programs.

In January 1973 the EPA issued new regulations to begin phasing out leaded gasoline, a major contributor to high lead levels, particularly in children in urban areas. It could also damage catalytic converters, key components in pollution reduction that started in the 1975 model cars. The EPA ordered that unleaded gasoline be generally available by July 1974 and set a schedule to reduce the lead content in gasoline progressively over the next five years.[56] Lead would be banned from use in soldering food cans, and in 1978 was completely removed from house paint. Over time, these steps successfully decreased lead levels in children. The EPA would further cut the lead allowed in gasoline in 1985 and finally completely ban leaded gas after January 1, 1996, producing dramatic drops in lead levels in the environment and the air.

Rachel Carson's concerns would find expression in two other bills. Drinking water policies, as in the 1944 Public Health Service Act, historically focused on preventing waterborne diseases such as cholera. Only in 1962 did the Public Health Service issue guidelines—nonenforceable guidelines—addressing other contaminants.

In 1970 the United States Public Health Service Water Supply Study revealed that many water systems failed to meet the 1962 standards. Carcinogens in the water supplies of New Orleans and other cities were reported in November 1973, amplified by a CBS Special broadcast, "Drinking Water May Be Dangerous to Your Health," in early 1974.[57] Congress responded with the Safe Drinking Water Act of 1974, targeting dangerous chemicals in water. Senator Warren Magnuson (D-WA), chair of the Senate Commerce Committee, had sent the committee report on the Senate bill to the White House on June 18, 1973, explaining, "While the Committee views the problem of unsafe drinking water as a matter which is and should be primarily the concern of state and local governments, the Committee has determined that the Federal government also has a responsibility to ensure the safety of the water its [people] drink."[58]

When the bill came to President Ford in December 1974, the administration was conflicted. Roy Ash, head of the Office of Management and Budget (OMB), opposed the bill, writing, "The issue raised by S. 433 is not whether it would add to the protection of the public health—it would. The issue is whether the degree of Federal takeover of State and local functions, and establishment of Federal grants to pay states . . . are too high a price to pay for the increased protection provided." In contrast, Council on Environmental Quality chair Russell Peterson argued, "The CEQ strongly recommends that you sign S. 433, the Safe Drinking Water Act. . . . The [Nixon] Administration proposed drinking water legislation in 1973 because available information indicated that public health was threatened by unsafe drinking water. Over the decade 1961–70 at least 130 outbreaks of disease or poisoning resulting in 46,374 illnesses and 20 deaths are known to have occurred."[59]

The OMB admitted that the "Administration would face a potentially massive Congressional and public outcry if the bill was vetoed . . . in the face of a strong Administration opposition to Federal enforcement, the bill passed the House by a vote of 296–84 and in the Senate by a voice vote. . . . The Federal enforcement role under the bill is generally the same in concept as that in the Clean Air Act and the Federal Water Pollution Control Act."[60] Train advised, "I recommend that the . . . bill be approved. The bill is similar in many ways and would accomplish the same objectives in essentially the same manner as would the Safe Drinking Water Act submitted to Congress by the Administration." President Ford signed the bill, commenting, "This bill today will provide us with the protection we need for drinking water."[61]

The act mandated that the EPA set standards for safe drinking water, identifying contaminants that could endanger health, then work with the states to meet the standards. Without having to prove certainty or even probability of harm, the EPA was empowered to set the "maximum (allowable) contaminant levels (MCLs)" and then mandate the best available technology to get below that threshold.[62]

In 1977 the EPA's national drinking water standards went into effect, requiring that forty thousand community drinking water systems and two hundred thousand other public water systems serving twenty-five or more persons test their water against these standards.[63] Utilities would have to notify customers if the MCL standards were not being met or if water quality declined. The new regulations set standards for microorganisms, ten inorganic chemicals, six pesticides, and radioactivity, as well as turbidity, or murkiness, of the water. States had the primary role in enforcement. By banning lead in water pipes for drinking water and water coolers, the Safe Drinking Water Act would drive lead levels down further.

Taking on Toxic Chemicals

Nixon's Environmental Message of February 1970 addressed the need to regulate nonagricultural chemicals. The CEQ had proposed that companies be required to test all new chemical substances for safety prior to allowing their marketing. Nixon, facing strong opposition from the Commerce Department, proposed a weaker bill, worrying that Congress would try to practice "oneupmanship" to require an even stronger bill.[64] But even the weaker administration proposal, introduced in 1971, did not become law, as a result of fierce opposition from the chemical industry, particularly Dow Chemical.[65] Train wrote that Dow had claimed the bill would cost the industry $2 billion a year, while the EPA estimated the cost of compliance at only $79–142.5 million. The bill twice passed both chambers but died in House-Senate conference committees.[66]

In 1975, two huge chemical spills revived the bill. The spillage of the pesticide kepone into the James River resulted in hospitalizations and a threat to the aquatic life of the Chesapeake Bay. Shortly afterward General Electric was found to have discharged large amounts of the carcinogenic chemical polychlorinated biphenyls (PCBs) into the Hudson River, closing the river to fishing.[67] Train pushed for legislation, telling the National Press Club, "We can no longer afford to wait for the basic authority to deal effectively with the problems of chemical pollution. It is time we gave the people of this country some reason to believe that, every time they take a breath or eat or touch, they are not taking their lives into their hands."[68] Responding to public outrage, the Senate Committee on Commerce held further hearings on the issue. The *Washington Post* editorialized, "It hardly seems unreasonable for Congress to require that substances not be marketed until their health effects have been addressed as well as possible, and no serious hazards have been found."[69]

The Commerce Committee unanimously sent S. 3149, the Toxic Substances Control Act, to the Senate floor on March 26, 1976. John Tunney (D-CA), whose subcommittee had directed the hearings, declared, "S. 3149 will close major gaps in the law that leave the public inadequately protected against the unregulated introduction of hazardous chemicals into the environment. . . . [Under the bill,] the EPA Administrator may require manufacturers to test or have tested chemical substances which he determines many present an unreasonable risk. . . . [T]his provision is applicable to both new and existing chemical substances."[70] James Pearson (R-KS), the ranking minority member on Tunney's subcommittee, explained, "The existence within S. 3149 of a strong premarket screening process is a key factor in the effective operation of this legislation."[71] Yet not every one supported the legislation. Strom Thurmond (R-SC) warned, "The Toxic Substances Control Act is probably the most serious threat the chemical industry has ever faced . . . it is unnecessary . . . it will stifle progress . . . it will drive industry overseas." . Howard Baker (R-TN) closed debate arguing, "The measure before us today is an innovative legislative effort and [will] evaluate and control these substances before they have a chance to become a problem."[72] The Senate then passed the bill by 60-13.

Six months later, after the House had passed a measure and the House-Senate conferees had agreed on a final bill, the Senate took it up again. Calling it "the most important environmental legislation to come before the 94th Congress," Magnuson declared himself "extremely pleased to state that the conference has now agreed on a strong premarket notification provision, which requires that 90 days prior to marketing new chemicals or existing substances for significant new uses, manufacturers must supply EPA with information in order that EPA can assess the safety of these chemicals."[73] Vance Hartke (D-IN) praised the final product: "While this legislation has gained acceptance by the mainstream of the chemical industry, it is also acceptable to environmental, public health and labor groups."[74] The Senate passed the Toxic Substances Control Act on September 28, 73–6. The House also passed the bill, by an equally veto-proof 319–45 margin. Train lobbied for the administration to support the bill, declaring, "It is time we started putting chemicals to the test, not people."[75] With the presidential election little more than a month away, President Ford signed the bill into law.

Science magazine called the Toxic Substances Control Act (TOSCA) "the first comprehensive regulation of the chemical industry."[76] The act gave the EPA the ability to track the estimated seventy-five thousand industrial chemicals produced in or imported into the United States. All new chemicals had to undergo testing and premanufacturing notification to the EPA.[77] The act exempted pesticides, tobacco, nuclear material, food, drugs, and cosmetics as governed by other statutes.[78] The act also directed the EPA to complete an inventory of all chemicals manufactured or processed in the United States by 1980.[79]

The EPA could require reporting or testing of chemicals it felt could pose an environmental or human health hazard, and could ban the manufacture or importation of chemicals causing excessive damage. On the other hand, the EPA administrator could exempt any chemical from the premarket clearance procedures if he felt it did not present a risk to health or the environment.[80] In addition, the act required schools to test for and remove asbestos when hazardous and to test for radon gas levels. The EPA would have to regularly inform the public about health hazards due to excessive radon exposure.[81]

TOSCA and FIFRA differed from many environmental statutes in regulating products rather than wastes. By stopping production of hazardous substances, it theoretically could prevent risks from emerging. Since production and sale clearly involved interstate commerce, there were no constitutional barriers to federal regulation.[82] Although TOSCA was a major step forward, it did not completely stop the problem of dangerous chemicals being released into the environment. The application process by companies for new products was confidential, preventing any public scrutiny of the chemicals before they were approved. The act did require that all chemicals imported into the United States go through strict testing.[83] The biggest problem was that systematic and up-to-date test data about these chemicals did not exist. EPA initially took the data from industry, but found that much of this data had been falsified. The process favored manufacturers of existing chemicals, who could delay the process, both for regulating old chemicals and registering new replacements, for years.[84]

In two ways, TOSCA was weaker than the amended FIFRA. Unlike the FIFRA, existing products (those produced before 1980) subject to TOSCA could be sold and distributed without prior EPA approval. The burden was on the EPA to act to ban or restrict the use of an existing product, while new chemicals introduced after 1980 were subject to more stringent regulation.[85] Environmental historian Richard Andrews noted the practical problems of the act, stating, "[the] EPA was now responsible for decisions involving tens of thousands of potentially hazardous substances, all of them commercially valuable rather than mere wastes. It had to bear the burden of proof for regulating them, which required scientific evidence that often did not exist, and for balancing their risks against their economic values."[86] Seeing it as one of the least effective statutes of the time, Hays concluded, "The nation's main law to control exposure to toxic substances fell into relative disuse."[87] Ruckelshaus commented in 2007, "Some of the things that EPA deals with are stalled because they are enormously complex to deal with."[88] The act did help to control some of the most egregious chemicals and limit the introduction of new untested agents. In his 2003 memoir, Train noted that, counter to the chemical industry claims, "TO-SCA has been law for about twenty-five years and would not seem to have destroyed either the chemical industry or the American economy."[89]

The Problems of Garbage Pile-Up

At the same time that government was wrestling with control of toxins, Congress and environmentalists were struggling with basic garbage. "The modern technology which has added much to our lives can also have a darker side," Johnson told Congress in a special message in 1965. "Its uncontrolled waste products are menacing the world we live in, our enjoyment and our health. The air we breathe, our water, our soil and wildlife, are being blighted by the poisons and chemicals which are the byproducts of technology and industry. . . . The same society which receives the rewards of technology must, as a cooperating whole, take responsibility for control."[90]

The Solid Waste Disposal Act, passed in 1965, created the Bureau of Solid Waste Management in the Department of Health, Education and Welfare to supply states with technical assistance and training, as well as fund research. It also set minimum safety requirements for landfills. But the program had relatively little funding and had not made a substantial difference by the end of the Johnson administration. Acting on the advice of his Scientific Advisory Committee, President Johnson had also ordered a study of the problem of solid waste, producing the 1968 National Survey of Community Solid Waste Practices.[91]

Nixon's staff recognized the problem's importance. In his 1970 environmental message, the president announced more research on "techniques for recycling materials, and on development and use of packaging and other materials which will degrade after use," but opposed "pouring more and more public money into collection and disposal of whatever happens to be privately produced and discarded."[92] Whitaker noted, "The Nixon administration did its best to restrict the federal government's role in solid waste management. . . . It seemed to [Nixon] that state and local governments were better equipped than the federal government to handle the problem."[93]

In his first environmental message, Nixon had urged action to deal with the problem of the estimated one million cars abandoned annually.[94] But the rise in steel prices made abandoned vehicles more valuable, while the development of automobile shredders helped separate out the metal. Among the solutions considered by the administration were deposits to be paid by buyers and returned at proper disposal, bounties for proper disposal, and loans to help businesses buy modern shredders. Yet the CEQ concluded, "The Council is not persuaded that the demand for auto scrap would be improved by such a system, nor that it would fact influence the economics affecting abandonment."[95] The CEQ proposed a ban on dumping solid waste into the oceans and Great Lakes, as well as requiring EPA permits for other dumping. While not agreeing to the details, Nixon thought the restriction worth pursuing.

Unwilling to wait, in 1970 Edmund Muskie introduced a bill with more funding for solid waste management than Nixon wanted. It called for the federal government picking up 75 percent of state or local solid waste planning costs, compared to Nixon's proposed 50 percent. It also funded more recycling research and expanded waste disposal facilities. In the fall of 1970 Congress passed the Resource Recovery Act, closer to Muskie's proposal than the administration's. For 1971–1973, it increased solid waste funding fourteenfold, a total of $400 million. A significant portion went for recycling, a point of agreement between Muskie and Nixon.[96] "Nixon nearly vetoed the Resource Recovery Act, almost solely on budgetary grounds," recalled Whitaker.[97] Instead, worried that the issue carried political vulnerability, the president signed the bill in late October, just before the midterm election.

In 1971, a CEQ proposal of tax incentives for recycling appealed to neither the administration nor Congress. Nor did another proposal to increase fees for disposing waste. In June 1971 Ruckelshaus initiated Operation 5000, which aimed to close five thousand of the fourteen thousand open dumps within the year. While this deadline was not met, it did begin replacing open dumps with more stringently regulated sanitary landfills.[98]

Congress took up additional regulation of waste disposal in 1976 with the proposed Resource Conservation and Recovery Act, seeking to regulate garbage, particularly the millions of tons of hazardous wastes dumped into the ground every year. The biggest controversy occurred in the Senate when Mark Hatfield (R-OR) proposed an amendment, the Beverage Container Reuse and Recycling Act of 1976, requiring beer and soda containers to be returnable for a 5-cent deposit. "This is not a new concept," pointed out Hatfield. "As recently as 1960, 95% of our soft drinks and 50% of our beer was packaged in refillable containers on which a deposit was paid."

He further noted, "Beverage containers, by the way, are currently the fastest growing category of municipal solid waste, increasing at a rate of 8% a year." Hatfield testified that the 15.4 billion beverage containers disposed of in 1959 had increased to 60 billion by 1973.[99] Hatfield's proposal received endorsements from the *Washington Post* and *Baltimore Sun*, with the latter stating, "The environmental, economic and esthetic arguments in favor of a ban on throwaway beverage containers are overwhelming. . . . [T]he Senate should accept the Hatfield amendment."[100] The *Sun* noted how the opposition of the powerful soda industry had blocked this idea from becoming law in the past.

Nevertheless, the Senate defeated the Hatfield amendment by a 60–26 vote, cutting across both party and ideological lines. Opposing the amendment, Nelson argued that such a complicated issue needed more consideration. The Senate now passed the bill by an 88–3 margin, with the opponents all being archconservatives opposed to any legislation in the area. The House passed a similar bill, producing the Resource Conservation and Recovery Act of 1976. When the legislation came to the White House, it received support from the EPA, CEQ, and OMB, with the Department of Defense opposed. Summarizing the bill for President Ford, his staff recommended approval, noting, "Local and county officials support the signing of this bill very strongly."[101] Ford signed the act.

The act allowed the EPA to control all aspects of the generation, transportation, treatment, storage, and disposal of hazardous waste. The act mandated industry to store, treat, and dispose of such wastes only in EPA-approved facilities and that the EPA would issue technology-based requirements for the building and operation of such facilities. All firms that generated large quantities of hazardous wastes had to keep "cradle to grave" records of them, including all offsite shipments.[102] The act aimed to prevent hazardous waste pollution rather than treat it; treatment would be taken up in the 1980 Superfund bill.

The second component of the act set regulations for the disposal of solid nonhazardous wastes. One important objective was to prevent substances leaching from the waste disposal sites into the groundwater, threatening health and the environment. The act set basic federal requirements for municipal landfills and other aspects of waste management but allowed states to design their own programs. Finally, the act aimed at reducing the quantity of waste and expanding waste recycling and recovery. The act did not greatly increase federal regulation or funding for solid waste management. The rigorous regulation of hazardous wastes was a notable exception.

The transformation of waste practices is one of the less-recognized environmental success stories of the 1970s. Uncovered dumps with open burning of often hazardous wastes disappeared, to be replaced by covered landfills lined to prevent contamination of the underlying soil and groundwater. Hazardous wastes were closely monitored, sharply reducing human exposure to these toxins.[103]

Protection Returns to the Sea

A frequent destination of all kinds of waste was the oceans, whose capacity for absorbing unwanted waste was considered almost boundless. Maritime dumping was a common practice, particularly by some cities disposing of municipal waste. "Although man's record as a steward of the natural resources of the earth has been a discouraging one, there has long been a certain comfort in the belief that the sea, at least, was inviolate, beyond man's ability to change and to despoil. But this belief, unfortunately, has proved to be naive," wrote Carson in a new preface to the 1961 edition of *The Sea Around Us*.[104] She was referring specifically to dumping nuclear wastes at sea, a concern it took Congress a decade to address.

In early 1970, the CEQ proposed legislation to govern dumping municipal waste, but conflict, partly over jurisdiction, interfered. That October, the CEQ issued a report on the subject, which Nixon released with his endorsement. In his 1971 environmental message, Nixon proposed legislation banning unregulated ocean dumping and limiting dumping of harmful materials.[105]

International action happened first. On February 15, 1972, twelve European nations signed a convention to end the dumping of poisonous wastes from ships or planes in the northeast Atlantic.[106] In June 1972, United Nations undersecretary-general Maurice Strong convened a UN Conference on the Human Environment in Stockholm. The conference endorsed several American proposals, including an ocean dumping agreement. A followup meeting in Britain created the Ocean Dumping Convention to regulate dumping in international waters.[107]

The UN effort helped spur Congress to act. The House took up a bill previously reported out by the Merchant Marine and Fisheries Committee. Wayne Aspinall, chair of the Interior and Insular Affairs Committee, proposed striking the section allowing the secretary of commerce to create marine sanctuaries. "This is an ocean dumping bill," argued Aspinall, "and the matter of marine sanctuaries has no place under it."[108] The section, he maintained, would transfer authority from the Department of the Interior to the Department of Commerce, without the approval of his committee. Responding to Aspinall, Merchant Marine and Fisheries chair Alton Lennon (D-NC) retorted, "His Committee has jurisdiction over the mineral resources of the outer Continental Shelf, but proposed Title III does not in any way include that jurisdiction." The issue was about "the living resources of the ocean," the jurisdiction of the Merchant Marine and Fisheries Committee, and the Department of Commerce.[109]

Aspinall's amendment, charged Thomas Pelly (R-WA), represented

a misguided and ill-conceived effort on the part of well-meaning individuals to protect the development of offshore oil resources which they view as threatened by a marine sanctuary law. This fear is groundless . . . the marine sanctuaries are not intended to prevent legitimate uses of the sea. They are intended to protect unique areas of the ocean bordering our country. . . . [A] sanctuary is not meant to be a marine wilderness where man will not enter. Its designation will insure [sic] very simply a balance between uses.[110]

After Aspinall and Dingell argued further over committee jurisdiction, Norman Lent (R-NY) offered an amendment allowing the secretary of commerce to block all development of an area being considered as a sanctuary, including offshore oil leases. The bill, Lent said, "for the first time, authorizes the establishment of select areas of our coastal waters for distinctive treatment . . . [This] acknowledges that our oceans are not an indestructible resource."[111]

Lent continued, "If one were to ask my colleagues who serve the coastal areas, 'What is one potential danger that would result in the most catastrophic destruction?' . . . their response would most likely cite the potential devastation that oil spills off our coasts creates. . . . We have the means at hand to prevent damage to these special areas before they have been despoiled by oil drilling operation. . . . I urge support of this amendment."[112] He entered into the Congressional Record several Long Island news stories and editorials opposing offshore drillings, and a letter from the chairman of the Suffolk County Legislature, John V. N. Klein, to President

Nixon, warning, "The potential for off shore drilling activities poses the greatest single environmental threat to Suffolk County since settlement in the early 1600s.'"[113]

Other Republicans joined Lent. Charles Teague (R-CA) reminded the House, "I represent the Santa Barbara area where, as members will recall, we had a disastrous accident about a year and half ago. . . . I do suggest to the Members who may not represent areas bordering the sea coast that oil wells in one's front yard are decidedly a mixed blessing." [114] Another coastal Republican, Bill Young, of Florida, warned, "Oil spillage from offshore drilling has become an ever-growing problem . . . until the oil companies prove they have the technology to prevent oil spills, we must impose strict regulation on oil exploration."[115] Still, the Lent amendment was rejected. Charles Sandman (R-NJ) then offered an amendment allowing the states to impose further requirements and liabilities. Republican Bill Frenzel, from definitively noncoastal Minnesota, endorsed it, saying, "In my judgement, the states . . . would like the ability to enhance the environment for their own people above that which the Federal government may determine to do."[116] The Sandman amendment passed by one vote. The House then passed the Marine Protection, Research and Sanctuaries Act 305–3. Aspinall was one of the three nos.

During the debate, among those pushing for a stronger bill were Republicans, mainly representing coastal districts, while Democrats were more divided. At the time, the oceans weren't partisan. It took the Senate a year to pass a similar bill.

In October 1972, again just before election day, President Nixon signed the Marine Protection, Research and Sanctuaries Act, declaring, "Our actions are part of what we hope and trust will be a global commitment to protecting the glory and majesty and life of the shining seas."[117] The act required EPA permits for ocean dumping of wastes, to be issued only when the administrator determined the dumping would not endanger human health, the marine environment, or economic opportunities. The EPA administrator could impose financial penalties for violations, and mandate actions to correct them. The Corps of Engineers could issue permits for dumping dredged material but needed EPA approval.

Environmentalists were frustrated that jurisdiction over future research was given to the National Oceanic and Atmospheric Administration, located in the antienvironmental Commerce Department. But the final act was stronger than both the Nixon and Muskie original proposals, completely banning the dumping of biological and chemical warfare agents, and all radiological wastes. The last aspect would become particularly important in the future, as the disposal of nuclear wastes became a pressing issue—as Carson had warned more than a decade earlier. The Ocean Dumping Ban Act of 1988 would eventually ban the dumping of any sewage sludge or industrial waste in the oceans.

Carson's legacy against the poisoning of the land has been legendary. She was also a voice in the battle against a toxic sea. The series of laws governing toxins, pesticides, ocean dumping, and solid waste passed with overwhelming support from both parties, underlining how the environmental concerns of the time crossed partisan and regional lines—especially on dumping and waste disposal. In March 2019 the Office of Response and Restoration at the National Oceanic and Atmospheric Administration—the foremost federal maritime agency—announced that it was "remembering Rachel Carson for Women's History month because she blazed a trail for the work we do in many ways. Rachel Carson encouraged Americans to love and explore our marine environments on every scale."[118] She helped set a tone not only on pesticides and ocean dumping but for the broader debate that would absorb Congress and the nation. "What we might call the Rachel Carson Paradigm," posited Zygmunt Plater in the *Loyola of Los Angeles Law Review* in 1994, "declared that, although humans naturally try to maximize their own accumulation of benefits and ignore negative effects of their actions, a society that wishes to survive and prosper must identify and take comprehensive account of the real interacting consequences of individual decisions, negative as well as positive, whether the marketplace accounts for them or not."[119]

Understanding that might be called the Green Years' Great Realization.

CHAPTER TWELVE

Land and Wilderness Management

KEY EVENTS:

Alaska Native Claims Settlement Act (1971)
Eastern Wilderness Act (1974)
Federal Land Policy and Management Act (1976)
National Forest Management Act (1976)

Battling for the quality of air and water—the vital components of life—absorbed major environmental effort during the Green Years. But underlying everything was the protection and preservation of the land, public and private, maintaining access for recreation, and preventing its destruction through exploitation. In the early 1970s legislators, advocates, and the Nixon administration struggled over numerous land issues, from western grazing to eastern wilderness to West Virginia coal mining to Alaska natives' rights. On land, perhaps the most fundamental issue, divisions became more partisan and more regional, but the time saw major advances with broad support.

In a country of more than three million square miles, with an intricate patchwork pattern of ownership, usage, and overlapping government authority, land issues would never be fully resolved. An overall resolution—a national land-use policy, pursued from different directions by the Nixon administration and Senate Interior Committee chairman Henry Jackson—collapsed along the way. But millions of acres were preserved from development and kept for recreation, some of the most destructive logging and mining practices were limited, and some order was brought to what had been chaotic federal supervision of vast stretches of America.

The Indigenous peoples who initially occupied what would become the United States had little concept of private land ownership. In sharp contrast, while treaty and purchase produced federal title to the great bulk of national land, "United States government policy was to promote the rapid transfer of public lands into private land, to generate both short-term revenues and long-term economic development."[1] Most of the public land would be given away by the end of the nineteenth century. By the 1960s, America's patchwork, uncoordinated land ownership was becoming an increasing problem. Ultimate authority was often left to local governments, who designed zoning management with limited expertise and resources and were vulnerable to powerful local interests. The situation created significant environmental issues, and uncontrolled development sprawled outside cities, swallowing rural areas. Ecologically important lands, such as wetlands and estuaries, were developed with no thought for public or long-term consequences. Each year 160,000 acres were paved over for highways and airports, another 420,000 acres became reservoirs, and another 420,000 open acres vanished into housing and commercial use.[2]

"An anachronistic tax structure that penalizes property owners who preserve open space or keep agricultural land in production is a serious impediment to sound land planning," Secretary of the Interior Stewart Udall warned about zoning in 1963. "Open space and other socially beneficial land use should be encouraged."[3] Udall also advocated conservation or scenic easements, with municipalities paying landowners to keep their property undeveloped.[4] Instead of letting the automobile dictate development, Udall urged planners to "put people first."

An estimated half of America's wetlands had been lost between 1780 and 1980, largely by drainage for agriculture.[5] Suburban growth accelerated the loss of wetlands. "Between 1950 and 1964," noted historian David Goldfield, "developers and local governments had drained one third of Long Island's wetlands to provide housing, airports, industrial plants, parking, recreational facilities, and garbage dumps." This prompted several New York congressmen in 1966 to propose permanent protection for sixteen thousand acres of wetlands on Long Island. Representative John Dingell (D-MI) proposed similar national legislation.[6]

Thinking Big on Big Expanses

Legal experts agreed that the interstate commerce clause gave the federal government authority over some land use, while federal funding could be used to induce other changes. In January 1970 Jackson proposed the National Land Use Policy Act, declaring, "Intelligent land-use planning and management provides the single most important institutional device for preserving and enhancing the environment."[7] It would mandate states to decide which lands to preserve in a wild state or for recreation, and which to use for industrial or residential purposes. Federal grants would assist the states, with penalties, in the form of decreased entitlement funding, for states failing to develop plans within three years. Supporters told Congress, "The need for this type of regulation is great," and "A coherent national land use policy is essential to our nation."[8] Secretary of the Interior Wally Hickel later declared, "Our greatest lack has been . . . the lack of imagination to care and plan for all of our property and all our people. . . . We must have a national land inventory."[9] President Richard Nixon supported such a policy, declaring, "We must create the administrative and regulatory mechanism to assure wise land use and to stop haphazard, wasteful, or environmentally damaging development."[10]

In April, Russell Train, John Whitaker, and John Ehrlichman met with Jackson and Senator Gordon Allott (R-CO). Ehrlichman, who had been a land use lawyer in Seattle, agreed to work closely with Jackson on the issue but did not commit the administration to specific legislation.[11] Train proposed a White House land use conference, but Whitaker wrote Ehrlichman, "I'm frankly suspicious. [The conference would be] a built-in chance for the doomsday boys to say we are not doing enough."[12] The White House abandoned the talks.

Instead, the administration had the Council on Environmental Quality (CEQ) develop its own land use bill, but the efforts were hampered by conflicts among departments, notably Transportation, Agriculture, Commerce, and Housing and Urban Development.[13] Train pushed for a bill, arguing, "Land use issues lie at the heart of many of the critical environmental decisions facing the nation."[14] In his 1971 environmental message, written by the CEQ, Nixon proposed a National Land Use Policy that would encourage the states, in cooperation with local governments, to regulate major developments.[15] He wanted it done by "establishing methods for protecting lands of critical environmental concern, methods for controlling large-scale development, and improving use of lands around key facilities and new communities."[16]

The administration's bill provided $20 million a year for five years to assist state planning and implementation. States failing to develop plans would lose federal funding. The Office of Management and Budget (OMB) objected to the price tag and cited the lack of clarity on federal guidelines, but Whitaker noted that everyone except the OMB supported the bill, and Nixon "simply deferred to Ehrlichman's expertise in land use, and Ehrlichman advised that this was a good piece of legislation."[17] While the Jackson plan applied to all lands, the CEQ proposal would mandate planning only for areas of "critical environmental importance."[18] Ehrlichman eliminated sanctions for noncompliance, fearing congressional opposition.[19] Still, conservative legislators protested both the cost and interference with state and local governments.

Through 1971 Jackson sought a compromise with the administration, finally accepting most of the CEQ proposal. "We eventually saw," explained his aide Steven Quarles, "that the states wouldn't realistically be able to set up a comprehensive program."[20] Interior Secretary Rogers Morton, who replaced Hickel, strongly backed the idea. Setting aside three million acres of California desert for recreational use in 1972, Morton commented, "What we really need is to develop a desert ethic. If we fail to instigate a land-use system in America now, the next generation will live in an intolerable environment."[21] Environmentalists, who had backed Jackson's original proposal, had concerns over the administration's plan. The Senate bill had required states to identify "areas of critical environmental concern"; the new bill called for identifying four "critical areas," including of "large scale development."[22] The Sierra Club's Michael McCloskey warned that this might facilitate the creation of large energy and other facilities, preempting state limitations. Nevertheless, on September 19, 1972, the Senate passed a bill acceptable to the administration and to Jackson.

But by this time conservatives in Congress opposed even this proposal. Representative Wayne Aspinall (D-CO) introduced a bill requiring federal agencies to review all public lands, which environmentalists saw as putting even established wilderness at risk for reclassification. One woman wrote to her senator, "I read that nearly 200 million acres of national forest, wildlife refuges etc. would be terminated. . . . [W]hat [Aspinall] proposes would be a disaster for the American people."[23] The House Interior Committee voted out (passed) Aspinall's bill on August 7, 1972, but as Train reported, it "was bottled up in the Rules Committee (with the encouragement of the Nixon White House)."[24] The bill died with the end of the congressional session.

Both the Jackson and the administration bills were reintroduced in the new Congress. On June 7, 1973, the Senate Interior Committee passed, 10–3, a synthesis of the two, and two weeks later the Senate passed it 64–21. The House subcommittee voted out a new bill, more closely resembling the Senate language, on September 13. Many of the provisions relating to public lands had been dropped. Sam Steiger (R-AZ) proposed an amendment giving states money to develop plans with little or no federal guidelines, while dropping any mandate to regulate ecologically important areas. Before recessing for Christmas, the full Interior Committee endorsed the subcommittee version over Steiger's plan.

In his State of the Union message on January 30, 1974, Nixon again called for early enactment of land use legislation. But on February 6 Steiger and twenty-one other House Republicans met with the president to complain that the administration's bill would, in Whitaker's words, "encroach on the states' zoning powers and on individual property rights."[25] On February 26 House minority leader John Rhodes (R-AZ) told the House Rules Committee that he and the administration favored what was now the Rhodes-Steiger bill over the subcommittee bill. The Rules Committee, with a vote of 9–4, now postponed floor consideration of the Interior Committee bill indefinitely.[26] After Morris Udall (D-AZ) held further hearings, on May 14 the Rules Committee reversed itself, and by an 8–7 vote sent the Interior Committee bill to the House floor. Nixon aide Kenneth Cole wrote to Rhodes reiterating, "The administration supports the Rhodes-Steiger Land Use Planning Act."[27] Jackson tried to get Nixon to defend either his own proposal or Jackson's bill, complaining, "I am concerned that the President's failure to stand by his position represents more than an abdication of leadership on one crucial legislative measure."[28]

Even after Udall accepted amendments stating that nothing in the bill threatened states' rights or private property, the Interior Committee/original administration proposal fell short in the House by fewer than twenty votes. Conservative groups persuaded Nixon, now facing imminent impeachment, not to push the legislation further. To account for the collapse of the entire project, Jackson suggested, "Impeachment politics," saying, "I am at a total loss to assign any other explanation."[29]

Watergate had shaped the land use law's prospects in another way, not by adding to the political pressure on Nixon but by subtraction. By the time the issue came up, the scandal had driven out a key White House voice. "It is . . . likely that Nixon had never felt any genuine commitment to land use, but had gone along with Ehrlichman, whom he had trusted to make sure that the administration's land use proposal did not infringe on states' zoning rights or on the rights of private property owners," explained Whitaker. By the time "Nixon heard charges from conservative lawmakers that the bill did in fact threaten constitutional rights, Ehrlichman was gone."[30] Environmental Protection Agency administrator Train's impression was the same: "Without Ehrlichman's persuasive counsel on the land use issue, Nixon simply had not the strength of interest or personal convictions to withstand conservative complaints about the legislation."[31]

Although national land use was dead, the debate did spur some states to develop their own rules. "Oregon was the first state in which new ideas about restricting sprawl and protecting open space through planning was put into play," wrote Samuel Hays. "In 1975 the state legislature approved a land-use planning system that emphasized preserving farmland by drawing a line around each town and city and requiring that development take place inside rather than outside that line."[32] But without national rules, land use planning varied widely from state to state. In some places regulations were quite extensive, limiting sprawl. Other places, such as Houston, saw massive sprawl.

Seeing the Forests and the Trees

Without an overall land use plan, Nixon-era battles focused on particular lands—such as the rich ecosystems that had awed and transfixed the first Europeans to arrive, the American forests. The forests of the United States had once seemed so vast that deforestation seemed unimaginable.[33] Yet by the mid-1800s these vast forests had been so depleted that wood started to be scarce. "There was enough wood for a thousand years, the optimists said, but the lumbermen levelled most of the forests in a hundred," recounted Stewart Udall. "Before the forest raids were finished, about half of the cutover woodlands had gone into farms and the other half was in sorry second growth or had been burned or logged into barrenness. By 1920 only one fifth of our primeval forest lands remained uncut."[34]

In 1877 Interior Secretary Carl Schurz proposed the first forest policy reform, calling for timbered lands to be appraised and sold for their market value. "The rapidity with which this country is being stripped of its forests must alarm every thinking man," warned Schurz. "The government . . . can preserve the forests still in its possession by keeping them under its control."[35] Congress ignored Schurz, instead enacting the Timber and Stone Act of 1878, which set the sale price of federal forestlands at $2.50

an acre, a tenth of their estimated value. Nearly fourteen million acres were sold under this act. The same year, the Free Timber Act allowed westerners to cut public lands timber for free for use in agriculture, mining or "other domestic purposes."[36] Predictably, overcutting followed. "In the old pioneer days, the American had but one thought about a tree, and that was to cut it down," Theodore Roosevelt told the American Forest Congress in 1905. "It took a long time to get the mind of our people, as a whole, accustomed to the fact that they had to alter their attitude towards the forest."[37]

The General Revision Act of 1891 repealed some of the most abused land laws, limiting homestead claims to 160 acres and requiring more explicit evidence of irrigation for arid lands. Most importantly, the act included a rider, at the urging of President Benjamin Harrison's secretary of the interior, John W. Noble, declaring, "The President of the United States may, from time to time, set aside and reserve . . . public lands wholly or in part covered by timber and undergrowth, whether of commercial value or not, as public reservations."[38] Udall noted, "The addition's potential did not penetrate the minds of the adjourning members. Had its scope been spelled out, the representatives of the forest states of the West would have opposed it almost to a man."[39]

With this rider, backed by foresters concerned about overcutting and western water providers seeking watershed protection, millions of acres would be reserved as national forests by the end of the nineteenth century.[40] Within a month of passage, President Harrison withdrew an estimated thirteen million acres of forestland and set up fifteen reserves under the Interior Department. In 1897 Congress granted the department permanent authority over these lands. That year, outgoing President Grover Cleveland reserved double the acreage that Harrison had set aside. "Outraged Senators demanded impeachment of the President and bills were passed to repeal Cleveland's proclamation then and there," reported Udall, "but a presidential veto and adjournment saved the day."[41]

In Theodore Roosevelt, the nation had its the first president with a passion for nature and wilderness. "It is safe to say that the prosperity of our people," he proclaimed, "depends directly on the energy and intelligence with which our natural resources are used."[42] Roosevelt, noted Richard Andrews, held the new belief that "both water resources and large areas of public lands should remain in government ownership, and that federal agencies staffed by professional agents should manage them."[43] Activist-author Bill McKibben conceded a century later, "There's plenty to dislike about Roosevelt. . . . But he was also the most significant environmental president in American history."[44]

Infuriated by the destruction of natural resources by certain companies, Roosevelt ripped up his prepared speech to tell a group of foresters, "I am against the land skinner every time."[45] Roosevelt's presidency saw the creation of new, more professional land agencies. The Newlands Reclamation Act of 1902 created the Reclamation Service, later renamed the Bureau of Reclamation, to manage funding for irrigation.

Roosevelt's most influential advisor on conservation was Gifford Pinchot, who believed that land should be protected for the people rather than being given away as cheaply as possible to foster development. Pinchot had been appointed chief forester in the Department of Agriculture in 1898, although the forest reserves were then under the Department of the Interior. "The man and the job were made for each other," assessed Udall. Pinchot "had the clear eye of a scientist, a naturalist's love of woods and open spaces, the moral fervor of an evangelist and a politician's intuition."[46]

Largely due to Pinchot's influence, in 1905 Congress transferred forest management to the Department of Agriculture and created the United States Forest Service within it. Pinchot's charge, that he authored himself, was to manage the forests for "the most productive use for the permanent good of the whole people, not the temporary benefit of individuals or companies."[47] Continuing his environmental program, in May 1908 Roosevelt organized the nation's first Conservation Conference at the White House, attended by forty-four of the forty-six state governors and many policymakers and experts.[48]

"By any standards, Gifford Pinchot was a magnificent bureaucrat," exulted Udall. "In his time, the Forest Service was the most exciting organization in Washington."[49] In 1910 Pinchot wrote, "We are prosperous because our forefathers bequeathed us a land of marvelous resources still unexhausted. . . . The forests have already begun to fail, as the direct result of the suicidal policy of forest destruction which the people of the United States have allowed themselves to pursue."[50] Pinchot introduced user fees—though well below market rates—for the lumber and grazing industry in the national forests.[51]

Under Roosevelt, the forest land under federal management steadily increased. Reacting, Congress in 1907 required congressional approval for any future western forest reservations. Roosevelt, after consulting with Pinchot, reserved sixteen million more acres before signing the bill.[52] In total, Roosevelt increased protected lands from 46.4 million acres to 194.4 million acres, including 172 million in the forest reserves, renamed the national forests.[53] "The object of our forest policy is not to preserve the forests because they are beautiful . . . or because they are refuges for the wild creatures of the wilderness," avowed Pinchot. "The forests are to be used by man. Every other consideration comes secondary."[54]

A different view was voiced by John Muir, founder of the Sierra Club, who believed in preserving wild lands for their own sake. "Pinchot and Muir were fast friends in 1896 at the time the two worked together with the National Forestry Commission," recounted Udall.

> When the Commission reached the Grand Canyon, the two left the party . . . the rest of the commission bedded down in a hotel, but Muir and Pinchot decided to sleep out on the rim of the canyon in freezing weather. "Muir was a storyteller in a million," Pinchot wrote, "It was such an evening as I have never had before or since." That night on the rim of the Grand Canyon was almost the last time the two men were on speaking terms.[55]

Their first clash was over sheep grazing in the national forests. "We were faced with this simple choice," argued Pinchot. "Shut out all the grazing and lose the Forest Reserves or let stock in under control and save the Reserves for the Nation."[56] Muir did not agree with Pinchot's willingness to compromise under political pressure, and their estrangement widened.

Land conservation moved east in 1911, when Roosevelt's successor, William Howard Taft, signed the Weeks Act, giving the federal government authority to purchase eastern lands for conservation purposes. Over the years, the Weeks Act would result in the purchase of over twenty million acres of mostly eastern private lands for restoration and management.

The Clarke-McNary Act of 1924 expanded the lands qualifying for purchase, established a state-federal fire control program, and promoted the planting of trees. Sponsor Charles L. McNary (R-OR), chairman of a Senate Select Committee on Reforestation, had written his brother, "I have an opportunity to do a grand piece of constructive work. . . . It will provide the first great plan to conserve and protect forests." McNary later pushed through another bill, the Woodruff-McNary Act of 1928, providing for federal ownership of forests and lands to preserve adjacent streams, and allowing the federal government to repossess timberlands for unpaid taxes.[57]

The Forest Service still saw its primary mission as producing commodities from forests. William Greeley, chief forester under Harding and Coolidge, declared that "the actual production of timber [was] the real objective" of the agency.[58] This perspective persisted, even after the agency's statutory mission became, in 1960, "multiple use/sustained yield management."[59]

The New Deal brought renewed efforts to protect forests as well as other lands. Franklin D. Roosevelt once described himself in *Who's Who* as a "tree grower." He called forests "the 'lungs' of our land, purifying the air and giving fresh strength to our people."[60] In Roosevelt's view, government spending to stimulate the economy included conservation projects. The Civilian Conservation Corps (CCC) took young unemployed men out of the cities and paid them to create trails, plant trees, build park lodges, and produce other projects providing access to nature and wilderness. The CCC planted almost three billion trees, built a million miles of forest roads and trails, helped reduce soil erosion, and aided habitat restoration. The program, concluded Andrews, "left as its legacy the most effective eight-year record of conservation work in U.S. history."[61] FDR also used the Weeks Act to purchase eleven million acres of deforested and eroded lands to add to national forests, national parks, and other public lands, compared to the five million acres purchased in the previous two decades.[62]

The recovery efforts of the 1930s halted with World War II and did not restart. "Historians have described the 1950s as the 'supreme period of development' for western resource industries, such as mining, lumber and energy," assessed James Morton Turner.[63] An alliance between the timber companies and the Forest Service, noted Irving Brant, "has been predominant in every controversy . . . involving conflict between conservation and commercial exploitation in the public lands."[64] Historian Bernard DeVoto called the American West "the plundered province."[65] With decreased lumber availability from private lands, the timber industry successfully pushed to expand logging in the national forests, where annual cuts rose from two billion board feet in 1939 to twelve billion by 1970. Twice as much timber was cut in the national forests from 1950 to 1966 as in the previous forty-five years.[66] Explained Brant, "President Eisenhower looked upon conservation with total indifference rather than hostility."[67]

At the same time, the national forests saw ever-increasing recreational use. In 1969 Forest Service chief Edward P. Cliff noted, "We had last year 150 million visitor days' use in the national forests for recreation. That's a lot of people, and they all drink and eat and create waste and garbage."[68]

Cliff continued, "Recreation is in competition with the use of the same land that timber production is going ahead on. We feel that on the national forests we can accommodate recreation and timber growing. . . . [A]s we establish new recreation area and wilderness area and new national parks are created on timbered acreages, timber land is being diverted to other uses."[69]

By this time the national forests encompassed 187 million acres, one-tenth of the nation's total land area.[70] The Forest Service decided in 1969 to increase the timber harvest, supported by the industry, while wilderness advocates objected. The National Timber Supply bill won support from both Jackson and the Nixon administration, which worried timber shortages would cause higher housing prices. The bill explicitly declared the primary purpose of the national forests to be timber production, a major change from the National Forest Multiple Use Act of 1960.[71] Edmund Muskie objected, "The timber-cutting bill is the first major environmental legislation to move before Congress since President Nixon signed [the National Environmental Policy Act]. If the law for environmental quality is to be meaningful for the country, it cannot be ignored or circumvented as was done in this case."[72]

John Saylor and others attacked the bill in the House, arguing that increased logging would detract from other uses and eliminate lands as possible future wilderness. Saylor complained, "It is incredible that the first environmental bill to be considered by Congress in this decade of the environment is one that will denude major watersheds and rape our great national forests."[73]

Environmental groups launched a lobbying campaign against the proposal. McCloskey recalled that Dingell "provided space for us to set up an operations room in Rayburn House Office Building. Teams lobbied every member of Congress. . . . One hundred and fifty thousand letters and wires from concerned constituents poured into Congress within a few weeks."[74] To gain support, the bill's backers added a fund from timber leases to promote other uses of the forest. It didn't help. Calling the bill "a well-camouflaged attack on the national forests," Saylor asked why, if there were a timber shortage, lumber was still being exported to Japan. The House killed the bill, 229–150.[75] Meanwhile, a Wilderness Society lawsuit produced a court ruling that, under the 1964 Wilderness Act, the Forest Service could not harvest timber on land adjoining designated "primitive areas" before completing its study of all lands considered for future wilderness status. Unable to pass a bill to increase the timber harvest, Nixon issued an executive action raising the cut, a move applauded by the timber industry—and attacked by environmentalists and by Saylor.[76]

Carving the National Forestry Management Act

Forestry practices had rarely taken account of the consequences. Clearcutting—removing all trees in an area—caused major erosion and stream damage, particularly on steep slopes, often destroying fisheries. Streamside logging, leading to increased water temperatures, further impaired fish populations, wiping out once-abundant salmon in many West Coast rivers and streams. Timber harvesting considered neither wildlife and recreation nor sustainability for future harvests. Logging had also destroyed most of the nation's old-growth forests. "It was often difficult for those in the private market," observed Hays, "to accept the notion that public natural resources were an important public asset."[77]

Some legislators had become openly skeptical about forest practices. In April 1971 Senator Frank Church (D-ID) questioned an executive from timber giant Weyerhaeuser about brochures showing flourishing forests in land that had been clear-cut. When the executive admitted that the pictures depicted a hoped-for future, Church snapped, "In other words, your forests don't actually look like this."[78] Church noted that this practice effectively violated the multiple-use mandate, saying, "A large piece of clear-cut land has obviously usurped other uses."[79] Yet many legislators continued to defer to the timber industry.

Then, in the early 1970s, West Virginia hunters and fishermen, together with the conservation group the Izaak Walton League and attorneys for the Sierra Club Legal Defense Fund, sued over the effects of clear-cutting on the fish and wildlife in the Monongahela National Forest. The plaintiffs based their suit on the Forest Management Act of 1897, which allowed harvesting only previously marked mature trees.[80] In December 1973, a federal court banned many common timber practices, such as some forms of clearcutting. The decision threatened to shut down logging across the nation.[81] Congress addressed the issue with the Forest and Rangeland Renewable Resources Planning Act of 1974, which required a periodic assessment of forest management, including timber inventories, estimated harvests, and recreational resources.[82] Senator Hubert Humphrey (D-MN) declared, "For too long we have marched backwards in our forest policies. In my judgement this Act comes to grips with tomorrow's resource problems now before we have [an] irreversible crisis in our forests."[83]

In 1976 Congress returned to the issue, with a bill drafted by Jim Moorman, head of the Sierra Club Legal Defense Fund, to limit clear-cutting and stress sustainability. The Senate passed it 90–0. The House process would be more contentious. On September 17 the House took up its own National Forest Management Act. "The need for prompt action on this legislation is well known," argued Al Ullman (D-OR), chairman of the Ways and Means Committee.

Recent Federal court decisions, based on the Organic Act of 1897, have effectively halted the timber sale program of the United States Forest Service in all or parts of six states. . . . I am especially pleased with . . . [these] aspects [of the bill]. . . . First, its emphasis on reforestation. . . . The second feature of the bill I am particularly pleased to see is that which incorporates the so-called Church subcommittee guidelines on timber management and clearcutting into law.[84]

George Brown (D-CA) offered an amendment to further limit clear-cutting, to harvest at only a sustainable level, and to require the secretary of agriculture to "take affirmative action to perpetuate habitats . . . and populations of native species of plants and wildlife." His amendment, Brown explained, "is substantially identical to the language contained in the Senate bill. . . . Despite the very specific and prescriptive language in the Organic Act, the Forest Service over a period of many years saw fit to disregard [it]. . . . We cannot say to the Forest Service, go out and practice good forestry. We need to give them some guidelines."[85]

Steve Symms (R-ID) disagreed, declaring, "In the committee bill we do have proper guidelines which deal with this subject, which would leave the flexibility somewhat better with professional foresters."[86] James Weaver (D-OR) endorsed Brown's amendment, arguing, "We will provide more jobs in our forests the more carefully we preserve our capital resources. . . . [I]n the past we squandered a whole lot of natural resources."[87] James Johnson (R-CO) responded, "The gentleman's amendment was considered. . . . He was voted down in the full committee and he was voted down in the sub-committee."[88] Brown's amendment was defeated again, on the House floor, nearly 2–1.

Weaver then offered his own sustainability amendment, noting, "The sustained yield language is the same as in the bill that was passed by the Senate."[89] John Melcher (D-MT) disagreed, insisting, "Environmental concerns have been considered by the Committee on Agriculture . . . we think that we have done a good job in enacting into the terms of this bill ample protection for environmental concerns." Les AuCoin (D-OR) warned, "To lock this policy into law is to fail to recognize the need for reasonable flexibility."[90] The Weaver amendment was defeated, along with a similar effort from Max Baucus (D-MT). The House then passed the compromise Agriculture Committee bill 305–24, with most of the opposition from urban liberals such as San Francisco's Philip Burton, Detroit's John Conyers and Henry Waxman of Los Angeles. Both Brown and Weaver supported it. Neither environmentalists nor the timber industry were entirely pleased, but it took clear steps forward.

On September 30, Representative Tom Foley (D-WA) brought up the conference bill, including Senate language requiring that "timber will be harvested from National Forest System lands only when soil, slope and watersheds will not be irreversibly damaged . . . clearcutting is used only when it is the optimum use and clear cuts are carried out in a manner consistent with the protection of soil, watershed, fish, wildlife, recreation, aesthetic resources and regeneration of the timber."[91] The bill was passed by Congress.

The final National Forest Management Act stopped large-scale clearcuts, banned many common logging practices, and required detailed logging plans for each national forest unit and a fifty-year management plan for each of the 120 national forests. The act required an inventory of damaged and denuded lands, and that "any lands not certified as satisfactory shall be returned to the backlog and scheduled for prompt treatment," with one-eighth of the backlog being reclaimed each year.[92] The act budgeted $200 million annually for reforestation and required the secretary of agriculture to report annually to Congress "on the amounts, types, and uses of herbicides and pesticides in the National Forest System, including the beneficial or adverse effects of such uses."[93] The Forest Service was now committed not to cut more than could be regrown. Brown had lost the battle but won the war. Finally, in selling timber, "the Federal Government [will] receive not less than the appraised value."[94] Theodore Roosevelt's idea finally became law. The act would take years to implement fully, as national forest timber harvests dropped from twelve billion board feet in the 1980s to two billion board feet in 1995.[95] A side result was increased timber imports and production of timber from private land.

The Battle for Alaska

The vastest stretches of federal land needing attention were in the new state of Alaska. The Alaska Statehood Act of 1958 gave the state twenty-five years to select 104 million acres, along with their mineral rights, for state ownership. Alaska tribes argued that they deserved ownership of their ancestral lands. Udall later explained,

> One of the other things I took most satisfaction in the last two years [in office]—and again, the President [Lyndon Johnson] and his people gave me support right down the line on this—was in championing the cause of the Alaskan natives and their desire to have land in Alaska. And I put a freeze on. I deliberately picked a head-on fight with the state of Alaska and said we weren't going to let them select further lands until the natives got their lands.[96]

The situation was complicated in February 1968 when a huge oil field was discovered at Prudhoe Bay on Alaska's Arctic coast. The oil companies now wanted to build a pipeline to Valdez, an all-weather port on the state's southern coast. In 1970 Interior Secretary Wally Hickel, an Alaskan, decided to issue permits for road construction necessary for the building of the pipeline. At this point five native villages along the proposed pipeline route filed suit, noting that they had not given permission for the pipeline to pass through their land. The Wilderness Society also sued, citing the pipeline's lack of an adequate environmental impact statement.[97]

Congress now opened debate on a bill giving Alaska natives land and money in exchange for their cooperation in allowing oil extraction and passage through their land. In summer 1970 the Senate voted to give the natives ten million acres and compensation equal to $1 billion. Natives felt the amount of land was insufficient, while environmentalists wanted to protect lands for later designation as wilderness.[98] On the House side, in October 1969 Saylor, Aspinall, and seven other members of the Subcommittee on Indian Affairs flew to Alaska to hold hearings, but failed to produce a bill in that Congress.

In 1971 the House considered a proposal to give Alaska natives eighteen million acres immediately and another twenty-two million after the state had completed its selection. Saylor and Morris Udall offered an amendment to prevent the state from choosing its land until the federal government completed its own land use plan, within five years. Up to one hundred million acres could be set aside by the interior secretary for possible wilderness during this period. "Alaska is the only place left under the American flag," argued Saylor, "where we can plan before the land has been ruined."[99] The amendment lost 217–178, and the House then passed the bill 334–63. Saylor and others persuaded Jackson and Alan Bible (D-NV), chair of the Senate Subcommittee on National Parks, to add wilderness language to the Senate bill. Testifying before the Senate Interior Committee, McCloskey implored, "There have been few moments in the history of our country when the fate of so much land had to be decided . . . This is the one great opportunity to do something right for once."[100] The Bible amendment gave the secretary of the interior six months to propose areas for potential protection.

The House-Senate conference committee met nine times before agreeing on final language, the Alaska Native Claims Settlement Act of 1971, giving natives forty million acres along with up to a billion dollars. The act also gave the Department of the Interior nine months to withdraw up to eighty million acres for wilderness or other protection and allowed the secretary three months to freeze unlimited acreage before natives or the state chose their land. The bill ended Stewart Udall's 1968 land freeze and explicitly provided a pipeline corridor. Nixon signed the act on December 18, 1971, four days after its passage.

The land to be protected would be decided by secretary of the interior Morton. McCloskey feared that the club had alienated Morton by campaigning against his nomination, but "when Morton was found recuperating in Stanford Medical Center from a cancer operation, [Sierra Club president Ed] Wayburn, a doctor attached to that hospital, would visit and chat about Alaska. Eventually Morton did the right thing."[101] Morton withdrew 127 million Alaska acres for possible protection. In 1980 the Alaska National Interest Lands Conservation Act finally protected 104 acres of wilderness.[102]

Setting Rules for Mining the Earth

Over a century of industrialization, Americans savaged the earth to extract natural resources. "In the effort to reach mineral riches, miners peeled away the very crust of the earth, gutted mountains with water cannons, clear-cut woodlands and destroyed the habitat of wildlife," wrote Benjamin Kline. "Minerals were necessary to build an industrial nation, and their extraction made some people wealthy—but again the environmental costs were high as pollution and wastes accumulated."[103]

Between 1866 and 1872 Congress enacted mining laws that were still largely unchanged 150 years later. "Mining companies could obtain valuable mineral assets for $2.50 per acre," related Andrews, "wherever on the public lands they might find them—prices that are still in effect today, a century and a quarter later—and persons under the guise of mining could enter and claim public lands for virtually any purpose, fulfill the minimum occupancy and improvement requirements, purchase them for a modest price, and control their future use." A General Accounting Office audit in 1974 found that 237 of 240 random claims had never been mined, and most were being used for other purposes.[104]

Legislation in 1920 and 1947 put fossil fuels and some minerals under a leasing system, but ignored other minerals, including precious metals. Mining interests' opposition to changing the law was formidable. In a 1969 interview Udall noted his effort to get Congress to rewrite the 1872 laws "consonant with sound conservation practices."[105] It didn't happen. It didn't happen under Nixon, either, despite an administration effort to require prospectors to obtain a license and to pay fair market value on any minerals produced.

Strip mining, surface ripping that was cheaper than deep mining, wreaked major damage on the land. In 1970 *Newsweek* reported, "More than 20,000 strip mines are cutting ugly scars across the landscape at an estimated rate of 153,000 acres annually. By 1980, according to a White House study, more than 5 million acres of America the beautiful will have been defaced in this way."[106] In 1965 Senator Gaylord Nelson (D-WI) introduced a bill to control strip mining and make mine operators responsible for land reclamation, charging, "Strip mining . . . destroys the land surface, increases erosion, pollutes rivers and streams, destroys natural beauty and threatens public safety."[107] Nelson introduced it in the next four sessions of Congress without success.

In 1967 the Department of the Interior, as required by the Appalachian Regional Development Act of 1965, recommended regulation of strip mining and reclamation of strip-mined lands, but the Johnson administration did not propose a bill.[108] Two years later the department adopted regulations requiring land reclamation, but later review found little enforcement.[109]

Saylor urged legislation enforcing strict rules on surface mining, requiring permits from the Interior Department and posting financial bonds to insure reclamation of the land. The bill also prohibited strip mining on steep slopes and created a $100 million fund to restore stripped lands. It passed the House 265–75 but died in the Senate.[110] In 1971 President Nixon recommended strip mining regulation in his environmental message to Congress, the first of four requests without effect. While the regulation found some support in the administration, the opposition of the powerful coal industry would affect both administration and congressional attitudes.

In 1971 Representative Ken Hechler (D-WV) introduced a bill to regulate strip mining, declaring, "I have seen what havoc and obliteration is left in the wake of strip mining. It has ripped the guts out of our mountains . . . and left a trail of utter despair for many honest and hardworking people," but his proposal did not make it out of the House Interior Committee.[111] In 1973 the Senate, driven by Jackson, passed by voice vote amendments from Nelson requiring restoration of mined areas, banning dumping downstream from mining cuts, and authorizing an excise tax to pay for restoration. The next year, the House passed a bill banning strip mining on land that could not be reclaimed and setting a fee on coal of thirty-five cents a ton to fund restoration. A conference bill passed both houses in December.

Morton and Train urged President Ford to sign it. In a memorandum on the bill, Ford's assistant Cole wrote,

> The environmental damage from strip mining is excessive and should be subject to effective control. A strip mining bill would provide industry with environmental ground rules and standards governing future production, the lack of which is said to be presently inhibiting expansion of coal mining. . . . Train states there is no reason to believe that the legislation will result in unacceptable increases in cost to the industry or losses of production.[112]

But with the Arab oil boycott following the Yom Kippur War, coal had become an energy as well as an environmental issue. Frank G. Zarb, head of the Federal Energy Administration, joined the coal companies in urging a veto, arguing that it would cut coal production and increase unemployment, and that reduced coal production would increase oil imports by 450,000 to 1.8 million barrels, costing consumers $5.6 billion.[113] The bill's supporters challenged these predictions, arguing that new jobs would be created in underground mining and land reclamation. Fearing the economic impact, Ford pocket vetoed the bill. When Congress repassed the bill in 1975, Ford again vetoed it. Before a vote to override the veto, Morris Udall told the House that the United Mine Workers and the AFL-CIO supported the bill, believing it would not cost jobs.[114] Still, the override motion fell three votes short of the two-thirds required. The bill passed Congress again in 1977, and the new president, Jimmy Carter, signed it.

The Wilderness Rises and Moves East

Years after its passage, the Wilderness Act of 1964 was still unfinished business. By 1971, seven years after the start of the Wilderness Act's ten-year review period, Congress had added only 1.4 million acres as wilderness of the 53 million acres to be reviewed.[115] In late 1970 the Forest Service began its Roadless Area Review and Evaluation (RARE), evaluating 1,449 roadless areas encompassing fifty-six million acres for possible wilderness designation.[116] Under lobbying from environmental groups, in 1971 the Nixon administration briefly considered an executive order to halt logging in roadless areas awaiting final designation, but decided not to issue the order. Whitaker noted that the decision was political, reflecting the "president's concern on overplaying the environment."[117]

In 1972 the completed study selected only six million acres as wilderness, releasing many more acres for multiple use development. Under agriculture secretary Earl Butz, the Forest Service still had increasing timber harvests as its highest priority.[118] The Sierra Club Legal Defense Fund filed suit in June 1972, arguing that the Forest Service had made decisions with inadequate public input and information. In August the court issued a preliminary injunction blocking all logging on roadless areas. The Forest Service then settled with the Sierra Club, dropping timber sales from roadless areas in 1973 and agreeing to follow NEPA requirements for full environmental impact statements on future roadless sales. The Forest Service's followup report, RARE II, released in 1977, expanded wilderness acreage from six million to fifteen million acres, with ten million additional acres set aside for further study.[119]

Full implementation of the Wilderness Act hung on a disagreement among agencies, and among environmentalists. The Forest Service maintained that wilderness areas had to be pristine, while the Fish and Wildlife Service argued that previously developed areas that had largely reverted to wildness could qualify. The National Park Service had its own idiosyncrasies in designation. At a Senate Interior Committee hearing in May 1972, Church complained, "I do not—and I think this Committee does not—want to see the promise of a truly diverse National Wilderness Preservation System cut short by unnecessarily restrictive policies."[120] Under pressure from Church and multiple citizens and groups, the National Park Service revised its policies. An Interior Department staffer promised, "Under these [new] guidelines, many of the areas previously excluded will be recommended for wilderness designation."[121]

Environmentalists had similar differences, particularly between the Wilderness Society and the Sierra Club. The Wilderness Society endorsed a flexibility like Fish and Wildlife's position, and under executive director Stewart Brandborg had doubled its membership by focusing on developing local organizations lobbying for wilderness status for areas nearby.[122] In contrast, the Sierra Club, under the volunteer head of its Wilderness Classification Committee, Francis Walcott, emphasized protection over access. Walcott argued that if overuse threatened wilderness, the club should support limiting access. The club's Pacific Northwest representative, Brock Evans, saw this strategy as politically disastrous, arguing, "We would be murdered in every debate if we become known as the nuts who do not want any people in the wilderness."[123]

These disagreements became important in the 1972 debate over protecting land in the East. The Sierra Club supported the proposed National Forest Wild Areas Act, sponsored by Senators George Aiken (R-VT) and Herman Talmadge (D-GA), to create a separate nonwilderness system of eastern lands with previous use, a designation allowing improvements and even some logging. Walcott said that he was reluctant "to insist on wilderness designation for [lands] which are really not that," and the bill noted that little land east of the Mississippi would fully meet the criteria of wilderness.[124] The Wilderness Society strongly rejected the proposal, instead backing Jackson's Eastern Wilderness Areas Act, which expanded the national wilderness system to include eastern lands without treating them differently. The Senate passed a bill in September 1972, but the House failed to act before the session ended.

When the new Congress met in January 1973, the Wilderness Society had found allies within the Sierra Club, and the club's board agreed to support Jackson's bill. In February 1974 the Forest Service agreed to support a bill if it explicitly limited "restored" wilderness to the East. In May, after a delay due to the Watergate scandal, the Senate Agriculture and Interior Committees jointly produced a new Eastern Wilderness act, a modification of Jackson's proposal.

The Senate debate was opened by Aiken, the ranking Republican on the Agriculture Committee, where he spent all his thirty-four years in the Senate. Aiken grew up on a farm in Vermont, wrote two books on horticulture, and always listed his occupation not as "senator" but "farmer." Legendary as a frugal Yankee, he would annually return any unspent office expense money to the Treasury. Fiscally conservative, he was socially liberal, a moving force behind the creation of the food stamp program, and a longtime advocate for preservation. Spending decades on the Foreign Relations Committee—he initially took the seat to keep Joe McCarthy from getting it—Aiken was an early critic of the Vietnam War, and became widely known for his proposed solution: the United States should declare victory and leave. Mike Mansfield, the longtime Democratic Senate majority leader, called Aiken the most solid man in the Senate.

"Since the enactment of the Wilderness Act of 1964, 95 wilderness areas have been designated in the United States," Aiken told the Senate. "Only four of these areas have been designated in the forests east of the 100th Meridian."[125] Endorsing the bill, Aiken explained, "The Interior Committee felt that rather than create a new system of wild areas in the eastern United States, it should extend the protection of the National Wilderness System to the eastern United States . . . the legislation creates 19 'instant' [wilderness] areas in 18 states and it designates 40 'study' areas which will be preserved for their wilderness potential." By agreement with western senators, Aiken explained, "western wilderness [will] be managed under the terms of the 1964 Act and the new Eastern wilderness will be managed under the more strict provisions" of the current bill. In the eastern wilderness, water or power projects were prohibited, along with any new mining.[126]

Talmadge, chair of the Agriculture Committee, promised that the bill "will preserve for future generations in the Eastern United States an opportunity to enjoy recreation in primitive wilderness areas. . . . In this bill, we recognize the fact that the Eastern National Forests have been acquired primarily from private ownership and, in the past, have been subject to highly developed works of man." After years of delay and disputes, explained Jackson, "all parties are united in their desire to correct the imbalance in the national effort to preserve wilderness and in their recognition that there are numerous areas in the East worthy of preservation." After objections from the Izaak Walton League, Jackson accepted an amendment increasing the term of protection from "three years after a President submits a recommendation to Congress" to a minimum of three full Congresses. The Senate then passed the Eastern Wilderness Act by acclamation.[127]

In the House, Aspinall had been removed by 1972 Colorado primary voters, and the Interior Committee chair was now held by James Haley (D-FL). Saylor and Haley proposed a bill protecting 471,186 acres as wilderness east of the Mississippi. To complaints that the proposal did not meet the criteria of the Wilderness Act, Saylor responded,

> I am the author of the Wilderness Act in this House. I know very well what it says and what it intended, and I know how it was intended to be applied in a practical program. I have spent more than 25 years of my life doing battle with these people. . . . If they want to come before me with a lot of hokum about "purity" and "diluting the high standards of the Wilderness Act" . . . they are welcome to do so, but ask them to come with their eyes opened and prepared for battle.[128]

In fall 1974 the House passed an amended measure, designating sixteen new wilderness areas and seventeen new wilderness study areas. Since Congress was preparing to adjourn, the Senate accepted the House version without the Senate's language differentiating between eastern and western lands. When the bill went to the president, the OMB recommended approval. Undersecretary of the Interior Whitaker urged, "We recommend the President approve the enrolled bill . . . the legislation represents a strong beginning towards enlarging the wilderness system in the eastern national forests."[129] The Forest Service agreed. In January President Ford signed the Eastern Wilderness Areas Act, protecting 207,000 acres in thirteen states east of the Mississippi, and setting aside another 125,000 acres in nine eastern states for study. By comparison, of the original 9.1 million acres in the Wilderness Act of 1964, just 26,000 were in the eastern United States.[130] There is now an 8,400-acre George D. Aiken Wilderness in Vermont.

The Nixon-Ford years saw a further expansion of wilderness areas in the West. Around the same time President Ford signed the Eastern Wilderness Act, he also signed the Omnibus Wilderness Act, protecting another 720,556 acres in seventeen wilderness areas across thirteen states.[131]

Protecting the Prairies and the Desert

Nonforested public lands—by 1960 half of the remaining 400 million public acres in the lower 48 states—received less attention.[132] Early on, observers noted that much of this land would require different treatment.[133] In 1878 Major John Wesley Powell conducted a detailed scientific survey of the Colorado River Basin, but his recommendation that planning and development needed to allow for the area's low rainfall was ignored. The year before, Congress had passed the Desert Land Act, allowing claimants to buy 640 acres of desert on the condition that they irrigate it. The irrigation requirement was largely ignored, but in the fourteen years before the act was repealed, 11 million acres were sold, mainly to large grazing operations and speculators.[134]

Soil destruction was clear even before the creation of the United States. Colonial planters recognized that tobacco stripped soil, forcing movement to new areas. Over time it became clear that other monocultures could have similar effects. The 1930s Dust Bowl in the Great Plains would later be traced to thirty years of monocultures depleting the grassland, eroding the topsoil, and ignoring the region's limited rainfall, leading to farms literally blowing away.[135] An estimated nine million acres were ruined and another fifty million severely damaged.[136] Theodore Roosevelt's proposal to charge for the use of federal grazing lands had been blocked by cattlemen's sharp opposition.[137] But in 1934 the Dust Bowl produced the Taylor Grazing Act, limiting grazing to designated areas. Representative Edward Taylor (D-CO) explained, "I fought for the conservation of the public domain under Federal leadership because the citizens were unable to cope with the situation. . . . [T]he livestock industry, through circumstances beyond its control, was headed for self-strangulation."[138] But while the Grazing Service created by the act blocked some overgrazing, domination by local users kept grazing fees well below market rates. Values other than livestock production, such as wildlife protection, were ignored.[139]

The next year, Congress established the Soil Conservation Service to manage the land against further destruction.[140] An Agriculture Department soil expert, Hugh Hammond Bennett, who had warned, Cassandra-like, of the danger of soil erosion during the 1920s, was named to head the service. Estimating the cost of erosion at $400 million a year, Bennett wrote, "Since the first crude plow uprooted the first square foot of sod . . . erosion of the soil has been a problem. . . . In the United States today, no problem is more urgent."[141] The Soil Conservation Service provided technical assistance to farmers and promoted soil-protective measures such as terracing, crop rotation, and planting and using trees as windbreaks.[142] In 1946 the Grazing Service merged with the General Land Office to form the Bureau of Land Management (BLM) to manage public lands not falling under the other agencies, labeled "the lands nobody knows."[143]

The 1960s saw increasing concern about damage done to nonforested land, particularly the 318 million acres of rangelands managed by the BLM. Overgrazing was damaging these lands, leading to erosion, damage to the soil and native plants, and habitat destruction. In 1975 the BLM reported only 17 percent of rangeland in good or excellent condition.[144] The BLM was strongly dominated by the livestock and mining industries. Political scientists Samuel Dana and Sally Fairfax assessed, "The bureau had no coherent mission, no authority. . . . It was rather like the lands it managed, a residual category, assigned to administer the loose ends of over 3500 statutes randomly enacted over the previous 150 years."[145]

Even with the massive giveaways of the nineteenth century, the federal government still owned one-third of the nation's land, with the proportion much higher in many western states. The land was mostly managed by the BLM, the least-funded and least-staffed agency. Thousands of contradictory laws, going back to the Northwest Ordinance of 1787, governed the public domain. In 1964 Congress passed the Classification and Multiple Use Act (CMUA), mandating the BLM to identify lands with multiple use values, specifically including outdoor recreation and wilderness.[146] The authority it granted the BLM was temporary, lapsing when the Public Land Law Review Commission (PLLRC) issued its report.[147] Historian James Skillen wrote, "Aspinall introduced and supported the CMUA . . . as a stopgap measure until the PLLRC could complete its investigation and make comprehensive legislative recommendations."[148]

During the 1960s Udall, who oversaw the BLM, tried to reform the agency. Karl Langstrom, BLM director from 1961 to 1963, declared new principles. Historian James Skillen wrote, "The government should receive full compensation for its property; federal-private land exchanges must serve a federal interest; lands that cannot be developed under existing laws would be retained."[149] Udall pushed for recreation to be considered an important part of multiple use management.[150] Against fierce opposition from ranchers and their congressional allies, Udall—and his successor, Wally Hickel—also tried to raise grazing fees to market levels.[151]

Through the second half of the 1960s, the Public Land Law Commission, chaired by Aspinall, met to review public lands regulation, hearing almost a thousand witnesses. "Some way or other," declared Aspinall, "we have got to bring into direct focus these 5000-plus public land laws that are now on our books, the 50,000-plus rules and regulations that are in effect and increasing daily." When a South Dakota congressman quoted Daniel Webster that the nation's lifeblood sprang from the soil, Aspinall quipped, "He also said that there wasn't anything west of the Mississippi River worth spending a cent on." Responding to environmentalists' urgings that non-financial values be considered, Aspinall argued, "There is a good expression that you can't live by bread alone. But the antithesis of that is you can't live without bread."[152] In the summer of 1970 Aspinall wrote to Nixon that the commission's recommendations were ready, and, in the words of an aide, he wanted "as much fanfare as possible." Nixon had to publicly accept the report; Whitaker's office noted that Aspinall "controls with an iron hand virtually all natural resource related legislation and funding in the West."[153]

The PLLRC presented its three-hundred-page report to President Nixon at a Rose Garden ceremony on June 23, 1970. The report included 137 specific major recommendations, 18 basic recommendations, and 250 supplementary recommendations, urging that the land be zoned for the most productive economic use.[154] Prioritizing mining, the PLLRC report declared, "*Mineral exploration and development should have a preference over some or all other uses on much of our public lands.*"[155] In Udall's estimation, the PLLRC had produced a "goodies-for-all report that apparently pleases nobody."[156]

Environmentalists and some leaders in the BLM and the Department of Interior, as well as Train at the EPA, opposed the idea that economic use should be the only criteria for land management. "Multiple use has become a misnomer," objected Justice William Douglas. "Land used for a highway preempts all other uses. Land used for strip mining is the same. Certain types of logging or even grazing may ruin most, if not all, other uses. . . . [T]he Public Land Law Review Commission in its 1970 report threw its weight on the side of dollars and against ecology."[157] McCloskey said that it proposed "replacing the concept of multiple use with dominant use—that is, frankly, setting aside many areas for grazing, mining or timbering as their principal use."[158] Having Aspinall chair the study, commented a writer for *Sports Illustrated*, was "a little like letting a rabbit decide the disposition of a lettuce field."[159] Critics pushed instead for a multiple-use mandate for the BLM, with wilderness included.

In July 1971 Jackson introduced the National Resource Land Management Act, drafted with input from the BLM, giving the BLM statutory authority for land classification, planning and multiple use. The bill ran into a roadblock in the House Subcommittee for Public Lands. Irving Senzel, BLM assistant director for legislation, reported, "Each of the hearings started with a statement that the bill was not acceptable to the Subcommittee [because it gave too] much authority to the Interior Secretary."[160] Aspinall introduced his own bill implementing the PLLRC's recommendations and curbing the secretary of the interior's power to protect public lands without congressional consent. Given the wide gulf between these positions, Congress could not reach agreement. Jackson would reintroduce his bill each year from 1971 to 1975.

These years saw the BLM sued successfully over the Trans-Alaska pipeline, offshore oil and gas leasing, and grazing, and for inadequate or missing environmental impact statements. This helped spur Congress to act. Early in 1976 the Senate, with environmentalist support, passed the Federal Lands Policy and Management Act, stressing the public interest rather than mining and ranching. In July the House took it up. With Aspinall gone, the House seemed more open to compromise. John Melcher (D-MT), chair of the Public Lands Subcommittee, opened the debate, calling the bill an implementation of the PLLRC report and "a major step in modernizing the public land laws. The bill . . . will establish a mission for the more than 450 million acres of public lands administered by the Bureau of Land Management."[161] Steiger, the subcommittee's ranking Republican, declared that the bill "is a long way from being perfect, but that does not take away from the fact that the existing unrevised laws are grossly imperfect."[162]

John Seiberling (D-OH) objected that the BLM did not have enough law enforcement authority to implement the regulations on its land, and to the provision allowing either house of Congress to review and potentially veto any withdrawals of land over five thousand acres. Joe Skubitz (R-KS) responded that the bill "seeks to reassert congressional control over the actions of the BLM, which, at most, have gone too far in the search for environment preservation."[163] To environmental critics, Melcher cited "three particular areas. The bill provides for range improvement, for improvement of habitat for both livestock and wildlife. . . . [It allows] BLM lands to be reviewed for possible inclusions of portions of land with the wilderness system. . . . Third, the bill does carry with it a provision for the California desert areas."[164] Tom Downey (D-NY) objected to "a grazing fee at less than fair market value."[165] Patsy Mink (D-HI) proposed increasing the level to trigger congressional oversight from five thousand acres to twenty-five thousand acres. Steiger replied, "We [should] have no acreage limitations . . . the previous Secretaries of the Interior have abused that withdrawal privilege."[166] Asked to give an example of abuse, Steiger fumed,

> Taking 1800 acres of southern Utah for preservation of the side blotched uta . . . it is a noxious lizard, some inch and a half in length, which abounds as a pest in the nearby community of Kanab. The sole purpose of protecting the side blotched uta, and the same with the sandhill tortoise and other esoteric creatures, half of which I think are fragments of the Secretary's imagination, is to prevent mining.[167]

Melcher, opposing the Mink amendment, noted that there had been only two parcels over five thousand acres withdrawn in the whole country in the prior year. The Mink amendment was defeated, 193–191.

Bob Eckhardt (D-TX) then proposed an amendment setting grazing fees at fair market value, leading Steiger to reply, "I have never seen so many people so dedicated to a subject about which they know so little."[168] The Eckhardt amendment was rejected. Seiberling offered an amendment strengthening the BLM's law enforcement authority and powers. Despite Jim Santini (R-NV) objecting that "the consequences of the amendment would be the establishment of a Federal police force on public lands," the Seiberling amendment was passed.[169] Conservatives now offered an amendment that any regulation or rule made by the secretaries of the interior and agriculture about public lands must be submitted to Congress for review. This amendment was rejected. A proposal by conservatives to send the bill back to the Interior Committee to incorporate such a plan was then rejected 198–128. The House then narrowly passed the Federal Land Policy and Management Act, 164–155, after numbers of both conservative and proenvironmental amendments had been rejected.

The final Senate-House conference committee bill would pass before the end of the year. The conference committee remained deadlocked on the issues of grazing fees, finally just mandating a study to decide if fees were "equitable to the United States and to the holders of grazing permits and leases."[170] The new law mandated that the BLM consider environmental issues in its policies and procedures, asking that the secretary of the interior "take any action necessary to prevent unnecessary or undue degradation of the land."[171] The bill declared, "The public lands [should] be managed in a manner that will protect the quality of scientific, scenic, historical, ecological, environmental, air and atmospheric, water resources, and archeological values."[172] The BLM was required to conduct an inventory and systematic evaluation of its public lands, including a comprehensive review of lands that could be considered wilderness. The BLM selected twenty-four million of fifty-seven million acres of roadless areas for review, with a goal of finishing this by 1991 and the land kept as wilderness in the interim.[173] The bill, declared Jackson, "represents a landmark achievement in the management of public lands for the United States. For the first time in the long history of public lands, one law provides comprehensive authority and guidelines for administration."[174]

The Green Years did not achieve the major advance that had once seemed so close: a national land use policy and structure. But the time's achievements on the landmass of the United States are the more impressive when set against the times to follow. By 1976 the wilderness system had only increased to 15 million acres, from the original 9.1 million acres in 1964. However, agency review, along with the new laws, would soon lead to a huge expansion of the area of protected wilderness. By 1994 the wilderness system would measure more than 100 million acres, much of it in Alaska.[175] Decades later, when any addition to the wilderness system would be a bitterly fought, interminable battle, the addition of tens of millions of acres set in motion by the efforts of the Green Years seems a massive leap forward. Nobody would claim that order and serenity had been achieved in the vast stretches of territory overseen by the Bureau of Land Management. But after a congressional battle, some greater clarity was achieved, an advance that looked even more substantial after decades when the Sagebrush Rebellion challenged the BLM's very authority, and resistance, occasionally violent, marked the reaction to the agency's efforts to collect grazing fees and limit use of battered landscapes.

The debate over the Federal Land Policy and Management Act displayed early evidence of the regional and partisan chasms that would impede future environmental reforms. The kind of legislators who could provide leadership across divisions—mountain state Democrats like Frank Church and Frank Moss in the Senate and John Melcher and Max Baucus in the House, and northeast Republicans such as John Saylor and George Aiken—would become endangered species themselves. The western Democrats would be replaced by conservative supporters of the grazing, mining, and logging industries, creating a larger gap with the more environmentally friendly Congressional representatives from more urban and suburban districts and states. But in the early 1970s, Capitol Hill backing for major environmental gains was often overwhelming, especially in the Senate. In the Green Years, congressional readiness to lead, and to support, produced a major legacy on lands.

CHAPTER THIRTEEN

The Years That Followed

The greatest burst of environmental activity was over. Yet the Carter administration would have significant achievements as the last gasp of the environmental tide, given what was to follow. Since then, the battle has too often been an effort to resist rollback.

Air, Water, Land, and Alaska in the Carter Years

In 1977 Congress passed the first major revision of the Clean Air Act, another bipartisan effort led by Edmund Muskie (D-ME) and Howard Baker (R-TN). But there was a difference. "Unlike in 1970 when there were few advocacy groups for or against clean air, we had created a lobbyist boom," wrote Baker. "Every day when we considered Clean Air act amendments and then conferred with the House on them, our venues were packed with lobbyists in long lines extending out the doors. . . . It was more difficult for members to find accommodation for competing views. There was more suspicion."[1]

The 1977 revisions created new performance standards, defined goals of preventing significant air quality deterioration, classified attainment and nonattainment areas, and set stricter motor vehicle emission standards.[2] Fighting auto industry efforts to weaken the law, Muskie, Baker, and Jennings Randolph (D-WV) accepted some modifications while retaining strong standards. The Senate bill was tougher than the House bill, which was strongly influenced by the auto industry and other advocates. "But because the Senate would not yield any further than it had with my amendment," recalled Baker, "the auto industry advocates had to accept that outcome."[3]

President Carter, in his first environmental message to Congress, called for action on water pollution, requesting $4.5 billion in each of the next ten years for municipal wastewater treatment. Congress responded with the Federal Water Pollution Control Act of 1977, requiring most cities to build water treatment facilities and providing federal grants to assist.[4] In the same message, Carter urged additions to the National Wild and Scenic Rivers system. Carter would add protection to thirty-four Alaska rivers totaling 3,427 miles, and, fifteen hours before he left office, the second-largest addition, protecting a group of rivers in northern California. In all, Carter would add five thousand miles to the system, increasing the miles of rivers protected by 300 percent.[5]

On March 30, 1977, Frank Church (D-ID) introduced the Endangered American Wilderness Act, protecting four hundred thousand acres of National Forest land. The act passed the Senate 89–3, with House passage and presidential signature following. Next, Church introduced three further bills to designate 1.3 million to 2.3 million acres in Idaho as wilderness, quoting the writer Edward Abbey, declaring, "Wilderness needs no defense—it needs more defenders."[6] Despite opposition from western conservatives, the Senate passed a bill designating 2.2 million acres as the River of No Return Wilderness—now the Frank Church River of No Return Wilderness—by 69–18. After the House approval with a vote of 271–137, Carter signed it into law in the summer of 1980.[7]

Representative Philip Burton (D-CA) engineered one of the biggest victories of the period, the National Parks and Recreation Act of 1978. It increased the rivers and mileage in the Wild and Scenic Rivers system by 40 percent, with seventeen more rivers set for further study. The bill also expanded national parks and wilderness areas in 144 different projects across forty-four states, a sweep that won it the label "parks barrel."[8] That year Congress also voted to add forty-eight thousand more acres to Redwood National Park, nearly doubling its size. In 1977 the push for control of strip mining was finally victorious when President Carter signed the Surface Mining Control and Reclamation Act.

Following the Alaska Native Claims Settlement Act of 1971, more than a hundred million acres were set aside for possible future protection. To complete the process, the House passed the Alaska National Interest Lands Conservation Act, 277–31. The bill made it through Senate committee to the floor with so little time left in the session that Senator Mike Gravel (D-AK), who had not taken much of a role up to then, could block enactment with the threat of a filibuster. "One man decided to prevent the other 99 senators from voting," complained Morris Udall, "and so we lost it."[9] In late 1978 Carter responded to the filibuster blocking the bill with executive action setting aside 113.5 million acres in Alaska, some as national monuments and some for temporary protection. "The top environmental priority of my administration, perhaps my entire life," explained Carter, "has been a carefully considered proper protection of the wild and precious land of Alaska."[10] In 1979 Udall, now chair of the House Interior Committee, introduced the bill again, warning, "Americans will never see a buffalo herd again and if we are not wise today, our grandchildren will not be able to see a caribou herd."[11] Udall's bill passed the House but met opposition in the Senate. Henry Jackson (D-WA) negotiated a compromise between developers and conservationists to pass it through the Senate, winning the gratitude of Secretary of the Interior Cecil Andrus.[12] In the bill, environmentalists accepted less restriction on development, particularly in the Arctic National Wildlife Range and the Tongass National Forest. But the bill still had to overcome opposition from Alaska's senators and the tradition that, in the words of James Morton Turner, "Congress rarely overrides a state's congressional delegation on matters of importance to the state."[13]

The final legislation placed 104 million acres in national parks and wildlife refuges while nearly doubling the land designated as wilderness. The act created twelve new national parks, fifty-six million acres of protected wilderness, twenty-five wild and scenic rivers, and eleven new national wildlife refuges. Senator Gaylord Nelson (D-WI) commented, "You'll never adopt anything like that again."[14]

In 1978 the nation learned of hazardous wastes contaminating the area around Love Canal in New York. The discovery brought to light thousands of similar abandoned waste sites across the country threatening public health and the environment. Addressing the issue, Congress produced the Comprehensive Environmental Response, Compensation and Liability Act, nicknamed Superfund. It allotted $1.6 billion for the cleanup of toxic waste sites and oil spills, funded by taxes on the petroleum and chemical industries.[15] The Environmental Protection Agency (EPA) would identify the sites, clean up the worst, and, when possible, force the responsible party to cover the costs. The money could also pay for cleanup in emergencies, or when the responsible party could not pay.[16]

The Superfund would ultimately prove disappointing. Due to the complexity of the problems, only a fraction of the most contaminated sites has been cleaned. It also failed to address ongoing ordinary chemical exposure. "While EPA has focused its entire hazardous waste program on industrial waste sites and abandoned dump sites, with little to show for it," judged H. Patricia Hynes, "problems of environmental contamination which don't fit that model are neglected," notably lead in urban soils and pesticides in farmers' wells.[17]

Finally, the Fish and Wildlife Conservation Act of 1980 recognized the "ecological, educational, esthetic, cultural, recreational, economic and scientific value" of all native species of wild vertebrates. It protected animals that were neither hunted or endangered, authorizing the Fish and Wildlife Service to allot $20 million over four years to state fish and wildlife agencies for "nongame conservation."[18]

In Reverse in the Reagan Era

The accomplishments during the Carter years were sizable—especially compared to the years that followed. Ronald Reagan not only defeated Carter handily, he brought along a Republican Senate. The new president and Senate were determined to reverse what they saw as excessive environmental regulation. Reagan gave industries a voice on any regulations affecting them. He cut the budgets and influence of the EPA and the Council on Environmental Quality (CEQ). Reagan's initial appointees to head the Department of Interior and the EPA, James Watt and Anne Gorsuch respectively, were overtly hostile to environmental regulations.[19] Watt had for years led the Mountain States Legal Foundation, specializing in antienvironmental legislation. Watt was forced out of Interior after two and a half years, after a congressional committee exposed leasing of Montana and Wyoming coal mining rights at a huge loss to the treasury.[20] Congress cited Gorsuch, who had been an attorney for a telephone company, for contempt for failing to produce EPA files on 160 toxic waste dumps, and she had to resign after being investigated for illegally manipulating Superfund money.

An important factor behind the Reagan administration's attacks on environmental policies was a shift in the West's congressional representation toward conservatives seeking to reduce the federal government's role in western lands. Barbara Dudley, former executive director of Greenpeace USA, credits the Reagan administration with a well-thought-out strategy to discredit environmental regulations, noting, "The brilliance of it was that they did not try to repeal laws . . . they enforced the laws against the

Moms and Pops . . . they built up this hatred for the environmental movement."[21] A Sierra Club task force had warned in 1979, "We are in terrible shape demographically—in general the states with the greatest BLM roadless acreage have the least population, including the least population of active conservationists."[22]

Turner wrote, "The ranchers, loggers, miners and off-road vehicle users who used the public domain were accustomed to playing by a set of rules that generally favored their interest."[23] These rural groups drove a political reaction against federal environmental regulations. "The Sagebrush Rebellion eventually petered out," observed journalist Philip Shabecoff, "because the 'rebels' were handed what they wanted by a compliant Interior Department: virtually unlimited access to federal lands and resources at bargain basement prices."[24] Dudley lamented, "The Wise Use [movement] outmaneuvered us."[25]

The Reagan years decimated the CEQ, which never recovered its status, level of staffing, or funding. Russell Train wrote that after his time as chairman, "Most presidents have initially tried to abolish CEQ and, when that became politically difficult, have let it continue by sufferance . . . CEQ often appears quite moribund as an institution."[26] He added wistfully, "With strong presidential support, CEQ has an almost limitless potential for creative environmental initiative."[27]

Reagan's attempts to weaken environmental laws would be somewhat limited by Congress's remaining Republican moderates. When the Endangered Species Act was reauthorized in 1982, Senator John Chafee (R-RI) made sure that its core survived. The revised law increased flexibility, allowing reintroduction of species into historic ranges, and permitting landowners to proceed with projects that might threaten species if the species were protected elsewhere. Conservative senator Alan Simpson (R-WY) praised Chafee for his compromise, "a more workable and credible framework for wildlife protection."[28]

Appalled by Reagan policies and huge EPA budget cuts, Train charged, "The EPA is rapidly being destroyed as an effective institution," a decline illustrated by Gorsuch's forced resignation and Superfund head Rita Lavelle's conviction for perjury.[29] Reagan surprised many when he brought back William Ruckelshaus to lead the EPA, where he restored professionalism and morale. "By the time I got back," Ruckelshaus explained, "the agency was in such a state of turmoil that the main thing that needed to be done was to calm it down and put it back to work."[30] J. Brooks Flippen wrote, "Even with Ruckelshaus's return, Reagan's two terms in office represented the worst environmental record of the modern era."[31] To Ruckelshaus himself, "When the Reagan Administration came in, the public was willing to give it a good deal of leeway on the means to achieve our environmental goals because it was clear some of the approaches we were taking were not going to work or were causing distortions. I don't think the public was ready to abandon—nor do I think it is now—its commitment to a clean environment."[32]

Back at the EPA, Ruckelshaus lobbied to strengthen the Clean Water Act, expanding it to cover non-source point pollution, from multiple sources. With reductions in municipal and industrial pollution, nonpoint pollution, from farm and other runoff, was the biggest uncontrolled source of tainted water. Proposals to deal with it ran into stiff resistance, particularly from agricultural interests. At the end of 1986 Congress passed legislation to strengthen the Clean Water Act, but President Reagan vetoed it. In the next Congress the Clean Water amendments passed overwhelmingly, 406–8 in the House and 93–6 in the Senate. Chafee urged the White House to sign the bill and claim credit."[33] When Reagan again vetoed the bill, Congress overrode him, allocating $20 billion for water treatment over nine years.

But regulation of nonpoint sources was weakened, limiting the EPA to providing technical assistance and funding for states' plans.[34] The result was fifty different and largely ineffective programs. Much later, a Clinton administration proposal on nonpoint pollution failed to advance in Congress.

Other changes shaped environmental options. "History will confirm that Ronald Reagan's legacy created a massive fiscal debt," mourned Stewart Udall, "restricting the options of his successor and of the American people for positive action on behalf of their air, water and land."[35] Conservatives built a case against regulation from the Fifth Amendment clause prohibiting government "taking [land] for public use without just compensation."[36] The 1922 Supreme Court case *Pennsylvania Coal Company v. Mahon* endorsed the clause as a limit on regulation. Dissenting, Justice Louis Brandeis argued, "Restriction imposed to protect the public health, safety, or morals from dangers threatened is not a taking."[37] In subsequent cases, courts would come down on either side.

The Reagan administration could point to one crucial environmental achievement. In 1974 two scientists, Sherwood Rowland and Mario

Modena, showed that chemicals called chlorofluorocarbons (CFCs), widely used in everything from refrigerants to aerosols, were contributing to the destruction of the atmosphere's ozone layer. In 1978, under President Carter, the United States banned CFC use in nonessential aerosols, yet in 1987, widely used CFC-containing products still generated an estimated $28 billion annually.[38] In 1985 British scientists noted a hole, or severe thinning, of the ozone layer over Antarctica, meaning that damaging ultraviolet radiation would increase.

Remarkably, in 1987 world leaders, with the Reagan administration in the forefront, agreed on the Montreal Protocol on Substances that Deplete the Ozone Layer, establishing policies to eliminate CFCs. "Industry preferred to face a stronger treaty, which would at least bind its foreign competitors," explained an American negotiator, "than unilateral U.S. controls with no treaty."[39] With increasing evidence of harm, the timetable was shortened in 1990 under the George H. W. Bush administration and again in 1997. By 2013 the production and use of CFCs had been reduced by over 95 percent, with a subsequent recovery of the ozone layer.[40] McCloskey commented, "With the ozone layer, we did demonstrate on a worldwide basis that scientific findings were heeded . . . showing that serious problems can be addressed by successful international action."[41]

Small Steps forward Since

Reagan's vice-president, George H. W. Bush, won the White House in 1988 calling for greater environmental protection, spurring a bipartisan coalition to strengthen the Clean Air Act. Democratic support increased when Senator Robert Byrd (D-WV), a supporter of the high-sulfur coal from his home state, was replaced as majority leader by George Mitchell (D-ME), a strong environmentalist.[42] Democratic congressional majorities would be bolstered by proenvironmental Republicans such as Chafee and Senator John Heinz (R-PA), while Bush persuaded other Republicans to support the amendments.

The Clean Air Act amendments of 1990 passed with overwhelming bipartisan support, 401–25 in the House and 89–10 in the Senate. The changes aimed to reduce acid rain and pollution emissions into the air in urban areas, and lower the emissions of two hundred airborne toxic chemicals. To reduce acid rain, caused by sulfur dioxide, in the most cost-efficient manner, the bill set up a system of marketable emission permits. Utilities could implement sulfur dioxide controls themselves or sell permits to another company that could do it for less. This plan was to prove very successful in reducing acid rain at a far lower cost than predicted. A 2010 analysis estimated that for annual costs of $3 billion, the changes had prevented eighteen thousand deaths and produced $108 billion in overall annual benefits.[43]

The 1990 Clean Air Act amendments gave the EPA power to determine the maximum achievable control technology for "major industrial facilities that emit one or more of the 189 substances presumed to be toxic," and then require the installation of such technology.[44] Conservatives attacked Bush and his EPA administrator, William Reilly, for the amendments, causing Bush to retreat on other environmental positions and weakening Reilly's position.[45]

By Bush's presidency, the threat of climate change was becoming clear. In its first report in 1970, the CEQ had noted, "Man may be changing his weather."[46] A book the same year warned, "The increasing carbon dioxide content of the upper atmosphere . . . has begun to alarm scientists because of the potential 'greenhouse effect' it may have in increasing the temperature of the earth's surface."[47] By 1983 the EPA reported, "It is probably too late to prevent the . . . warming expected to result in the next sixty years from rising atmospheric concentrations of carbon dioxide and other greenhouse gases."[48] In 1988, a year of high temperatures, drought, and fires, NASA scientist James Hansen testified to Congress, "We can state with about 99% confidence that current temperatures represent a real warming trend rather than a chance fluctuation."[49] The Bush administration refused to sign an international treaty on carbon dioxide emissions, despite its acceptance by most countries, until it was watered down to insignificance.[50]

In 1997, under Bush's successor, Bill Clinton, the United States joined the Kyoto Climate Change Accord, requiring developed countries to reduce greenhouse gas emissions to 1990 levels by 2012. Developing countries were exempted from restrictions. Partly due to this exemption, the Republican-controlled Senate refused to ratify the treaty. The Clinton administration made some progress on warming by asserting that the EPA could regulate carbon dioxide under the Clean Air Act.

Clinton's proposed broad-based energy tax, meant to reduce greenhouse gases, was weakened to pass the House and still could not pass the Senate. Manufacturers, truckers, farm lobbies, and the oil industry strongly opposed it, arguing that the tax would cost jobs and hurt consumers. Many House Democrats who supported the energy bill were defeated in the 1994

Republican landslide, with the energy issue prominent.[51] The issues of energy costs and independence constantly complicated debates over dealing with global warming and increasingly the debates over pollution. Under Clinton, in 1994 Congress passed the California Desert Protection Act, designating seven million acres of new wilderness.[52] By the mid-1990s, after many states had banned phosphate-containing detergents, the industry voluntarily quit manufacturing them.[53]

By the end of the century the environment was fully a partisan issue. For many Republicans, noted Flippen, "the environment had joined taxes and a litany of social concerns such as abortion and gay rights as wedge issues, defining partisan allegiances." Republican House whip Tom DeLay (R-TX) called the EPA "the Gestapo of government."[54] Senator John McCain (R-AZ) was a lonely GOP voice insisting in 1996, "We need to assure the public that in the 105th Congress the Republican environmental agenda will consist of more than coining new epithets for environmental extremists. . . . We Republicans are responsible for much of the negative perception of our environmental record."[55] Defending the agency he'd twice led, Ruckelshaus warned, "To the extent that people discredit this agency charged with protecting the public health and the environment, it weakens it. It weakens, even more importantly, the trust that the American people have that the government is trying to do the right thing."[56]

George W. Bush succeeded Clinton after Democratic candidate Al Gore, the strongest environmentalist among political leaders for a generation, was narrowly nosed out in the electoral college after losing by 537 votes in Florida, where nearly 100,000 votes were drawn off by the Green Party. Bush, commented Flippen, "launched a frontal attack on the environment that surpassed even the Reagan era's."[57] In 2004 Train, for the first time in his life, voted for a Democratic presidential candidate, John Kerry, charging that Bush had declared "war on the environment."[58] But despite Republican majorities in both houses, the Bush administration failed to weaken the Clean Air Act. The Republican House now succeeded in passing a law that environmentalists saw as gutting the Endangered Species Act. However, in the Senate, Lincoln Chafee (R-RI), like his father a rare pro-environment Republican, blocked action.[59]

Bush initially seemed open to taking on climate change. His first EPA administrator, Christine Whitman, declared that climate change was a major issue that needed action.[60] But facing opposition from conservatives and energy companies, Bush decided not to regulate carbon dioxide under the Clean Air Act, noting that the knowledge about the cause of climate change was incomplete.[61] Asked whether the Clean Air Act covered carbon dioxide, in April 2007 the Supreme Court affirmed, 5–4, the "existence of a causal connection between man-made greenhouse gas emissions and global warming," deciding that carbon dioxide fit the Clean Air Act definition of an air pollutant.[62]

In 2009 Bush was succeeded by Democrat Barack Obama. The Democratic Congress passed the Omnibus Public Land Management Act, adding two million acres of wilderness, with compromises building wide bipartisan support. Congress also strengthened the regulation of toxic substances in 2016.[63] A major energy bill with carbon emissions limits passed the House but failed in the Senate, and then featured prominently the following November in a Republican wave retaking the House.

Further attempts to restrict greenhouse gases, notably carbon dioxide, were unsuccessful until the Paris Climate Accord of 2015, signed by almost every nation, mandating carbon dioxide limits internationally. The agreement committed member nations, cheered Secretary of State Kerry, "that we keep pace with the technology and that we accelerate the global transition to a clean energy economy."[64] To reduce US emissions, Obama issued an executive order creating a Clean Power Plan and raising car fuel economy standards. In 2016 the United States agreed with other nations to phase out hydrofluorocarbons, extremely potent greenhouse gases. In 2016 the International Civil Aviation Organization, with US support, adopted an agreement for carbon-neutral growth. "It was the single most effective year for the environment I can remember," judged Kerry, "since groundbreaking legislation was passed in the early 70s."[65] Whether or not this judgment was correct, the gains would be negated by the 2016 presidential election.

After the election of Donald Trump, the United States abandoned any attempts to control climate change. Trump and many Republicans in Congress derided climate change as a hoax, denying human responsibility for any warming. Senator James Inhofe (R-OK), a key committee chairman, labeled climate change "the greatest hoax ever perpetuated on the American people."[66] Trump withdrew the United States from the Paris Climate Accord.

The Trump administration attacked environmental regulations in multiple areas. During the 2016 campaign Trump declared that he wanted to eliminate the EPA, saying, "What they do is a disgrace. Every week they come out with new regulations."[67] Matt Gaetz (R-FL) introduced a bill to abolish it, while Representative Rob Bishop (R-UT) declared it time to "repeal and replace" the Endangered Species Act.[68] Yet even the most antienvironmental Congress in over half a century could pass only a few rollbacks of environmental law, perhaps most notably opening the Arctic National Wildlife Refuge for development. "While Republicans had much success in . . . expanding coal, oil, and gas development both onshore and offshore after the 1980s," wrote Turner and Isenberg, "efforts to transfer public lands to the states or roll back the scope of environmental laws [have] largely fizzled."[69] With the Democrats' 2018 recapture of the House, the window for antienvironmental legislation closed, although the Trump administration proposed further administrative changes to roll back environmental regulations.

From 2016 to 2020, progress against climate change was limited to the state level and the business sector, with improved efficiency and costs leading to a rapid expansion of renewable energy sources. The election of President Joseph Biden marked a revived federal recognition of the problem of climate change. Whether the clear progress in reducing the cost of renewable energy and its increasing adoption can occur fast enough to prevent the worst scenarios of climate change remains to be answered.

Those Who Shaped the Green Years

The years after 1976 saw the Green Years' major figures take quite different paths.

When John Blatnik retired from Congress in 1974, the *St. Paul Pioneer Press* commented, "Humphrey, McCarthy and Mondale, of course, all have run or are running for the presidency, but none has exercised more power or had a more lasting influence on Minnesota or the nation than Blatnik."[70] He died in 1991, and his tombstone reads, "He cared, he served."[71]

Russell Train, after leaving the EPA in 1976, became head of the American branch of the World Wildlife Fund (WWF), leading it to sizable expansion and increased prominence. He maintained an interest in the environment until his death in 2012 at ninety-two.

Stewart Udall never repeated his success as interior secretary. After some years as an environmental consultant he returned to the Southwest as an attorney representing clients with radiation poisoning from atomic testing. He resumed writing, particularly books about the West and the environment. Udall died on March 20, 2010, the last survivor of the original Kennedy cabinet. On June 8, 2010, President Obama issued a proclamation renaming the Interior Building after him, declaring, "Stewart Udall left an indelible mark on this Nation and inspired countless Americans who will continue his fight for clean air, clean water, and to maintain our many national treasures."[72]

Frank Church prominently opposed the Vietnam War, joining with Kentucky Republican John Sherman Cooper in a series of amendments that first prohibited use of American combat troops in Laos or Thailand in 1969 and then in Cambodia in 1970. In 1975 he chaired the high-profile Senate Select Committee on Intelligence, delaying his presidential campaign until March 1976. Church won several primaries but could not catch up to Jimmy Carter. In the Reagan landslide of 1980 Church lost his seat by 4,262 votes, a margin of less than 1 percent in a state where federal environmental policy had become highly unpopular.[73] Less than four years later he died of pancreatic cancer at fifty-nine. Congress subsequently renamed the Idaho wilderness area the Frank Church River of No Return Wilderness.

Henry "Scoop" Jackson remained one of the most powerful voices in the Senate, and a firm hawk. The Jackson-Vanik Amendment, enacted over White House opposition, denied "most favored nation" trading status to countries refusing to allow their citizens to emigrate, prying a way out for many Soviet Jews. With his hawkish foreign policy views not affecting his liberal domestic stances, Jackson declined offers to be secretary of state or defense from Republican presidents. Although he won multiple awards from environmental groups, his foreign policy positions—and support for nuclear power and the supersonic transport airplane—also alienated many generally dovish environmentalists. Jackson, noted his aide Ben Wattenberg, "believed in the possibility and necessity of reconciling environmental protection with robust economic growth."[74] These positions have overshadowed his crucial contributions to environmental protection.

Jackson ran unsuccessfully for president twice, in 1972 and 1976. Easily reelected repeatedly to the Senate, he lost the Interior Committee chair when Republicans captured the Senate in 1980. Jackson won his sixth term in the Senate in 1982. One of Jackson's last proposals was for a second Outdoor Recreation Resources Review Commission, which he called "an opportunity to rediscover the constructive and bipartisan spirit that has been hallmark of much of the environmental and recreation-related legislation of the past two decades."[75] On September 1, 1983, Jackson died at seventy-one of a sudden rupture of his aorta.[76]

After a 1971 redistricting added suburban areas to Wayne Aspinall's district, his antienvironmental stances and his support of the uranium industry toppled him in the 1972 primary. The political activist group Environmental Action had placed him at the top of its "Dirty Dozen" target list. Back in Colorado, Aspinall consulted for mining companies and other western resource users. Moving right, attacking the federal government's public land decisions and pushing for more state control, he worked with Watt and the Sagebrush Rebellion before dying in 1983.

Even as his Pennsylvania district became increasingly Democratic, John Saylor continued to win reelection by wide margins. Along with support at home from both coal companies and labor unions, he was repeatedly honored by national environmental groups. The Izaak Walton League and the Sierra Club gave him their highest awards; the only other political leader to receive the Sierra Club John Muir Award was Jackson. "Whenever conservation had needed a friend in Congress," David Brower wrote Saylor, "you were there."[77] After repeated heart problems, Saylor died on October 28, 1973. Tributes poured in from both sides of the aisle.[78] Wilderness Society leader Stewart Brandborg called him "my and our great champion . . . he was undoubtedly one of the very best (and one of the earliest) environmental advocates."[79] Despite suggestions from Senator Mark Hatfield (R-OR) and others, nothing has been named for Saylor. But in Blatnik's words, Saylor's "legacy is written in countless clear-flowing streams, and in national parks and protected natural areas across America."[80]

In addition to environmentalism, Gaylord Nelson became known for efforts to protect consumers and for early opposition to the Vietnam War. By his third term he was named the best-liked senator by his colleagues. Like Church, he lost his seat in 1980. Nelson then became chairman of the Wilderness Society, which during the 1980s exploded from forty-two thousand to three hundred thousand members, partly in reaction to Reagan's policies. Clinton awarded Nelson the Presidential Medal of Freedom, the nation's highest civilian award, in 1995. Nelson resigned as chairman of the Wilderness Society in 2000 but remained an active voice until his death in 2005 at eighty-nine.

In 1977 Warren Magnuson left the chair of the Commerce Committee to take over the even more powerful Appropriations Committee. After thirty-six years in the Senate, Magnuson was swept out in the 1980

Republican tide by the moderate Republican state attorney general, Slade Gorton. "Senator Magnuson did more to better the quality of life for his fellow human beings than any other U.S. Senator," assessed Jackson. "That's a mighty big statement and I do not make it lightly."[81] Magnuson died of congestive heart failure in his Seattle home on May 20, 1989.[82]

John Dingell served in the House until 2015, for a record sixty years. In 1981 he became chair of the House Energy and Commerce Committee, with oversight over the EPA under Reagan. When Dingell retired in 2016 his seat was won by his second wife, Debbie; going back to his father's service, the seat has been held by the family since 1934. After retiring, Dingell remained politically involved, denouncing Donald Trump as "a clear and present danger to the United States of America."[83] After Dingell died in 2019 Congress passed a permanent reauthorization of the Land and Water Conservation Fund as the John D. Dingell, Jr. Conservation, Management and Recreation Act

William Ruckelshaus left the Environmental Protection Agency in April 1973 to become acting FBI director and then deputy attorney general. He was fired, following the resignation of Attorney General Elliot Richardson, when both men refused President Nixon's order to fire Watergate special prosecutor Archibald Cox in what became known as the "Saturday Night Massacre." Ruckelshaus practiced law before moving to Seattle in 1975 to become senior vice-president of Weyerhaeuser from 1976 until 1983. In 1976 President Ford was leaning to Ruckelshaus as his running mate, until conservatives persuaded him to choose Kansas senator Bob Dole instead. After a close battle with Ronald Reagan for the top spot, Train wrote, "Ford had simply not been in a position to risk a possible floor fight on the vice-presidential nomination."[84] In 1983, following Gorsuch's resignation, White House chief of staff James Baker asked Ruckelshaus to serve again as EPA administrator. Ruckelshaus improved morale at the agency, noting, "the mood swung from despair to jubilation . . . what the Burford [Gorsuch's married name] people had done was really terrible."[85] In 1985 Ruckelshaus returned to Seattle to practice law and serve on multiple boards involved in environmental issues. He died in 2019.

Howard Baker became nationally known as vice-chairman of the Senate special committee investigating the Watergate scandal, as he repeatedly asked, "What did the president know, and when did he know it?" He went on to become Senate minority leader in 1977, and after an unsuccessful run for president in 1980, spent four years as majority leader until 1985. After leaving the Senate, Baker became White House chief of staff for President Reagan in the wake of the Iran-Contra scandal, and under George W. Bush served as ambassador to Japan. Baker, perhaps due to his support of things anathema to environmentalists such as the supersonic transport and modification of the Endangered Species Act, never was as recognized for his environmental contributions as he deserved. Yet, looking back in 2005, at the end of his public career, Baker wrote, "I hope to be best remembered for my role in shaping the Clean Air Act of 1970."[86]

Edmund Muskie served in the Senate until 1980, becoming the first chairman of the new Senate Budget Committee, until he became secretary of state amid the Iran hostage crisis. He remained in Washington practicing law until his death in 1996. "Although the Clean Air Act and Clean Water Act are not known as the 'Muskie' Act[s] they might well be," concluded Joel Goldstein. "Indeed . . . members of the Supreme Court treat Muskie's intent as the relevant lodestar for understanding these acts. The justices recognize him as the creator of the regulatory framework."[87] In 2014 legal historian Richard Lazarus assessed, "Decades after their first enactment, the basic legal architecture that [Muskie] and his staffers like Leon Billings constructed remains largely in place." Lazarus noted how Muskie's environmental influence persisted:

> Senator Muskie has not served in the Senate since 1980, yet judges and advocates continue to debate Muskie's views in determining the legality of EPA actions. . . . Congressional intent in the context of federal environmental laws may be fairly equated with the intent of Senator Ed Muskie of Maine. Federal courts in their opinions have cited the views of Senator Muskie in the enactment of federal environmental statutes in at least 293 separate cases . . . [the Supreme Court] Justices have cited Muskie in 22 different cases. They include 8 Clean Air cases and 11 Clean Water Cases.[88]

Alan Lockward wrote in the *Atlantic* that the Clean Air Act, only a part of Muskie's legacy, had saved $22 trillion in healthcare costs.[89] Senate majority leader George Mitchell, a later senator from Maine, praised Muskie as, "by universal acclaim, the greatest environmental legislator in American history."[90]

Lady Bird Johnson continued her beautification efforts on a smaller scale in Texas after leaving the White House. After her husband died in January

1973, she served as a regent of the University of Texas and oversaw the family radio and television interests. On her seventieth birthday in 1982, she donated money and land to establish the National Wildflower Research Center near Austin. She died on July 11, 2007, at the age of ninety-five.

Lyndon Baines Johnson left public life at the end of his presidency, rarely leaving the Johnson ranch, and feeling isolated away from his life in Washington.[91] He died in 1973.

CHAPTER FOURTEEN

What Happened in the Green Years?

Looking back from today, the environmental progress over the Green Years seems almost unimaginable. The high tide of legislation and advance was produced by a meeting of men and moment, of attitude and opportunity that fifty years of politics and pollution have since made as distant as a clear horizon.

The Johnson Treatment

The achievements of the first four years cannot be understood without Lyndon Johnson. His National Park director, George Hartzog, testified to the president's deep involvement in land legislation, recalling, "I suppose the greatest interest that . . . that I have observed has been in this area of scenic rivers and trails, and then in the redwoods, which very early in the proposals he took a very personal interest in."[1] At Johnson's request, at the end of his administration, Stewart Udall catalogued the conservation achievements of his department, including passage of the Wilderness and Wild and Scenic Rivers Acts, new programs to control water and air pollution, and creating forty-six new units in the national park system and thirty-nine new wilderness areas.[2] Udall also noted changing the focus of the Interior Department from western resource development to broader national earth issues. Wayne Aspinall later commented of Johnson, "I suppose as much as any president he knew the working of the legislative department or branch of government. . . . It makes all the difference in the world if you have a knowledgeable president and a president who has the ambition to get things done."[3]

In his memoirs, Johnson recalled hearing from Udall toward the end of his administration, "History tells us that two Presidents this century—the Roosevelts—quickened the land conscience of the nation . . . and established sound policies of stewardship. I believe the Johnson years will undeniably be regarded as a 'third wave' of the conservation movement that will quantitatively compare very favorably with those of these two predecessor Presidents." Johnson concluded, "I believe that assessment will stand the test of time."[4]

Looking back, Udall cited the Johnson administration's start on tackling pollution, foreshadowing the future awareness of the problem. "We decided to clean things up; we decided to develop new attitudes and approaches toward the American environment. As I say, Johnson was very receptive and very good on these things. If you could come in with a water pollution bill or an air pollution bill, let's go, gung-ho . . . it came through loud and clear that the president said we were going to do this, and everybody better get busy."[5] Thus, the Air Quality Act, the Water Quality Act, the Clean Water Restoration Act, the Solid Waste Disposal Act, Aircraft Noise Abatement Act, and the Motor Vehicle Air Pollution Control Act were all passed under Johnson. Laurance Rockefeller judged that the Johnson legislation was "magnificently inclusive of virtually all the major areas of conservation need—air pollution, water pollution. You have it, they're all here."[6]

Some contemporaries did give Johnson credit for his environmental efforts. "The man from the Texas hill country had a deep love for the land," praised *Audubon* magazine in 1973, "and his efforts to preserve and restore it not only laid the foundation for the environmental crusade of the 1970s, but enriched the quality of life for all Americans."[7] Political scientist Lynton Caldwell wrote in 1970 that Johnson had "anticipated the environmental quality issue in his Great Society address, on May 22, 1964 . . . the fact that he had publicly identified himself with the environmental issue strengthened its position in American political life."[8]

Historian Martin Melosi concluded, "The overarching goal of the administration—if there was one—was to wed concern over the environment to the larger goals of the Great Society. This meant either identifying with continuing congressional efforts or writing new legislation."[9] The Sierra Club's Michael McCloskey stated, "When he became president, he became progressive. He had a matchless record as president."[10] On the productivity of the 1965 congressional session, House Speaker John W. McCormack cited "the dynamic, insistent, unrelenting, tireless . . . leadership of President Lyndon Baines Johnson."[11] And crucially, pushing on environmental issues with Johnson was a determined and resourceful secretary of the interior, Stewart Udall. A department that had been largely a service agency for western ranchers and loggers suddenly had an energetic conservation agenda—a national conservation agenda. "Johnson aggressively used the power of the presidency," noted historian Adam Rome, "to draw public attention to environmental problems."[12] Almost all of the Nixon era's most prominent environmental laws, with the notable exception of the National Environmental Policy Act (NEPA), would involve strengthening laws originally from the Johnson administration.

Nixon Reconsidered

Richard Nixon, after resigning in disgrace and receiving a pardon from his successor, Gerald Ford, was initially a public pariah. Over time, he worked to rebuild himself as a foreign policy oracle in books, articles, and interviews. In none of them did he mention the environment.[13] For Nixon, the environment was clearly of secondary interest. Yet, while sometimes wanting weaker, less costly measures, he did not stand in the way of environmental progress. Unlike most of his Republican successors, Nixon was not hostile to environmental measures, and signed most of the ones that came to his desk. "The list of what the Nixon administration accomplished domestically," wrote Evan Thomas, "makes Nixon look like a great liberal as well as one of the last of the big spenders."[14] Nixon aide John C. Whitaker gave him higher praise, writing of the environmental progress of the time, "Much of the credit belongs, in the author's opinion, to Richard Nixon. Nixon was there at the right moment. He grasped the issue quickly and presented a comprehensive and broad legislative environmental agenda."[15] Looking back in 2003, Russell Train commented, "In striking contrast to the situation today, the United States was the clear world leader during the 1970s in terms of both domestic environmental policy and international environmental cooperation."[16]

Some advocates, critical at the time, later had second thoughts about him. Nixon's record, conceded Robert Cahn, was "much better than some of us, who sought so much more, are usually willing to admit." The environmental messages in particular carried "support of land use planning, creation of the Environmental Protection Agency, support for expansion of wilderness and urban parks, cutting down on pesticide use, and eliminating the use of poison in the control of predators on public lands."[17] Years later, the Sierra Club's David Brower reflected that if environmentalists had tried to court instead of criticize Nixon's administration, "We could have advanced our cause. . . . [Nixon] had great promise and did great things, but we deserted him."[18] "In terms of the environment," concluded Greenpeace's Barbara Dudley, "Richard Nixon was to the left of Barack Obama and Bill Clinton."[19] McCloskey viewed it differently, noting that Nixon "perceived that he would be opposed [in 1972] by either [Henry] Jackson or [Edmund] Muskie . . . the two environmental champions. When he was reelected, he didn't need to worry about that. . . . [S]uddenly he was no help at all . . . it was almost as if everything before has been opportunistic."[20] Nixon's own historic view was revealing. In 1991, Nixon, after giving a speech in New York, told William Reilly, George H. W. Bush's EPA administrator, "I know you. You're at EPA, and I founded EPA. I'm an environmentalist too."[21] Nixon died on April 22, 1994, the twenty-fourth anniversary of the first Earth Day.

A Changing Society Changes Attitudes

"Now our rate of change is very great," mused Supreme Court Justice William O. Douglas in 1972. "The problems of air and water pollution, the poisoning of fish, pheasants and other wildlife, and the general problem of waste and littering date from about 1945, when we made revolutionary technological changes in our productive enterprises."[22] Historians such as Samuel Hays have often tied environmental attitudes to socioeconomic status, noting that a wealthier population with more leisure time could afford a taste for wilderness, which also tracked with higher education levels. Hays noted that support for the environment ran highest in prosperous regions, such as the Northeast and the Pacific Coast, with less enthusiasm in economically hard-pressed areas.[23] Taking a more national view, political scientist Grant McConnell wrote in 1970, "As the nation has become richer, however, economic values have lost their old urgency and other more important matters have emerged . . . the values of natural beauty and wilderness are critical examples here."[24]

The change also produced new constituencies. Rome argued that the 1960s saw increasing environmental concern from scientists, liberals, young people, middle-class women, and traditional conservationists that blossomed, but did not stop, with Earth Day. "In the early 1960s, the major women's magazines all published pieces about water pollution and the articles highlighted the threat to domestic life," noted Rome. "The

League of Women Voters played a vital role in the battle against water pollution. . . . In many cities, women organized aggressively to stop air pollution . . . in many communities, women also led campaigns to preserve open space."[25] Some key events—the publication of *Silent Spring*, the Santa Barbara oil spill, the periodic slaughter from chemical spills, and the burning of the polluted rivers—drove the movement. It helped that many environmental issues, from polluted skies to garbage strewn at the roadside, were visually dramatic, helping to rouse the public to demand changes.

Bipartisanship and the Environmental Mood of the Times

During the Green Years, the strong environmental mood of the country—and these constituencies—helped drive the legislative changes. Dudley noted key drivers of action: "You have a river burning and smog-filled air and you had a moderate Republican party."[26] McCloskey observed, "Throughout the sixties there was a rising tide toward environmental interests . . . it paved the way for the Wilderness Act. . . . [T]he other big thing was the Republicans were not the antienvironmental party."[27]

The progress of the Green Years was achieved by Democrats and Republicans together. "The creation of the Clean Air Act of 1970 marked an important turning point in our nation's history, but it also revealed what is possible when two men from opposing parties work together to effect positive change," wrote former vice-president Al Gore in 2005. "There is stark contrast between what goes on now in the relationship between the two parties and the kind of relationship that Senator Howard Baker (R-TN) and Senator Ed Muskie (D-ME) enjoyed."[28] McCloskey stated, "The 1970 Clean Air Act was basically the product of Ed Muskie's strength in the Senate. . . . [W]e didn't lobby at all."[29]

In 1970, a reporter asked Muskie, "Do you see the environmental problem becoming so political that the results are likely to be watered down in the coming two years?" No, the senator said firmly; instead, "the competition for credit" would produce tougher laws, not weaker ones.[30] In fact, Nixon often accepted a stronger environmental bill than he wanted, a strategy to avoid giving Democrats political ammunition. In some cases, such as the creation of the EPA, Nixon himself offered a strong proposal to win credit. After one rare Nixon environmental veto, the Clean Water Act, large numbers of Republicans joined Democrats to override his rejection. For years, apportionment gave rural legislators outsized power in

Congress. In the early 1960s the Supreme Court's "one man, one vote" decision increased the proportion of urban and suburban lawmakers. Historian Richard Andrews noted that the change produced more environmentally minded legislators, since rural lawmakers tended to favor traditional resource extraction industries.[31]

Still, Senate Democrats from largely rural states such as Clinton Anderson and Henry Jackson as chairmen of the Interior Committee, Frank Church as a key member, and Muskie as chair of the Subcommittee on Air and Water Pollution, were key to passing much of the Green Years' legislation.[32] While public mood in favor of environmental progress might have driven progress without them, they were key players in passing strong legislation. Udall commented in a 1969 interview:

> Historically, I think without doubt one of the biggest brakes on conservation action had been the fact that the committees [that] handle most conservation legislation are dominated by westerners. The westerners themselves are dominated by the local desires and local pressures of the cattlemen, lumbermen, stockmen, and so on—in other words they're user oriented rather than conservation oriented. . . . It goes back to Teddy Roosevelt's time . . . the one tactic . . . I used to offset this was to curry favor with and work closely with congressmen who were either not westerners or were not typical western congressmen.[33]

This would become even truer later, as the western Democrats were replaced with more conservative Republicans. Udall noted the key role of allies such as John Saylor, Jackson, and Senator Thomas Kuchel (R-CA), in environmental achievements, explaining, "So you had to work with those people and kind of surround and put pressures on the more slow-moving types like Congressman Aspinall."[34]

During this period, environmental groups increasingly focused on working in Washington for legislation and policy. "Unlike those demonstrating against the war in Vietnam," observed McCloskey, "we did not feel excluded from or disenfranchised by the normal political process."[35] Compared with the antiwar movement, pointed out Hays, "The Washington-based environmental movement of the 1970s emphasized practical gains rather than affirmation of ideologies."[36] McCloskey noted that for the environmental movement, at a time when other pressures were splitting movements and communities apart, "The period of 1972–77 was particularly productive. These were the years when so many of America's basic laws and programs to protect the environment were set in place."[37] Looking back, McCloskey recalled, "The very breadth of what happened in the first six years, you couldn't replicate it."[38]

The environmental groups themselves mushroomed. In 1965 the ten largest environmental organizations had a combined membership below 500,000 and a budget less than $10 million. By 1990, overall memberships had increased to 7.2 million, with budgets totaling $514 million. The number of smaller, local and state environmental groups also exploded, to an estimated 10,000 by 1992.[39] From 7,000 members in 1950, the Sierra Club, led by Brower, increased to 100,000 in 1970. Membership of the National Audubon Society, energized by dangers to birds from pesticides to loss of habitat, rocketed from 17,000 in 1950 to 100,000 in 1970.[40] Beginning in 1960, executive director Tom Kimball transformed the National Wildlife Federation. Once made up of local hunting and fishing groups, the federation began to accept individual members in 1961. Its bimonthly magazine, *National Wildlife*, began to emphasize environmental issues. By 1970 the federation had 540,000 members. The federation strongly supported the Great Society environmental agenda, telling its members in a 1965 issue of *National Wildlife* that an updated version of Gifford Pinchot's wise-use principle required saving streams "in their wild, free state," while preserving wilderness and other open spaces.[41]

As the pace of progress slowed in subsequent decades, environmental groups would be criticized as being too willing to compromise. "Compromise, which produced some limited gains for the movement in the 1970s," complained Mark Dowie, "in the 1980s became the habitual response of the environmental establishment."[42] McCloskey, however, noted that much followup legislation would pass later, "a fair amount after 1976. . . . [I]n terms of controversy and its size, the Alaska National Lands bill was monumental."[43]

Why Then and Not at Other Times

Environmental issues were of marginal importance to most American political leaders and to the public before the presidency of Theodore Roosevelt. The limited steps before Roosevelt involved protecting a small portion of the national forests. Roosevelt brought a strong environmental advocacy that focused on protecting wild and historic areas, along with actions to protect animals. Particularly with his creation of national monuments, Roosevelt dragged enough reluctant legislators with him to drive changes.

Environmental issues found few legislative or executive advocates until the next Roosevelt became president. Franklin Delano Roosevelt expanded protection of lands. The Civilian Conservation Corps alone repaired more of the nation's outdoor infrastructure than anything before or since. But for politicians and most Americans, environmental issues were overshadowed by the challenges of the Great Depression and then World War II under Roosevelt, and by the Cold War during the Truman and Eisenhower administrations.

While John F. Kennedy had little personal interest in the environment and an overflowing agenda, a cadre of leaders who were interested and had power began to emerge in his time, including secretary of the interior Stewart Udall and legislators such as Saylor and Muskie. A growing concern about pollution and other environmental degradation supported their efforts, setting the stage for the Green Years that followed.

Leadership in Congress

James Morton Turner credits the Democratic Party for the gains of the Green Years, noting, "Democrats consistently took the lead on conservation and environmental issues in the 1960s and 1970s. . . . With Democrats in control of both chambers of Congress between 1955 and 1980, their power was considerable. . . . The Democratic faith in the role of government, which many Republicans shared, was instrumental in making possible the legislative advances for environmental protection in the 1960s and 1970s."[44] Hays estimated that in the Congress of the time, two-thirds of Democrats supported environmental protection with one-third opposed, while the proportions were reversed for Republicans.[45] Yet almost all environmental laws passed from 1964 to 1976 commanded huge bipartisan support. The NEPA passed in the House 374–15, the Clean Air Act 374–1, and the Clean Water Act 366–11. They all passed in the Senate without dissent. McCloskey explained this differently, stating, "Very often our opponents were asleep at the switch. . . . They didn't realize the implications [of the legislation]."[46]

Forty years later, John Dingell said, in an explanation sounding very alien to twenty-first-century Congress-watchers, "NEPA and the Endangered Species Act were passed because we used the legislative process to build broad, bipartisan support for passage. We gathered the facts and were patient while experts reviewed them. At every opportunity, we shared credit with our colleagues, especially colleagues from across the aisle. In life and legislation, you can achieve anything if you don't mind letting the other fellow take the credit for it."[47] Historian Richard Lazarus noted the difference: "While Muskie's Congress represents lawmaking at its best, Congress since 1990 has been the exact opposite: Congress at its worst. The spirit of bipartisanship and constructive compromise that Muskie fostered and that was crucial to his success has since collapsed. While we once had environmental law because of Congress, we now have environmental law without Congress."[48]

A now largely vanished feature of Congress during the Green Years was friendships and socialization between Democrats and Republicans. "When I entered Congress, it was largely a place of comity and mutual respect across the aisle," remembered Dingell.[49] Dingell, a Democrat, was one of the Republican Saylor's closest friends in Congress. For years, Dingell hunted with Republicans like James Baker and Alan Simpson, recalling, "Hunting was more than a way to relax and be in nature; it was also a way to form a bond between me and a number of friends and colleagues from the other party."[50] House Republican leader and later president Gerald Ford, Dingell recalled, "likely worked better with me and my Democratic colleagues than members of his own party."[51] McCormack explained about serving with the Republican Nixon, "We were a constructive party because we felt that a party not in control of the White House owed a responsibility to the people to act constructively."[52]

These sentiments sound almost unknown in today's Congress, where members race home after brief compressed weeks of work to fundraise and focus on their constituencies. Moreover, most legislators, particularly Republicans, are more vulnerable to a primary challenge from a true believer, critical of their cooperation with the other party, than from a general election foe. It is in the more marginal districts that there is a greater willingness to accept ideas such as climate change, yet it is these legislators who are most often swept away, as when the Democrats recaptured the House in 2018.

One impediment to further environmental progress may have been the departure of so many of the major congressional champions of the issue. Saylor died unexpectedly in 1973. John Blatnik retired the following year. Muskie left the Senate in 1980 to briefly become secretary of state. The Reagan landslide in 1980 took out Church, Warren Magnuson, and

Gaylord Nelson. Jackson died in 1983. Baker left Congress in 1985. Only Dingell remained to carry the institutional memory of successful cooperation for the next thirty years.

In assessing the environmental achievements of the time, the influence of these individuals has been greatly overlooked. If Jackson had not been an aggressive advocate in his many years as chairman of the Senate Interior Committee, legislation such as the Wild and Scenic Rivers Act and the National Trails Act might have had a harder path. Certainly, it is unlikely that the National Environmental Policy, or a North Cascades National Park, would exist. Other legislation, such as the National Land and Policy Management Act and the Alaska Native Claims settlement acts, with their provisions for land for additional wilderness and parks, might have turned out less favorably from an environmental perspective. In environmental history, Jackson's opposition on Washington home state issues such as the supersonic transport and timber harvest may have overshadowed his great green achievements.

Aspinall's obstruction in the House showed what might have happened if a less environmentally friendly and committed senator had chaired the Interior Committee. Conversely, Udall noted how much stronger environmental legislation could have passed if Saylor had been the chair, rather than the ranking minority member, of the House Interior Committee. Similarly, much of the oceangoing environmental legislation needed Magnuson as chair of the Senate Commerce Committee. Certainly, the Clean Air Acts and Clean Water Acts were shaped and promoted by the way Muskie used his subcommittee chairmanship and legislative acumen, along with his alliance with Baker.

The Green Begins to Fade

Public sentiment also drove political progress. "It is quite remarkable, nevertheless, that the social protest which characterized Earth Day could be channeled so effectively into political gains in Congress," observed Turner. "One way to explain this paradox is to emphasize the exceptional nature of the politics surrounding Earth Day; the mass outpouring of popular concern for the environment made possible such far-reaching policies."[53] On the environment, as with civil rights, citizen action and legislative efforts drove each other forward. As early as April 1970, Saylor worried that environmental enthusiasm might be short-lived, warning, "To date, the environmental concern is a fad. When the American people are asked to pay for cleaning up and restoring the natural landscape, then we will discover if there is a real environmental concern that can move legislation."[54] Over the next decades, the ever-louder argument that environmental protection was too expensive has made Saylor prophetic.

Ford, Nixon's successor, brought friendships with many House Democrats to his presidency. Ford was not an antienvironmental zealot, yet the twin issues of inflation and energy limited his environmental commitment. "Ford was a thoroughly decent man," recounted Train. "At the same time, he had little or no·interest in the environment."[55] Ford's instincts, judged Cahn, "led him to believe that environmental improvements were gained only at the expense of business and the economy."[56]

Even with a Democratic Congress, Jimmy Carter's administration brought relatively little environmental progress, partly because the Carter White House did not work well with that Congress. "The Carter people . . . weren't worth a pinch of owl shit," concluded Dingell in naturalistic terms. "I had the Devil's own time getting the Carter people to see the big picture. Like their boss, they could see every damned tree, but they couldn't see the forest."[57] Carter also retreated from some of his earlier environmental advocacy, such as limiting dam building, in the face of protests from unhappy legislators. Train was more charitable, suggesting gently, "Environmental concerns did not have the same urgency for the public as they had in the late 1960s and early 1970s, probably because laws enacted in those decades had begun to address the most pressing environmental issues and an institutional structure had been put in place, principally at EPA, to carry out those laws."[58]

By then the national mood was different from the prosperous 1960s when everything seemed possible. The 1973 energy crisis led Nixon and his advisors to blame environmental regulations for limiting energy production. Other factors, from the Arab oil embargo to the manipulations of the major oil companies, also played a role in the energy crunch. Still, the energy shortages provided cover to allow rollback, or at least the slowing, of implementing environmental regulations. The combined problems of inflation and high unemployment—"stagflation"—that marked the rest of the 1970s also weakened focus on environmental goals. "Environmentalism spoke for the spiritual and nonutilitarian values of natural resources," explained J. Brooks Flippen. "In times of economic strain—indicative of the Ford and Carter years—they became to many a luxury that the nation could no longer afford."[59]

Yet environmentalism had not disappeared, as President Ronald Reagan discovered after nominating radical antienvironmentalists to roll back environmental protections. The moves drew a strong pushback and spurred a steep increase in environmental memberships.[60] By 1988, Earth Day coordinator Denis Hayes could declare, "In terms of sustainability the [environmental] movement has exceeded our expectations."[61] A 1990 Gallup poll found that 76 percent of Americans called themselves environmentalists.[62] McCloskey wrote, "The environmental movement has made commendable progress. . . . [I]t has suffered almost no crushing defeats . . . none of its remedial programs have been repealed in their entirety . . . it has endured, defended its achievements, recruited more adherents, widened its orbit of interests, tackled new issues and won a firm place in public regard."[63]

The GOP Changes

Why did the Republican party, which deserves shared credit for so much early environmental progress, come to regard environmental protection as a Democratic plot? On the crucial environmental issue of today, climate change, most Republicans in Congress deny that it even exists. "Throughout the 1970s," pointed out Turner and Andrew Isenberg, "the Republican Party (1) viewed environmental issues with a sense of urgency that demanded action, (2) put faith in scientific research and professional expertise, and (3) embraced an essential role for government . . . to safeguard the environment." In contrast, they wrote, "Since the 1980s, the Republican Party has increasingly (1) viewed environmental concerns as alarmist and exaggerated, (2) cast doubt on scientific research and dismissed professional expertise, and (3) viewed many environmental regulations as unnecessary burdens on the economy and as threats to individual freedom."[64]

One change is the new geography of the Republican Party over the last four decades. Hays pointed out that economies focusing on extractive industries such as agriculture, grazing, mining, and lumber are the least supportive of environmental limitations. The current Republican Party primarily represents such areas.[65] Moderate northeastern Republicans, once the strongest environmental voices in the party, are today virtually extinct.

Western environmental skeptics have shaped the twenty-first-century Republican Party, further sharpening partisan differences. When the Wilderness Act was passed in 1964, the Senate included seventeen Democrats and seven Republicans from western states. By the end of 1980 a host of western Democratic senators had been replaced by conservative Republicans, giving the GOP a majority among western senators that would persist for the next three decades. Republicans gained similar success in the House. In 1994, western Republicans ran against regulation and for development, and picked up House seats across the West as they won control of the chamber. Meanwhile, moderate to conservative southern Democrats have been almost entirely replaced by more conservative Republicans.

Republicans' movement toward older and less-educated voters may also contribute to a policy shift. Hays noted that environmental values rise with levels of education, being more prominent in younger people.[66] In the 1960s and 1970s, most college graduates voted Republican, helping influence their representatives in that direction.[67] At that time, Turner and Isenberg pointed out, "much of the early support for environmental reform came from middle-class, white, and largely Republican suburbanites."[68]

The two parties' environmental attitudes have increasingly diverged. "Until 1990, about 40% of the Republican members of Congress would support environmental measures," observed McCloskey. "Then, during the next 25 years Republican support in Congress fell to just five or ten percent."[69] Turner and Isenberg note that Democratic and Republican legislators' votes on environmental issues have become more and more divergent in each decade, with the biggest change occurring in the 1990s.[70]

Yet the change in attitudes reflects more than simply conservatives' replacement of moderates within Republican ranks. In the 1960s and 1970s, even staunch conservatives agreed that environmental progress might be an area requiring government regulation. Conservative theorist Friedrich Hayek, legendary in his opposition to government regulation, accepted it on the environment, since "certain harmful effects of deforestation, or some methods of farming, or of the smoke and noise of factories cannot be confined to the owner of the property in question."[71] In 1970 Barry Goldwater declared, "While I am a great believer in the free competitive enterprise system and all that it entails, I am an even stronger believer in the right of our people to live in a clean and pollution-free environment. When pollution is found, it should be halted at its source, even if this requires stringent government action."[72] Yet by 1996 John McCain, in Goldwater's seat, was a lonely conservative insisting, "We must learn that protecting the environment requires the bipartisan cooperation necessary for progress on all the great issues of the day," and over the next two decades would be ever more isolated as a Republican voice for action on climate change.[73] Later conservatives, associating environmentalism with liberal Democrats, saw environmental regulations as overbearing and an assault on personal liberty and business interests.

A dramatic shift came with Reagan's election to the presidency in 1980. As governor of California from 1967 to 1975, Reagan had been an environmental moderate, particularly pushing to reduce air pollution. But in 1980 Reagan campaigned against environmental laws, often ignoring facts, such as by claiming that acid rain might be caused mainly by the eruption of Mount St. Helens.[74] The New Right, Chris Mooney observed, "nourished a strong anti-East Coast, anti-intellectual animus that easily translated into distrust of the American scientific community."[75] Donald Trump's dismissal of the urgency of environmental issues, his disregard for scientific expertise, and his refusal to accept the need for government action to protect the environment is in this tradition, although even the Reagan administration was able to set aside ideology to deal with ozone depletion. Increasingly, noted Turner and Isenberg, "Conservatives have managed to tie their environmental policy ideas to . . . a distrust of government, science and secular intellectuals; and a faith in the market, technological innovation, and perhaps above all in a God who has provided a cornucopia of resources for human use."[76]

Today, Republicans attack regulation as hurting economic growth. Ironically, this would have been a stronger argument in the 1960s and 1970s, when the cost of regulation was not really known. But over the forty years since, environmental protection has typically brought concrete health benefits far exceeding their cost. "EPA kept track of jobs that were lost in closure of factories that were too old and dirty to be cleaned up," related McCloskey. "It found that fewer than 40,000 cumulatively lost jobs could be attributed to that cause. On the other side of the ledger, some studies estimated that more a million new jobs were being created by environmental programs."[77] Economic growth was once thought to require increased energy consumption. The experience of the last few decades shows that the two are disconnected, with per capita energy usage dropping even as Americans use more powered devices, with increased efficiency covering the gap.

Business Reacts

After some uncertainty, business has led what Hays has called a "massive onslaught against environmental policies and programs."[78] Some conservatives, such as Lewis Powell before his Supreme Court appointment, urged businesses to mobilize against the new regulations. As one strategy, Mooney noted, "businesses turned to funding intellectuals and research organizations that would promote their own goals and interests, rather than more objective study."[79] Extractive industries such as oil and coal led the assault.

The spearpoint of the campaign has been an attack on environmental science and scientists. "Rules by new agencies such as EPA and OSHA necessarily required a firm scientific basis," wrote Mooney. "Yet this, in turn, created a strong incentive for companies subject to potentially costly regulation to sponsor their own contrary science, a powerful technique for blocking or rebutting proposed agency action."[80] The Republican war on science began during the Nixon administration. Angered by testimony against the proposed supersonic transport by a member of his Presidential Scientific Advisory Committee, Nixon, following his 1972 reelection, abolished the committee, as well as the position of presidential science advisor. Reagan's budget director David Stockman, in opposing scientific input in the White House, explained, "We know what we want to do and they'll only give us contrary advice."[81] In 1994, when the Republicans won the House of Representatives, they dismantled the nonpartisan Office of Technology Assessment, which had produced 750 scientific studies for Congress since its establishment in 1972.

Over time, the environmental regulations of the Green Years galvanized very wealthy conservatives to create conservative institutions such as think tanks to challenge them, and later the very idea of climate change. "Financed by wealthy benefactors, the anti-environmental think tanks remained the main source of anti-environmental ideological support," observed Hays.[82] "By the end of the 1970s conservative nonprofits had achieved power that was almost unthinkable," concluded journalist Jane Mayer. "Enormously wealthy right-wing donors had transformed themselves from the ridiculed, self-serving 'economic royalists' of FDR's day into the respected 'other side' of a two-sided debate."[83] Republicans increasingly "relied on analyses prepared by lobbyists and ideologically committed think tanks like the Heritage Foundation."[84] Building on the tactics of the tobacco industry, industries opposed to environmental regulations trotted out their own scientists and claimed scientific uncertainty to delay action. This strategy was used by the Reagan administration to avoid action on acid rain, and is used by today's Republicans to block moves against climate change.

The breakdown of a common mainstream media credible to people of all persuasions has contributed to this polarization. Once Democrats and Republicans all listened to Walter Cronkite, David Brinkley, and other not overtly political newscasters. Now Republicans who most often watch Fox News are fed a steady diet of antienvironmental claims.

When the issue of climate change was first raised in the sixties there were enough uncertainties and more pressing problems to consign it to temporary oblivion. When the threat had become clearer in the eighties the Reagan administration had little appetite for perceived antibusiness policies to deal with an issue of the future. Attempts to deal with it under Presidents George H. W. Bush and Bill Clinton met resistance, while George W. Bush's administration focused on the challenges of the 9/11 attack and the wars that followed. It is simplistic, but not without a grain of truth, to suggest that because the issue is not as visually obvious as smog-filled skies and garbage-filled roads, it is harder to explain and win support for action. Even today the more powerful hurricanes and expanded forest fires that reflect the change so far are dismissed by climate change deniers as chance events of nature.

Republican rejection of climate change is relatively recent. In 2008 GOP presidential nominee McCain openly acknowledged it as a major problem. Former House Speaker Newt Gingrich once called for action on the issue. Yet in 2015 Lazarus noted, "Because the associated political obstacles of enacting national climate legislation has so far proven overwhelming, EPA has been relegated to relying on the statutory authorities set forth in Muskie's Clean Air Act Legislation."[85]

One element driving the change has been increasing Republican dependence on campaign donors such as the Koch brothers, whose company is integrally involved in fossil fuels. Mayer reported that the Republican capture of the House in 2010 dramatically changed the Energy and Commerce Committee: "The new Republican leadership stocked the committee with oil industry advocates, many of whom owed huge campaign debts to the Kochs. Koch Industries PAC . . . had donated to twenty-two of the committee's thirty-one Republican members."[86] Political scientist Lee Drutman found that because the wealthiest Republican donors were the most opposed to taxes and regulations, "the more Republicans depend upon 1% of the 1% donors, the more conservative they tend to be."[87]

From 2003 to 2010, huge amounts of money were spent to minimize the public perception of the threat of climate change. Republican pollster Frank Luntz told conservatives, "Should the public come to believe that the scientific issues are settled, their views on global warming will change accordingly. Therefore, you need to continue to make the lack of scientific certainty a primary issue."[88] In line with this strategy, observed environmentalist Alden Meyer, "ExxonMobil has manufactured uncertainty about the human causes of global warning just as tobacco companies denied their products caused cancer."[89] The sharp partisan split has prevented virtually any new environmental legislation in recent decades. Lately, wrote Turner and Isenberg, "Most of the heavy lifting in recent environmental politics has been done through administrative orders, administrative rulemaking, congressional appropriations and the courts."[90] And any order from one administration can be, and recently has been, reversed by the next.

The Road Forward

Environmentalists are torn about the best approach going forward. Years ago, Barry Commoner warned, "The older national environmental organizations in their Washington offices have taken the soft political road of negotiation, compromising with the corporations on the amount of pollution that is acceptable."[91] The 1980s saw the growth of "radical environmentalism," such as Earth First!, wielding militant tactics such as civil disobedience and industrial sabotage. The radical strategies drew lots of publicity, but also questions about whether they helped or hurt the environmental cause, before collapsing in the 1990s. The question, McCloskey noted, is "whether it is wise to work within the context of the basic social, political and economic institutions to achieve stepwise progress, or whether prime energies must be directed at changing those institutions." From his perspective, argued McCloskey, "We may be 'reformist' and all, but we know how to work within the context of the institutions of society."[92] And, he pointed out, "We do know things would be a lot worse if we had not been on the job."[93]

McCloskey pointed out, "The environmental movement is the most successful political movement in the United States since WWII . . . in terms of the depth and breadth in change."[94] He argued that the difficulties moving forward were not specific to environmentalism, saying, "The same dilemma faces every progressive movement."[95] While rebutting Republican antienvironmental arguments, McCloskey wrote, "Environmentalists would be well advised to examine the thinking of conservatives to see whether they can improve their approach so as to reduce some of their objections."[96]

On McCloskey's side, former director of the Izaak Walton League Paul Hansen argued, "History shows us that environmental progress always comes in half loaves. President Lyndon Johnson said, 'A person not willing to settle for a half loaf has never been hungry.'" Environmentalists needed to be willing to compromise and work with other parties to achieve progress, Hansen insisted: "Success requires the broader support that comes from a more inclusive and collaborative approach that accepts compromise. . . . Going forward conservation cannot succeed from a confrontational or insular base of advocates."[97] Similarly, Turner pointed out that "the Wilderness Act's architects, such as Howard Zahniser, were willing to make specific accommodations for grazing, mining, motorboats, and, in one instance, a road to move the Wilderness Act through Congress. That is why every major wilderness bill since has included similar compromises and exceptions."[98]

Other environmental voices have called for deeper organizing. "Instead of simply thinking like experts," urged Robert Gottlieb, "environmentalists need to think—and act—like organizers, driven by the passions for change and the ability to make persuasive the notion that environmental and social transformation is not only imperative, but possible."[99] Noting the transformation of many environmental groups into professional staff dependent on foundation support, Dudley argued, "We need movements again . . . the Populist movement did not get foundation money."[100] Agreeing, Bill McKibben wrote, "It's going to take the inspired political movement of millions of Americans to get our country on track to solving [climate change]."[101]

Taking on industries that can massively outspend them has always been a challenge for environmentalists. "Rachel Carson forewarned that industry will always be prepared to keep regulation at a minimum," noted Dowie, "by purchasing more scientific expertise than the [environmental] movement."[102] On the legal front, conservatives have counterattacked, "litigating for regulatory relief and private property rights," before an increasingly conservative judiciary.[103] One study found that industry deploys ten times the lobbyists and spends ten times as much lobbying Congress as environmentalists.[104] Andrews concluded that "the environmental movement would have a difficult time since it fought for long-term nonmarket values against more concrete short-term self-interests."[105]

The media have had a hard time with environmental issues, often carefully explaining both sides of issues such as climate change, even when the science supporting one side was overwhelming. "Since most environmental issues involved undramatic cumulative change," judged Hays, "they were rarely well covered."[106] Climate scientist Mike Hulme argues that there are also problems with using the language of "climatic Apocalypse"; namely, "it frequently leads to disempowerment, apathy and skepticism among its audience."[107] The debate often ignores the economic benefits of environmental protection while focusing only on the potential costs. Whole new industries based on controlling pollution and reducing waste have emerged. By mandating emissions cuts that challenged existing capacity, regulation has spurred technological innovation. However, it has been easier to point out existing jobs in danger, such as in coal mining, than the greater number of jobs being created in solar and wind.

Some environmentalists and historians, such as Dowie and Andrews, question the success of the Green Years, complaining that the weakness of some laws allowed the persistence of pollution and toxins. William Ruckelshaus rejoined, "[Consider] where we would be today supposing the federal colossus had continued to slumber and no response had followed the public demands of the late 1960s. Instead of the improvements we've witnessed, we'd have endured even greater degradation."[108]

The Green Years—and the years since—argue the need for three elements for any future burst of environmental progress. First, it takes a strongly proenvironmental president, or at least one, like Nixon, amenable to public pressure on the issue. Without one, as the administrations of Trump and George W. Bush show, forward movement is impossible. Equally necessary is a Congress with influential environmentally minded legislators, preferably holding key committee chairs. Currently, it would be hard to expect that from the Republican Party. In fact, most Republican legislators espouse antienvironmental stands even when polling shows support for such environmental programs from Republicans in the populace. Should enough Republicans recapture a party environmental tradition extending from Theodore Roosevelt to Baker—and to McCain—the task would be immensely easier. And considering the current requirement of supermajority support for any Senate action, some bipartisan support would be a virtual necessity.

Third, both president and Congress must be pressured by a strong public demand for environmental action. McCloskey stated, "All we can do is organize and campaign and hope it produces something useful . . . there are no philosopher-kings in charge of the world."[109] Ruckelshaus commented in a 1993 interview, "Public opinion remains absolutely essential for any-thing to be done on behalf of the environment."[110] The achievements of the Green Years were attained only by legislators feeling that their con-stituents demanded action. Such a tidal wave of public sentiment could overwhelm all the industry lobbyists and subsidized scientists. Yet until the rising seas threaten to engulf Fox News, it is hard to envision a sweeping bipartisan demand for strong action.

The threat of climate change differs from all previous environmental issues in being both all-encompassing and intensely urgent. McKibben notes how the effect of humans on the environment now far outstrips prior impacts.[111] The disastrous effects of temperature changes so far would be dwarfed by the impact of continually increasing greenhouse gas emissions. The effects would be, as a recent *New England Journal of Medicine* editorial understated, "frighteningly broad"; a global temperature increase of two degrees Celsius would raise sea levels and badly hurt agricultural condi-tions, and many projections forecast an even higher increase.[112]

"If enough of us stop looking away and decide that climate change is worthy of Marshall levels of response," hopes Naomi Klein, "then it will become one and the political class will have to respond."[113] Yet, conceded Dudley, "A crisis works. . . . [I]t doesn't seem to be working yet."[114] Mc-Closkey commented, "Climate is the most momentous issue the environ-mental movement has faced. . . . [I]t has made good progress by ordinary standards, but ordinary standards are not enough."[115]

And while debates over wilderness lands could seem geographically dis-tant to many Americans, the effects of global warming are increasingly direct. Since 1994, Turner and Isenberg note, polls have steadily shown at least 70 percent of Americans agreeing that the nation should do what-ever is necessary to help the environment.[116] While climate denial echoes through our political climate, seven of ten Americans surveyed in October 2017 believed that global warming was real. Effective action against global warming will take an effort at least comparable to the Green Years; for one thing, a climate drive needs to be international. But the Green Years provide a model and a pattern, in and out of Congress, for historic coor-dinated action to protect the land and water around us. The challenge is daunting, but we have seen before that Americans have been known to take up a challenge.

In policy as on the calendar, a green season can come again.

Notes

Chapter 1. Earth Day, 1970

1. Carolyn Merchant, *The Columbia Guide to American Environmental History* (New York: Columbia University Press, 2002), 182.

2. United Press International, "Americans Rally to Make It Again Beautiful Land," *Chicago Tribune*, April 23, 1970, 3.

3. John Guernsey, "Pollution Foes Clean Up Portland; Even Bridge, Statue Get Brush," *Oregonian* (Portland, OR), April 23, 1970, 15.

4. Guernsey, "Pollution Foes Clean Up Portland," 15.

5. "'E-Day' Here Runs Gamut," *Dominion News* (Morgantown, WV), April 23, 1970, 8.

6. Associated Press, "N.C. Communities Mark Earth Day," *Robesonian* (Lumberton, NC), April 23, 1970, 1.

7. Ed Meagher, "No Smog on L.A. Earth Day," *Los Angeles Times*, April 23, 1970, 35.

8. Meagher, 35.

9. Stephen Seplow, "Rally to 'Save Our Earth,'" *Des Moines Register*, April 23, 1970, 6.

10. Seplow, 6.

11. Associated Press, "Daughters of American Revolution Raps Earth Day as Subversive," *Sacramento Bee*, April 23, 1970, 25.

12. Guernsey, "Pollution Foes Clean Up Portland," 15.

13. Meagher, "No Smog on L.A. Earth Day," 35.

14. Bill Christofferson, *The Man from Clear Lake: Earth Day Founder Senator Gaylord Nelson* (Madison: University of Wisconsin Press, 2004), 4.

15. Christofferson, 4.

16. Guernsey, "Pollution Foes Clean Up Portland," 15.

17. Victor B. Scheffer, *The Shaping of Environmentalism in America* (Seattle: University of Washington Press, 1991), 125.

18. Scheffer, *Shaping of Environmentalism in America*, 124.

19. Edmund Muskie, speech in Environmental Action, *Earth Day—The Beginning: A Guide for Survival* (New York: Bantam Books, 1970).

20. Gladwin Hill, "Millions Join Earth Day Observances across the Nation," *New York Times*, April 23, 1970, 1.

21. Guernsey, "Pollution Foes Clean Up Portland," 15.

22. "The Dawning of Earth Day," *Time*, April 27, 1970.

23. Christofferson, *Man from Clear Lake*, 1.

24. Hill, "Millions Join Earth Day Observances," 1.

25. "'E-Day' Here Runs Gamut," 8.

26. Meagher, "No Smog on L.A. Earth Day," 35.

27. Adam Rome, *The Genius of Earth Day: How a 1970 Teach-In Unexpectedly Made the First Green Generation* (New York: Hill and Wang, 2013), 140.

28. Philip Shabecoff, *A Fierce Green Fire* (New York: Hill and Wang, 1993), 113.

29. Gaylord A. Nelson, "Earth Day—Where Do We Go From Here," speech at Catalyst Conference, University of Illinois, Urbana–Champaign, October 6, 1990, cited in Christofferson, 7.

30. Udall quoted in Christofferson, *Man from Clear Lake*, 244.

31. Godfrey Sperling Jr., "The State of Government," *Christian Science Monitor*, January 3, 1963.

32. Christofferson, *Man from Clear Lake*, 295.

33. Gaylord A. Nelson to John Fitzgerald Kennedy, August 29, 1963, Name File, White House Central Files, Lyndon Baines Johnson Library and Museum, University of Texas, Austin.

34. Nelson to Kennedy, August 29, 1963.

35. Milo Mason, "Interview: Gaylord Nelson," Natural Resources and environment (ABA), summer 1995, quoted in Christofferson, *Man from Clear Lake*, 305.

36. Mason, "Interview: Gaylord Nelson," quoted in Christofferson, 316.

37. Gaylord A. Nelson, interview by Bill Christofferson, January 9, 1993, in Christofferson, *Man from Clear Lake*, 516.

38. Dennis W. Brezina, interview with Donald A. Richie, August 17, 2005, Senate Historical Office, United States Senate.

39. Charles Russell, "College Teach-Ins on Environment Crisis Proposed," *Seattle Post Intelligencer*, September 21, 1969.

40. Russell, "College Teach-Ins."

41. Brezina, interview.

42. "The Man in the News," *Des Moines Register*, April 23, 1970, 6.

43. Christofferson, *Man from Clear Lake*, 518.

44. Joe Uehlein, "Labor and Environmentalists Have Been Teaming Up since the First Earth Day," *Grist*, April 22, 2010, https://grist.org/article/2010 -04-21-labor-and-environmentalists-have-been-teaming-up-since-the-first /full/.

45. Uehlein, "Labor and Environmentalists."

46. Brezina, interview.

47. Denis Hayes, interview by Bill Christofferson, June 28, 2001, in Christofferson, *Man from Clear Lake*, 519.

48. Dennis Hayes, interview with Robert Gottlieb, 1991, in Gottlieb, *Forcing the Spring: The Transformation of the American Environmental Movement* (Washington, DC: Island, 2005), 150.

49. Gaylord A. Nelson," History of Earth Day," Wilderness Society flyer, quoted in Christofferson, *Man from Clear Lake*, 520.

50. Gaylord Nelson, interview with Robert Gottlieb, 1991, in Gottlieb, *Forcing the Spring*, 149.

51. Gaylord A. Nelson, 116 Cong. Rec. 82–87 (1970).

52. E. W. Kenworthy, "Senator Nelson to Ask for Anti-pollution Measure," *New York Times*, January 19, 1970, 29.

53. Brezina, interview.

54. Gaylord A. Nelson, Earth Day speech, University of Wisconsin, Madison, April 21, 1970, videotape, visual materials archive, Wisconsin Historical Society, quoted in Christofferson, *Man from Clear Lake*, 7.

55. Nan Robertson, "Earth Day, like Mother's, Pulls Capital Together, *New York Times*, April 23, 1970, quoted in Christofferson, 529.

56. Hill, "Millions Join Earth Day Observances," 1.

57. Nelson quoted in Shabecoff, *Fierce Green Fire*, 107.

58. Associated Press, "Daughters of American Revolution," 25.

59. Associated Press, "N.C. Communities Mark Earth Day," 1.

60. Hill, "Millions Join Earth Day Observances," 1.

61. "'E-Day' Here Runs Gamut," 8.

62. Mark Dowie, *Losing Ground: American Environmentalism as the Close of the Twentieth Century* (Cambridge: MIT Press, 1995), 3.

63. Scheffer, *Shaping of Environmentalism*, 19.

64. Dennis Hayes, speech in Environmental Action, *Earth Day—The Beginning.*

65. Kirkpatrick Sale, *The Green Revolution: The American Environmental Movement, 1962–1992* (New York: Hill and Wang, 1993), 24.

66. Gottlieb, *Forcing the Spring*, 153.

67. Associated Press, "N.C. Communities Mark Earth Day," 1.

68. John C. Whitaker, *Striking a Balance: Environment and Natural Resources Policy in the Nixon-Ford Years* (Washington, DC: American Enterprise Institute for Public Policy Research, 1976), 6.

69. Dan Rather, CBS-TV Network Special, April 22, 1970, quoted in Whitaker, *Striking a Balance*, 7.

70. "'E-Day' Here Runs Gamut," 8.

71. Hill, "Millions Join Earth Day Observances," 1.

72. Associated Press, "N.C. Communities Mark Earth Day," 1.

73. "Is Earth Day 'A Hell of a Waste of Time,'" *Sacramento Bee*, April 23, 1970, 19.

74. Gottlieb, *Forcing the Spring*, 154.

75. Hill, "Millions Join Earth Day Observances," 1.

76. Seplow, "Rally to 'Save Our Earth,'" 6.

77. Seplow, 6.

78. Gottlieb, *Forcing the Spring*, 154.

79. Gottlieb, 155.

80. "Dawning of Earth Day."

81. Hill, "Millions Join Earth Day Observances," 1.

82. "'E-Day' Here Runs Gamut," 8.

83. Meagher, "No Smog on L.A. Earth Day," 35.

84. Guernsey, "Pollution Foes Clean Up Portland," 15.

85. "Dawning of Earth Day."

86. "Dawning of Earth Day."

87. Brezina, interview.

88. Rome, *Genius of Earth Day*, 274.

89. Sale, *Green Revolution*, 25.

90. Hill, "Millions Join Earth Day Observances," 1.

91. Brezina, interview.

92. Hill, "Millions Join Earth Day Observances," 1.

93. Hill, 1.

94. J. Brooks Flippen, *Nixon and the Environment* (Albuquerque: University of New Mexico Press, 2000), 5.

95. Quoted in Rome, *Genius of Earth Day*, 221–222.

96. Rome, 240.

97. Flippen, *Nixon and the Environment*, 100.

98. Flippen, 107.

99. Nelson, interview by Christofferson, January 9, 1993, in Christofferson, *Man from Clear Lake*.

Chapter 2. Wilderness at Last

1. Lyndon B. Johnson, speech, May 22, 1964, Ann Arbor, MI, UShistory.org /documents/great-society.htm.

2. Johnson, speech, May 22, 1964.

3. Benjamin Kline, *First along the River: A Brief History of the U.S. Environmental Movement* (San Francisco: Acada Books, 1997), 21.

4. William Bradford, *Of Plymouth Plantation, 1620–1647*, ed. Samuel Eliot Morison (New York: Alfred A. Knopf, 2002) 62.

5. Roderick Nash, *Wilderness and the American Mind*, 3rd ed. (New Haven, CT: Yale University Press, 1982), 43.

6. George Catlin, *North American Indians: Being Letters and Notes on their Manners, Customs and Conditions, Written during Eight Years Travel amongst the Wildest Tribes of Indians in North America* (London, 1841), quoted in Nash, 101.

7. Henry David Thoreau, *Walden and Civil Disobedience* (New York: Signet Classics, 1960), 66.

8. Henry David Thoreau, *Walden* (New York: New American Library, 1960), quoted in Nash, *Wilderness and the American Mind*, 102.

9. George P. Marsh, *Man and Nature; or Physical Geography as Modified by Human Nature* (New York: Charles Scribner, 1864).

10. Marsh.

11. Marsh.

12. Marsh.

13. Bill McKibben, ed., *American Earth: Environmental Writing since Thoreau* (Washington, DC: Library of America, 2008), 71.

14. An Act Authorizing a Grant to the State of California of the "Yo-Semite Valley," and of the Land Embracing the "Mariposa Big Tree Grove" 13 Stat. 325 (1864).

15. Ron Chernow, *Grant* (New York: Penguin Books, 2017), 739.

16. Carolyn Merchant, *The Columbia Guide to American Environmental History* (New York: Columbia University Press, 2002), 135.

17. 18 Cong. Rec. 153, 154 (1886).

18. Nash, *Wilderness and the American Mind*, 115.

19. William H. H. Murray, *Adventures in the Wilderness; Or, Camp-life in the Adirondacks* (Boston: Fields, Osgood, 1869), 22.

20. New York Laws, 1892, ch. 709, p. 1439, quoted in Nash, *Wilderness and the American Mind*, 120.

21. Stewart L. Udall, *The Quiet Crisis and the Next Generation* (Layton, UT: Gibbs Smith, 1988), 115.

22. John Muir, *Our National Parks* (Boston: Houghton Mifflin, 1901), quoted in Kline, *First along the River*, 50.

23. Linne Marsh Wolfe, ed., *John of the Mountains: The Unpublished Journals of John Muir* (Boston: Houghton, Mifflin, 1938), 317, quoted in Doug Scott, *The Enduring Wilderness: Protecting Our Natural Heritage through the Wilderness Act* (Golden, CO: Fulcrum, 2004), 22.

24. Frederick Jackson Turner, "The Problem of the West," *Atlantic*, September 1896, https://www.theatlantic.com/magazine/archive/1896/09/the-problem-of -the-west/525699/.

25. Roosevelt, *African Game Trails*, in *Works*, vol. 5, xxvii, and Roosevelt, "The Strenuous Life," in *Works*, vol. 15, 267, 281, quoted in Nash, *Wilderness and the American Mind*, 150.

26. American Antiquities Act 1906,16 USC431-433.

27. Quoted in Char Miller, *Public Lands, Public Debates: A Century of Controversy* (Corvallis: Oregon State University Press, 2012), 72.

28. Irving Brant, *Adventures in Conservation with Franklin D. Roosevelt* (Flagstaff, AZ: Northland, 1988), 254.

29. Miller, *Public Lands, Public Debates*, 73.

30. Theodore Roosevelt, speech at the Grand Canyon, *Coconino Sun* (Flagstaff, AZ), May 9, 1903, available at http:www.kaibab.org/gc/gcps/teddy.htm.

31. Brant, *Adventures in Conservation*, 252.

32. Richard N. L. Andrews, *Managing the Environment, Managing Ourselves: A History of American Environmental Policy* (New Haven, CT: Yale University Press, 1999), 150.

33. Paul Walden Hansen, *Green in Gridlock: Common Goals, Common Ground, and Compromise* (College Station, TX: Texas A&M University Press, 2013), 77.

34. Mark Dowie, *Losing Ground: American Environmentalism at the Close of the Twentieth Century* (Cambridge: MIT Press, 1995), 17.

35. Miller, *Public Lands*, 73.

36. Draft of H.R. 8668 to establish a National Park Service, 1916, quoted in

David J. Webber, *Outstanding Environmentalists of Congress* (Washington, DC: U.S. Capitol Historical Society, 2002), 39.

37. Udall, *Quiet Crisis and the Next Generation*, 123.

38. Report of the Secretary of the Interior, 65th Cong., 3rd Sess., H. Doc. 1455, 110, quoted in Douglas H. Strong, *Dreamers and Defenders: American Conservationists* (Lincoln: University of Nebraska Press, 1988), 118.

39. Andrews, *Managing the Environment*, 157.

40. Udall, *Quiet Crisis and the Next Generation*, 124.

41. Paul S. Sutter, *Driven Wild: How the Fight against Automobiles Launched the Modern Wilderness Movement* (Seattle: University of Washington Press, 2002), 71.

42. Aldo Leopold, "The Wilderness and Its Place in Forest Recreational Policy," *Journal of Forestry* 19, no. 7 (November 1921): 719.

43. Aldo Leopold, "Wilderness as a Form of Land Use," *Journal of Land and Public Utility Economics* 1 (October 1925): 404, 400.

44. Aldo Leopold, "The Last Stand of the Wilderness," *American Forests and Forest Life* 31, no. 382 (1925): 602; repr. in *American Forests and Forest Life* (Winter 2014), https://www.americanforests.org/magazine/article/aldo-leopolds-the-last-stand-of-the-wilderness/.

45. Regulation L-20, October 30, 1929, as quoted in Dennis M. Roth, *The Wilderness Movement and the National Forests* (College Station, TX: Intaglio Press, 1988), 3, quoted in Scott, *Enduring Wilderness*, 29.

46. Aldo Leopold, *A Sand County Almanac: And Sketches Here and There* (1949; repr. Oxford University Press, 2020), 186.

47. Benton MacKaye, "Why the Appalachian Trail?" *Living Wilderness* 1, no. 1 (September 1935): 7, quoted in Sutter, *Driven Wild*, 192.

48. "Wilderness as Minority Right," *Service Bulletin* of the US Forest Service, August 27, 1928, quoted in Robert Gottlieb, *Forcing the Spring: The Transformation of the American Environmental Movement* (Washington, DC: Island, 2005), 48.

49. Sutter, *Driven Wild*, 194.

50. Gottlieb, *Forcing the Spring*, 50.

51. Robert Marshall, "The Universe of the Wilderness is Vanishing," *Nature* 9, no. 4 (April 1937): 236, quoted in Scott, *Enduring Wilderness*, 24.

52. Elizabeth C. Flint, "Robert Marshall, the Man and His Aims," *Sunday Missoulian* (Missoula, MT), November 19, 1939, quoted in Nash, *Wilderness and the American Mind*, 203.

53. Scott, *Enduring Wilderness*, 31.

54. Wilderness Society, January 21, 1935, box 11, folder 14, Wilderness Society Papers, quoted in Sutter, *Driven Wild*, 242.

55. James Morton Turner, *The Promise of Wilderness: American Environmental Politics since 1964* (Seattle: University of Washington Press, 2012), 25.

56. Robert Marshall to Harold Ickes, "Suggested Program for Preservation of Wilderness Areas," April 1934, record group 79, file 601–12, Parks-General Lands-General-Wilderness Areas, pt. 1, National Archives, quoted in Scott, *Enduring Wilderness*, 18.

57. Harold Ickes, US Department of the Interior, Memorandum for the Press, January 3, 1939, National Archives Record Group 48, NPS 1933–42, quoted in Scott, 34.

58. H.R. 3648, 76th Congress, 1st session, introduced February 2, 1939, and S.1188, introduced February 6, 1939, National Archive Record Group 95, U, Legislation, Federal, S.1188, quoted in Scott, 34.

59. Scott, 35.

60. Gottlieb, *Forcing the Spring*, 51.

61. Sutter, *Driven Wild*, 257.

62. C. Frank Keyser, Committee on Merchant Marine and Fisheries, *The Preservation of Wilderness Areas: An Analysis of Opinion on the Problem by C. Frank Keyser, Regional Economist*, Legislative Reference Service, Library of Congress, August 24, 1949, Committee Print 19, 10, quoted in Scott, *Enduring Wilderness*, 42.

63. Udall, *Quiet Crisis and the Next Generation*, 216.

64. Turner, *Promise of Wilderness*, 23.

65. Howard Zahniser, "The Wilderness Bill and Foresters," March 14, 1957, quoted in Scott, *Enduring Wilderness*, 5.

66. John Saylor, 102 Cong. Rec. 12,583 (1956), quoted in Thomas G. Smith, *Green Republican: John Saylor and the Preservation of America's Wilderness* (Pittsburgh, PA: University of Pittsburgh Press, 2006), 114.

67. Smith, *Green Republican*, 113.

68. Richard Allan Baker, *Conservation Politics: The Senate Career of Clinton P. Anderson* (Albuquerque: University of New Mexico Press, 1985), 102.

69. Thomas G. Smith, *Stewart L. Udall: Steward of the Land* (Albuquerque: University of New Mexico Press, 2017), 93.

70. 103 Cong. Rec. 1906 (1957).

71. John Saylor, quoted in *Johnston (PA) Tribune-Democrat*, August 16, 1964, quoted in Smith, *Green Republican*, 2.

72. Smith, 48.

73. Smith, 62.

74. John Saylor, 99 Cong. Rec. A5069 (1953), quoted in Smith, 67.

75. Smith, 70.

76. Smith, 76.

77. Smith, 84.

78. Brant, *Adventures in Conservation*, 307.

79. David Brower to John Saylor, March 13, 1954, folder 11, box 66, Sierra Club Records, quoted in Smith, *Green Republican*, 85.

80. Nash, *Wilderness and the American Mind*, 212.

81. Ulysses S. Grant, *Proceedings before the United States Department of the Interior: Hearings on Dinosaur National Monument, Echo Park and the Split Mountain Dams*, 319, quoted in Nash, 213.

82. Nash, 219.

83. "National Forests: Play Area Trends to Wilds Is Cited," *New York Times*, March 17, 1957.

84. Clinton Anderson, 103 Cong. Rec. 958–59 (1957), quoted in Baker, *Conservation Politics*, 104.

85. Wayne Aspinall to David Brower, January 2, 1959, folder 26, box 90, Sierra Club Records, quoted in Smith, *Green Republican*, 120.

86. Smith, *Stewart L. Udall*, 94.

87. Wayne N. Aspinall," Irrigation and Federal Participation in Colorado," July 18–20, 1977, Western States College, Gunnison, CO, speech transcript, Vivian Passer Collection, quoted in Steven C. Schulte, *Wayne Aspinall and the Shaping of the American West* (Boulder: University Press of Colorado, 2002), 2.

88. Wayne Aspinall, interview with Steven Schulte, January 10, 1978, quoted in Schulte, 45.

89. Schulte, 53.

90. John Aspinall to Grace Saylor, October 28, 1973, folder 40, box 36, Wayne Aspinall Papers, University of Colorado, Boulder, quoted in Smith, *Green Republican*, 144.

91. Schulte, *Wayne Aspinall*, 74.

92. Smith, *Stewart L. Udall*, 60.

93. Stewart L. Udall, interview with Joe Frantz, April 18, 1969, Lyndon Baines Johnson Presidential Library Oral Histories, Lyndon Baines Johnson Presidential Library, University of Texas at Austin.

94. Udall, interview, April 18, 1969.

95. Schulte, *Wayne Aspinall*, 94.

96. Louis Cassels, "Man in a Hurry Who Loves His Work," *Desert News*, May 13, 1961, quoted in Smith, *Stewart L. Udall*, 136.

97. Stewart L. Udall, interview with Joe B. Frantz, May 19, 1969, Lyndon Baines Johnson Presidential Library Oral Histories.

98. Clinton P. Anderson, *Outsider in the Senate* (New York: World, 1970), quoted in Webber, *Outstanding Environmentalists of Congress*, 12.

99. Baker, *Conservation Politics*, 34.

100. Clinton Anderson, "The Wilderness of Aldo Leopold," *Living Wilderness* 19 (1954–55): 44–46, quoted in Nash, *Wilderness and the American Mind*, 224.

101. *The Wilderness Act: Hearings on S. 174 Before the Committee on Interior and Insular Affairs*, 87th Cong. 347 (1961).

102. Elynor S. Johnson to Senator Henry Jackson, February 10, 1961, Henry Jackson Papers, Special Collections, University of Washington Library, Seattle; Phyllis H. Bryant to Senator Henry Jackson, February 3, 1961, Henry Jackson Papers.

103. Don A. Gillis to Senator Henry Jackson, February 11, 1961, Henry Jackson Papers.

104. Katherine C. Snow to Senator Henry Jackson, February 15, 1961, Henry Jackson Papers.

105. Ray E. Johnson to Senator Henry Jackson, February 21, 1961, Henry Jackson Papers.

106. 103 Cong. Rec. 958–959 (1957), quoted in Baker, *Conservation Politics*, 140.

107. Zahniser to Anderson, July 14, 1961, box 642, Clinton Anderson Papers, Library of Congress, quoted in Baker, 141.

108. 107 Cong. Rec. 18,045–18,046 (1961).

109. 107 Cong. Rec. 18,045–18,047 (1961), quoted in Baker, *Conservation Politics*, 142.

110. Baker, 127.

111. Wayne N. Aspinall to William E. Bray, February 28, 1961, box 93, folder "L-11-a-1," Wayne Aspinall Papers, UDA, quoted in Schulte, *Wayne Aspinall*, 125.

112. "Statement by Hon. Wayne N. Aspinall (D-CO), Chairman of the Committee on Interior and Insular Affairs of the House of Representatives, December 21, 1961," box 16, folder 45, Wayne N. Aspinall Papers, University of Colorado at Boulder, quoted in Schulte, 132.

113. Senate, Interior and Insular Affairs Committee, Hearings, National Wilderness Preservation Act, 107, quoted in Richard A. Cooley and Geoffrey Wandesforde-Smith, eds., *Congress and the Environment* (Seattle: University of Washington Press, 1970), 56.

114. Wallace Stegner, "Wilderness Letter," December 3, 1960, full text available at "Wallace Stegner," The Wilderness Society, https://www.wilderness.org/articles/article/wallace-stegner.

115. Schulte, *Wayne Aspinall*, 97–98.

116. Udall, *Quiet Crisis and the Next Generation*, 180.

117. Stewart Udall, "To Save the Wonder of Wilderness," *New York Times Magazine*, May 27, 1962, 39–40, quoted in Smith, *Stewart L. Udall*, 154.

118. David Brower, address to 4th Biennial Conference on Northwest Wilderness, Seattle, April 14–15, 1962.

119. Charles E. Randall, "White House Conference on Conservation," *Journal of Forestry* 60 (1962): 457–458, quoted in Smith, *Stewart L. Udall*, 154.

120. Schulte, *Wayne Aspinall*, 134.

121. Schulte, 135.

122. Udall, *Quiet Crisis and the Next Generation*, 220.

123. Smith, *Stewart L. Udall*, 161.

124. Paul Brooks, "Congressman Aspinall vs. The People of the United States," *Harper's*, March 1963, 61.

125. Brooks, 61.

126. Citizens Committee on Natural Resources, press release, October 29, 1962, quoted in Schulte, *Wayne Aspinall*, 142.

127. Stewart Udall, report to the president, July 24, 1962, folder 7, box 98, Stewart Udall Papers, University of Arizona, Tucson, quoted in Smith, *Stewart L. Udall*, 161.

128. Brooks, "Congressman Aspinall," 60–63.

129. Brooks, 63.

130. Wayne Aspinall to John Saylor, September 21, 1962, box 37, John Saylor Papers, quoted in Smith, *Green Republican*, 179.

131. Wayne N. Aspinall, 108 Cong. Rec. (1962), quoted in Schulte, *Wayne Aspinall*, 139.

132. Wayne N. Aspinall to Howard Zahniser, October 1, 1962, box 20, folder 38, Wayne Aspinall Papers, University of Colorado at Boulder, quoted in Schulte, 141.

133. Wayne N. Aspinall, letter, December, 1962, box 20, folder 22, Wayne N. Aspinall Papers, University of Colorado at Boulder, quoted in Schulte, 144.

134. Stewart Udall, handwritten penciled note, January 14, 1963, folder 2, box 109, Stewart Udall Papers, quoted in Smith, *Stewart L. Udall*, 175.

135. Stewart Udall, conservation tour notes, folder 4, box 112, Stewart L. Udall Papers, quoted in Smith, 183.

136. David Goldfield, *The Gifted Generation: When Government Was Good* (New York: Bloomsbury, 2017), 293.

137. 109 Cong. Rec. 5923 (1963).

138. 109 Cong. Rec. 5926 (1963).

139. 109 Cong. Rec. 5936 (1963).

140. 109 Cong. Rec. 5942 (1963).

141. 109 Cong. Rec. 5887 (1963).

142. 109 Cong. Rec. 5888 (1963).

143. 109 Cong. Rec. 5944 (1963).

144. 145 Cong. Rec. S11,126–S11,127 (daily ed. September 21, 1999).

145. Brooks, "Congressman Aspinall," 60–63.

146. Smith, *Stewart L. Udall*, 179.

147. Brooks, "Congressman Aspinall," 60–63.

148. Senator Henry M. Jackson to a constituent, March 15, 1963, Senate Interior and Insular Affairs Committee S.2 S.4(cont.), Record Group 46, National Archives, as quoted in Roth, *Wilderness Movement and the National Forests*, 9–10, quoted in Scott, *Enduring Wilderness*, 62.

149. Smith, *Stewart L. Udall*, 180.

150. Interview with Robert Wolf, Establishment of Public Land Law Review Commission, November 5, 1981, quoted in Baker, *Conservation Politics*, 209.

151. Interview with Wolf, November 5, 1981, quoted in Baker, 209.

152. Howard Zahniser to Harvey Broome, May 3, 1963, Wilderness Society files, quoted in Scott, *Enduring Wilderness*, 55.

153. Udall, *Quiet Crisis and the Next Generation*, 220.

154. Howard Zahniser, letter to Paul Brooks, December 19, 1962, box 5: 102, folder NWPS-Wilderness Bill-Advocacy-Correspondence, June–December, 1962, quoted in Schulte, *Wayne Aspinall*, 145.

155. *Daily Sentinel*, April 17, 1963, quoted in Schulte, *Wayne Aspinall*, 147.

156. Smith, *Stewart L. Udall*, 187.

157. Udall, *Quiet Crisis and the Next Generation*, 220.

158. Wayne N. Aspinall, interview with Steven Schulte, June 14, 1974, quoted in Schulte, *Wayne Aspinall*, 151.

159. Wayne N. Aspinall to Dan Hughes, December 4, 1963, box 140, folder "L-11-a-3," Wayne Aspinall Papers, UDA, quoted in Schulte, 152.

160. Udall, interview, April 18, 1969.

161. Smith, *Stewart L. Udall*, 194.

162. Wayne Aspinall, interview with Joe Frantz, June 14, 1974, Lyndon Baines Johnson Presidential Library Oral Histories.

163. Lyndon Baines Johnson, *Vantage Point: Perspectives of the Presidency, 1963–1969* (New York: Holt, Rinehart and Winston, 1971), 336, quoted in Smith, *Stewart L. Udall*, 194.

164. Lyndon B. Johnson, speech, May 22, 1964, Ann Arbor, MI, UShistory.org/documents/great-society.htm.

165. Lynton K. Caldwell, "Natural Beauty and the Politics of Environmental Analysis (unpublished manuscript), 1966, 17, quoted in Cooley and Wandesforde-Smith, *Congress and the Environment*, xiv.

166. Johnson, *Vantage Point*, 337.

167. Howard Zahniser, Hearings, National Wilderness Preservation System, part 4, 1054, quoted in Smith, *Green Republican*, 186.

168. Zahniser, Wilderness Preservation System, Hearings, 1964, p. 1182, Schulte, *Wayne Aspinall*, 155.

169. John Dingell Jr., Wilderness Preservation System, Hearings, 1964, p. 1126, quoted in Schulte, 156.

170. Editorial, *Washington Post*, April 30, 1964.

171. Wayne Aspinall, Hearings, National Wilderness Preservation System, pt. 4,1291, quoted in Smith, *Green Republican*, 186.

172. *Wilderness Preservation System: Hearings Before the Subcommittee on Public Lands of the Committee on Interior and Insular Affairs* 88th Cong. 1394 (1964).

173. *Wilderness Preservation System: Hearings Before the Subcommittee on Public Lands of the Committee on Interior and Insular Affairs*, 88th Cong. 1394 (1964), quoted in Smith, *Green Republican*, 186.

174. Wayne Aspinall, 110 Cong. Rec. 10,214 (1964), quoted in Smith, 188.

175. Anderson, *Outsider in the Senate*, quoted in Schulte, *Wayne Aspinall*, 157.

176. Smith, *Green Republican*, 190.

177. 110 Cong. Rec. 17,427 (1964).

178. 110 Cong. Rec. 17,430 (1964).

179. 110 Cong. Rec. 17,430 (1964).

180. 110 Cong. Rec. 17,434 (1964).

181. 110 Cong. Rec. 13,437 (1964).

182. 110 Cong. Rec. 20,627 (1964).

183. 110 Cong. Rec. 20,602 (1964), quoted in Scott, *Enduring Wilderness*, 4.

184. 110 Cong. Rec. 20,630 (1964), quoted in Schulte, *Wayne Aspinall*, 160.

185. 110 Cong. Rec. 20,629–20,630 (1964).

186. 110 Cong. Rec. 20,627 (1964), quoted in Turner, *Promise of Wilderness*, 37.

187. 110 Cong. Rec. 20,627 (1964), quoted in Turner, 37.

188. Scott, *Enduring Wilderness*, 132.

189. Schulte, *Wayne Aspinall*, 165.

190. Aspinall, interview, June 14, 1974.

191. Wayne N. Aspinall to Stewart Udall, November 27, 1964, folder 12, box 115, Stewart L. Udall Papers, quoted in Smith, *Stewart L. Udall*, 201.

192. Anderson, *Outsider in the Senate*, 236, quoted in Baker, *Conservation Politics*, 228.

193. Stewart L. Udall, interview with Joe B. Frantz, December 16, 1969, Lyndon Baines Johnson Library Oral Histories.

194. Doris Kearns Goodwin, *Leadership in Turbulent Times* (New York: Simon and Schuster, 2018), 335.

195. Lyndon Baines Johnson, "Remarks upon Signing the Wilderness Bill and the Land and Water Conservation Fund Bill," September 3, 1964, made available online by Gerhard Peters and John T. Woolley, The American Presidency Project https://www.presidency.ucsb.edu/node/241689.

196. William O. Douglas, foreword to *The Wild Cascades: Forgotten Parklands*, quoted in Scott, *Enduring Wilderness*, xi.

197. Representative John Dingell, debate on H.R. 19007, 116 Cong. Rec. 32,754 (1970), quoted in Scott, 73.

198. Hansen, *Green in Gridlock*, 17.

199. 116 Cong. Rec. 36,758 (1970).

200. David R. Brower, "De Facto Wilderness: What Is Its Place?" in *Wildlands in Our Civilization* (San Francisco: Sierra Club, 1964), 103, 109, quoted in Scott, 77.

201. Udall, *Quiet Crisis and the Next Generation*, 221.

202. Stewart M. Brandborg, "Executive Director's Report to Council 1966–67," box 2, Wilderness Society Archives, Denver Public Library, Denver, CO, quoted in Scott, *Enduring Wilderness*, 63.

203. Lyndon Johnson to Stewart Udall, January 29, 1965, folder 1, box 145, Stewart Udall Papers, and James Reston, *New York Times*, November 4, 1964, both quoted in Smith, *Stewart L. Udall*, 198.

204. Webber, *Outstanding Environmentalists*, 85.

205. Lyndon B. Johnson to Stewart Udall, January 29, 1965, folder 1, box 140, Stewart L. Udall Papers, quoted in Smith, *Stewart L. Udall*, 201.

206. Cooley and Wandesforde-Smith, *Congress and the Environment*, 61.

207. Turner, *Promise of Wilderness*, 396.

208. Lyndon B. Johnson, letter to Congress, March 29, 1968, quoted in Scott, *Enduring Wilderness*, 13.

209. 110 Cong. Rec. 17,449 (1964), quoted in Hansen, *Green in Gridlock*, 63.

210. 145 Cong. Rec. S11,126–S11,127 (daily ed. September 21, 1999).

Chapter 3. Money, Beauty, and Recreation

1. Lyndon B. Johnson, *My Hope for America* (New York: Random House, 1964), 51, quoted in John P. Crevelli, "The Final Act of the Greatest Conservation President," *Prologue* 12 (Winter 1980): 173–191.

2. Richard Goodwin, "Preservation of Natural Beauty," *Stewart Udall Papers* (June 1964), quoted in Lewis L. Gould, *Lady Bird Johnson and the Environment* (Lawrence: University Press of Kansas, 1988), 39.

3. Laurance Rockefeller, interview with Joe B. Frantz, August 5, 1969, Lyndon Baines Johnson Oral Histories, Lyndon Baines Johnson Presidential Library, University of Texas at Austin.

4. Joseph Califano, quoted in Stewart Udall, note on telephone conversation, December 18, 1965, folder 2, box 123, Stewart Udall Papers, University of Arizona, Tucson, quoted in Thomas G. Smith, *Stewart L. Udall: Steward of the Land* (Albuquerque: University of New Mexico Press, 2017), 213.

5. Lyndon Johnson, "Presidential Policy Paper No. 3: Conservation of Natural Resources," November 1, 1964, made available online by Gerhard Peters and John T. Woolley, The American Presidency Project, https://www.presidency.ucsb.edu/node/241697.

6. Stewart L. Udall, interview with Joe B. Frantz, May 19, 1969, Lyndon Baines Johnson Oral Histories.

7. Wayne Aspinall, 110 Cong. Rec. 16,520 (1964), quoted in Thomas G. Smith, *Green Republican: John Saylor and the Preservation of America's Wilderness* (Pittsburgh, PA: University of Pittsburgh Press, 2006), 188.

8. Smith, *Green Republican*, 267.

9. *Land and Water Conservation Fund: Hearings on S. 859 Before the Committee on Interior and Insular Affairs*, 88th Cong. 176 (1963).

10. Richard Allan Baker, *Conservation Politics: The Senate Career of Clinton P. Anderson* (Albuquerque: University of New Mexico Press, 1985), 154.

11. Edward C. Crafts, interview with David G. McComb, April 2, 1969, Lyndon Baines Johnson Oral Histories.

12. Baker, *Conservation Politics*, 161.

13. Udall, interview, May 19, 1969.

14. Lyndon Baines Johnson, "Special Message to the Congress on Conservation and Restoration of Natural Beauty," February 8, 1965, made available online by Lyndon Baines Johnson Presidential Library, http://www.lbjlibrary.net/collections/selected-speeches/1965/02-08-1965.html.

15. Lyndon Johnson, "Annual Message to the Congress on the State of the Union," January 4, 1965, in *Public Papers of the Presidents of the United States: Lyndon B. Johnson, 1965* (Washington, DC: Government Printing Office, 1966), 1:8.

16. Smith, *Stewart L. Udall*, 204.

17. Robert Dallek, *Flawed Giant: Lyndon Johnson and His Times, 1961–1973* (New York: Oxford University Press, 1998), 229.

18. Lyndon B. Johnson, "Remarks to the Delegates to the White House Conference on Natural Beauty," May 25, 1965, American Presidency Project, http://www.presidency.ucsb.edu/ws/?pid=26993.

19. Henry L Diamond, "The Land, the City and the Human Spirit," *Environmental Forum* 3, no. 8 (1984): 12–13, quoted in Victor B. Scheffer, *The Shaping of Environmentalism in America* (Seattle: University of Washington Press, 1991), 154.

20. Rockefeller, interview, August 5, 1969.

21. Mark K. Updegrove, *Indomitable Will: LBJ in the Presidency* (New York: Crown, 2012), 307–308.

22. Lady Bird Johnson to Emily Crow, May 12, 1942, Cp-Cz folder, selected names, box 14, Lady Bird Johnson Archives, University of Texas, Austin, quoted in Gould, *Lady Bird Johnson and the Environment*, 17.

23. Ken Givens, "A Brief History of the Early Years of One Austin Texas Radio Station KTBC" (typescript, 1981), in Barker Texas History Center, Austin, 4, quoted in Gould, 19.

24. Gould, 33.

25. Gould, 51.

26. Edward C. Crafts, interview with David G. McComb, May 12, 1969, Lyndon Baines Johnson Oral Histories.

27. Updegrove, *Indomitable Will*, 309.

28. Martin V. Melosi, "Lyndon Johnson and Environmental Policy," in *Lyndon Johnson and Environmental Policy*, vol. 2 of *The Johnson Years*, ed. Robert A. Divine (Lawrence: University Press of Kansas, 1987), 119.

29. Edward P. Cliff, interview with Joe Frantz, January 6, 1969, Lyndon Baines Johnson Oral Histories.

30. Gould, *Lady Bird Johnson and the Environment*, 60.

31. Gould, 92.

32. *Department of the Interior and Related Agencies Appropriations for 1969: Hearings Before a Subcommittee of the Committee on Appropriations*, 90th Cong. 500 (1968).

33. Gould, *Lady Bird Johnson and the Environment*, 148.

34. Lyndon B. Johnson, "Letter to the President of the Senate and to the Speaker of the House Transmitting Bills to Improve Highway Beauty," May 26, 1965, made available online by Gerhard Peters and John T. Woolley, The American Presidency Project, https://www.presidency.ucsb.edu/node/241402.

35. Lady Bird Johnson interview with Harry Middleton, November 15, 1995, Lyndon Baines Johnson Oral Histories.

36. Ogden Nash, "Song of the Open Road," *New Yorker*, October 15, 1932, quoted in William O. Douglas, *The Three Hundred Year War: A Chronicle of Ecological Disaster* (New York: Random House, 1972), 152.

37. Gould, *Lady Bird Johnson and the Environment*, 138.

38. *Highway Beautification: Hearings Before the Subcommittee on Roads of the Committee on Public Works, House of Representatives*, 89th Cong. 4 (1965).

39. Patrick McNamara, as quoted in Paul Southwick to Lawrence O'Brien, April 14, 1965, Bill Moyers Files, HB, box 79, White House Central Files, quoted in Gould, *Lady Bird Johnson and the Environment*, 148.

40. Richard A. Cooley and Geoffrey Wandesforde-Smith, eds., *Congress and the Environment* (Seattle: University of Washington Press, 1970), 38–39.

41. Elizabeth Brenner Drew, "Lady Bird's Beauty Bill," *Atlantic*, December 1965, 71, quoted in Gould, *Lady Bird Johnson and the Environment*, 154.

42. *Washington Post*, September 30, 1965, quoted in Gould, 161.

43. Liz Carpenter to Lady Bird Johnson, October 4, 1965, White House Social Files/BF, Highway Beautification Act, box 14, quoted in Gould, 162.

44. Lyndon Johnson, "Remarks at the Signing of the Highway Beautification Act of 1965," October 22, 1965, in *Public Papers of the Presidents*, 2:1072–1073.

45. Cooley and Wandesforde-Smith, *Congress and the Environment*, 152.

46. Senator Warren Magnuson, press release, Warren Magnuson Papers, Special Collections, University of Washington Library.

47. Leo D. Bloch to Senator Warren Magnuson, February 17, 1967, Warren Magnuson Papers.

48. Douglas, *Three Hundred Year War*, 152.

49. Gould, *Lady Bird Johnson and the Environment*, 196.

50. Gould, 220.

51. Stewart L. Udall, *The Quiet Crisis and the Next Generation* (Layton, UT: Gibbs Smith, 1988), 177.

52. George Hartzog Jr., interview with Joe Frantz, December 20, 1968, Lyndon Baines Johnson Oral Histories.

53. Lyndon B. Johnson, as quoted in Gordon L. Hall, *Lady Bird and Her Daughters* (Philadelphia: M. Smith, 1967), 232, quoted in Crevelli, "Final Act."

54. Julian E. Zelizer, *The Fierce Urgency of Now: Lyndon Johnson, Congress, and the Battle for the Great Society* (New York: Penguin, 2015), 221.

55. Doris Kearns Goodwin, *Leadership in Turbulent Times* (New York: Simon and Schuster, 2018), 329–330.

56. Goodwin, 330.

57. Henry Jackson, interview with Michael L. Gillette, March 13, 1978, Lyndon Baines Johnson Oral Histories.

58. Richard L. Strout, "Johnson's Treadmill Spins," *Christian Science Monitor*, April 5, 1965, quoted in Zelizer, *The Fierce Urgency of Now*, 221.

59. Stewart L. Udall, interview with Joe Frantz, April 18, 1969, Lyndon Baines Johnson Oral Histories.

60. Lyndon B. Johnson, "Special Message to the Congress Proposing Measures to Preserve America's Natural Heritage," February 23, 1966, made available online by Gerhard Peters and John T. Woolley, The American Presidency Project, https://www.presidency.ucsb.edu/node/238149.

61. Stewart L. Udall, interview with Joe B. Frantz, December 16, 1969, Lyndon Baines Johnson Oral Histories.

62. Stewart Udall, *Hearing before the Subcommittee on National Parks and Recreation of the Committee on Interior and Insular Affairs, on H.R. 8578, to Amend Title I of the Land and Water Conservation Fund Act of 1965*, 90th Cong., 2nd Sess. (Washington, DC: GPO, 1968), 28–31, quoted in Smith, *Green Republican*, 275.

63. *Land and Water Conservation Fund Act Amendments: Hearings on H.R. 8578 and Related Bills Before the Subcommittee on National Parks and Recreation of the Committee on Interior and Insular Affairs*, 90th Cong. 11, 10 (1968).

64. *Land and Water Conservation Fund Act Amendments*, 130.

65. Wayne Aspinall and John Saylor to House of Representatives, May 20, 1968, Henry Jackson Papers, Special Collections, University of Washington Library, Seattle.

66. "The Conservation Fund," *New York Times*, May 19, 1968.

67. Editorial, *Washington Post*, July 10, 1968.

68. Crafts, interview, April 2, 1969.

69. Crafts, interview, April 2, 1969.

70. Melville Grosvenor, letter to Lyndon Baines Johnson, October 16, 1968, Lyndon Baines Johnson Library, quoted in Joseph A. Califano Jr., *The Triumph and Tragedy of Lyndon Johnson: The White House Years* (New York: Touchstone, 1991), 338.

Chapter 4. Lands, Rivers, and Trails

1. Laurance Rockefeller, interview with Joe. B. Frantz, August 5, 1969, Lyndon Baines Johnson Oral Histories, Lyndon Baines Johnson Presidential Library, University of Texas at Austin.

2. Thomas G. Smith, *Stewart L. Udall: Steward of the Land* (Albuquerque: University of New Mexico Press, 2017), 214.

3. Lyndon B. Johnson, "Special Message to Congress Proposing Measures to Preserve America's Natural heritage," February 23, 1966, The American Presidency Project, http://www.presidency.ucsb.edu/ws/?pid=28097.

4. Stewart L. Udall, interview with Joe B. Frantz, May 19, 1969, Lyndon Baines Johnson Oral Histories.

5. Udall, interview, May 19, 1969.

6. Udall, interview, May 19, 1969.

7. Lyndon B. Johnson to Stewart Udall, December 23, 1965, FG145, box 204, Lyndon B. Johnson Papers, quoted in Smith, *Stewart L. Udall*, 219.

8. Tim Palmer, *Wild and Scenic Rivers: An American Legacy* (Corvallis: Oregon State University Press, 2017), 18.

9. Palmer, 24.

10. Thomas G. Smith, *Green Republican: John Saylor and the Preservation of America's Wilderness* (Pittsburgh, PA: University of Pittsburgh Press, 2006), 221.

11. Report of the Senate Select Committee on National Water Resources, 87th Cong., 2nd session, January 31, 1961, quoted in Palmer, *Wild and Scenic Rivers*, 28.

12. Report of the Outdoor Recreation Resources Review Commission, January 30, 1962, quoted in Palmer, 28.

13. Palmer, 29.

14. Stewart L. Udall, *The Quiet Crisis and the Next Generation* (1963; repr., Layton, UT: Gibbs Smith, 1988), quoted in Palmer, 30.

15. Palmer, 31.

16. Stewart Udall, interview with LeRoy Ashby and Rod Gramer, June 11, 1979, quoted in LeRoy Ashby and Rod Gramer, *Fighting the Odds: The Life of Senator Frank Church* (Pullman: Washington State University Press, 1994), 345.

17. "Distinguished Young Americans," p. 17, CP, 10.1, box 1, Frank Church Papers, Boise State University, quoted in Ashby and Gramer, 12.

18. Carl Pease to Frank Church, March 7, 1961, quoted in Ashby and Gramer, 146.

19. Smith, *Green Republican*, 221.

20. Smith, *Stewart L. Udall*, 213.

21. Smith, *Green Republican*, 221.

22. John Saylor to Frank Romeo, October 25, 1966, box 37, John Saylor Papers, quoted in Smith, 220.

23. Smith, 224.

24. John Saylor to Theodore Bingham, June 16, 1966, box 33, John Saylor Papers, quoted in Smith, 225.

25. James MacGregor Burns, ed., *To Heal and to Build: The Programs of President Lyndon B. Johnson* (New York: McGraw-Hill, 1968), 300.

26. Stewart Udall, interview with Robert G. Kaufman, February 17, 1995, quoted in Robert G. Kaufman, *Henry M. Jackson: A Life in Politics* (Seattle: University of Washington Press, 2000), 164.

27. Kaufman, *Henry M. Jackson*, 15.

28. Jackson, "Address to the Bellingham Sportsmen," September 7, 1957, Henry M. Jackson 35603/233/43, quoted in Kaufman, 164.

29. Kaufman, 164.

30. Daniel Patrick Moynihan, interview with Robert G. Kaufman, July 28, 1996, quoted in Kaufman, 167.

31. Kaufman, 176.

32. John Saylor, 111 Cong. Rec. 8,042 (1965), quoted in Smith, *Stewart L. Udall*, 237.

33. David Brower, letter to Stewart Udall, April 29, 1966, folder 13, box 6, Harold C. Bradley Papers, Sierra Club Members Papers, quoted in Smith, 240.

34. Morris K. Udall, *Too Funny to Be President* (New York: Henry Holt, 1988), 46, quoted in Donald W. Carson and James W. Johnson, *Mo: The Life and Times of Morris K. Udall* (Tucson: University of Arizona Press, 2001), 121.

35. John Saylor, 112 Cong. Rec. 17,782 (1966), quoted in Smith, *Stewart L. Udall*, 241.

36. David Brower, interview, November 6, 1969, quoted in Roderick Nash, *Wilderness and the American Mind*, 3rd ed. (New Haven, CT: Yale University Press, 1982), 230.

37. Steven C. Schulte, *Wayne Aspinall and the Shaping of the American West* (Boulder: University Press of Colorado, 2002), 198.

38. Carson and Johnson, *Mo*, 124.

39. Nash, *Wilderness and the American Mind*, 230.

40. *Albuquerque Tribune*, November 18, 1966, quoted in Schulte, *Wayne Aspinall*, 201.

41. Carson and Johnson, *Mo*, 123.

42. Nash, *Wilderness and the American Mind*, 230.

43. "Sierra Club–Misc. Corresp." folder, box 1, Brower Papers, Sierra Club Members Papers, San Francisco, quoted in Douglas H. Strong, *Dreamers and Defenders: American Conservationists* (Lincoln: University of Nebraska Press, 1988), 209.

44. Wayne N. Aspinall, Colorado River Basin Project, Hearings, 1967, quoted in Schulte, *Wayne Aspinall*, 207.

45. *Denver Post*, June 25, 1967, quoted in Schulte, 208.

46. Stewart L. Udall, interview with Joe B. Frantz, December 16, 1969, Lyndon Baine Johnson Oral Histories.

47. Tim Palmer, *Endangered Rivers and the Conservation Movement* (Berkeley: University of California Press, 1986), 145, quoted in Smith, *Green Republican*, 225.

48. Smith, 226.

49. Carson and Johnson, *Mo*, 133.

50. Udall, *Too Funny to Be President*, quoted in Carson and Johnson, 124.

51. Carson and Johnson, 128.

52. Wilderness Society Archives, Denver Public Library, Denver, CO.

53. Mr. and Mrs. George Hudson to Senator Henry Jackson, June 4, 1967, Henry Jackson Papers, Special Collections, University of Washington.

54. Hal Bacon to Senator Henry Jackson, May 26, 1967, Henry Jackson Papers.

55. Anthony J. Golden to Senator Henry Jackson, February 1, 1967, Henry Jackson Papers.

56. Department of the Interior Administrative History, vol 1, pt. 1, History of the Implementation of the Land and Water Conservation Fund Program, Johnson papers, Lyndon B. Johnson Presidential Library, University of Texas, Austin, quoted in John P. Crevelli, "The Final Act of the Greatest Conservation President," *Prologue* 12 (Winter 1980): 173–191.

57. John Saylor to Theodore Bingham, Editor, *Dayton Journal Herald*, June 16, 1966, box 33, John Saylor Papers, quoted in Smith, *Green Republican*, 228.

58. Wayne Aspinall, Hearings, Subcommittee on National Parks and Recreation, House Committee on Interior and Insular affairs, 90th Cong., 2nd Session (Washington, DC: GPO, 1968), 243, quoted in Smith, 228.

59. Sam Steiger, Minutes, Executive Session, House Subcommittee on National Parks and Recreation, June 10, 1968, box 33, John Saylor Papers, quoted in Palmer, *Wild and Scenic Rivers*, 36.

60. John Saylor to Stewart Udall, July 22, 1968, box 33, John Saylor Papers, quoted in Smith, *Green Republican*, 217.

61. Edward Crafts to Senator Henry Jackson, September 5, 1968, Henry Jackson Papers.

62. 114 Cong. Rec. 26,588 (1968), quoted in Smith, *Green Republican*, 232.

63. Smith, 234.

64. Stewart Udall, interview with LeRoy Ashby and Rod Gramer, June 11, 1979.

65. Bill Hall, interview with LeRoy Ashby and Rod Gramer, April 8, 1979, quoted in Ashby and Gramer, *Fighting the Odds*, 345.

66. Ashby and Gramer, 348.

67. Frank Church to Bob Johnson, December 2, 1965, Frank Church Papers, Boise State University, quoted in Ashby and Gramer, 345.

68. John Noble Wilford, "Corps of Engineers Caught Up in Battle of Builders against the Preservers," *New York Times*, September 22, 1968.

69. Udall, interview, December 16, 1969.

70. Clifford M. Hardin, press release, 1970, Wilderness Society Archives, Denver Public Library.

71. J. Michael McCloskey, *In the Thick of It: My Life in the Sierra Club* (Washington, DC: Island, 2005), 66.

72. Lyndon Johnson, "Remarks on the Proposed Redwoods National Park in Northern California," June 25, 1964, made available online by Gerhard Peters and John T. Woolley, The American Presidency Project, https://www.presidency.ucsb.edu/node/239219.

73. Lyndon B. Johnson, Message to Congress, February 23, 1966, quoted in Burns, *To Heal and to Build*, 299.

74. Smith, *Stewart L. Udall*, 281.

75. McCloskey, *In the Thick of It*, 57.

76. Wayne N. Aspinall to Richard D. Lamm, February 3, 1967, box 276, folder "L-11-d," Wayne Aspinall Papers, University of Denver Archives, Denver, quoted in Schulte, *Wayne Aspinall*, 229.

77. Lyndon B. Johnson to Wayne Aspinall, July 10, 1967, box 226, folder Aspinall, Wayne, Cong., Name Files, Lyndon B. Johnson Presidential Papers, Lyndon B. Johnson Presidential Library, quoted in Schulte, 229.

78. 113 Cong. Rec. 30,744 (1967).

79. 113 Cong. Rec. 30,747 (1967).

80. 113 Cong. Rec. 30,748 (1967).

81. 113 Cong. Rec. 30,744–30,758 (1967).

82. 113 Cong. Rec. 30,750, 30,751 (1967).

83. 113 Cong. Rec. 30,752–30,753 (1967).

84. 113 Cong. Rec. 30,753, 30,755 (1967).

85. Letter to Senator Henry Jackson, Henry Jackson Papers.

86. Morris Udall, Hearings, North Cascades National Park, 614, quoted in Smith, *Green Republican*, 286.

87. Wayne Aspinall, 114 Cong. Rec., 21,387 (1968), quoted in McCloskey, *In the Thick of It*, 80.

88. Schulte, *Wayne Aspinall*, 231.

89. 114 Cong. Rec. 21,387 (1968), quoted in Smith, *Green Republican*, 261.

90. Wayne N. Aspinall to C. E. Moritz, August 5, 1968, box 310, folder "L-11-d," Wayne Aspinall Papers, University of Denver Archives, quoted in Schulte, *Wayne Aspinall*, 232.

91. Smith, *Stewart L. Udall*, 282.

92. Udall, interview, December 16, 1969.

93. Michael McCloskey, interview with Gregg Coodley, September 18, 2019.

94. L. V. Venable to Senator Henry Jackson, February 10, 1961, Henry Jackson Papers.

95. McCloskey, *In the Thick of It*, 44.

96. Richard A. Cooley and Geoffrey Wandesforde-Smith, eds., *Congress and the Environment* (Seattle: University of Washington Press, 1970), 74.

97. Christina Powers to Senator Henry Jackson, March 5, 1968, Henry Jackson.

98. Nancy Riddell to Senator Henry Jackson, April 5, 1968, Henry Jackson Papers.

99. Elmer P. Lawrence to Senator Henry Jackson, April 19, 1968, Henry Jackson.

100. Omak Chamber of Commerce to Senator Henry Jackson, February 22, 1968, Henry Jackson Papers.

101. Udall, interview with Kaufman, quoted in Kaufman, *Henry M. Jackson*, 168.

102. Letter from Senator Henry Jackson, April 1, 1968, Henry Jackson Papers.

103. Wild Cascades, February–March 1968, 3, quoted in Cooley and Wandesforde-Smith, *Congress and the Environment*, 78.

104. *Seattle Times*, June 4, 1968, 10, cited in Cooley and Wandesforde-Smith, 79.

105. Udall, interview with Kaufman, quoted in Kaufman, *Henry M. Jackson*, 168.

106. Udall, interview, December 16, 1969.

107. Bill Christofferson, *The Man from Clear Lake: Earth Day Founder Senator Gaylord Nelson* (Madison: University of Wisconsin Press, 2004), 357; Benton MacKaye, "The Appalachian Trail: A Project in Regional Planning," *Journal of the American Institute of Architects* (October 1921).

108. Lyndon B. Johnson, Message to Congress on Natural Beauty, 1965, quoted in Christofferson, 360.

109. Lyndon B. Johnson, Message to Congress, February 23, 1966, quoted in Burns, *To Heal and to Build*, 299–300.

110. Udall, interview, December 16, 1969.

111. 112 Cong. Rec. 7393 (1966).

112. Smith, *Green Republican*, 273.

113. 114 Cong. Rec. 21,431 (1968).

114. Senator Henry Jackson to Hollis Day, April 21, 1967, Henry Jackson Papers.

115. William Walmat to Senator Henry Jackson, September 15, 1968, Henry Jackson Papers.

116. Stewart Udall, oral history interview, October 31, 1969, 3, Lyndon B. Johnson Presidential Library, quoted in Crevelli, "Final Act."

117. Edward C. Crafts, interview with David G. McComb, May 12, 1969, Lyndon Baine Johnson Oral Histories.

118. Crevelli, "Final Act."

119. Crafts, interview, May 12, 1969.

120. Stewart L. Udall, interview with Joe Frantz, October 31, 1969, Lyndon Baines Johnson Oral Histories.

121. W. DeVier Pierson, Oral History Interview, March 19, 1969, 18–19, Lyndon B. Johnson Presidential Library.

122. Wayne Aspinall Oral History Interview, June 19, 1079, 27, Lyndon B. Johnson Presidential Library, quoted in Crevelli, "Final Act."

123. Udall, interview, October 31, 1969.

124. Crevelli, "Final Act."

125. Crafts, interview, May 12, 1969.

126. Stewart Udall to Lyndon and Lady Bird Johnson, February 6, 1969, folder 1, box 182, Stewart Udall Papers, quoted in Smith, *Stewart L. Udall*, 293.

127. Lady Bird Johnson to Stewart Udall, February 14, 1969, folder 2, box 145, Stewart L. Udall Papers, quoted in Smith, 293.

128. Joseph A. Califano, Jr., *The Triumph and Tragedy of Lyndon Johnson: The White House Years* (New York: Touchstone, 1991), 340.

129. Cooley and Wandesforde-Smith, *Congress and the Environment*, xv.

130. Rockefeller, interview, August 5, 1969.

131. Stewart L. Udall to the president, October 17, 1968. White House Central Files, Ex NR, quoted in Martin V. Melosi, "Lyndon Johnson and Environmental Policy," in *Vietnam, the Environment, and Space*, vol. 2 of *The Johnson Years*, ed. Robert A. Divine (Lawrence: University Press of Kansas, 1987), 117.

132. Lyndon Baines Johnson, *Vantage Point: Perspectives of the Presidency 1963–1969* (New York: Holt, Rinehart and Winston, 1971), 338.

Chapter 5. Tackling Pollution in the Johnson Years

1. Edmund S. Muskie, *Journeys* (Garden City, NY: Doubleday, 1972), 83.

2. Muskie, 84.

3. William O. Douglas, *The Three Hundred Year War: A Chronicle of Ecological Disaster* (New York: Random House, 1972), 21.

4. Robert Gottlieb, *Forcing the Spring: The Transformation of the American Environmental Movement* (Washington, DC: Island, 2005), 95.

5. Frederick Law Olmsted, Harlan Page Kelsey, et al., *The Smoke Nuisance* (Philadelphia, PA: American Civic Association, 1908), 4, 6.

6. David C. Brill, ed., *Cleaning America's Air: Progress and Challenges* (Knoxville, TN: Howard Baker Jr. Center for Public Policy Publications, 2005), 2.

7. *Times* (London), April 20, 1953, 7, quoted in E. Melanie DuPuis, ed., *Smoke and Mirrors: The Politics and Culture of Air Pollution* (New York: New York University Press, 2004), 164.

8. Brill, *Cleaning America's Air*, 2.

9. J. Brooks Flippen, *Nixon and the Environment* (Albuquerque: University of New Mexico Press, 2000), 91.

10. Ralph L. Larsen, "Air Pollution from Motor Vehicles," *Annals of the New York Academy of Sciences* 136, no. 12 (1966): 298, quoted in Victor B. Scheffer, *The Shaping of Environmentalism in America* (Seattle: University of Washington Press, 1991), 57.

11. Richard N. L. Andrews, *Managing the Environment, Managing Ourselves: A History of American Environmental Policy* (New Haven, CT: Yale University Press, 1999), 208.

12. Muskie, *Journeys*, 84.

13. Brill, *Cleaning America's Air*, 2–3.

14. 110 Cong. Rec., 6261 (1964).

15. Muskie, *Journeys*, 85–86.

16. Theo Lippman Jr., and Donald C. Hansen, *Muskie* (New York: W. W. Norton, 1971), 142.

17. Robert Dallek, *Flawed Giant: Lyndon Johnson and His Times, 1961–1973* (New York: Oxford University Press, 1998), 229.

18. Donald F. Hornig, interview with David G. McComb, December 4, 1968, Lyndon Baines Johnson Oral Histories, Lyndon Baines Johnson Presidential Library, University of Texas at Austin.

19. Martin Melosi, "Lyndon Johnson and Environmental Policy," in *Vietnam, the Environment, and Space*, vol. 2 of *The Johnson Years*, ed. Robert A. Divine (Lawrence: University Press of Kansas, 1987), 134.

20. Press release, Johnson to Hornig, November 4, 1965, FG 11-9, box 122, quoted in Melosi, 134.

21. David Goldfield, *The Gifted Generation: When Government Was Good* (New York: Bloomsbury, 2017), 295.

22. Brill, *Cleaning America's Air*, 3.

23. "Don't Breathe Deeply," *Saturday Evening Post*, July 31, 1965, 88, quoted in Goldfield, *Gifted Generation*, 295.

24. Andrews, *Managing the Environment*, 209.

25. Lyndon B. Johnson, message to Congress, January 1967, quoted in James MacGregor Burns, ed., *To Heal and to Build: The Programs of President Lyndon B. Johnson* (New York: McGraw-Hill, 1968), 304.

26. Air Pollution Control, 42 U.S.C. §§ 1857–1857l (Supp. V, 1970), quoted in Char Miller and Hal Rothman, eds., *Out of the Woods: Essays in Environmental History* (Pittsburgh, PA: University of Pittsburgh Press, 1997), 130.

27. Lippman and Hansen, *Muskie*, 148.

28. Lyndon B. Johnson, "Remarks on Signing the Air Quality Act of 1967," November 21, 1967, quoted in Burns, *To Heal and to Build*, 301.

29. Johnson, "Remarks on Signing the Air Quality Act of 1967," November 21, 1967, quoted in Irwin Unger and Debi Unger, *LBJ: A Life* (New York: John Wiley and Sons, 1999), 435.

30. "Remarks at the Signing of the Water Quality Act of 1965," October 2, 1965, in *Public Papers of the Presidents of the United States: Lyndon B. Johnson, 1965* (Washington DC: Government Printing Office, 1966), 2:1035.

31. Flippen, *Nixon and the Environment*, 66.

32. Brill, *Cleaning America's Air*, 3.

33. Birch Bayh, interview with Paige E. Mulhollen, February 12, 1969, Lyndon Baines Johnson Oral Histories.

34. Andrews, *Managing the Environment*, 42.

35. Lemuel Shattuck et al., *Report of the Sanitary Commission of Massachusetts* (Cambridge, MA, Harvard University Press, 1948; facsimile of Report of a General

Plan for the Promotion of Public and Personal Health, Dutton and Wentworth, Boston, 1850), quoted in Peninah Neimark and Peter Rhoades Mott, *The Environmental Debate*, 2nd ed. (Amenia, NY: Grey House, 2011), 82.

36. Gottlieb, *Forcing the Spring*, 91.

37. Paul Charles Milazzo, *Unlikely Environmentalists: Congress and Clean Water, 1945–1972* (Lawrence: University Press of Kansas, 2006), 1.

38. Milazzo, 2.

39. Flippen, *Nixon and the Environment*, 4.

40. Andrews, *Managing the Environment*, 204.

41. Philip K. Micklin, "Water Quality: A Question of Standards," in *Congress and the Environment*, ed. Richard A. Cooley and Geoffrey Wandesforde-Smith (Seattle: University of Washington Press, 1970), 132.

42. Milazzo, *Unlikely Environmentalists*, 31.

43. Andrews, *Managing the Environment*, 204

44. Carolyn Merchant, *The Columbia Guide to American Environmental History* (New York: Columbia University Press, 2002), 115.

45. John C. Whitaker, *Striking a Balance: Environment and Natural Resources Policy in the Nixon-Ford Years* (Washington, DC: American Enterprise Institute for Public Policy Research, 1976), 23.

46. Harvey Lieber, *Federalism and Clean Waters: The 1972 Water Pollution Control Act* (Lexington, MA: Lexington Books, 1975), 12.

47. Jerry Sonosky, interview by Paul Charles Milazzo, October 28, 1998, quoted in Milazzo, *Unlikely Environmentalists*, 22.

48. David J. Webber, *Outstanding Environmentalists of Congress* (Washington, DC: U.S. Capitol Historical Society, 2002), 19.

49. *Water Pollution Control Act: Hearings on S. 890 and H.R. 9540 Before the Subcommittee on Rivers and Harbors of the Committee on Public Works, House of Representatives*, 84th Cong. 111 (1956).

50. Jerry Sonosky, interview with Paul Charles Milazzo, October 28, 1998, quoted in Milazzo, *Unlikely Environmentalists*, 35.

51. Walter A. Rosenbaum, *The Politics of Environmental Concern* (New York: Praeger, 1973), 137.

52. Webber, *Outstanding Environmentalists*, 19.

53. Lieber, *Federalism and Clean Waters*, 12

54. Milazzo, *Unlikely Environmentalists*, 36.

55. Lyndon Baines Johnson, *Vantage Point: Perspectives of the Presidency, 1963–1969* (New York: Holt, Rinehart and Winston, 1971), 337.

56. Milazzo, *Unlikely Environmentalists*, 52.

57. *Water Resources Activities in the United States—Water Quality Management*, 86th Cong., 2nd Sess., February 1960, Committee Print No. 32, 4–5, quoted in Milazzo, 53.

58. "Special Message to the Congress on Natural Resources," February 23, 1961, in *Public Papers of the Presidents: John F. Kennedy, 1961* (Washington, DC: Government Printing Office, 1962): 116.

59. Environmental Protection Agency, *Legal Compilation: Statutes and Legislative History, Executive Orders, Regulations, Guidelines and Reports* (Washington, DC: Government Printing Office, 1973), 457.

60. Cooley and Wandesforde-Smith, *Congress and the Environment*, 133.

61. Bill Christofferson, *The Man from Clear Lake: Earth Day Founder Senator Gaylord Nelson* (Madison: University of Wisconsin Press, 2004), 366.

62. Julian E. Zelizer, *The Fierce Urgency of Now: Lyndon Johnson, Congress, and the Battle for the Great Society* (New York: Penguin, 2015), 220.

63. Lyndon B. Johnson quoted in memorandum from Kermit Gordon, March 6, 1965, box 24, Presidential Papers, Lyndon B. Johnson Presidential Library, University of Texas, Austin, quoted in Goldfield, *Gifted Generation*, 294.

64. Muskie, *Journeys*, 79–80.

65. Milazzo, *Unlikely Environmentalists*, 65.

66. Joel K. Goldstein, "Edmund S. Muskie: The Environmental Leader and Champion," *Maine Law Review* 67, no. 2 (2015).

67. Milazzo, *Unlikely Environmentalists*, 65.

68. Muskie, *Journeys*, 82.

69. Edmund Muskie to Bernard Asbell, in Asbell, *The Senate Nobody Knows* (Garden City, NY: Doubleday, 1978), 120–121, quoted in Lewis L. Gould, *The Most Exclusive Club: A History of the Modern United States Senate* (New York: Basic Books, 2005), 228.

70. Milazzo, *Unlikely Environmentalists*, 69.

71. Lady Bird Johnson, interview with Michael L. Gillette, November 15, 1981, Lyndon Baine Johnson Oral Histories.

72. Ron Linton, interview with Paul Charles Milazzo, July 28, 1998, quoted in Milazzo, *Unlikely Environmentalists*, 70.

73. Goldstein, "Edmund S. Muskie."

74. *Troubled Waters*, narrated by Henry Fonda, documentary produced by the United States Senate Subcommittee on Air and Water Pollution of the Senate Committee on Public Works, 1965, quoted in Milazzo, *Unlikely Environmentalists*, 75.

75. Elinor Langer, "Water Pollution: Federal Role Is Strengthened by Law Authorizing New Agency and Quality Standards," *Science* 150 (October 8, 1965): 258, quoted in Milazzo, 78.

76. Zelizer, *Fierce Urgency of Now*, 220–221.

77. *Water Pollution Control Act Amendments: Hearings on S. 649, H.R. 3166, H.R. 4571, H.R. 6844 Before the Committee on Public Works*, 88th Cong. 238 (1964).

78. Lyndon B. Johnson, "Remarks at the Signing of the Water Quality Act of 1965," October 2, 1965, http://www.presidency.ucsb.edu/ws/?pid=27289

79. Johnson, *Vantage Point*, 337–38.

80. Johnson, 338.

81. Johnson, 338.

82. John Bird, "Our Dying Waters," *Saturday Evening Post*, April 23, 1966, 34, quoted in Goldfield, *Gifted Generation*, 296.

83. Lyndon B. Johnson, "State of the Union Address," January 12, 1966, https://www.infoplease.com/primary-sources/government/presidential-speeches/state-union-address-lyndon-b-johnson-january-12-1966.

84. Lyndon B. Johnson, "Special Message to the Congress Proposing Measures to Preserve America's Natural Heritage," February 23, 1966, made available online by Gerhard Peters and John T. Woolley, The American Presidency Project, https://www.presidency.ucsb.edu/node/238149.

85. Goldfield, *Gifted Generation*, 294.

86. "Nelson Proposes Aid to Cut Industrial Waste," *Milwaukee Journal*, October 15, 1966, quoted in Christofferson, *Man from Clear Lake*, 457.

87. Goldstein, "Edmund S. Muskie."

88. Ronald Reagan to Lyndon B. Johnson, June 1, 1967, box 26, Presidential Papers, Lyndon B. Johnson Presidential Library, quoted in Goldfield, *Gifted Generation*, 299.

89. Zelizer, *Fierce Urgency of Now*, 221.

90. Lyndon B. Johnson, *Vantage Point*, 337

91. Bird, "Our Dying Waters," quoted in Goldfield, *Gifted Generation*, 295.

92. Robert F. Kennedy, quoted in Bird, "Our Dying Waters," quoted in Goldfield, 296.

93. "The People-Water Crisis," *Newsweek* 66 (August 23, 1965): 48–52, quoted in Milazzo, *Unlikely Environmentalists*, 77–78.

94. Christofferson, *Man from Clear Lake*, 367.

95. Andrews, *Managing the Environment*, 206.

96. Webber, *Outstanding Environmentalists*, 56.

97. Milazzo, *Unlikely Environmentalists*, 179.

98. Rosenbaum, *Politics of Environmental Concern*, 141.

99. *Water Pollution—1968, Part I: Hearings on Activities of the Federal Water Pollution Control Administration—Water Quality Standards, Before the Subcommittee on Air and Water Pollution of the Committee on Public Works*, 90th Cong. A23 (1968).

100. Milazzo, *Unlikely Environmentalists*, 142.

101. Cooley and Wandesforde-Smith, *Congress and the Environment*, 143.

Chapter 6. The Green Nixon

1. Julian E. Zelizer, *The Fierce Urgency of Now: Lyndon Johnson, Congress, and the Battle for the Great Society* (New York: Penguin, 2015), 310; Joseph A. Califano Jr., interview with Tim Naftali, April 3, 2007, Richard Nixon Presidential Library and Museum, Yorba Linda, CA; H. R. Haldeman, interview with Raymond H. Geselbracht, August 11, 1987, Richard Nixon Presidential Library and Museum.

2. John C. Whitaker, *Striking a Balance: Environment and Natural Resources Policy in the Nixon-Ford Years* (Washington, DC: American Enterprise Institute for Public Policy Research, 1976), 1.

3. James Kilpatrick, "Call for Action," *Pittsburgh Press*, reported in 115 Cong. Rec., 28,791 (1969), quoted in Thomas G. Smith, *Green Republican: John Saylor*

and the Preservation of America's Wilderness (Pittsburgh, PA: University of Pittsburgh Press, 2006), 266.

4. William O. Douglas, *The Three Hundred Year War: A Chronicle of Ecological Disaster* (New York: Random House, 1972), 199.

5. John Steele Gordon, "The American Environment: The Big Picture is More Heartening than All the Little Ones," *American Heritage*, October 1993, 45, quoted in Benjamin Kline, *First along the River: A Brief History of the U.S. Environmental Movement* (San Francisco: Acada Books, 1997), 84.

6. Zelizer, *Fierce Urgency of Now*, 318.

7. Evan Thomas, *Being Nixon: A Man Divided* (New York: Random House, 2015), 411.

8. John Whitaker, interview by Evan Thomas, in Thomas, *Being Nixon*, 411.

9. Edward Nixon, interview with Tim Naftali, April 7, 2007, Richard Nixon Presidential Library and Museum.

10. Thomas, *Being Nixon*, 339.

11. Joan Hoff, *Nixon Reconsidered* (New York: Basic Books, 1994), 118, quoted in Thomas, 341.

12. Roy L. Ash, interview with Raymond H. Geselbracht and Frederick J. Graboske, January 13, 1988, Richard Nixon Presidential Library and Museum.

13. National Environment Policy Act of 1969, Pub. L. No. 91-190, 83 Stat. 852 (1970), quoted in Carolyn Merchant, *The Columbia Guide to American Environmental History* (New York: Columbia University Press, 2002), 181.

14. Quoted in Russell Train, *A Memoir* (Washington, DC: Published by the author, 2000), 174.

15. Lynton K. Caldwell, *Environment as a Focus for Public Policy*, ed. Robert V. Bartlett and James N. Gladden (College Station: Texas A&M University Press, 1995), 30–31. Emphasis in original.

16. Caldwell, 162.

17. J. Brooks Flippen, *Nixon and the Environment* (Albuquerque: University of New Mexico Press, 2000), 48.

18. Peninah Neimark and Peter Rhoades Mott, eds., *The Environmental Debate*, 2nd ed. (Amenia, NY: Grey House, 2011), 218.

19. Martin V. Melosi, "Lyndon Johnson and Environmental Policy," in *Vietnam, the Environment, and Space*, vol. 2 of *The Johnson Years*, ed. Robert A. Divine (Lawrence: University Press of Kansas, 1987), 126–127.

20. Robert G. Kaufman, *Henry M. Jackson: A Life in Politics* (Seattle: University of Washington Press, 2000), 202.

21. Bill Van Ness, interview with Robert C. Kaufman, May 2, 1995, quoted in Kaufman, 203.

22. George Hartzog Jr., interview with Joe Frantz, December 20, 1968, Lyndon Baines Johnson Oral Histories, Lyndon Baines Johnson Presidential Library, University of Texas at Austin.

23. Kaufman, *Henry M. Jackson*, 203.

24. Daniel Dreyfus, interview with Robert. C. Kaufman, December 31, 1996, quoted in Kaufman, *Henry M. Jackson*, 203.

25. *National Environmental Policy: Hearing on S. 1075, S. 237, and S. 1752 Before the Committee on Interior and Insular Affairs*, 91st Cong. 37–38 (1969).

26. Report of the Natural Resources and Environment Transition Task Force, December 5, 1968, Folder "Task Force Reports, Transition Period, 1968–1969," box 1, Transition Task Force Reports, White House Central Files (hereafter WHCF), Richard Nixon Presidential Materials Project (hereafter RNPMP), quoted in J. Brooks Flippen, *Conservative Conservationist: Russell E. Train and the Emergence of American Environmentalism* (Baton Rouge: Louisiana State University Press, 2006), 61.

27. Richard A.Cooley and Geoffrey Wandesforde-Smith, eds., *Congress and the Environment* (Seattle: University of Washington Press, 1970), 216.

28. Report of the Natural Resources and Environment Task Force, December 5, 1968, Folder "Task Force Reports, Transition Period, 1968–69," Transition Task Force Reports, WHCF, RNPMP, quoted in Flippen, *Conservative Conservationist*, 62.

29. Richard Nixon, inaugural address, January 20, 1969, made available online by Gerhard Peters and John T. Woolley, The American Presidency Project, https://www.presidency.ucsb.edu/node/239549.

30. Flippen, *Conservative Conservationist*, 67.

31. Russell E. Train, *Politics, Pollution, and Pandas: An Environmental Memoir* (Washington, DC: Island, 2003), 78–79.

32. Walter J. Hickel, *Who Owns America?* (Englewood Cliffs, NJ: Prentice-Hall, 1971), 13.

33. Victor B. Scheffer, *The Shaping of Environmentalism in America* (Seattle: University of Washington Press, 1991), 47.

34. Stewart L. Udall, interview with Joe Frantz, July 29, 1969, Lyndon Baines Johnson Oral Histories.

35. Walter Hickel, interview with Timothy Naftali, April 25, 2008, Presidential Materials, Richard Nixon Presidential Library and Museum.

36. Hickel, *Who Owns America?*, 95.

37. Kirkpatrick Sale, *The Green Revolution: The American Environmental Movement, 1962–1992* (New York: Hill and Wang, 1993), 19.

38. Hickel, interview, April 25, 2008.

39. Senator Henry Jackson, speech to 11th Biennial Wilderness Conference, San Francisco, March 15, 1969, Henry Jackson Papers, Special Archives, University of Washington Library.

40. Cooley and Wandesforde-Smith, *Congress and the Environment*, 221.

41. Kaufman, *Henry M. Jackson*, 203.

42. Cooley and Wandesforde-Smith, *Congress and the Environment*, 222.

43. *National Environmental Policy: Hearing on S. 1075, S. 237, and S. 1752 Before the Committee on Interior and Insular Affairs*, 91st Cong. 206 (1969).

44. Whitaker, *Striking a Balance*, 28.

45. Whitaker, 30.

46. Whitaker, 31.

47. Robert Cahn, *Footprints on the Planet: A Search for an Environmental Ethic* (New York: Universe Books, 1978), 25.

48. Lynton Caldwell, "Environment: A New Focus for Public Policy?" *Public Administration Review*, 1963.

49. Richard Andrews, *Environmental Policy and Administrative Change* (Lanham, MD: Lexington Books, 1976), 9, quoted in Flippen, *Nixon and the Environment*, 35.

50. Senator Henry M. Jackson, "A National Policy for the Environment," address before the National Audubon Society, Saint Louis, Missouri, April 26, 1969, quoted in Cooley and Wandesforde-Smith, *Congress and the Environment*, 229.

51. Ronald Ritz to Senator Henry Jackson, November 1, 1969, Henry Jackson Papers, Special Collections, University of Washington Library, Seattle.

52. Train, *Politics, Pollution, and Pandas*, 69.

53. Memo, Russell Train to John Ehrlichman, November 3, 1969, folder 485-OA2977, Environment, box 63, Emil Krogh Files, WHSF, RNPMP, quoted in Flippen, *Conservative Conservationist*, 85.

54. Train, *Politics, Pollution, and Pandas*, 69.

55. Flippen, *Conservative Conservationist*, 85.

56. Kaufman, *Henry M. Jackson*, 204.

57. Paul Charles Milazzo, *Unlikely Environmentalists: Congress and Clean Water, 1945–1972* (Lawrence: University Press of Kansas, 2006), 127.

58. Kaufman, *Henry M. Jackson*, 204; Laurance S. Rockefeller to Senator Henry Jackson, September 24, 1969, Henry Jackson Papers.

59. "Agree Upon Changes," 115 Congressional Record 29,056 (1969), quoted in Paul Milazzo, *Unlikely Environmentalists, Congress and Clean Water 1945–72* (Lawrence: University Press of Kansas, 2006), 130.

60. Milazzo, *Unlikely Environmentalists*, 130.

61. Kaufman, *Henry M. Jackson*, 204.

62. 115 Cong. Rec. 26,579 (1969).

63. Mrs. E. D. Blocker to Senator Henry Jackson, March 5, 1969, Henry Jackson Papers.

64. Flippen, *Conservative Conservationist*, 96.

65. John McPhee, *Encounters with the Archdruid* (New York: Farrar, Straus and Giroux, 1971), 87.

66. J. Michael McCloskey, *In the Thick of It: My Life in the Sierra Club* (Washington, DC: Island, 2005), 104.

67. Train, *Politics, Pollution, and Pandas*, 61.

68. Hickel, *Who Owns America?*, 125.

69. Train, *Politics, Pollution, and Pandas*, 64.

70. H. R. Haldeman, interview with Raymond H. Geselbracht and Fred J. Graboske, August 13, 1987, Richard Nixon Presidential Library and Museum.

71. H. R. Haldeman, with Raymond H. Geselbracht, August 11, 1987, Richard Nixon Presidential Library and Museum.

72. Whitaker, *Striking a Balance*, 28.

73. Flippen, *Nixon and the Environment*, 48.

74. Train, *Politics, Pollution, and Pandas*, 70.

75. Train, 72.

76. Richard Nixon, "Statement about the National Environmental Policy Act of 1969," January 1, 1970, made available online by Gerhard Peters and John T. Woolley, The American Presidency Project, https://www.presidency.ucsb.edu /node/239921.

77. Flippen, *Conservative Conservationist*, 86.

78. Flippen, *Nixon and the Environment*, 51.

79. Rick Perlstein, *Nixonland: The Rise of a President and the Fracturing of America* (New York: Scribner, 2008), 460.

80. John Mallon to Senator Henry Jackson, December 8, 1969, Henry Jackson Papers.

81. Austin K. Van Dusen to Senator Henry Jackson, November 5, 1969, Henry Jackson Papers.

82. John Whitaker to Richard Nixon, January 28, 1970, folder January–April, 1 of 4, January, 1970, box 2, John Whitaker Files, WHCF, RNPMP, quoted in Flippen, *Nixon and the Environment*, 53.

83. Cahn, *Footprints on the Planet*, 24.

84. Cahn, 27.

85. Flippen, *Conservative Conservationist*, 88.

86. Executive Order, Protection and Enhancement of Environmental Quality, March 5, 1970, folder "The Environmental Coalition, 1 of 2," box 61, Charles Colson Files, WHSF, RNPMP, quoted in Flippen, *Nixon and the Environment*, 51.

87. Train, *Politics, Pollution, and Pandas*, 90.

88. Train, 81.

89. Train, 91.

90. Cahn, *Footprints on the Planet*, 32.

91. Cahn, 32.

92. Train, *Politics, Pollution, and Pandas*, 105.

93. Train, 101.

94. Cahn, *Footprints on the Planet*, 41.

95. Richard M. Nixon, Presidential Statement, January 19, 1971, quoted in Cahn, *Footprints on the Planet*, 42.

96. Cahn, 42–43.

97. Cahn, 43.

98. Richard Nixon, "Annual Message to the Congress on the State of the Union," January 22, 1970, in *Public Papers of the Presidents of the United States: Richard Nixon, 1970* (Washington, DC: Government Printing Office, 1971), 11–12.

99. Nixon, 13.

100. Train, *Politics, Pollution, and Pandas*, 89.

101. Cahn, *Footprints on the Planet*, 33.

102. Cahn, 35.

103. Cahn, 36.

104. Hickel, *Who Owns America?*, 129.

105. Richard Nixon, "Annual Message to the Congress on the State of the Union," January 22, 1971, made available online by Gerhard Peters and John T. Woolley, The American Presidency Project, https://www.presidency.ucsb.edu/node /240562.

106. William Ruckelshaus, interview with Timothy Naftali, April 12, 2007, Presidential Materials, Richard Nixon Presidential Library and Museum.

107. Council on Environmental Quality, *President's 1971 Environmental Program* (Washington, DC: US Government Printing Office, 1971), quoted in Train, *Politics, Pollution, and Pandas*, 104.

108. Cahn, *Footprints on the Planet*, 36.

109. Victor Yannacone, as quoted in Gilbert Rogin, "All He Wants to Do Is Save the World," *Sports Illustrated*, February 3, 1969, 29, quoted in Adam Rome, *The Genius of Earth Day: How a 1970 Teach-In Unexpectedly Made the First Green Generation* (New York: Hill and Wang, 2013), 193.

110. David Brower, as quoted in Luther J. Carter, "Environmental Pollution: Scientists Go to Court," *Science* 158 (December 22, 1967): 1556, quoted in Rome, 194.

111. Victor Yannacone, "Sue the Bastards," *Earth Day—The Beginning, Environmental Action*, 199, quoted in Rome, 195.

112. Scheffer, *Shaping of Environmentalism in America*, 26.

113. Calvert Cliffs Coordinating Committee, Inc. v. Atomic Energy Commission, Environmental Law Reporter 1 (1971), 20353–54, quoted in Milazzo, *Unlikely Environmentalists*, 136–137.

114. Russell E. Train, letter to IRS Commissioner Randolph Thrower, September 30, 1970, quoted in Train, *Politics, Pollution, and Pandas*, 95.

115. Senator James Eastland, quoted in *St. Petersburg Times*, October 13, 1971, quoted in Walter A. Rosenbaum, *The Politics of Environmental Concern* (New York: Praeger, 1973), 188.

116. Milazzo, *Unlikely Environmentalists*, 149.

117. Joseph L. Sax, "The Public Trust Doctrine in Natural Resource Law: Effective Judicial Intervention," *Michigan Law Review* 68 (1970): 474, quoted in Richard N. L. Andrews, *Managing the Environment, Managing Ourselves: A History of American Environmental Policy* (New Haven, CT: Yale University Press, 1999), 240.

118. Mark Dowie, *Losing Ground: American Environmentalism at the Close of the Twentieth Century* (Cambridge: MIT Press, 1995), 37.

119. Margaret McKeown, "Supreme Court Justice William O. Douglas Was Not Just a Legal Giant, but Also a Powerful Environmentalist," *Seattle Times*, August 16, 2018.

120. Sierra Club v. Morton, 405 U.S. 727, April 19, 1972, quoted in Bill

McKibben, ed., *American Earth: Environmental Writing since Thoreau* (Washington, DC: Library of America, 2008), 355.

121. Sierra Club v. Morton, 405 U.S. 727, April 19, 1972, quoted in Cahn, *Footprints on the Planet*, 238.

122. Milazzo, *Unlikely Environmentalists*, 237–238.

123. Cahn, *Footprints on the Planet*, 37.

124. Cahn, 39.

125. Warm Springs Dam Task Force v. Gribble, 417 U.S. 1301, 1309 (1974).

126. Kaufman, *Henry M. Jackson*, 202.

127. Kaufman, 208.

128. Henry M. Jackson, "The Environmental Responsibility of Business and Society," National Soft Drink Association, San Francisco, November 18, 1969, 3560-4/233/23, Henry M. Jackson Papers, Special Collections, University of Washington Library, quoted in Kaufman, 206–207.

129. Train, *Politics, Pollution, and Pandas*, 93–97.

130. Train, 117.

131. Andrews, *Managing the Environment*, 315.

132. Flippen, *Nixon and the Environment*, 226.

133. Douglas, *Three Hundred Year War*, 175.

134. Richard Nixon, "Special Message to the Congress on Environmental Quality," February 10, 1970, made available online by Gerhard Peters and John T. Woolley, The American Presidency Project, https://www.presidency.ucsb.edu/node/240088.

135. Richard M. Nixon, *Public Papers of the Presidents, Nixon, 1970*, Special Message to Congress on Environmental Quality, 95, quoted in Whitaker, *Striking a Balance*, 42.

136. *New York Times*, February 11, 1970, 46, quoted in Flippen, *Nixon and the Environment*, 74.

137. Melosi, "Lyndon Johnson and Environmental Policy," 124–125.

138. Robert H. Finch, interview with Michael L. Gillette, February 23, 1989, Lyndon Baines Johnson Oral Histories.

139. Memo, Russell Train to John Ehrlichman, March 23, 1970, Public Papers of Russell Train, Library of Congress, quoted in Flippen, *Conservative Conservationist*, 92.

140. "Q and A: Russell Train, Green Legislator Pioneer," *American Forests*, Autumn 2006, 39, quoted in Char Miller, *Public Lands, Public Debates: A Century of Controversy* (Corvallis: Oregon State University Press, 2012), 126.

141. Memo, Russell Train to John Ehrlichman, March 23, 1970, Public Papers of Russell Train, Library of Congress, quoted in Train, *Politics, Pollution, and Pandas*, 102.

142. Whitaker, *Striking a Balance*, 70.

143. Finch, interview, February 23, 1989.

144. Flippen, *Nixon and the Environment*, 85.

145. Whitaker, *Striking a Balance*, 56.

146. Scheffer, *Shaping of Environmentalism in America*, 144.

147. Perlstein, *Nixonland*, 517.

148. John Whitaker to Roy Ash, July 9, 1970, folder "May–August, 1970, 3 of 4, July 1970," box 2, John Whitaker Files, WHCF, RNPMP, quoted in Flippen, *Nixon and the Environment*, 88.

149. Letter from Senator Henry Jackson, March 2, 1970, Henry Jackson Papers.

150. David C. Brill, ed., *Cleaning America's Air: Progress and Challenges* (Knoxville, TN: Howard Baker Jr. Center for Public Policy Publications, 2005), 15.

151. Ruckelshaus, interview, April 12, 2007.

152. Ruckelshaus, interview, April 12, 2007.

153. H. Patricia Hynes, *The Recurring Silent Spring* (Elmsford, NY: Pergamon, 1989), 49.

154. J. Lewis, "The Birth of the EPA," *EPA Journal*, quoted in Hynes, 20.

155. Robert W. Collin, *The Environmental Protection Agency: Cleaning Up America's Act* (Westport, CT: Greenwood, 2006), 119.

156. William Ruckelshaus, interview with Michael Gorn, January 1993, EPA Oral History Series.

157. Lois R. Ember, "EPA Administrators Deem Agency's First 25 Years Bumpy but Successful," *Chemical & Engineering News*, October 30, 1995, 19, quoted in Kline, *First along the River*, 95.

158. Train, *Politics, Pollution, and Pandas*, 103.

159. Flippen, *Nixon and the Environment*, 88.

160. Ruckelshaus, interview, January 1993.

161. Ruckelshaus, interview, April 12, 2007.

162. Brill, *Cleaning America's Air*, 15.

163. Brill, 15.

164. Ruckelshaus, interview, April 12, 2007.

165. Ruckelshaus, interview, April 12, 2007.

166. Ruckelshaus, interview, April 12, 2007.

167. Ruckelshaus, interview, January 1993.

168. Andrews, *Managing the Environment*, 235.

169. Andrews, 231.

170. Flippen, *Nixon and the Environment*, 226.

171. Senator Warren Magnuson, press release, May 27, 1965, Warren Magnuson Papers, Special Collections, University of Washington Library, Seattle, WA.

172. Nixon, "State of the Union," 1970, 12.

173. *Public Papers of the Presidents, Nixon, 1970* (Washington, DC: General Printing Office, 1970), 101, quoted in Flippen, *Nixon and the Environment*, 67.

174. Hickel, *Who Owns America?*, 182.

175. Flippen, *Nixon and the Environment*, 67.

176. Richard M. Nixon, "Special Message to the Congress on Environmental Quality," February 10, 1970, *Public Papers of the Presidents of the United States*, 101, quoted in Whitaker, *Striking a Balance*, 34.

177. Nixon, "Special Message to the Congress on Environmental Quality."

178. Cahn, *Footprints on the Planet*, 109.

179. Milazzo, *Unlikely Environmentalists*, 155.

180. Stewart Udall, *Arizona Republic*, June 28, 1970.

181. Rome, *Genius of Earth Day*, 218.

182. Press release, Air Pollution, Backing Words with Action, Edmund Muskie, August 16, 1970, folder 3, "1970 Press File- Ledger Syndicate Columns, 1970—So Goes the Nation," box 1533, USSSO, Edmund Muskie Archives, quoted in Flippen, *Nixon and the Environment*, 97.

183. Andrews, *Managing the Environment*, 233.

184. Flippen, *Conservative Conservationist*, 101.

185. Milazzo, *Unlikely Environmentalists*, 157.

186. Andrews, *Managing the Environment*, 234.

187. Leon Billings, "In the Shadow of Greatness," in Brill, *Cleaning America's Air*, 12.

188. J. Lee Annis Jr., *Howard Baker: Conciliator in an Age of Crisis* (Lanham, MD: Madison Books, 1995), 75.

189. William H. Frist, *Tennessee Senators, 1911–2001: Portraits of Leadership in a Century of Change*, with James Lee Annis Jr. (Lanham, MD: Madison Books, 1999), 142.

190. Billings, "In the Shadow of Greatness," in Brill, *Cleaning America's Air*, 12.

191. Howard H. Baker Jr., *No Margin for Error: America in the Eighties* (New York: Times Books, 1980), 39.

192. Howard H. Baker Jr., "U.S. Environmentalism, Comity and the Clean Air Act," in Brill, *Cleaning America's Air*, 8.

193. Bernard Asbell, *The Senate Nobody Knows* (Garden City, NY: Doubleday, 1978), 167.

194. Brill, *Cleaning America's Air*, 8.

195. Asbell, *Senate Nobody Knows*, 376.

196. Brill, *Cleaning America's Air*, 9.

197. Kline, *First along the River*, 95.

198. Annis, *Howard Baker*, 78.

199. Baker, *No Margin for Error*, 39.

200. Annis, *Howard Baker*, 80.

201. Bill Christofferson, *The Man from Clear Lake: Earth Day Founder Senator Gaylord Nelson* (Madison: University of Wisconsin Press, 2004), 564.

202. Flippen, *Nixon and the Environment*, 98.

203. Russell Train to John Ehrlichman, December 14, 1970, Public Papers of Russell Train, Library of Congress, quoted in Flippen, *Conservative Conservationist*, 101.

204. Edmund Muskie to Bernard Asbell, in Asbell, *Senate Nobody Knows*, 210.

205. Karl Braithwaite to Bernard Asbell, in Asbell, *Senate Nobody Knows*, 355.

206. Russell Train to Richard Nixon, October 1, 1970, Public Papers of Russell Train, Library of Congress, quoted in Flippen, *Conservative Conservationist*, 102.

207. Douglas, *Three Hundred Year War*, 22.

208. Douglas, 23.

209. Rosenbaum, *Politics of Environmental Concern*, 159.

210. Flippen, *Conservative Conservationist*, 102.

211. Flippen, *Nixon and the Environment*, 116.

212. Flippen, *Nixon and the Environment*, 116.

213. Eliot Cutler to Bernard Asbell, in Asbell, *Senate Nobody Knows*, 192.

214. Ruckelshaus, interview, April 12, 2007.

215. Ruckelshaus, interview, April 12, 2007.

216. Ruckelshaus, interview, April 12, 2007.

217. Richard Nixon, quoted in Tom Wicker, *One of Us* (New York: Random House, 1991), 515–516, quoted in Flippen, *Nixon and the Environment*, 142.

218. Flippen, 143.

219. Edmund S. Muskie, *Journeys* (Garden City, NY: Doubleday, 1972), 86.

220. Muskie, 94.

221. Ruckelshaus, interview, April 12, 2007.

222. Ruckelshaus, interview, April 12, 2007.

223. 115 Cong. Rec. 7,959 (1969).

224. 115 Cong. Rec. 17,560 (1969).

225. Nixon, "Special Message to the Congress on Environmental Quality."

226. Nixon, "Special Message to the Congress on Environmental Quality."

227. John Whitaker quoted in Johnathan Aitken, *Nixon: A Life* (Washington, DC: Regnery, 1993), 398, quoted in Flippen, *Nixon and the Environment*, 91.

228. Flippen, 92.

229. Richard M. Nixon, "Special Message to Congress on Environmental Quality," February 10, 1970.

230. Whitaker, *Striking a Balance*, 187.

231. Richard M. Nixon, remarks of the president following a helicopter tour of the proposed Gateway East Recreation Area, May 10, 1971, Office of the White House Press Secretary, quoted in Whitaker, 191.

232. McCloskey, *In the Thick of It*, 133.

233. Hartzog, interview, December 20, 1968.

234. Council on Environmental Quality, "Environmental Quality: The First Annual Report of the Council on Environmental Quality" (Washington, DC: US Government Printing Office, 1970), vii, quoted in Rome, *Genius of Earth Day*, 230.

235. Dennis W. Brezina, interview with Donald A. Richie, August 17, 2005, Senate Historical Office, United States Senate.

236. Brezina, interview, August 17, 2005.

237. Brezina, interview, August 17, 2005.

238. Rome, *Genius of Earth Day*, 239.

239. Christofferson, *Man from Clear Lake*, 566.

240. Flippen, *Conservative Conservationist*, 89.

241. Train, *Politics, Pollution, and Pandas*, 80.

242. Richard Reeves, *President Nixon: Alone in the White House* (New York: Simon and Schuster, 2001), 172, quoted in Train, *Politics, Pollution, and Pandas*, 80.

Chapter 7. High Tide on Nixon Water Policy

1. J. Brooks Flippen, *Nixon and the Environment* (Albuquerque: University of New Mexico Press, 2000), 181.

2. William O. Douglas, *The Three Hundred Year War: A Chronicle of Ecological Disaster* (New York: Random House, 1972), 35.

3. Paul Charles Milazzo, *Unlikely Environmentalists: Congress and Clean Water, 1945–1972* (Lawrence: University Press of Kansas, 2006), 145.

4. Thomas G. Smith, *Green Republican: John Saylor and the Preservation of America's Wilderness* (Pittsburgh, PA: University of Pittsburgh Press, 2006), 274.

5. Walter J. Hickel, *Who Owns America?* (Englewood Cliffs, NJ: Prentice-Hall, 1971), 213.

6. Richard Nixon, Remarks on Transmitting a Special Message to Congress on Environmental Quality, February 10, 1970, *Public Papers of the Presidents, 1970*, 95, quoted in John C. Whitaker, *Striking a Balance: Environment and Natural Resources Policy in the Nixon-Ford Years* (Washington, DC: American Enterprise Institute for Public Policy Research, 1976), 79.

7. Richard Nixon, "Special Message to the Congress on Environmental Quality," February 10, 1970, made available online by Gerhard Peters and John T. Woolley, The American Presidency Project, https://www.presidency.ucsb.edu /node/240088.

8. Nixon, "Special Message to the Congress on Environmental Quality."

9. Nixon, "Special Message to the Congress on Environmental Quality."

10. Russell E. Train, Diary, February 5, 1970, quoted in Russell E. Train, *Politics, Pollution, and Pandas: An Environmental Memoir* (Washington, DC: Island, 2003), 85.

11. *Water Pollution Control Legislation—1971 (Proposed Amendments to Existing Legislation): Hearings Before the Committee on Public Works*, 92nd Cong. 225 (1971).

12. Whitaker, *Striking a Balance*, 75.

13. Richard Nixon, Memo to John Ehrlichman, March 13, 1969, folder "335 Domestic Policy, 2 of 2," box 31, John Ehrlichman Files, WHSF, Richard Nixon Presidential Materials Project, quoted in Flippen, *Nixon and the Environment*, 48.

14. Flippen, 220.

15. Milazzo, *Unlikely Environmentalists*, 195.

16. John Tunney to Edmund Muskie, June 3, 1971, folder "Tunney Standard," box 4, RG46.18, NARA, quoted in Milazzo, 197.

17. Leon Billings to Edmund Muskie, "National Minimum Water Quality Standards, July 19, 1971, folder "Memos," box 4, RG46.18, NARA, quoted in Milazzo, 202.

18. Milazzo, 204.

19. Leon Billings to Edmund Muskie, "National Minimum Water Quality

standards," Folder "Executive Sessions-Water," pp. 1–3, box 4, RG46.18, NARA, quoted in Milazzo, 209.

20. Milazzo, 212.

21. US Senate, Committee on Public Works, Federal Water Pollution Control Acts of 1971, Senate Report No. 92-414 to Accompany S.2770, 92nd Cong., 1st Sess., 1971, p. 3, quoted in Harvey Lieber, *Federalism and Clean Water: The 1972 Water Pollution Control Act* (Lexington, MA: Lexington Books, 1975), 15.

22. Milazzo, *Unlikely Environmentalists*, 217.

23. William Ruckelshaus, interview with Timothy Naftali, April 12, 2007, Presidential Materials, Richard Nixon Presidential Library and Museum, Yorba Linda, CA.

24. Senate Committee on Public Works Executive Session, September 30, 1971, pp. 48–49, folder 6, box 3045, quoted in Milazzo, *Unlikely Environmentalists*, 221–222.

25. Edmund S. Muskie, "Clean Water Act of 1972: Its Meaning for Users and Investors," Remarks to Bradley, Woods and Company Dinner Seminar, Sheraton Park Hotel, Washington, DC, December 12, 1972.

26. Lieber, *Federalism and Clean Waters*, 7.

27. Train, *Politics, Pollution, and Pandas*, 87.

28. Milazzo, *Unlikely Environmentalists*, 223.

29. Richard Nixon, "Special Message to the Congress Urging Legislation to Avoid Further Pollution in the Santa Barbara Channel," June 11, 1970, in *Public Papers of the Presidents of the United States: Richard Nixon, 1970* (Washington, DC: Government Printing Office, 1971), 497.

30. Gaylord A. Nelson, "America's Last Chance," remarks to midwinter meeting, State Bar of Wisconsin, Milwaukee, February 19, 1965, Nelson Senate Papers, quoted in Bill Christofferson, *The Man from Clear Lake: Earth Day Founder Senator Gaylord Nelson* (Madison: University of Wisconsin Press, 2004), 106.

31. J. Brooks Flippen, *Conservative Conservationist: Russell E. Train and the Emergence of American Environmentalism* (Baton Rouge: Louisiana State University Press, 2006), 104.

32. Train, *Politics, Pollution, and Pandas*, 125.

33. Douglas, *Three Hundred Year War*, 88.

34. Flippen, *Nixon and the Environment*, 103.

35. Douglas, *Three Hundred Year War*, 88.

36. *Toxic Substances Control Act of 1971 and Amendment: Hearings on S. 1478 Before the Subcommittee on the Environment of the Committee on Commerce*, 92nd Cong. 407 (1972).

37. Peter Vanderpoel, "Washington's Poor Advice," *Minneapolis Tribune*, October 7, 1971, quoted in Christofferson, *Man from Clear Lake*, 370.

38. Christofferson, 371.

39. 30 Stat. 1152, 33 U.S.C. 401-15, quoted in Milazzo, *Unlikely Environmentalists*, 166.

40. United States v. Standard Oil Co., 384 U.S. 224 (1966), quoted in Milazzo, 167.

41. Milazzo, 168–169.

42. Hickel, *Who Owns America?*, 105.

43. SCNR, *Our Waters and Wetlands: How the Corps of Engineers Can Help Prevent Their Destruction and Pollution*, 91st Cong., 2nd Sess., March 18, 1970, H.R. 917, pp. 14–18, quoted in Milazzo, *Unlikely Environmentalists*, 170.

44. Department of the Army, Office of the Chief of Engineers, "Civil Regulatory Function: Illegal Deposits in Navigable Waters," Circular No. 1145-2-1, S-1, February 17, 1967, quoted in Milazzo, 167.

45. Lieber, *Federalism and Clean Waters*, 24.

46. Milazzo, *Unlikely Environmentalists*, 173.

47. Milazzo, 175.

48. Lieber, *Federalism and Clean Waters*, 24.

49. Walter A. Rosenbaum, *The Politics of Environmental Concern* (New York: Praeger, 1973), 144.

50. Ruckelshaus, interview, April 12, 2007.

Chapter 8. The Atmosphere Changes

1. Nixon quoted in Haldeman Personal Notes, February 9, 1971, Folder "Notes, January–March, 1971 (January 1–February 15, 1971), Part I," box 43, H.R. Haldeman Files, WHSF, Richard Nixon Presidential Materials Project (hereafter RNPMP), quoted in J. Brooks Flippen, *Conservative Conservationist: Russell E. Train and the Emergence of American Environmentalism* (Baton Rouge: Louisiana State University Press, 2006), 111.

2. Nixon quoted in Haldeman Personal Notes, February 9, 1971, Folder "Notes, January–March, 1971 (January 1–February 15, 1971), Part I," box 43, H.R. Haldeman Files, WHSF, RNPMP, quoted in J. Brooks Flippen, *Nixon and the Environment* (Albuquerque: University of New Mexico Press, 2000), 135.

3. Evan Thomas, *Being Nixon: A Man Divided* (New York: Random House, 2015), 412.

4. Flippen, *Nixon and the Environment*, 148.

5. Russell Train to John Whitaker, November 24, 1970, folder EX FG251, EQC, box 1, Cabinet Committee on the Environment Files, WHCF, RNPMP, quoted in Flippen, 106.

6. Henry M. Jackson, Speech before American Law Institute, September 28, 1971, Folder 2, Speeches and Writings, "Law, Lawyers and the Environment" ABA, ALI, Smithsonian, box 236, Accession No. 3560-5, PHJ, quoted in Flippen, 105.

7. Henry M. Jackson, Speech before American Law Institute, September 28, 1971, quoted in Flippen, 150.

8. William Ruckelshaus, interview with J. Brooks Flippen, April 2, 1998.

9. Flippen, *Nixon and the Environment*, 137.

10. Walter A. Rosenbaum, *The Politics of Environmental Concern* (New York: Praeger, 1973), 160.

11. Rosenbaum, 163.

12. Letter, Maurice Stans to Richard Nixon, April 12, 1971, Folder "Meetings

Files, Beginning April 11, 1971," box 84, President's Office Files, WHSF, RNPMP, quoted in Flippen, *Nixon and the Environment*, 139.

13. Lowry Wyatt, "Economy and the Environment: The Need for Integrity," *Vital Speeches of the Day* 37, no. 16 (June 1, 1971), 509, quoted in Flippen, 196.

14. Memo, John Whitaker to John Ehrlichman, September 1, 1971, folder "July–October, 1971, 3 of 4, September, 1971," box 4, John Whitaker Files, WHCF, RNPMP, quoted in Flippen, 148.

15. William Ruckelshaus, interview with J. Brooks Flippen, April 2, 1998.

16. Flippen, 203.

17. William Ruckelshaus, "Environmental Regulation: The Early Days at EPA," *EPA Journal*, March 1988, 109.

18. Richard N. L. Andrews, *Managing the Environment, Managing Ourselves: A History of American Environmental Policy* (New Haven, CT: Yale University Press, 1999), 233.

19. William Ruckelshaus, interview with Timothy Naftali, April 12, 2007, Presidential Materials, Richard Nixon Presidential Library and Museum.

20. Ruckelshaus, interview, April 12, 2007.

21. William Ruckelshaus, application for suspension of the 1975 Motor Vehicle Exhaust Emission Standards, decision of the administrator, EPA, mimeographed, May 12, 1972, 17, Environmental Protection Agency, quoted in John C. Whitaker, *Striking a Balance: Environment and Natural Resources Policy in the Nixon-Ford Years* (Washington, DC: American Enterprise Institute for Public Policy Research, 1976), 99.

22. Whitaker, 100.

23. Whitaker, 94.

24. Philip Berry, interview by J. Brooks Flippen, June 19, 1998, quoted in Flippen, *Nixon and the Environment*, 172.

25. Rosenbaum, *Politics of Environmental Concern*, 124.

26. Roy L. Ash, interview with Raymond H. Geselbracht and Frederick J. Graboske, January 13, 1988, Richard Nixon Presidential Library and Museum, Yorba Linda, CA.

27. Roy L. Ash, interview with Frederick J. Graboske, August 4, 1988, Richard Nixon Presidential Library and Museum.

28. Roy L. Ash, interview with Tim Naftali, April 9, 2007, Richard Nixon Presidential Library and Museum.

29. Flippen, *Conservative Conservationist*, 142.

30. Russell Train, interview with J. Brooks Flippen, July 8, 1988, quoted in Flippen, *Nixon and the Environment*, 146.

31. Flippen, *Conservative Conservationist*, 132.

32. Russell Train, *Washington Evening Star and Daily News*, June 14, 1973, 1, quoted in Flippen, 133.

33. Nixon's Handwritten Comments on Daily New Summaries, June 15, 1972, Folder "Annotated News Summaries, June 7–23, 1972, 1 of 2," box 40, President's Office Files, WHSF, RNPMP, quoted in Flippen, *Nixon and the Environment*, 172.

34. Flippen, *Conservative Conservationist*, 113.

35. John Ehrlichman to John Whitaker, August 20, 1971, Folder "July–October, 1971, 2 of 4, August 1971," box 4, John Whitaker Files, WHCF, RNPMP, quoted in Flippen, *Nixon and the Environment*, 110.

36. Flippen, 180.

37. Russell Train, quoted in *Washington Post*, December 8, 1971, 6, quoted in Flippen, *Conservative Conservationist*, 113.

38. Summary, Second Annual Report, Council on Environmental Quality, August 1971, Folder "CEQ 1971-72, 2 of 3," box 123, John Whitaker Files, WHCF, RNPMP, quoted in Flippen, *Nixon and the Environment*, 147.

39. Whitaker, *Striking a Balance*, 82.

40. Nixon quoted in John Ehrlichman to John Connolly, December 8, 1971, folder "Recycling 1971–72, 3 of 3," box 98, John Whitaker Files, WHCF, RNPMP, quoted in Flippen, *Conservative Conservationist*, 110.

41. Bernard Asbell, *The Senate Nobody Knows* (Garden City, NY: Doubleday, 1978), 82.

42. US Senate, Committee on Public Works, A Legislative History of the Water Pollution Control Act Amendments of 1972, 93rd Cong., 1st Sess., January 1973, vol. II, p. 1264, quoted in Harvey Lieber, *Federalism and Clean Waters: The 1972 Water Pollution Control Act* (Lexington, MA: Lexington Books, 1975), 55.

43. US Senate, Committee on Public Works, A Legislative History of the Water Pollution Control Act Amendments of 1972, 93rd Cong., 1st Sess., January 1973, vol. II, p. 1325, quoted in Harvey Lieber, *Federalism and Clean Waters: The 1972 Water Pollution Control Act* (Lexington, MA: Lexington Books, 1975), 55.

44. Lieber, 55.

45. Lieber, 42.

46. Claude E. Barfield, "Environmental Report: Administration Fights Goals, Costs of Senate Water Quality Bill," *National Journal*, January 15, 1972, 93, quoted in Lieber, 46.

47. Edmund Muskie, press release, Water Pollution Bill, November 17, 1971, folder "Water Bill, I, 1971-2, 2 of 3," John Whitaker Files, WHCF, RNPMP, quoted in Flippen, *Nixon and the Environment*, 156.

48. Lieber, *Federalism and Clean Waters*, 61.

49. Paul Charles Milazzo, *Unlikely Environmentalists: Congress and Clean Water, 1945–1972* (Lawrence: University Press of Kansas, 2006), 228.

50. Milazzo, 229.

51. Karen DeW. Lewis, "Washington Pressures: NAM Turns Pragmatic in Opposing Federal Restraints on Industry," *National Journal*, June 3, 1972, 940, quoted in Milazzo, 228.

52. Edward E. David to John Blatnik, December 10, 1971, folder 199, box 28, Arthur Maass Papers, Records Collections. Office of History, Headquarters, US Army Corps of Engineers, quoted in Milazzo, 230.

53. Lieber, *Federalism and Clean Waters*, 63.

54. Flippen, *Nixon and the Environment*, 180.

55. Milazzo, *Unlikely Environmentalists*, 231.

56. Nixon quoted in Memorandum for the Presidents' File, Herbert Stein, June 26, 1972, Folder "Meetings File, Beginning June 18, 1972," box 89, President's Office File, WHSF, RNPMP, quoted in Flippen, *Nixon and the Environment*, 181.

57. Howard Baker to Richard Nixon, August 4, 1972, folder "EXHE 9-4, Water Pollution-Purification, January 1, 1971–, 2 of 3," box 36, Health Files, WHCF, RNPMP.

58. Flippen, 182.

59. Congressional Research Service, *A Legislative History of the Water Pollution Control Act Amendments of 1972* (Washington, DC: US Government Printing Office, 1973).

60. Senate Consideration of the Report of the Conference Committee, October 4, 1972, quoted in Milazzo, *Unlikely Environmentalists*, 236.

61. Lieber, *Federalism and Clean Waters*, 79.

62. John A. Blatnik, radio broadcast, 1972 (no other information available), quoted in David J. Webber, *Outstanding Environmentalists of Congress* (Washington, DC: U.S. Capitol Historical Society, 2002), 20.

63. Kalur v. Resor, 1 ELR 20637, 20641 (D.D.C. 1971).

64. *A Legislative History of the Water Pollution Control Act Amendments of 1972, Prepared by the Environmental Policy Division of the Congressional Research Service of the Library of Congress*, vol. 1, 93rd Cong. 153 (1973).

65. John Anderson et al. to Richard Nixon, Oct. 13, 1972, folder "EX HE 9–4, Water Pollution-Purification, January 1, 1971–, 3 of 3, box 36, Health Files, WHCF, RNPMP, quoted in Flippen, *Nixon and the Environment*, 182.

66. Whitaker to President Nixon, "Decision on Possible Veto of Water Pollution Bill," May 17, 1972, pp. 3–5, folder "Water Bill—2 of 3," box 114, John Whitaker Papers, quoted in Milazzo, *Unlikely Environmentalists*, 250.

67. Flippen, *Nixon and the Environment*, 180.

68. Webber, *Outstanding Environmentalists*, 20.

69. Nixon, Public Papers of the Presidents, 1972, 992, quoted in Flippen, *Nixon and the Environment*, 183.

70. *Legislative History of the Water Pollution Control Act Amendments of 1972*, 137, 138, emphasis in original.

71. *New York Times*, October 19, 1972, 1, 46, quoted in Flippen, *Nixon and the Environment*, 183.

72. Federal Water Pollution Control Act (Clean Water Act), Pub. L. No. 92-500, 86 Stat. 816 (1972).

73. James L. Sundquist, *The Decline and Resurgence of Congress* (Washington, DC: Brookings Institution, 1981), 202–203.

74. Richard Nixon to William Ruckelshaus, November 22, 1972, folder "EX FG 9–4, Water Pollution-Purification, January 1, 1971–, 3 of 3," box 36, Health Files, WHCF, RNPMP, quoted in Flippen, *Nixon and the Environment*, 187.

75. Flippen, 141.

76. John Whitaker, Memorandum to Russell E. Train, March 3, 1972, quoted in Russell E. Train, *Politics, Pollution, and Pandas: An Environmental Memoir* (Washington, DC: Island, 2003), 110–111.

77. Robert Cahn, *New York Times*, September 6, 1972, 12, quoted in Flippen, *Conservative Conservationist*, 131.

78. Flippen, *Nixon and the Environment*, 184.

79. Policy Paper for Natural Resources, 1973, Earl Butz, January 30, 1973, folder "Environment-General, 1972–1973, 1 of 2," box 60, John Whitaker Files, WHCF, RNPMP, quoted in Flippen, 190.

80. Train, *Politics, Pollution, and Pandas*, 79.

81. Council on Environmental Quality, *The President's 1973 Environmental Program* (Washington, DC: Government Printing Office, 1973), 3, 12.

82. President's handwritten notes, March 13, 1973, folder "Annotated News Summaries, March 1–7, 1973, 3 of 3," box 49, President's Office Files, WHSF, RNPMP, quoted in Flippen, 192.

83. Flippen, 191.

84. Flippen, *Conservative Conservationist*, 137.

85. Flippen, *Nixon and the Environment*, 191.

86. Nixon quoted in Stanley Kutler, ed., *The Abuse of Power* (New York: Free Press, 1997).

87. Russell E. Train, *Politics, Pollution and Pandas* (Washington, DC: Island, 2003), 151.

88. Nixon quoted in Memorandum for the President's File, July 26, 1973, folder "Meetings File, Beginning July 22, 1973," box 92, President's Office Files, WHSF RNPMP, quoted in Flippen, 199–200.

89. Train, *Politics, Pollution, and Pandas*, 156.

90. Train, 167.

91. Train, 169.

92. Russell Train, *Washington Post*, March 4, 1973, 4, quoted in Flippen, *Conservative Conservationist*, 145.

93. Lois R. Ember, "EPA Administrators Deem Agency's First 25 Years Bumpy but Successful," *Chemical & Engineering News Archive*, October 30, 1995, 19, quoted in Benjamin Kline, *First along the River: A Brief History of the U.S. Environmental Movement* (San Francisco: Acada Books, 1997), 97.

94. Ken Cole to Richard Nixon, February 27, 1974, folder "HE 9–1, Air Pollution, September 1, 1973–, 2 of 2," box 31, Health Files, WHCF, RNPMP, quoted in Flippen, *Nixon and the Environment*, 213.

95. Train, *Politics, Pollution, and Pandas*, 177.

96. Train, 178.

97. *Washington Post*, March 23, 1974, 1, quoted in Flippen, *Conservative Conservationist*, 147.

98. Russell E. Train, "An Environmental Sell-Out Will Not Turn Energy

Faucets on Full," *American Lung Association Bulletin* 60, no. 2 (March 1974): 2–3, quoted in Flippen, *Conservative Conservationist*, 148.

99. Train, *Politics, Pollution, and Pandas*, 178–179; Train is quoting from his testimony before Senate Committee on Public Works, July 16, 1993.

100. Milazzo, *Unlikely Environmentalists*, 252.

Chapter 9. Saving the Oceans

1. Walter Hickel, interview with Timothy Naftali, April 25, 2008, Presidential Materials, Richard Nixon Presidential Library and Museum, Yorba Linda, CA.

2. *Water Pollution, 1969: Hearings on S. 7 and S. 544 Before the Subcommittee on Air and Water Pollution of the Committee on Public Works*, 91st Cong. 342 (1969).

3. William O. Douglas, *The Three Hundred Year War: A Chronicle of Ecological Disaster* (New York: Random House, 1972), 14.

4. Douglas, 14.

5. Martin V. Melosi, "Lyndon Johnson and Environmental Policy," in *Vietnam, the Environment, and Space*, vol. 2 of *The Johnson Years*, ed. Robert A. Divine (Lawrence: University Press of Kansas, 1987), 133.

6. Walter A. Rosenbaum, *The Politics of Environmental Concern* (New York: Praeger, 1973), 12.

7. Douglas, *Three Hundred Year War*, 103.

8. Russell E. Train, memo to Legislative Counsel, September 15, 1969, Public Papers of Russell Train, Library of Congress.

9. J. Brooks Flippen, *Conservative Conservationist: Russell E. Train and the Emergence of American Environmentalism* (Baton Rouge: Louisiana State University Press, 2006), 78.

10. John C. Whitaker, *Striking a Balance: Environment and Natural Resources Policy in the Nixon-Ford Years* (Washington, DC: American Enterprise Institute for Public Policy Research, 1976), 151.

11. Flippen, *Conservative Conservationist*, 78.

12. *Christian Science Monitor*, June 23, 1969, 13, quoted in J. Brooks Flippen, *Nixon and the Environment* (Albuquerque: University of New Mexico Press, 2000), 179.

13. Nixon handwritten comments, Daily News Summary, June 24, 1969, folder "Annotated News Summaries, June, 1969," box 30, President's Office Files, WHSF, Richard Nixon Presidential Materials Project (hereafter RNPMP), quoted in Flippen, 42.

14. Coastal Zone Management Act of 1972, 16 USC 1451-1464, Office for Coastal Management, National Oceanic and Atmospheric Administration, quoted in Donna R. Christie and Richard G. Hildreth, *Coastal and Ocean Management Law* (Saint Paul, MN: West Academic, 1999), 61.

15. Whitaker, *Striking a Balance*, 154.

16. Whitaker, 155.

17. Senator Warren Magnuson, press release, May 27, 1975, Warren Magnuson Papers, Special Collections, University of Washington Library, Seattle.

18. Christie and Hildreth, *Coastal and Ocean Management Law*, 62.

19. Senator Warren Magnuson, press release, July 16, 1975, Warren Magnuson Papers.

20. Christie and Hildreth, *Coastal and Ocean Management Law*, 65.

21. Richard N. L. Andrews, *Managing the Environment, Managing Ourselves: A History of American Environmental Policy* (New Haven, CT: Yale University Press, 1999), 291.

22. "Special Message to the Congress Outlining the 1972 Environmental Program," February 8, 1972, in *Public Papers of the Presidents of the United States: Richard Nixon, 1972* (Washington, DC: Government Printing Office, 1974), 181.

23. Douglas, *Three Hundred Year War*, 7.

24. Stewart L. Udall, *The Quiet Crisis and the Next Generation* (Layton, UT: Gibbs Smith, 1988), 62–63.

25. Douglas, *Three Hundred Year War*, 7.

26. 118 Cong. Rec., 7,685, 7,686, 7,690 (1972).

27. 118 Cong. Rec. 7,690, 7,691 (1972).

28. 16 USC section 1361.

29. Christie and Hildreth, *Coastal and Ocean Management Law*, 235.

30. Christie and Hildreth, 244.

31. Marine Mammal Protection Act, 16 U.S.C. § 1381 (1985).

32. Christie and Hildreth, *Coastal and Ocean Management Law*, 245.

33. Christie and Hildreth, 247.

34. Christie and Hildreth, 236.

35. 16 USC section 1401.

36. 16 USC Section 1378.

37. Russell E. Train, *Politics, Pollution, and Pandas: An Environmental Memoir* (Washington, DC: Island, 2003), 142.

38. Victor B. Scheffer, *The Shaping of Environmentalism in America* (Seattle: University of Washington Press, 1991), 161.

39. *Seattle Post-Intelligencer*, December 10, 1980, quoted in Shelby Scates, *Warren G. Magnuson and the Shaping of Twentieth-Century America* (Seattle: University of Washington Press, 1997), 69.

40. Scates, 75.

41. Scates, 177.

42. Warren Magnuson, "The Wet War: A Struggle for the Oceans," series of articles in Hearst Newspapers, June 1959, quoted in Scates, *Warren G. Magnuson*, 179.

43. W. Featherstone Reid, interview with Shelby Scates, March 20, 1995.

44. Lyndon B. Johnson, quoted by Irv Hoff, interview with Shelby Scates, June 1994, quoted in Scates, *Warren G. Magnuson*, 185.

45. Warren G. Magnuson, interview with Shelby Scates, Palm Springs, January 8, 1981.

46. Eugene McCarthy, interview, December 1971, quoted in Scates, 217.

47. Lady Bird Johnson, interview with Michael L. Gillette, November 15, 1981,

Lyndon Baine Johnson Oral Histories, Lyndon Baines Johnson Presidential Library, University of Texas at Austin.

48. Magnuson, Oral History, Warren G. Magnuson file, Lyndon Baines Johnson Presidential Library, quoted in Scates, *Warren G. Magnuson*, 195.

49. Scates, 255.

50. Ralph Nader, interview, December 12, 1995, quoted in Scates, 222.

51. Jerry Grinstein, interview with Shelby Scates, June 2 1995, quoted in Scates, 247.

52. Warren Magnuson, interview with Michael L. Gillette, March 14, 1978, Lyndon Baine Johnson Oral Histories.

53. Magnuson, interview, March 14, 1978.

54. Andrews, *Managing the Environment*, 159.

55. Warren G. Magnuson File, Lyndon B. Johnson Presidential Library, quoted in Scates, *Warren G. Magnuson*, 262.

56. Senator Warren Magnuson, press release, March 5, 1975, Warren Magnuson Papers.

57. 122 Cong. Rec. 119 (1976).

58. 122 Cong. Rec. 123 (1976).

59. 122 Cong. Rec. 123 (1976).

60. 122 Cong. Rec. 126 (1976).

61. 122 Cong. Rec. 126 (1976).

62. 122 Cong. Rec. 130 (1976).

63. 122 Cong. Rec. 132 (1976).

64. 122 Cong. Rec. 138 (1976).

65. 122 Cong. Rec. 139 (1976).

66. 122 Cong. Rec. 1,299 (1976).

67. 122 Cong. Rec. 1,181 (1976).

68. 122 Cong. Rec. 1,191 (1976).

69. 122 Cong. Rec. 1,297 (1976).

70. 122 Cong. Rec. 1,299 (1976).

71. 122 Cong. Rec. 1,303 (1976).

72. 122 Cong. Rec. 1,311 (1976).

73. Christie and Hildreth, *Coastal and Ocean Management Law*, 193.

74. Christie and Hildreth, 193.

75. Christie and Hildreth, 198–199.

Chapter 10. Protecting Endangered Species

1. Benjamin Franklin to Richard Jackson, May 5, 1753, in Albert Henry Smyth, ed., *The Writings of Benjamin Franklin*, by Benjamin Franklin (New York: Macmillan, 1905), 3:135.

2. Peninah Neimark and Peter Rhoades Mott, eds., *The Environmental Debate*, 2nd ed. (Amenia, NY: Grey House, 2011), 57–58.

3. John Russell Bartlett, ed., *Records of the Colony of Rhode Island and Providence Plantations in New England*, vol. 1, *1636 to 1663* (Providence, RI: A. Crawford Greene, 1856), 113, 85.

4. Thomas R. Dunlap, *Saving America's Wildlife: Ecology and the American Mind, 1850–1990* (Princeton, NJ: Princeton University Press, 1988), 5.

5. Dan Flores, *American Serengeti: The Last Big Animals of the Great Plains* (Lawrence: University Press of Kansas, 2016), 122–123.

6. Shannon C. Petersen, *Acting for Endangered Species: The Statutory Ark* (Lawrence: University Press of Kansas, 2002), 7–8.

7. George Catlin, *Letters and Notes on the Manners, Customs and Conditions of the North American Indians* (London, 1841), 259, quoted in Bill McKibben, ed., *American Earth: Environmental Writing since Thoreau* (Washington, DC: Library of America, 2008), 41.

8. Mario R. DiNunzio, ed., *Theodore Roosevelt: An American Mind, A Selection from His Writings*, by Theodore Roosevelt (New York: St. Martin's, 1994), 242.

9. Brian Czech and Paul R. Krausman, *The Endangered Species Act: History, Conservation Biology, and Public Policy* (Baltimore: Johns Hopkins University Press, 2001), 8.

10. James S. Macdonald Jr., *The Founding of Yellowstone into Law and Fact*, www.yellowstone-online.com.

11. Udall, *Quiet Crisis and the Next Generation*, 65.

12. Czech and Krausman, *Endangered Species Act*, 11.

13. Vincent Zisweiler, *Extinct and Vanishing Animals: A Biology of Extinction and Survival* (London: English Universities Press, 1967), 95.

14. Jeremy Bentham, *An Introduction to the Principles of Morals and Legislation* (London, 1789), quoted in Peter Singer, *Animal Liberation* (New York: Random House, 1975), 8, quoted in Dunlap, *Saving America's Wildlife*, 20.

15. Philip Shabecoff, *A Fierce Green Fire: The American Environmental Movement* (New York: Hill and Wang, 1993), 42.

16. Dunlap, *Saving America's Wildlife*, 22.

17. Dunlap, 9.

18. Roderick Nash, *Wilderness and the American Mind*, 3rd ed. (New Haven, CT: Yale University Press, 1982), 152.

19. Dunlap, *Saving America's Wildlife*, 11.

20. Aldo Leopold, *Game Management* (New York: Charles Scribner's Sons, 1933; repr., Madison: University of Wisconsin Press, 1987), 13.

21. Petersen, *Acting for Endangered Species*, 4.

22. Dunlap, *Saving America's Wildlife*, 39.

23. Theodore Roosevelt, letter to Frank M. Chapman, Bird Lore, April 1899.

24. Samuel P. Hays, *A History of Environmental Politics since 1945* (Pittsburgh, PA: University of Pittsburgh Press, 2000), 88.

25. Dunlap, *Saving America's Wildlife*, 37.

26. Hunt v. United States, 278 U.S. 96 (1928).

27. Horace M. Albright, "The National Park Service's Policy on Predatory Mammals," *Journal of Mammalogy* 12, no. 2 (1931): 185–186, quoted in Dunlap, 79.

28. Carolyn Merchant, *The Columbia Guide to American Environmental History* (New York: Columbia University Press, 2002), 177.

29. Benjamin Kline, *First along the River: A Brief History of the U.S. Environmental Movement*, 4th ed. (Lanham, MD: Rowman & Littlefield, 2011), 69.

30. Franklin Delano Roosevelt to Henry L. Stimson, December 1, 1941, quoted in Udall, *Quiet Crisis and the Next Generation*, 145.

31. Richard N. L. Andrews, *Managing the Environment, Managing Ourselves: A History of American Environmental Policy* (New Haven, CT: Yale University Press, 1999), 173.

32. Dunlap, *Saving America's Wildlife*, 98.

33. Frank Graham Jr., *Since Silent Spring* (Boston: Houghton Mifflin, 1970), 183.

34. Victor B. Scheffer, *The Shaping of Environmentalism in America* (Seattle: University of Washington Press, 1991), 97.

35. Graham, *Since Silent Spring*, 184.

36. Starker Leopold, "Predator and Rodent Control in the United States," in *Transactions of the Twenty-Ninth North American Wildlife and Natural Resources Conference* (Baltimore: Monumental, 1964), 27, quoted in John C. Whitaker, *Striking a Balance: Environment and Natural Resources Policy in the Nixon-Ford Years* (Washington, DC: American Enterprise Institute for Public Policy Research, 1976), 140.

37. Rachel Carson, "Rachel Carson Answers Her Critics," *Audubon* 65–66 (September–October 1963): 262, quoted in Douglas H. Strong, *Dreamers and Defenders: American Conservationists* (Lincoln: University of Nebraska Press, 1971), 192.

38. John Dingell Jr., interview with Office of the Historian, February 3, 2012, United States House of Representatives.

39. Robert Draper, *Do Not Ask What Good We Do: Inside the U.S. House of Representatives* (New York: Free Press, 2012), 173.

40. "Wildlife Species Face Extinction," *New York Times*, January 9, 1966, 48.

41. "Wildlife Species Face Extinction," 48.

42. *Predatory Mammals: Hearings Before the Subcommittee on Fisheries and Wildlife Conservation of the Committee on Merchant Marine and Fisheries*, 89th Cong. 1 (1966).

43. Scheffer, *Shaping of Environmentalism in America*, 158.

44. Czech and Krausman, *Endangered Species Act*, 21.

45. Thomas G. Smith, *Stewart L. Udall: Steward of the Land* (Albuquerque: University of New Mexico Press, 2017), 225.

46. "Civilization's Prey," *New York Times*, September 9, 1967, 30.

47. Wayne Aspinall Papers, 1968, Special Collections, University of Denver Library.

48. "Traffic in Savagery," *New York Times*, September 19, 1968, 46.

49. Dunlap, *Saving America's Wildlife*, 146.

50. "Washington Records: The President," *New York Times*, December 6, 1969, 25, quoted in Petersen, *Acting for Endangered Species*, 26.

51. Dunlap, *Saving America's Wildlife*, 146.

52. Walter Hickel, interview with Timothy Naftali, April 25, 2008, Presidential Materials, Richard Nixon Presidential Library and Museum, Yorba Linda, CA.

53. J. Brooks Flippen, *Nixon and the Environment* (Albuquerque: University of New Mexico Press, 2000), 153.

54. Mike Frome, "Prejudice, Predators and Politics," *Field and Stream*, December 1967, quoted in Saylor's testimony in *Predator Control and Related Problems: Hearings Before the Subcommittee on Agriculture, Environmental, and Consumer Protection of the Committee on Appropriations*, 92nd Cong. 273 (1972).

55. *Predatory Mammals and Endangered Species: Hearings Before the Subcommittee on Fisheries and Wildlife Conservation of the Committee on Merchant Marine and Fisheries*, 92nd Cong. 246 (1972).

56. Russell E. Train, *Politics, Pollution, and Pandas: An Environmental Memoir* (Washington, DC: Island, 2003), 94.

57. Richard Nixon, "Special Message to the Congress Outlining the 1972 Environmental Program," made available online by Gerhard Peters and John T. Woolley, The American Presidency Project, https://www.presidency.ucsb.edu /node/255047; Smith, *Green Republican*, 277.

58. Dunlap, *Saving America's Wildlife*, 140.

59. Whitaker, *Striking a Balance*, 141.

60. Whitaker, 143.

61. Mrs. Michael Curran to Senator Henry Jackson, February 26, 1972, Henry Jackson Papers, Special Collections, University of Washington Library, Seattle.

62. William O. Douglas, *The Three Hundred Year War: A Chronicle of Ecological Disaster* (New York: Random House, 1972), 6.

63. Stewart Udall, *1976: Agenda for Tomorrow* (New York: Harcourt, Brace and World, 1968), 115.

64. John D. Dingell Jr., foreword to The Endangered Species Act, D. J. Rohlf (Palo Alto, CA: Stanford Environmental Law Society, 1989), quoted in Czech and Krausman, *Endangered Species Act*, 23.

65. Richard Nixon, *Public Papers of the Presidents 1972* (Washington, DC: US Government Printing Office, 1974), 183, quoted in Petersen, *Acting for Endangered Species*, 27.

66. *Endangered Species Act of 1973: Hearings on S. 1592 Before the Subcommittee on the Environment of the Committee on Commerce*, 93rd Cong. 50 (1973).

67. *Endangered Species Act of 1973: Hearings on S. 1592.*

68. *Endangered Species Act of 1973: Hearings on S. 1592.*

69. *Endangered Species Act of 1973: Hearings on S. 1592.*

70. *Endangered Species Act of 1973: Hearings on S. 1592.*

71. *Endangered Species Act of 1973: Hearings on S. 1592.*

72. *Endangered Species Act of 1973: Hearings on S. 1592.*

73. Statement of Senator Stevens, reprinted in Committee on Environment and Public Works, *Legislative History*, 361, quoted in Petersen, *Acting for Endangered Species*, 29.

74. 119 Cong. Rec. 30,162 (1973).

75. 119 Cong. Rec. 30,162–30,163 (1973).

76. 119 Cong. Rec. 30,164 (1973).

77. 119 Cong. Rec. 30,164 (1973).

78. 119 Cong. Rec. 30,165 (1973).

79. 119 Cong. Rec. 30,166 (1973).

80. 119 Cong. Rec. 30,167 (1973).

81. John D. Dingell Jr., *The Dean: The Best Seat in the House*, with David Bender (New York: HarperCollins, 2018), 206.

82. Dingell, 206.

83. Petersen, *Acting for Endangered Species*, 29.

84. Petersen, 29.

85. Richard Nixon, Public Papers of the Presidents, 1973, 1027, quoted in Petersen, 30.

86. Roy Ash to Richard Nixon, December 23, 1973, folder "EX NR Fish-Wildlife, 6 of 7, May–December, 1973," box 3, Natural Resources Files, WHCF, Richard Nixon Presidential Materials Project, quoted in Flippen, *Nixon and the Environment*, 211.

87. Endangered Species Act, 16 U.S.C., section 2b, 1973, quoted in Czech and Krausman, *Endangered Species Act*, 24.

88. Endangered Species Act, 16 U.S.C., section 3, 1973, quoted in Czech and Krausman, 24.

89. Czech and Krausman, 24.

90. Czech and Krausman, 148.

91. Petersen, *Acting for Endangered Species*, 31.

92. Statement of Senator Williams, reprinted in Committee on Environment and Public Works, Legislative History, 374, quoted in Petersen, 32.

93. Richard Nixon, Public Papers of the Presidents, 1973, 1027, quoted in Petersen, 32.

94. Petersen, 30.

95. Petersen, 33.

96. *Tennessee Valley Authority v. Hill*, 437 U.S. 153 (1978), quoted in Czech and Krausman, *Endangered Species Act*, 36.

97. B. J. Bergman, "Leader of the Pack," *Sierra* 8, no. 6, 54, quoted in Czech and Krausman, 149.

98. Michael McCloskey, "The Environmental Movement after Fifty Years: How Much Influence Did It Exert?" unpublished memo, March 2019.

99. Lewis Regenstein, *The Politics of Extinction: The Shocking Story of the World's Endangered Wildlife* (New York: Macmillan, 1975), 149.

100. Petersen, *Acting for Endangered Species*, 125.

Chapter 11. Tracking Toxins across Land and Sea

1. Samuel P. Hays, *A History of Environmental Politics since 1945* (Pittsburgh, PA: University of Pittsburgh Press, 2000), 13.

2. John C. Whitaker, *Striking a Balance: Environment and Natural Resources*

Policy in the Nixon-Ford Years (Washington, DC: American Enterprise Institute for Public Policy Research, 1976), 22.

3. Walter A. Rosenbaum, *The Politics of Environmental Concern* (New York: Praeger, 1973), 41–42.

4. Victor B. Scheffer, *The Shaping of Environmentalism in America* (Seattle: University of Washington Press, 1991), 91.

5. Clarence Cottam and Elmer Higgins, *DDT: Its Effect on Fish and Wildlife*, Fish and Wildlife Service, US Department of the Interior, circ. 11 (Washington, DC: Government Printing Office, 1946), quoted in Bill Christofferson, *The Man from Clear Lake: Earth Day Founder Senator Gaylord Nelson* (Madison: University of Wisconsin Press, 2004), 466.

6. Frank Graham Jr., *Since Silent Spring* (Boston: Houghton Mifflin, 1970), 21.

7. David Goldfield, *The Gifted Generation: When Government Was Good* (New York: Bloomsbury, 2017), 285, quoted in Linda Lear, *Rachel Carson: Witness for Nature* (New York: Henry Holt, 1997).

8. Goldfield, *Gifted Generation*, 286, quoted in Lear, *Rachel Carson*.

9. Rachel Carson, *The Sea around Us* (New York: Oxford University Press, 1961), xiii.

10. Rachel Carson, letter to Paul Brooks, quoted in Graham, *Since Silent Spring*, 44.

11. Velsicol Chemical Corporation letter to Houghton Mifflin, Summer 1962, quoted in H. Patricia Hynes, *The Recurring Silent Spring* (Elmsford, NY: Pergamon, 1989), 16.

12. Paul Brooks, *The House of Life: Rachel Carson at Work* (Boston: Houghton Mifflin, 1972), 293, quoted in Scheffer, *Shaping of Environmentalism*, 120.

13. Rachel Carson, *Silent Spring* (1962; repr., Boston: Houghton Mifflin, 2002), 85.

14. Carson, 12.

15. Carson, 219, 239. Emphasis in the original, 5.

16. Stewart L. Udall, *The Quiet Crisis and the Next Generation* (Layton, UT: Gibbs Smith, 1988), 201.

17. Goldfield, *Gifted Generation*, 283, quoted in Lear, *Rachel Carson*.

18. Report of the Presidential Scientific Advisory Committee: Pesticides Report, May 15, 1963, 38–39, Papers of John F. Kennedy, Presidential Papers, President's Office Files, Departments and Agencies, https://www.jfklibrary.org/asset-viewer/archives /JFKPOF/087/JFKPOF-087-003?image_identifier=JFKPOF-087-003-p0044.

19. "Rachel Carson Stands Vindicated," *Christian Science Monitor*, May 16, 1963.

20. Brooks, *House of Life*, 308, quoted in Hynes, *Recurring Silent Spring*, 45.

21. Rachel Carson, *Silent Spring* (Boston: Houghton-Mifflin, 1962), quoted in Graham, *Since Silent Spring*, 96.

22. Douglas H. Strong, *Dreamers and Defenders: American Conservationists* (Lincoln: University of Nebraska Press, 1988), 193.

23. Udall, *Quiet Crisis and the Next Generation*, 202.

24. Secretary of the Interior, Memorandum to Heads of Bureaus and Offices, May 7, 1964, US Department of the Interior, quoted in Graham, *Since Silent Spring*, 105.

25. Stewart L. Udall, interview with Joe B. Frantz, December 16, 1969, Lyndon Baines Johnson Oral Histories, Lyndon Baines Johnson Presidential Library, University of Texas at Austin.

26. Richard N. L. Andrews, *Managing the Environment, Managing Ourselves: A History of American Environmental Policy* (New Haven, CT: Yale University Press, 1999), 216.

27. Jamie L. Whitten, *That We May Live* (Princeton, NJ: Van Nostrand, 1966), quoted in Hynes, *Recurring Silent Spring*, 115.

28. Lyndon B. Johnson, "Remarks upon Signing the Pesticide Control Bill," May 12, 1964, made available online by Gerhard Peters and John T. Woolley, The American Presidency Project, https://www.presidency.ucsb.edu/node/238626.

29. John W. Finney, "President Signs a Pesticide Bill," *New York Times*, May 13, 1964, 49.

30. Graham, *Since Silent Spring*, 211.

31. William O. Douglas, *The Three Hundred Year War: A Chronicle of Ecological Disaster* (New York: Random House, 1972), 78.

32. UPI, "Drop DDT from Pesticide Lists, Nelson Urges," *Milwaukee Sentinel*, June 20, 1966.

33. J. Brooks Flippen, *Nixon and the Environment* (Albuquerque: University of New Mexico Press, 2000), 44.

34. "Nelson Says Ban on DDT Nonexistent," *Milwaukee Sentinel*, March 2, 1970, quoted in Christofferson, *Man from Clear Lake*, 474.

35. Lee DuBridge to John Ehrlichman, July 3, 1970, folder "Pesticides, 1970 (1969–1970), 3 of 3," box 90, John Whitaker Files, White House Central Files (hereafter WHCF), Richard Nixon Presidential Materials Project (hereafter RNPMP), quoted in Flippen, *Nixon and the Environment*, 44.

36. EPA Consolidated DDT Hearings, Opinion and Order of the Administrator, *Federal Register* 37, no. 131 (July 7, 1972), 13,373, quoted in Whitaker, *Striking a Balance*, 134.

37. William Ruckelshaus, interview with Timothy Naftali, April 12, 2007, Presidential Materials, Richard Nixon Presidential Library and Museum, Yorba Linda, CA.

38. Ruckelshaus, interview, April 12, 2007.

39. Whitaker, *Striking a Balance*, 126.

40. Chronology of DDT Events, June 30, 1971, folder "Pesticides-General, DDT, 3 Materials, 1971," box 91, John Whitaker Files, WHCF, RNPMP, quoted in Flippen, *Nixon and the Environment*, 132.

41. Ruckelshaus, interview, April 12, 2007.

42. Whitaker, *Striking a Balance*, 128.

43. *To Amend the Federal Insecticide, Fungicide and Rodenticide Act: Hearings on*

H.R. 10729 Before the Subcommittee on the Environment of the Committee on Commerce, 92nd Cong. 1 (1972).

44. *Hearings on H.R. 10729*, 91.

45. *Hearings on H.R. 10729*, 134.

46. "Statement on Signing the Federal Environmental Pesticide Control Act of 1972," October 21, 1972, in *Public Papers of the Presidents of the United States: Richard Nixon, 1972* (Washington, DC: Government Printing Office, 1974), 1005.

47. Christofferson, *Man from Clear Lake*, 475.

48. Hays, *History of Environmental Politics*, 129.

49. Andrews, *Managing the Environment*, 243.

50. Whitaker, *Striking a Balance*, 130.

51. Hynes, *Recurring Silent Spring*, 149.

52. Hynes, 150.

53. Whitaker, *Striking a Balance*, 132.

54. Whitaker, 138.

55. Robert Gottlieb, *Forcing the Spring: The Transformation of the American Environmental Movement* (Washington, DC: Island, 2005), 318.

56. Gottlieb, 322.

57. Martin V. Melosi, *The Sanitary City: Urban Infrastructure in America from Colonial Times to the Present* (Baltimore: Johns Hopkins University Press, 2000), 392–393.

58. "Safe Water Drinking Act S.433," box 15, Legislative Case Files, White House Records Office, Gerald R. Ford Presidential Library, University of Michigan, Ann Arbor.

59. "Safe Water Drinking Act."

60. "Safe Water Drinking Act."

61. "Safe Water Drinking Act."

62. John G. Spankling and Gregory S. Weber, *The Law of Hazardous Wastes and Toxic Substances* (Saint Paul, MN: Thomson West, 2007), 155–156.

63. Spankling and Weber, 152.

64. Whitaker, *Striking a Balance*, 144.

65. J. Brooks Flippen, *Conservative Conservationist: Russell E. Train and the Emergence of American Environmentalism* (Baton Rouge: Louisiana State University Press, 2006), 174.

66. Russell E. Train, *Politics, Pollution, and Pandas: An Environmental Memoir* (Washington, DC: Island, 2003), 208.

67. Flippen, *Conservative Conservationist*, 174.

68. Train, *Politics, Pollution, and Pandas*, 209.

69. Editorial, *Washington Post*, February 28, 1976.

70. 122 Cong. Rec. 8,281 (1976).

71. 122 Cong. Rec. 8,283 (1976).

72. 122 Cong. Rec. 8,303 (1976).

73. 122 Cong. Rec. 32,852 (1976).

74. 122 Cong. Rec. 32,855–32,856 (1976).

75. "Safe Drinking Water Act."

76. John Walsh, "EPA and Toxic Substances Law: Dealing with Uncertainty," *Science* 202, no. 4368 (November 10, 1978): 598.

77. Andrews, *Managing the Environment*, 245.

78. Scheffer, *Shaping of Environmentalism*, 151.

79. Spankling and Weber, 156.

80. Whitaker, *Striking a Balance*, 144.

81. Benjamin Kline, *First along the River: A Brief History of the U.S. Environmental Movement* (San Francisco: Acada Books, 1997), 98.

82. Spankling and Weber, *Law of Hazardous Wastes*, 57–58.

83. Flippen, *Nixon and the Environment*, 229.

84. Andrews, *Managing the Environment*, 246.

85. Spankling and Weber, *Law of Hazardous Wastes*, 74.

86. Andrews, *Managing the Environment*, 245.

87. Hays, *History of Environmental Politics*, 213.

88. Ruckelshaus, interview, April 12, 2007.

89. Train, *Politics, Pollution, and Pandas*, 210.

90. *Journal of the Senate of the United States of America*, 89th Cong. (Washington, DC: Government Printing Office, 1965), 149.

91. Martin V. Melosi, "Lyndon Johnson and Environmental Policy," in *Vietnam, the Environment, and Space*, vol. 2 of *The Johnson Years*, ed. Robert A. Divine (Lawrence: University Press of Kansas, 1987), 139.

92. Richard Nixon, "Special Message to the Congress on Environmental Quality," February 10, 1970, made available online by Gerhard Peters and John T. Woolley, The American Presidency Project, https://www.presidency.ucsb.edu/node/240088.

93. Whitaker, *Striking a Balance*, 111.

94. Whitaker, 118.

95. Council on Environmental Quality, First Annual Report, 116, quoted in Whitaker, 119.

96. Rosenbaum, *Politics of Environmental Concern*, 247.

97. Whitaker, *Striking a Balance*, 112.

98. Andrews, *Managing the Environment*, 247.

99. 122 Cong. Rec. 21,405 (1976).

100. "Bottle Ban," *Baltimore Sun*, June 30, 1976, 18.

101. Jim Cannon, October 20, 1976, box 68, Legislation Case Files, White House Records Office, Gerald R. Ford Presidential Library.

102. Andrews, *Managing the Environment*, 248.

103. Andrews, 248.

104. Carson, *Sea Around Us*, xi.

105. Train, *Politics, Pollution, and Pandas*, 97.

106. Douglas, *Three Hundred Year War*, 34.

107. Donna R. Christie and Richard G. Hildreth, *Coastal and Ocean Management Law* (Saint Paul, MN: West Academic, 1999), 320.

108. 117 Cong. Rec. 31,134 (1971).

109. 117 Cong. Rec. 31,134 (1971).

110. 117 Cong. Rec. 31,136 (1971).

111. 117 Cong. Rec. 31,138 (1971).

112. 117 Cong. Rec. 31,138 (1971).

113. 117 Cong. Rec. 31,139 (1971).

114. 117 Cong. Rec. 31,144 (1971).

115. 117 Cong. Rec. 31,146 (1971).

116. 117 Cong. Rec. 31,151 (1971).

117. Nixon, *Public Papers of the Presidents: Nixon, 1972* (Washington, DC: US Government Printing Office, 1972), 1051–1052, quoted in Flippen, *Nixon and the Environment*, 178.

118. Megan Ewald, "Rachel Carson: Biologist, Writer, Role Model," March 7, 2019, *NOAA Office of Response and Restoration Blog*, https://blog.response.restoration.noaa.gov/rachel-carson-biologist-writer-role-model.

119. Zygmunt Plater, "From the Beginning: A Fundamental Shift of Paradigms: A Theory and Short History of Environmental Law," *Loyola of Los Angeles Law Review* 27, no. 3 (1994): 982.

Chapter 12. Land and Wilderness Management

1. Richard N. L. Andrews, *Managing the Environment, Managing Ourselves: A History of American Environmental Policy* (New Haven, CT: Yale University Press, 1999), 72.

2. John C. Whitaker, *Striking a Balance: Environment and Natural Resources Policy in the Nixon-Ford Years* (Washington, DC: American Enterprise Institute for Public Policy Research, 1976), 23.

3. Stewart L. Udall, *The Quiet Crisis and the Next Generation* (Layton, UT: Gibbs Smith, 1988), 166.

4. Udall, 167.

5. J. R. McNeill, *Something New under the Sun: An Environmental History of the Twentieth-Century World* (New York: W. W. Norton, 2000), 187.

6. David Goldfield, *The Gifted Generation: When Government Was Good* (New York: Bloomsbury, 2017), 296–297.

7. 116 Cong. Rec. 1,757 (1970).

8. Paul Holmes to Senator Henry Jackson, June 1, 1972, Henry Jackson Papers, Special Collections, University of Washington Library, Seattle; Thomas A. Rosenau to Senator Henry Jackson, May 28, 1971, Henry Jackson Papers.

9. Walter J. Hickel, *Who Owns America?* (Englewood Cliffs, NJ: Prentice-Hall, 1971), 312.

10. Richard Nixon, "Special Message to the Congress Outlining the 1972 Environmental Program," February 8, 1972, made available online by Gerhard Peters

and John T. Woolley, The American Presidency Project, https://www.presidency.ucsb.edu/node/255047.

11. Whitaker, *Striking a Balance*, 155.

12. John Whitaker to John Ehrlichman, June 29, 1970, folder "May–August, 1970, 2 of 4, June, 1970," box 2, John Whitaker Files, White House Central Files (hereafter WHCF), Richard Nixon Presidential Materials Project (hereafter RNPMP), quoted in J. Brooks Flippen, *Conservative Conservationist: Russell E. Train and the Emergence of American Environmentalism* (Baton Rouge: Louisiana State University Press, 2006), 117.

13. Flippen, *Nixon and the Environment*, 102.

14. Russell Train, *Birmingham News*, June 19, 1973, 28, quoted in Flippen, *Conservative Conservationist*, 117.

15. Rosenbaum, *Politics of Environmental Concern*, Walter A. Rosenbaum, *The Politics of Environmental Concern* (New York: Praeger, 1973), 285.

16. Richard Nixon, "Special Message to the Congress Proposing the 1971 Environmental Program," February 8, 1971, made available online by Gerhard Peters and John T. Woolley, The American Presidency Project, https://www.presidency.ucsb.edu/node/240587.

17. Whitaker, *Striking a Balance*, 158.

18. Flippen, *Conservative Conservationist*, 117.

19. Flippen, *Nixon and the Environment*, 195.

20. James Noone, "Senate, House Differ in Approaches to Reform of Nation's Land Use Laws," *National Journal*, July 22, 1972, 1193, quoted in Whitaker, *Striking a Balance*, 160.

21. William O. Douglas, *The Three Hundred Year War: A Chronicle of Ecological Disaster* (New York: Random House, 1972), 175.

22. 118 Cong. Rec. 31,187 (1972), quoted in J. Michael McCloskey, *In the Thick of It: My Life in the Sierra Club* (Washington, DC: Island, 2005), 139.

23. Mrs. William Franks to Senator Henry Jackson, June 10, 1972, Henry Jackson Papers.

24. Train, *Politics, Pollution, and Pandas*, 108.

25. Whitaker, *Striking a Balance*, 162.

26. Whitaker, 163.

27. Letter from Kenneth R. Cole, Jr., assistant to the President for domestic affairs, to Congressman John. J. Rhodes, May 14, 1974.

28. Henry M. Jackson, Press Release, March 13, 1973, folder 85, "Letter to the President on Land Use Stuff," box 260, Accession No. 3560–5, Papers of Henry Jackson, quoted in Flippen, *Nixon and the Environment*, 196.

29. J. V. F., "Land Use Bill Defeated: Udall Charges 'Impeachment Politics,'" *BioScience* 24, no. 8 (August 1974): 470.

30. Whitaker, *Striking a Balance*, 165.

31. Train, *Politics, Pollution, and Pandas*, 108.

32. Samuel P. Hays, *A History of Environmental Politics since 1945* (Pittsburgh, PA: University of Pittsburgh Press, 2000), 71.

33. Joseph M. Petulla, *American Environmental History: The Exploitation and Conservation of Natural Resources.* (San Francisco: Boyd & Fraser, 1977), 51.

34. Udall, *Quiet Crisis and the Next Generation*, 99.

35. *Annual Report of the Secretary of the Interior for the Fiscal Year Ended June 30, 1877* (Washington, DC: Government Printing Office, 1877), xvi.

36. Timber and Stone Act, 45th Congress, 2nd Sess., ch. 151 20 Stat. 89, 1878, quoted in Andrews, *Managing the Environment*, 102.

37. Mario R. DiNunzio, ed., *Theodore Roosevelt: An American Mind, A Selection from His Writings*, by Theodore Roosevelt (New York: St. Martin's, 1994), 286.

38. 22 Cong. Rec. 1,103 (1890), quoted in Udall, *Quiet Crisis and the Next Generation*, 100.

39. Udall, 101.

40. Andrews, *Managing the Environment*, 106.

41. Udall, *Quiet Crisis and the Next Generation*, 101.

42. Theodore Roosevelt, "Natural Resources—Their Wise Use or Their Waste," address at the opening of the conference on the Conservation of Natural Resources, May 13, 1908, in *Selected Speeches and Writings of Theodore Roosevelt*, ed. Gordon Hunter (New York: Vintage Books, 2014), 152.

43. Andrews, *Managing the Environment*, 146.

44. Bill McKibben, ed., *American Earth: Environmental Writing since Thoreau* (Washington, DC: Library of America, 2008), 129.

45. Theodore Roosevelt, Address to Forest Congress, Washington, DC, January 5, 1905.

46. Udall, *Quiet Crisis and the Next Generation*, 102.

47. Gifford Pinchot, 1905, quoted in Andrews, *Managing the Environment*, 146.

48. Udall, *Quiet Crisis and the Next Generation*, 134.

49. Udall, 103–104.

50. Gifford Pinchot, "The Fight for Conservation," 1910, in McKibben, *American Earth*, 173.

51. Andrews, *Managing the Environment*, 147.

52. Udall, *Quiet Crisis and the Next Generation*, 105.

53. Andrews, *Managing the Environment*, 146.

54. Kline, *First along the River: A Brief History of the U.S. Environmental Movement* (San Francisco: Acada Books, 1997), 58.

55. Udall, *Quiet Crisis and the Next Generation*, 118.

56. Udall, 120.

57. Steve Neal, *McNary of Oregon: A Political Biography* (Portland: Oregon Historical Society Press, 1985), 91, quoted in David J. Webber, *Outstanding Environmentalists of Congress* (Washington, DC: U.S. Capitol Historical Society, 2002), 49–50.

58. William Greeley, "The Initial Statement and Transcript of the Testimony of Col. W. B. Greeley," *Lumber World Review*, February 10, 1921, 34.

59. Andrews, *Managing the Environment*, 313.

60. Franklin D. Roosevelt, "Statement on Being Awarded the Schlich Forestry Medal," January 29, 1935, made available online by Gerhard Peters and John T. Woolley, The American Presidency Project, https://www.presidency.ucsb.edu /node/209004.

61. Andrews, *Managing the Environment*, 163.

62. Andrews, 174.

63. James Morton Turner, *The Promise of Wilderness: American Environmental Politics since 1964* (Seattle: University of Washington Press, 2012), 21.

64. Irving Brant, *Adventures in Conservation with Franklin D. Roosevelt* (Flagstaff, AZ: Northland, 1988), 24.

65. Bernard DeVoto, "The West against Itself," *Harper's*, January 1947.

66. Andrews, *Managing the Environment*, 194.

67. Brant, *Adventures in Conservation*, 313.

68. Edward P. Cliff, interview with Joe Frantz, January 6, 1969, Lyndon Baines Johnson Oral Histories, Lyndon Baines Johnson Presidential Library, University of Texas at Austin.

69. Cliff, interview, January 6, 1969.

70. Rosenbaum, *Politics of Environmental Concern*, 192.

71. Richard A. Cooley and Geoffrey Wandesforde-Smith, eds., *Congress and the Environment* (Seattle: University of Washington Press, 1970), 240.

72. Muskie quoted in E. W. Kenworthy, "Sierra Club and Muskie Accuse the Administration of Disregarding New Environmental Policy Act," *New York Times*, February 22, 1970, 44, quoted in Flippen, *Nixon and the Environment*, 93.

73. 116 Cong. Rec. 2,312 (1970).

74. McCloskey, *In the Thick of It*, 111.

75. 116 Cong. Rec. 5,113, 5,117 (1970), quoted in Smith, *Green Republican*, 278.

76. Thomas G. Smith, *Green Republican: John Saylor and the Preservation of America's Wilderness* (Pittsburgh, PA: University of Pittsburgh Press, 2006), 279.

77. Hays, *History of Environmental Politics*, 90.

78. Gary Eisler, "Forest Practices Debated in Washington," *Not Man Apart* (June 1971): 1–2, quoted in LeRoy Ashby and Rod Gramer, *Fighting the Odds: The Life of Senator Frank Church* (Pullman: Washington State University Press, 1994), 353.

79. Eisler, "Forest Practices Debated in Washington," quoted in Ashby and Gramer, *Fighting the Odds*, 354.

80. Flippen, *Nixon and the Environment*, 198.

81. Paul Walden Hansen, *Green in Gridlock: Common Goals, Common Ground, and Compromise* (College Station: Texas A&M University Press, 2013), 62.

82. Char Miller, *Public Lands, Public Debates: A Century of Controversy* (Corvallis: Oregon State University Press, 2012), 110.

83. Hubert Humphrey, in Conservation Milestones, 40 Records of the Council on Environmental Quality, Washington, DC, 1984, quoted in Victor B. Scheffer, *The Shaping of Environmentalism in America* (Seattle: University of Washington Press, 1991), 156.

84. 122 Cong. Rec. 31,039 (1976).

85. 122 Cong. Rec. 31,047 (1976).

86. 122 Cong. Rec. 31,048 (1976).

87. 122 Cong. Rec. 31,048 (1976).

88. 122 Cong. Rec. 31,047 (1976).

89. 122 Cong. Rec. 31,054 (1976).

90. 122 Cong. Rec. 31,055–31,056, 31,056 (1976).

91. 122 Cong. Rec. 34,045–34,046 (1976).

92. National Forest Management Act, 16 U.S.C. § 1601 (1976).

93. National Forest Management Act, Pub. L. No. 94-588 90 Stat. 2951 (1976).

94. National Forest Management Act, 16 U.S.C. § 472a (1976).

95. Hansen, *Green in Gridlock*, 62.

96. Stewart L. Udall, interview with Joe Frantz, July 29, 1969, Lyndon Baines Johnson Oral Histories.

97. Flippen, *Nixon and the Environment*, 90.

98. Smith, *Green Republican*, 292.

99. 117 Cong. Rec. 36,861 (1969).

100. McCloskey, *In the Thick of It*, 138.

101. McCloskey, 137.

102. Smith, *Green Republican*, 303.

103. Kline, *First along the River*, 44.

104. Andrews, *Managing the Environment*, 99.

105. Stewart L. Udall, interview with Joe B. Frantz, December 16, 1969, Lyndon Baines Johnson Oral Histories.

106. Kenneth Auchincloss, "The Ravaged Environment," *Newsweek*, January 26, 1970, 39, quoted in Scheffer, *Shaping of Environmentalism*, 67.

107. "US Strip Mining Control Sought," *Charleston (WV) Gazette*, October 27, 1965, quoted in Bill Christofferson, *The Man from Clear Lake: Earth Day Founder Senator Gaylord Nelson* (Madison: University of Wisconsin Press, 2004), 574.

108. Whitaker, *Striking a Balance*, 174.

109. Rosenbaum, *Politics of Environmental Concern*, 227.

110. Smith, *Green Republican*, 271.

111. Ken Hechler quoted in *New York Times*, October 15, 1972, quoted in Rosenbaum, *Politics of Environmental Concern*, 218.

112. Ken Cole, memorandum, December 1974, box 17, White House Records Office Legislation Case Files, Gerald R. Ford Presidential Library, University of Michigan, Ann Arbor.

113. Ken Cole, memorandum, December 1974.

114. Donald W. Carson and James W. Johnson, *Mo: The Life and Times of Morris K. Udall* (Tucson: University of Arizona Press, 2000), 185.

115. Turner, *Promise of Wilderness*, 101.

116. Turner, 114.

117. John C. Whitaker, Memorandum to John D. Ehrlichman Regarding Possible Presidential Executive Order, July 27, 1971, JWP, box 118, folder "Wilderness Areas 4," quoted in Turner, 113.

118. Flippen, *Nixon and the Environment*, 228.

119. Andrews, *Managing the Environment*, 169.

120. Senator Frank Church, Statement before Senate Public Lands Committee, 1972, TWSR, box 157, folder "Oregon: Mt. Hood National Forrest, 1970–72."

121. Nathaniel P. Reed to Stewart Brandborg, August 22, 1972, HCP, box 1:1, folder "Correspondence, 1972," quoted in Turner, *Promise of Wilderness*, 129.

122. Turner, 69.

123. Brock Evans to Francis Walcott, "Criticism of the Region Five Multiple Use Management Guides for Wilderness," December 12, 1969, Sierra Club PNWP, accession 2678-09, box 6, folder "Wilderness Management," quoted in Turner, 89.

124. Francis Walcott to Shirley Taylor, Florida chapter, Sierra Club, December 13, 1972, Sierra Club NLOR, box 133, folder 7, 1, quoted in Turner, 87.

125. 120 Cong. Rec. 17,184 (1974).

126. 120 Cong. Rec. 17,184 (1974).

127. 120 Cong. Rec. 17,191 (1974).

128. 119 Cong. Rec. 849 (1973), quoted in Smith, *Green Republican*, 341.

129. "Eastern Wilderness," January 3, 1975, S. 3433, box 20, Legislative Case Files, Gerald R. Ford Presidential Library.

130. "Eastern Wilderness."

131. "Omnibus Wilderness," January 3, 1975, box 21, Legislative Case Files, Gerald R. Ford Presidential Library.

132. Phillip O. Foss, *Politics and Grass: The Administration of Grazing in the Public Domain* (Seattle: University of Washington Press, 1960), 195.

133. Roderick Nash, *The American Environment: Readings in Conservation* (Reading, MA: Addison-Wesley, 1968), 28.

134. Andrews, *Managing the Environment*, 102.

135. Carolyn Merchant, *The Columbia Guide to American Environmental History* (New York: Columbia University Press, 2005), 97.

136. Andrews, *Managing the Environment*, 169.

137. Petulla, *American Environmental History*, 311.

138. Petulla, 366.

139. Andrews, *Managing the Environment*, 169.

140. Kline, *First along the River*, 68.

141. Hugh Hammond Bennett, *Soil Conservation* (New York: McGraw-Hill, 1939), v, quoted in Philip Shabecoff, *A Fierce Green Fire: The American Environmental Movement* (New York: Hill and Wang, 1993), 75.

142. Andrews, *Managing the Environment*, 170.

143. Turner, *Promise of Wilderness*, 53.

144. Scheffer, *Shaping of Environmentalism*, 36.

145. Samuel Trask Dana and Sally K. Fairfax, *Forest and Range Policy: Its Development in the United States*, 2nd ed. (New York: McGraw-Hill, 1980), 187.

146. James R. Skillen, *The Nation's Largest Landlord: The Bureau of Land Management in the American West* (Lawrence: University Press of Kansas, 2009), 45.

147. Skillen, 48.

148. Skillen, 49.

149. Skillen, 54.

150. Skillen, 57.

151. Skillen, 76.

152. Aspinall Papers.

153. Thomas P. Holley to John Whitaker, March 34, 1970, folder "Public Land Law Review, Grazing, 1969–1970, 2 of 2," box 96, John Whitaker Files, WHCF, RNPMP, quoted in Flippen, *Nixon and the Environment*, 95.

154. Turner, *Promise of Wilderness*, 116.

155. *One Third of the Nation's Land: A Report to the President and to the Congress by the Public Land Law Review Commission* (Washington, DC: Public Land Law Review Commission, 1970), 22. Emphasis in the original.

156. Stewart L. Udall, "Conflicting Claims over *A Third of the Nation*," *Newsday*, July 8, 1970, quoted in Skillen, 82.

157. Douglas, *Three Hundred Year War*, 139.

158. McCloskey, *In the Thick of It*, 116.

159. Harold Peterson, "Moving in for a Land Grab," *Sports Illustrated*, June 20, 1970, https://vault.si.com/vault/1970/07/13/moving-in-for-a-land-grab.

160. Irving Senzel, "Genesis of a Law, Part 1," *American Forests* 84, no. 1 (1978): 63, quoted in Skillen, *Nation's Largest Landlord*, 86.

161. 122 Cong. Rec. 23,435 (1976).

162. 122 Cong. Rec. 23,435 (1976).

163. 122 Cong. Rec. 23,436 (1976).

164. 122 Cong. Rec. 23,437 (1976).

165. 122 Cong. Rec. 23,441 (1976).

166. 122 Cong. Rec. 23,451 (1976).

167. 122 Cong. Rec. 23,451 (1976).

168. 122 Cong. Rec. 23,457, 23,459 (1976).

169. 122 Cong. Rec. 23,466 (1976).

170. 43 U.S.C. §1751.

171. 43 U.S.C. §1732.

172. 43 U.S.C. §1701.

173. Turner, *Promise of Wilderness*, 241.

174. *Legislative History of the Federal Land Policy and Management Act of 1976 (Public Law 94-579)* (Washington, DC: Government Printing Office, 1978), vi, quoted in Skillen, *Nation's Largest Landlord*, 110.

175. Turner, *Promise of Wilderness*, 396.

Chapter 13. The Years That Followed

1. Howard H. Baker Jr., "U.S. Environmentalism, Comity and the Clean Air Act," in David C. Brill, ed., *Cleaning America's Air: Progress and Challenges* (Knoxville, TN: Howard Baker Jr. Center for Public Policy Publications, 2005), 9.

2. Baker, "U.S. Environmentalism, Comity and the Clean Air Act," 4.

3. Baker, 11.

4. Victor B. Scheffer, *The Shaping of Environmentalism in America* (Seattle: University of Washington Press, 1991), 150.

5. Tim Palmer, *Wild and Scenic Rivers: An American Legacy* (Corvallis: Oregon State University Press, 2017), 37.

6. "An Interview on Wilderness with Senator Frank Church," *Western Wildlands* (Fall 1977), 3, quoted in LeRoy Ashby and Rod Gramer, *Fighting the Odds: The Life of Senator Frank Church* (Pullman: Washington State University Press, 1994), 586.

7. Ashby and Gramer, 591.

8. Palmer, *Wild and Scenic Rivers*, 37.

9. Scheffer, *Shaping of Environmentalism*, 157.

10. White House Press Office, "Alaskan Lands Status Report," July 12, 1980, 3, quoted in Roderick Nash, *Wilderness and the American Mind*, 3rd ed. (New Haven, CT: Yale University Press, 1982), 298.

11. Morris Udall, as quoted in Julius Discha, "How the Alaska Act Was Won," *Living Wilderness* 44 (1981): 8.

12. Robert G. Kaufman, *Henry M. Jackson: A Life in Politics* (Seattle: University of Washington Press, 2000), 348.

13. James Morton Turner, *The Promise of Wilderness: American Environmental Politics since 1964* (Seattle: University of Washington Press, 2012), 164.

14. Gaylord Nelson, as quoted in Rocky Barker, "Cecil Andrus Knew How to Take a Stand," *High Country News*, February 20, 1995, quoted in Bill Christofferson, *The Man from Clear Lake: Earth Day Founder Senator Gaylord Nelson* (Madison: University of Wisconsin Press, 2004), 576.

15. J. Brooks Flippen, *Conservative Conservationist: Russell E. Train and the Emergence of American Environmentalism* (Baton Rouge: Louisiana State University Press, 2006), 196.

16. Christofferson, *Man from Clear Lake*, 577.

17. H. Patricia Hynes, *The Recurring Silent Spring* (Elmsford, NY: Pergamon, 1989), 69.

18. Scheffer, *Shaping of Environmentalism*, 159.

19. Carolyn Merchant, *The Columbia Guide to American Environmental History* (New York: Columbia University Press, 2005), 183.

20. Scheffer, *Shaping of Environmentalism*, 179.

21. Barbara Dudley, interview with Gregg Coodley, August 28, 2019.

22. "Report of BLM Wilderness Task Force, SC," June 18, 1979, Sierra Club NLOR, box 139, folder 6, quoted in Turner, *Promise of Wilderness*, 238.

23. Turner, 239.

24. Philip Shabecoff, *A Fierce Green Fire: The American Environmental Movement* (New York: Hill and Wang, 1993), 209.

25. Dudley, interview, August 28, 2019.

26. Russell E. Train, *Politics, Pollution, and Pandas: An Environmental Memoir* (Washington, DC: Island, 2003), 117.

27. Train, 118.

28. *Endangered Species Act Amendments of 1982: Hearing on S. 2309 Before the Subcommittee on Environmental Pollution of the Committee on Environment and Public Works*, 97th Cong. 188 (1982).

29. Flippen, *Conservative Conservationist*, 203.

30. Lois B. Ember, "EPA Administrators Deem Agency's First 25 Years Bumpy but Successful," *Chemical & Engineering News*, October 30, 1995, 21, quoted in Benjamin Kline, *First along the River: A Brief History of the U.S. Environmental Movement* (San Francisco: Acada Books, 1997), 106.

31. Flippen, *Conservative Conservationist*, 204–205.

32. Kline, *First along the River*, 106.

33. James Morton Turner and Andrew C. Isenberg, *The Republican Reversal: Conservatives and the Environment from Nixon to Trump* (Cambridge, MA: Harvard University Press, 2018), 131.

34. Turner and Isenberg, 133.

35. Stewart Udall, *The Quiet Crisis and the Next Generation* (Layton, UT: Gibbs Smith, 1988), 262, quoted in Scheffer, *Shaping of Environmentalism in America*, 178–179.

36. Richard N. L. Andrews, *Managing the Environment, Managing Ourselves: A History of American Environmental Policy* (New Haven, CT: Yale University Press, 1999), 67.

37. Pennsylvania Coal Co. v. Mahon, 260 U.S. 393, 417 (1922).

38. Paul Walden Hansen, *Green in Gridlock: Common Goals, Common Ground and Compromise* (College Station: Texas A&M University Press, 2013), 28.

39. Richard Elliot Benedick, *Ozone Diplomacy: New Directions in Safeguarding the Planet*, enlarged ed. (Cambridge, MA: Harvard University Press, 1998), 64.

40. Hansen, *Green in Gridlock*, 29.

41. McCloskey, interview by Gregg Coodley, September 18, 2019.

42. Brill, *Cleaning America's Air*, 4.

43. Turner and Isenberg, *Republican Reversal*, 120.

44. Brill, *Cleaning America's Air*, 5.

45. Flippen, *Conservative Conservationist*, 215.

46. Council on Environmental Quality, First Annual Report (Washington, DC, 1970), 93, quoted in Scheffer, *Shaping of Environmentalism*, 60.

47. Richard A. Cooley and Geoffrey Wandesforde-Smith, eds., *Congress and the Environment* (Seattle: University of Washington Press, 1970), 242.

48. Environmental Protection Agency, one page press release on two 1983 publications: "Can We Delay a Greenhouse Warming?" and "Projecting Future Sea Level Rise," Washington, DC, 1983, quoted in Scheffer, *Shaping of Environmentalism in America*, 60.

49. *Greenhouse Effect and Global Climate Change: Hearing Before the Senate Committee on Energy and Natural Resources*, 100th Cong., part 2, 43 (1988) (prepared statement of James E. Hansen, NASA Goddard Institute for Space Studies).

50. Kirkpatrick Sale, *The Green Revolution: The American Environmental Movement, 1962–1992* (New York: Hill and Wang, 1993), 75.

51. Turner and Isenberg, *Republican Reversal*, 161.

52. Turner, *Promise of Wilderness*, 258.

53. Christofferson, *Man from Clear Lake*, 368.

54. Tom DeLay, quoted in Michael Schaller and George Rising, *The Republican Ascendency: American Politics, 1968–2001* (Wheeling, IL: Harlan Davidson, 2002), 132, quoted in Flippen, *Conservative Conservationist*, 216.

55. John McCain, "Nature is Not a Liberal Plot: Extreme Anti-Environmentalism Hurts the GOP," *New York Times*, November 22, 1996.

56. Ruckelshaus, interview with Timothy Naftali, April 12, 2007, Presidential Materials, Richard Nixon Presidential Library and Museum, Yorba Linda, CA.

57. Flippen, *Conservative Conservationist*, 219.

58. Russell E. Train, *Seattle Post Intelligencer*, September 8, 2004, quoted in Flippen, 222.

59. Turner and Isenberg, *Republican Reversal*, 91.

60. Turner and Isenberg, 169.

61. Turner and Isenberg, 170.

62. Massachusetts v. EPA 549 U.S. 497 (2007), quoted in Turner and Isenberg, 180.

63. Michael McCloskey, "The Environmental Movement after Fifty Years: How Much Influence Did It Exert?" unpublished memo, March 2019.

64. John Kerry, *Every Day Is Extra* (New York: Simon and Schuster, 2018), 576.

65. Kerry, 577.

66. James Inhofe, *How the Global Warming Conspiracy Threatens Your Future* (Washington, DC: WND Books, 2012), quoted in Turner and Isenberg, *Republican Reversal*, 2.

67. Sara Jerde, "Trump Says He Will Cut the EPA as Prez: 'We'll be Fine with the Environment,'" *Live Wire*, October 18, 2015, quoted in Turner and Isenberg, 1.

68. Joshua Zaffos, "House Republicans Want to 'Repeal and Replace' the ESA," *High Country News*, December 28, 2016, quoted in Turner and Isenberg, 93.

69. Turner and Isenberg, 94.

70. *St. Paul Pioneer Press*, 1974, quoted in David J. Webber, *Outstanding Environmentalists of Congress* (Washington, DC: U.S. Capitol Historical Society, 2002).

71. Webber, *Outstanding Environmentalists of Congress*, 22.

72. Barack Obama, "Statement on the Death of Stewart L. Udall," March 20, 2010, made available online by Gerhard Peters and John T. Woolley, The American Presidency Project, https://www.presidency.ucsb.edu/node/216474.

73. Ashby and Gramer, *Fighting the Odds*, 604.

74. Ben Wattenberg, interview with Henry Kaufman, March 16, 1995, quoted in Kaufman, *Henry M. Jackson*, 205.

75. Senator Henry M. Jackson, posthumous testimony, Senate Energy and Natural Resources Committee, on S.1090, National Outdoor Recreation Resources Review Act of 1983, September 1, 1983, quoted in Webber, *Outstanding Environmentalists*, 33.

76. Kaufman, *Henry M. Jackson*, 432.

77. David Brower, telegram to John Saylor, October 20, 1970, 1970 scrapbook, John Saylor Papers, Indiana University of Pennsylvania Saylor Special Collection, quoted in Thomas G. Smith, *Green Republican: John Saylor and the Preservation of America's Wilderness* (Pittsburgh, PA: University of Pittsburgh Press, 2006), 283.

78. *Memorial Services Held in the House of Representatives and Senate of the United States, Together with Tributes Presented in Eulogy of John P. Saylor,* 93rd Cong. 3–4 (1974), quoted in Smith, 316.

79. Stewart Brandborg, letter to Thomas G. Smith, December 10, 1997, quoted in Smith, 317.

80. *Memorial Services,* 131.

81. Shelby Scates, *Warren G. Magnuson and the Shaping of Twentieth-Century America* (Seattle: University of Washington Press, 1997), 322.

82. Scates, 327.

83. John D. Dingell, *The Dean: The Best Seat in the House,* with David Bender (New York: HarperCollins, 2018), 282.

84. Train, *Politics, Pollution, and Pandas,* 221.

85. Ruckelshaus, interview with Michael Gorn, January 1993, EPA Oral History Series.

86. Baker, "U.S. Environmentalism, Comity and the Clean Air Act," 7.

87. Joel K. Goldstein, "Edmund S. Muskie: The Environmental Leader and Champion." *Maine Law Review* 67, no. 2 (2015): 225–232.

88. Richard Lazarus, "Senator Ed Muskie's Enduring Legacy in the Courts," *Maine Law Review* 67, no. 2 (2015): 240–250.

89. Alan H. Lockwood, "How the Clean Air Act Has Saved $22 Trillion in Health Care Costs," *Atlantic,* September 7, 2012.

90. Webber, *Outstanding Environmentalists,* 58.

91. Doris Kearns Goodwin, *Lyndon Johnson and the American Dream* (New York: St. Martin's, 1991), 542.

Chapter 14. What Happened in the Green Years?

1. George Hartzog Jr., interview with Joe Frantz, December 20, 1968, Lyndon Baines Johnson Oral Histories, Lyndon Baines Johnson Presidential Library, University of Texas at Austin.

2. Thomas G. Smith, *Stewart L. Udall: Steward of the Land* (Albuquerque: University of New Mexico Press, 2017), 283.

3. Wayne Aspinall, interview with Joe Frantz, June 14, 1974, Lyndon Baines Johnson Oral Histories.

4. Lyndon Baines Johnson, *Vantage Point: Perspectives of the Presidency, 1963–1969* (New York: Holt, Rinehart and Winston, 1971), 336.

5. Stewart L. Udall, interview with Joe Frantz, April 18, 1969, Lyndon Baines Johnson Oral Histories.

6. Laurance Rockefeller, interview with Joe. B. Frantz, August 5, 1969, Lyndon Baines Johnson Oral Histories.

7. Cynthia Wilson, "Lyndon Johnson, Conservationist," *Audubon* 75 (March

1973): 122, quoted in Martin V. Melosi, "Lyndon Johnson and Environmental Policy," in *Vietnam, the Environment, and Space*, vol. 2 of *The Johnson Years*, ed. Robert A. Divine (Lawrence: University Press of Kansas, 1987), 122–123.

8. Lynton K. Caldwell, *Environment: A Challenge for Modern Society* (Garden City, NY: Natural History Press, 1970), 54.

9. Melosi, "Lyndon Johnson and Environmental Policy," 128.

10. Michael McCloskey, interview with Gregg Coodley, September 18, 2019.

11. 111 Cong. Rec. 28,699 (1965).

12. Adam Rome, *The Genius of Earth Day: How a 1970 Teach-In Unexpectedly Made the First Green Generation* (New York: Hill and Wang, 2013), 19.

13. J. Brooks Flippen, *Nixon and the Environment* (Albuquerque: University of New Mexico Press, 2000), 221.

14. Evan Thomas, *Being Nixon: A Man Divided* (New York: Random House, 2015), 410.

15. John C. Whitaker, *Striking a Balance: Environment and Natural Resources Policy in the Nixon-Ford Years* (Washington, DC: American Enterprise Institute for Public Policy Research, 1976), 337.

16. Russell E. Train, *Politics, Pollution, and Pandas: An Environmental Memoir* (Washington, DC: Island, 2003), 123.

17. Robert Cahn, *Footprints on the Planet: A Search for an Environmental Ethic* (New York: Universe Books, 1978), 44.

18. David Brower, interview with J. Brooks Flippen, April 7, 1998, quoted in Flippen, *Nixon and the Environment*, 228.

19. Barbara Dudley, interview with Gregg Coodley, August 28, 2019.

20. McCloskey, interview, September 18, 2019.

21. William Reilly, interview with Flippen, June 26, 1998, quoted in Flippen, *Nixon and the Environment*, 231.

22. William O. Douglas, *The Three Hundred Year War: A Chronicle of Ecological Disaster* (New York: Random House, 1972), 15.

23. Samuel P. Hays, *A History of Environmental Politics since 1945* (Pittsburgh, PA: University of Pittsburgh Press, 2000), 25.

24. Grant McConnell, *Private Power and American Democracy* (New York: Alfred A. Knopf, 1966), quoted in Richard A. Cooley and Geoffrey Wandesforde-Smith, eds., *Congress and the Environment* (Seattle: University of Washington Press, 1970), 13.

25. Rome, *Genius of Earth Day*, 30.

26. Dudley, interview, August 28, 2019.

27. McCloskey, interview, September 18, 2019.

28. Al Gore, "Riders on the Blue Marble Must Confront Climate Change," in David C. Brill, ed., *Cleaning America's Air: Progress and Challenges* (Knoxville, TN: Howard Baker Jr. Center for Public Policy Publications, 2005), 36.

29. McCloskey, interview, September 18, 2019.

30. Muskie, interview with Mitchell Krause, May 11, 1970, transcript, folder 9, "1970 Press File, Speeches, May," box 1533, USSSO, Edmund Muskie Archives,

Bates College Library, Maine, quoted in Flippen, *Nixon and the Environment*, 99.

31. Richard N. L. Andrews, *Managing the Environment, Managing Ourselves: A History of American Environmental Policy* (New Haven, CT: Yale University Press, 1999), 222.

32. Clinton Anderson, interview with T. H. Baker, May 20, 1969, Lyndon Baines Johnson Oral Histories; Frank Church, interview with Paige E. Mulhollen, May 1, 1969, Lyndon Baines Johnson Oral Histories.

33. Stewart L. Udall, interview with Joe B. Frantz, December 16, 1969, Lyndon Baines Johnson Oral Histories.

34. Udall, interview, December 16, 1969.

35. J. Michael McCloskey, *In the Thick of It: My Life in the Sierra Club* (Washington, DC: Island, 2005), 129.

36. Hays, *Environmental Politics since 1945*, quoted in Kirkpatrick Sale, *The Green Revolution: The American Environmental Movement, 1962–1992* (New York: Hill and Wang, 1993), 35.

37. McCloskey, *In the Thick of It*, 128.

38. McCloskey, interview, September 18, 2019.

39. Benjamin Kline, *First along the River: A Brief History of the U.S. Environmental Movement* (San Francisco: Acada Books, 1997), 89.

40. Rome, *Genius of Earth Day*, 47.

41. Rome, 50.

42. Mark Dowie, *Losing Ground: American Environmentalism at the Close of the Twentieth Century* (Cambridge: MIT Press, 1995), 6.

43. McCloskey, interview, September 18, 2019.

44. James Morton Turner, *The Promise of Wilderness: American Environmental Politics since 1964* (Seattle: University of Washington Press, 2012), 40.

45. Hays, *History of Environmental Politics*, 118.

46. McCloskey, interview, September 18, 2019.

47. John D. Dingell, *The Dean: The Best Seat in the House*, with David Bender (New York: HarperCollins, 2018), 208.

48. Richard Lazarus, "Senator Ed Muskie's Enduring Legacy in the Courts," *Maine Law Review* 67, no. 2 (2015): 240–250.

49. Dingell, *Dean*, xvi.

50. Dingell, 216.

51. Dingell, 213.

52. John W. McCormack, interview with T. H. Baker, September 23, 1968, Lyndon Baines Johnson Oral Histories.

53. Turner, *Promise of Wilderness*, 135.

54. 116 Cong. Rec. 10,346 (1970).

55. Train, *Politics, Pollution, and Pandas*, 233.

56. Cahn, *Footprints on the Planet*, 53.

57. Dingell, *Dean*, 214.

58. Train, *Politics, Pollution, and Pandas*, 257.

59. Flippen, *Nixon and the Environment*, 222.

60. Flippen, 224.

61. Sale, *Green Revolution*, 77.

62. Sale, 80.

63. Michael McCloskey, "The Environmental Movement After Fifty Years: How Much Influence Did It Exert?" unpublished article, March 2019, 79.

64. James Morton Turner and Andrew C. Isenberg, *The Republican Reversal: Conservatives and the Environment from Nixon to Trump* (Cambridge, MA: Harvard University Press, 2018), 6–7.

65. Hays, *History of Environmental Politics*, 188.

66. Hays, 188.

67. Turner and Isenberg, *Republican Reversal*, 30.

68. Turner and Isenberg, 34.

69. Michael McCloskey, "Why Republicans Have Turned Against Environmental Measures," unpublished article, April, 2019, 1.

70. Turner and Isenberg, *Republican Reversal*, 16.

71. Friedrich Hayek, *The Road to Serfdom*, ed. Bruce Caldwell (Chicago: University of Chicago Press, 2007), 87, quoted in Turner and Isenberg, 29.

72. Barry Goldwater, *The Conscience of a Majority* (Englewood Cliffs, NJ: Prentice Hall, 1970), 212, quoted in Turner and Isenberg, 31.

73. John McCain, "Nature Is Not a Liberal Plot: Extreme Anti-environmentalism Hurts the GOP," *New York Times*, November 22, 1996.

74. Turner and Isenberg, *Republican Reversal*, 52.

75. Chris Mooney, *The Republican War on Science* (New York: Basic Books, 2005), 30.

76. Turner and Isenberg, *Republican Reversal*, 205.

77. McCloskey, *In the Thick of It*, 202.

78. Samuel Hays, *Beauty, Health and Permanence: Environmental Politics in the United States, 1955–1985* (New York: Cambridge University Press, 1987), 307.

79. Mooney, *Republican War on Science*, 32.

80. Mooney, 30.

81. Mooney, 36.

82. Hays, *History of Environmental Politics*, 215.

83. Jane Mayer, *Dark Money: The Hidden History of the Billionaires behind the Rise of the Radical Right* (New York: Random House, 2016), 175.

84. Mooney, *Republican War on Science*, 54.

85. Lazarus, "Senator Ed Muskie's Enduring Legacy."

86. Mayer, *Dark Money*, 514.

87. Lee Drutman, "Are the 1% of the 1% Pulling Politics in a Conservative Direction?," Sunlight Foundation, June 26, 2013, https://sunlightfoundation .com/2013/06/26/1pct_of_the_1pct_polarization/.

88. Frank Luntz quoted by Isaac Chotiner, "Frank Luntz's Tarnished Legacy," *New Republic*, January 29, 2007.

89. "Scientists' Report Documents ExxonMobil's Tobacco-like Disinformation Campaign on Global Warming Science," *Union of Concerned Scientists*,

January 2007, http:/ucsusa.org/new/press_release/ExxonMobil-globalwarming-tobacco.html.

90. Turner and Isenberg, *Republican Reversal*, 16.

91. Sale, *Green Revolution*, 58.

92. Michael McCloskey, memo to Sierra Club Board of Directors, January 1986, quoted in Sale, 61.

93. McCloskey, *In the Thick of It*, 364.

94. McCloskey, interview, September 18, 2019.

95. McCloskey, interview, September 18, 2019.

96. Michael McCloskey, "Why Republicans Have Turned against Environmental Measures," unpublished memo, April 2019.

97. Paul Walden Hansen, *Green in Gridlock: Common Goals, Common Ground and Compromise* (College Station: Texas A&M University Press, 2013), 12.

98. Turner, *Promise of Wilderness*, 39.

99. Robert Gottlieb, *Forcing the Spring: The Transformation of the American Environmental Movement* (Washington, DC: Island, 2005), 409.

100. Dudley, interview, August 28, 2019.

101. Bill McKibben, *Fight Global Warming Now: The Handbook for Taking Action in Your Community* (New York: Henry Holt, 2007), xvi.

102. Dowie, *Losing Ground*, 39.

103. Dowie, 78.

104. Dowie, 85.

105. Andrews, *Managing the Environment*, 411.

106. Hays, *History of Environmental Politics*, 220.

107. Mike Hulme, *Why We Disagree about Climate Change: Understanding Controversy, Inaction and Opportunity* (Cambridge: Cambridge University Press, 2009), 348.

108. William Ruckelshaus, speech before the Vermont Natural Resources Council, September 10, 1983, quoted in Philip Shabecoff, *Fierce Green Fire: The American Environmental Movement.* (New York: Hill and Wang, 1993), 258.

109. McCloskey, interview, September 18, 2019.

110. Ruckelshaus, interview, 1993.

111. Bill McKibben, *The End of Nature* (New York: Random House, 1989), 9.

112. Renee Salas, Debra Malina, and Caren Solomon, "Prioritizing Health in a Changing Climate," *New England Journal of Medicine* 381, no. 8 (August 22, 2019): 773–774.

113. Naomi Klein, *This Changes Everything: Capitalism vs. the Climate* (New York: Simon and Schuster, 2014), 6.

114. Dudley, interview, August 28, 2019.

115. McCloskey, interview, September 18, 2019.

116. Pew Research Center, March 2016 Political Survey, http://www.people-press.org/files/2016/03/03-31-2016-Political-topline-for-release.pdf, quoted in Turner and Isenberg, *Republican Reversal*, 215.

Bibliography

Archival Sources

Aspinall, Wayne. Papers. Special Collections. University of Colorado Boulder Library. Boulder, CO.

Aspinall, Wayne. Papers. Special Collections. University of Denver Library, Denver, CO.

Jackson, Henry. Papers. Special Collections. University of Washington Library, Seattle.

Johnson, Lyndon Baine. Oral Histories. Lyndon Baines Johnson Presidential Library, University of Texas at Austin.

Magnuson, Warren. Papers. Special Collections. University of Washington Library, Seattle.

National Archives, Washington, DC.

Nixon, Richard. Presidential Materials. Richard Nixon Presidential Library and Museum, Yorba Linda, CA.

Senate Historical Office, United States Senate, Washington, DC.

White House Records Office Legislation Case Files. Gerald R. Ford Presidential Library, University of Michigan, Ann Arbor.

Wilderness Society Archives. Denver Public Library, Denver, CO.

Primary and Secondary Sources

Aitken, Jonathan. *Nixon: A Life.* Washington, DC: Regnery, 1993.

Albright, Horace M. "The National Park Service's Policy on Predatory Mammals." *Journal of Mammalogy* 12, no. 2 (1931): 185–186.

Anderson, Clinton P. *Outsider in the Senate.* New York: World, 1970.

Anderson, Clinton. "The Wilderness of Aldo Leopold." *Living Wilderness* 19 (1954–55): 44–46.

Andrews, Richard. *Environmental Policy and Administrative Change.* Lanham, MD: Lexington Books, 1976.

Andrews, Richard N. L. *Managing the Environment, Managing Ourselves: A History of American Environmental Policy.* New Haven, CT: Yale University Press, 1999.

Annis, J. Lee, Jr. *Howard Baker: Conciliator in an Age of Crisis.* Lanham, MD: Madison Books, 1995.

Asbell, Bernard. *The Senate Nobody Knows.* Garden City, NY: Doubleday, 1978.

Ashby, LeRoy, and Rod Gramer. *Fighting the Odds: The Life of Senator Frank Church.* Pullman: Washington State University Press, 1994.

Baker, Howard H., Jr. *No Margin for Error: America in the Eighties*. New York: Times Books, 1980.

Baker, Richard Allan. *Conservation Politics: The Senate Career of Clinton P. Anderson*. Albuquerque: University of New Mexico Press, 1985.

Bartlett, John Russell, ed. *Records of the Colony of Rhode Island and Providence Plantations in New England*, vol. 1, *1636 to 1663*. Providence, RI: A. Crawford Greene, 1856.

Benedick, Richard Elliot. *Ozone Diplomacy: New Directions in Safeguarding the Planet*. Enlarged ed. Cambridge, MA: Harvard University Press, 1998.

Bennett, Hugh Hammond. *Soil Conservation*. New York: McGraw-Hill, 1939.

Bentham, Jeremy. *An Introduction to the Principles of Morals and Legislation*. London, 1789.

Bradford, William. *Of Plymouth Plantation, 1620–1647*. Edited and with an introduction by Samuel Eliot Morison. New York: Alfred A. Knopf, 2002.

Brant, Irving. *Adventures in Conservation with Franklin D. Roosevelt*. Flagstaff, AZ: Northland, 1988.

Brill, David C., ed. *Cleaning America's Air: Progress and Challenges*. Knoxville, TN: Howard Baker Jr. Center for Public Policy Publications, 2005.

Brooks, Paul. *The House of Life*. Boston: Houghton Mifflin, 1972.

Brower, David, "Address to 4th Biennial Conference on Northwest Wilderness," Seattle, April 14–15, 1962.

Brower, David R. "De Facto Wilderness: What Is Its Place?" In *Wildlands in Our Civilization*, edited by David R. Brower. San Francisco: Sierra Club, 1964.

Burns, James MacGregor, ed. *To Heal and to Build: The Programs of President Lyndon B. Johnson*. New York: McGraw-Hill, 1968.

Cahn, Robert. *Footprints on the Planet: A Search for an Environmental Ethic*. New York: Universe Books, 1978.

Caldwell, Lynton K. *Environment: A Challenge for Modern Society*. Garden City, NY: Natural History Press, 1970.

Caldwell, Lynton K. *Environment as a Focus for Public Policy*. Edited by Robert V. Bartlett and James N. Gladden. College Station: Texas A&M University Press, 1995.

Califano, Joseph A., Jr. *The Triumph and Tragedy of Lyndon Johnson: The White House Years*. New York: Simon & Schuster, 1991.

Carson, Donald W., and James W. Johnson. *Mo: The Life and Times of Morris K. Udall*. Tucson: University of Arizona Press, 2001.

Carson, Rachel. *The Sea Around Us*. New York: Oxford University Press, 1961.

Carson, Rachel. *Silent Spring*. 1962. Reprint, Boston: Houghton Mifflin, 2002.

Carter, Luther J. "Environmental Pollution: Scientists Go to Court." *Science* 158 (December 22, 1967).

Catlin, George. *Letters and Notes on the Manners, Customs and Conditions of the North American Indians*. London, 1841.

Catlin, George. *North American Indians: Being Letters and Notes on their Manners, Customs and Conditions, Written during Eight Years Travel amongst the Wildest Tribes of Indians in North America*. London, 1841.

Chernow, Ron. *Grant.* New York: Penguin Books, 2017.

Christie, Donna R., and Richard G. Hildreth. *Coastal and Ocean Management Law.* Saint Paul, MN: West Academic, 1999.

Christofferson, Bill. *The Man from Clear Lake: Earth Day Founder Senator Gaylord Nelson.* Madison: University of Wisconsin Press, 2004.

Collin, Robert W. *The Environmental Protection Agency: Cleaning Up America's Act.* Westport, CT: Greenwood, 2006.

Cooley, Richard A., and Geoffrey Wandesforde-Smith, eds. *Congress and the Environment.* Seattle: University of Washington Press, 1970.

Cottam, Clarence, and Elmer Higgins. *DDT: Its Effect on Fish and Wildlife.* Fish and Wildlife Service, US Department of the Interior, circ. 11. Washington, DC: Government Printing Office, 1946.

Council on Environmental Quality. *The President's 1973 Environmental Program.* Washington, DC: Government Printing Office, 1973.

Crevelli, John P. "The Final Act of the Greatest Conservation President." *Prologue* 12 (Winter 1980): 173–191.

Czech, Brian, and Paul R. Krausman. *The Endangered Species Act: History, Conservation Biology, and Public Policy.* Baltimore: Johns Hopkins University Press, 2001.

Dallek, Robert. *Flawed Giant: Lyndon Johnson and His Times, 1961–1973.* New York: Oxford University Press, 1998.

Dana, Samuel Trask, and Sally K. Fairfax. *Forest and Range Policy: Its Development in the United States,* 2nd ed. New York: McGraw-Hill, 1980.

Diamond, Henry L. "The Land, the City and the Human Spirit." *Environmental Forum* 3, no. 8 (1984).

Dingell, John D. *The Dean: The Best Seat in the House.* With David Bender. New York: HarperCollins, 2018.

DiNunzio, Mario R., ed. *Theodore Roosevelt: An American Mind, A Selection from His Writings.* By Theodore Roosevelt. New York: St. Martin's, 1994.

Discha, Julius. "How the Alaska Act Was Won." *Living Wilderness* 44 (1981).

Douglas, William O. *The Three Hundred Year War: A Chronicle of Ecological Disaster.* New York: Random House, 1972.

Douglas, William O. Foreword to *The Wild Cascades: Forgotten Parklands,* by Harvey Manning and Ansel Adams. San Francisco: Sierra Club, 1969.

Dowie, Mark. *Losing Ground: American Environmentalism at the Close of the Twentieth Century.* Cambridge: MIT Press, 1995.

Draper, Robert. *Do Not Ask What Good We Do: Inside the U.S. House of Representatives.* New York: Free Press, 2012.

Dunlap, Thomas R. *Saving America's Wildlife: Ecology and the American Mind, 1850–1990.* Princeton, NJ: Princeton University Press, 1988.

DuPuis, E. Melanie, ed. *Smoke and Mirrors: The Politics and Culture of Air Pollution.* New York: New York University Press, 2004.

Ember, Lois R. "EPA Administrators Deem Agency's First 25 Years Bumpy but Successful." *Chemical & Engineering News Archive,* October 30, 1995, 18–23.

Flippen, J. Brooks. *Conservative Conservationist: Russell E. Train and the Emergence of American Environmentalism.* Baton Rouge: Louisiana State University Press, 2006.

Flippen, J. Brooks. *Nixon and the Environment.* Albuquerque: University of New Mexico Press, 2000.

Flores, Dan. *American Serengeti: The Last Big Animals of the Great Plains.* Lawrence: University Press of Kansas, 2016.

Foss, Philip O. *Politics and Grass: The Administration of Grazing in the Public Domain.* Seattle: University of Washington Press, 1960.

Frist, William H. *Tennessee Senators, 1911–2001: Portraits of Leadership in a Century of Change.* With James Lee Annis Jr. Lanham, MD: Madison Books, 1999.

Goldfield, David. *The Gifted Generation: When Government Was Good.* New York: Bloomsbury, 2017.

Goldstein, Joel K. "Edmund S. Muskie: The Environmental Leader and Champion." *Maine Law Review* 67, no. 2 (2015): 225–232.

Goldwater, Barry. *The Conscience of a Majority.* Englewood Cliffs, NJ: Prentice Hall, 1970.

Goodwin, Doris Kearns. *Leadership in Turbulent Times.* New York: Simon and Schuster, 2018.

Goodwin, Doris Kearns. *Lyndon Johnson and the American Dream.* New York: St. Martin's, 1991.

Gore, Al. *The Assault on Reason: Our Information Ecosystem, from the Age of Print to the Age of Trump.* New York: Penguin Books, 2017.

Gottlieb, Robert. *Forcing the Spring: The Transformation of the American Environmental Movement.* Washington, DC: Island, 2005.

Gould, Lewis L. *Lady Bird Johnson and the Environment.* Lawrence: University Press of Kansas, 1988.

Gould, Lewis L. *The Most Exclusive Club: A History of the Modern United States Senate.* New York: Basic Books, 2005.

Graham, Frank, Jr. *Since Silent Spring.* Boston: Houghton Mifflin, 1970.

Greeley, William. "The Initial Statement and Transcript of the Testimony of Col. W. B. Greeley." *Lumber World Review,* February 10, 1921, 34–35.

Hansen, Paul Walden. *Green in Gridlock: Common Goals, Common Ground, and Compromise.* College Station: Texas A&M University Press, 2013.

Hayek, Friedrich. *The Road to Serfdom.* Edited by Bruce Caldwell. Chicago: University of Chicago Press, 2007.

Hays, Samuel. *Beauty, Health and Permanence: Environmental Politics in the United States, 1955–1985.* New York: Cambridge University Press, 1987,

Hays, Samuel P. *A History of Environmental Politics since 1945.* Pittsburgh, PA: University of Pittsburgh Press, 2000.

Hickel, Walter J. *Who Owns America?* Englewood Cliffs, NJ: Prentice-Hall, 1971.

Hoff, Joan. *Nixon Reconsidered.* New York: Basic Books, 1994.

Hulme, Mike. *Why We Disagree about Climate Change: Understanding Controversy, Inaction and Opportunity.* Cambridge: Cambridge University Press, 2009.

Hynes, H. Patricia. *The Recurring Silent Spring*. Elmsford, NY: Pergamon, 1989.

Inhofe, James. *How the Global Warming Conspiracy Threatens Your Future*. Washington, DC: WND Books, 2012.

J. V. F. "Land Use Bill Defeated: Udall Charges 'Impeachment Politics.'" *BioScience* 24, no. 8 (August 1974): 470–471.

Johnson, Lyndon B. *My Hope for America*. New York: Random House, 1964.

Johnson, Lyndon Baines. *Vantage Point: Perspectives of the Presidency, 1963–1969*. New York: Holt, Rinehart and Winston, 1971.

Journal of the Senate of the United States of America, 89th Cong. Washington, DC: Government Printing Office, 1965.

Kaufman, Robert G. *Henry M. Jackson: A Life in Politics*. Seattle: University of Washington Press, 2000.

Kerry, John. *Every Day Is Extra*. New York: Simon and Schuster, 2018.

Klein, Naomi. *This Changes Everything: Capitalism vs. the Climate*. New York: Simon and Schuster, 2014.

Kline, Benjamin. *First along the River: A Brief History of the U.S. Environmental Movement*. San Francisco: Acada Books, 1997.

Kline, Benjamin. *First along the River: A Brief History of the U.S. Environmental Movement*. 4th ed. Lanham, MD: Rowman & Littlefield, 2011.

Kutler, Stanley, ed. *The Abuse of Power*. New York: Free Press, 1997.

Langer, Elinor. "Water Pollution: Federal Role Is Strengthened by Law Authorizing New Agency and Quality Standards." *Science* 150 (October 8, 1965): 198–260.

Larsen, Ralph L. "Air Pollution from Motor Vehicles." *Annals of the New York Academy of Sciences* 136, no. 12 (1966): 277–301.

Lazarus, Richard. "Senator Ed Muskie's Enduring Legacy in the Courts." *Maine Law Review* 67, no. 2 (2015): 240–250.

Leopold, Aldo. *Game Management*. New York: Charles Scribner's Sons, 1933. Reprinted with new foreword by Laurence R. Jahn. Madison: University of Wisconsin Press, 1987.

Leopold, Aldo. "The Last Stand of the Wilderness." *American Forests and Forest Life* 31, no. 382 (1925): 602. Reprinted in *American Forests and Forest Life* (Winter 2014), https://www.americanforests.org/magazine/article/aldo-leopolds-the -last-stand-of-the-wilderness/.

Leopold, Aldo. *A Sand County Almanac: And Sketches Here and There*. 1949. Reprint, Oxford University Press, 2020.

Leopold, Aldo. "The Wilderness and Its Place in Forest Recreational Policy," *Journal of Forestry* 19, no. 7 (November 1921): 718–721.

Leopold, Aldo. "Wilderness as a Form of Land Use," *Journal of Land and Public Utility Economics* 1 (October 1925): 398–404.

Leopold, Starker. "Predator and Rodent Control in the United States." In *Transactions of the Twenty-Ninth North American Wildlife and Natural Resources Conference*. Baltimore: Monumental, 1964.

Lieber, Harvey. *Federalism and Clean Waters: The 1972 Water Pollution Control Act*. Lexington, MA: Lexington Books, 1975.

Lippman, Theo, Jr., and Donald C. Hansen. *Muskie*. New York: W. W. Norton, 1971.

MacKaye, Benton. "The Appalachian Trail: A Project in Regional Planning." *Journal of the American Institute of Architects* (October 1921).

MacKaye, Benton. "Why the Appalachian Trail?" *Living Wilderness* 1, no. 1 (September 1935).

Marshall, Robert. "The Universe of the Wilderness is Vanishing." *Nature* 9, no. 4 (April 1937).

Mayer, Jane. *Dark Money: The Hidden History of the Billionaires behind the Rise of the Radical Right*. New York: Random House, 2016.

McCloskey, J. Michael. *In the Thick of It: My Life in the Sierra Club*. Washington, DC: Island, 2005.

McCloskey, Michael. "The Environmental Movement after Fifty Years: How Much Influence Did It Exert?" Unpublished memo, last modified March 2019. In possession of Gregg Coodley.

McCloskey, Michael. "Why Republicans Have Turned against Environmental Measures." Unpublished memo, April 2019. In possession of Gregg Coodley.

McConnell, Grant. *Private Power and American Democracy*. New York: Alfred A. Knopf, 1966.

McKibben, Bill, ed. *American Earth: Environmental Writing since Thoreau*. Washington, DC: Library of America, 2008.

McKibben, Bill. *The End of Nature*. New York: Random House, 1989.

McKibben, Bill. *Fight Global Warming Now: The Handbook for Taking Action in Your Community*. New York: Henry Holt, 2007.

McNeill, J. R. *Something New under the Sun: An Environmental History of the Twentieth-Century World*. New York: W. W. Norton, 2000.

McPhee, John. *Encounters with the Archdruid*. New York: Farrar, Straus and Giroux, 1971.

Melosi, Martin V. "Lyndon Johnson and Environmental Policy." In *Vietnam, the Environment, and Space*, vol. 2 of *The Johnson Years*, ed. Robert A. Divine, 113–149. Lawrence: University Press of Kansas, 1987.

Melosi, Martin V. *The Sanitary City: Urban Infrastructure in America from Colonial Times to the Present*. Baltimore: Johns Hopkins University Press, 2000.

Merchant, Carolyn. *The Columbia Guide to American Environmental History*. New York: Columbia University Press, 2002.

Milazzo, Paul Charles. *Unlikely Environmentalists: Congress and Clean Water, 1945–1972*. Lawrence: University Press of Kansas, 2006.

Miller, Char. *Public Lands, Public Debates: A Century of Controversy*. Corvallis: Oregon State University Press, 2012.

Miller, Char, and Hal Rothman, eds. *Out of the Woods: Essays in Environmental History*. Pittsburgh, PA: University of Pittsburgh Press, 1997.

Mooney, Chris. *The Republican War on Science*. New York: Basic Books, 2005.

Muir, John. *Our National Parks*. Boston: Houghton Mifflin, 1901.

Murray, William H. H. *Adventures in the Wilderness; Or, Camp-life in the Adirondacks*. Boston: Fields, Osgood, 1869.

Muskie, Edmund S. *Journeys*. Garden City, NY: Doubleday, 1972.

Nash, Roderick. *The American Environment: Readings in Conservation*. Reading, MA: Addison-Wesley, 1968.

Nash, Roderick. *Wilderness and the American Mind*. 3rd ed. New Haven, CT: Yale University Press, 1982.

Neal, Steve. *McNary of Oregon: A Political Biography*. Portland: Oregon Historical Society Press, 1985.

Neimark, Peninah, and Peter Rhoades Mott, eds. *The Environmental Debate*. 2nd ed. Amenia, NY: Grey House, 2011.

Olmsted, Frederick Law, Harlan Page Kelsey, et al. *The Smoke Nuisance*. Philadelphia, PA: American Civic Association, 1908.

One Third of the Nation's Land: A Report to the President and to the Congress by the Public Land Law Review Commission. Washington, DC: Public Land Law Review Commission, 1970.

Palmer, Tim. *Endangered Rivers and the Conservation Movement*. Berkeley: University of California Press, 1986.

Palmer, Tim. *Wild and Scenic Rivers: An American Legacy*. Corvallis: Oregon State University Press, 2017.

Perlstein, Rick. *Nixonland: The Rise of a President and the Fracturing of America*. New York: Scribner, 2008.

Petersen, Shannon C. *Acting for Endangered Species: The Statutory Ark*. Lawrence: University Press of Kansas, 2002.

Petulla, Joseph M. *American Environmental History: The Exploitation and Conservation of Natural Resources*. San Francisco: Boyd & Fraser, 1977.

Plater, Zygmunt. "From the Beginning, A Fundamental Shift of Paradigms: A Theory and Short History of Environmental Law." *Loyola of Los Angeles Law Review* 27, no. 3 (1994): 981–1008.

Public Papers of the Presidents of the United States: John F. Kennedy, 1961. Washington, DC: Government Printing Office, 1962.

Public Papers of the Presidents of the United States: Lyndon B. Johnson, 1965. 2 vols. Washington, DC: Government Printing Office, 1966.

Public Papers of the Presidents of the United States: Richard Nixon, 1970. Washington, DC: Government Printing Office, 1971.

Public Papers of the Presidents of the United States: Richard Nixon, 1972. Washington, DC: Government Printing Office, 1974.

Randall, Charles E. "White House Conference on Conservation." *Journal of Forestry* 60 (1962).

Reeves, Richard. *President Nixon: Alone in the White House*. New York: Simon and Schuster, 2001.

Regenstein, Lewis. *The Politics of Extinction: The Shocking Story of the World's Endangered Wildlife*. New York: Macmillan, 1975.

Rome, Adam. *The Genius of Earth Day: How a 1970 Teach-In Unexpectedly Made the First Green Generation*. New York: Hill and Wang, 2013.

Roosevelt, Theodore. "Natural Resources—Their Wise Use or Their Waste." Address at the opening of the conference on the Conservation of Natural Resources, May 13, 1908. In *Selected Speeches and Writings of Theodore Roosevelt*, edited and with an introduction by Gordon Hunter, 148–152. New York: Vintage Books, 2014.

Rosenbaum, Walter A. *The Politics of Environmental Concern*. New York: Praeger, 1973.

Roth, Dennis M. *The Wilderness Movement and the National Forests*. College Station, TX: Intaglio Press, 1988.

Ruckelshaus, William. "Environmental Regulation: The Early Days at EPA." *EPA Journal* (March 1988).

Salas, Renee, Debra Malina, and Caren Solomon. "Prioritizing Health in a Changing Climate." *New England Journal of Medicine* 381, no. 8 (2019): 773–774.

Sale, Kirkpatrick. *The Green Revolution: The American Environmental Movement, 1962–1992*. New York: Hill and Wang, 1993.

Sax, Joseph L. "The Public Trust Doctrine in Natural Resource Law: Effective Judicial Intervention." *Michigan Law Review* 68 (1970).

Scates, Shelby. *Warren G. Magnuson and the Shaping of Twentieth-Century America*. Seattle: University of Washington Press, 1997.

Schaller, Michael, and George Rising. *The Republican Ascendency: American Politics, 1968–2001*. Wheeling, IL: Harlan Davidson, 2002.

Scheffer, Victor B. *The Shaping of Environmentalism in America*. Seattle: University of Washington Press, 1991.

Schulte, Steven C. *Wayne Aspinall and the Shaping of the American West*. Boulder: University Press of Colorado, 2002.

Scott, Doug. *The Enduring Wilderness: Protecting Our Natural Heritage through the Wilderness Act*. Golden, CO: Fulcrum, 2004.

Senzel, Irving. "Genesis of a Law, Part 1." *American Forests* 84, no. 1 (1978): 30–32, 61–64.

Shabecoff, Philip. *A Fierce Green Fire: The American Environmental Movement*. New York: Hill and Wang, 1993.

Skillen, James R. *The Nation's Largest Landlord: The Bureau of Land Management in the American West*. Lawrence: University Press of Kansas, 2009.

Smith, Thomas G. *Green Republican: John Saylor and the Preservation of America's Wilderness*. Pittsburgh, PA: University of Pittsburgh Press, 2006.

Smith, Thomas G. *Stewart L. Udall: Steward of the Land*. Albuquerque: University of New Mexico Press, 2017.

Smyth, Albert Henry, ed. *The Writings of Benjamin Franklin*. By Benjamin Franklin. 10 vols. New York: Macmillan, 1905–1907.

Spankling, John G., and Gregory S. Weber. *The Law of Hazardous Wastes and Toxic Substances*. Saint Paul, MN: Thomson West, 2007.

Strong, Douglas H. *Dreamers and Defenders: American Conservationists*. Lincoln: University of Nebraska Press, 1971.

Sundquist, James L. *The Decline and Resurgence of Congress*. Washington, DC: Brookings Institution, 1981.

Sutter, Paul S. *Driven Wild: How the Fight against Automobiles Launched the Modern Wilderness Movement*. Seattle: University of Washington Press, 2002.

Thomas, Evan. *Being Nixon: A Man Divided*. New York: Random House, 2015.

Thoreau, Henry David. *Walden*. New York: New American Library, 1960.

Thoreau, Henry David. *Walden and Civil Disobedience*. New York: Signet Classics, 1960.

Train, Russell E. "An Environmental Sell-Out Will Not Turn Energy Faucets on Full." *American Lung Association Bulletin* 60, no. 2 (March 1974): 2–3.

Train, Russell. *A Memoir*. Washington, DC: Published by the author, 2000.

Train, Russell E. *Politics, Pollution, and Pandas: An Environmental Memoir*. Washington, DC: Island, 2003.

Turner, James Morton. *The Promise of Wilderness: American Environmental Politics since 1964*. Seattle: University of Washington Press, 2012.

Turner, James Morton, and Andrew C. Isenberg. *The Republican Reversal: Conservatives and the Environment from Nixon to Trump*. Cambridge, MA: Harvard University Press, 2018.

Udall, Morris K. *Too Funny to Be President*. New York: Henry Holt, 1988.

Udall, Stewart. *1976: Agenda for Tomorrow*. New York: Harcourt, Brace and World, 1968.

Udall, Stewart L. *The Quiet Crisis and the Next Generation*. Layton, UT: Gibbs Smith, 1988.

Unger, Irwin, and Debi Unger. *LBJ: A Life*. New York: John Wiley and Sons, 1999.

Updegrove, Mark K. *Indomitable Will: LBJ in the Presidency*. New York: Crown, 2012.

Walsh, John. "EPA and Toxic Substances Law: Dealing with Uncertainty." *Science* 202, no. 4368 (November 10, 1978): 598–602.

Webber, David J. *Outstanding Environmentalists of Congress*. Washington, DC: U.S. Capitol Historical Society, 2002.

Whitaker, John C. *Striking a Balance: Environment and Natural Resources Policy in the Nixon-Ford Years*. Washington, DC: American Enterprise Institute for Public Policy Research, 1976.

Whitten, Jamie L. *That We May Live*. Princeton, NJ: Van Nostrand, 1966.

Wicker, Tom. *One of Us*. New York: Random House, 1991.

"Wilderness as Minority Right." *Service Bulletin* of the US Forest Service, August 27, 1928.

Wilson, Cynthia. "Lyndon Johnson, Conservationist." *Audubon* 75 (March 1973).

Wolfe, Linne Marsh, ed. *John of the Mountains: The Unpublished Journals of John Muir*. Boston: Houghton, Mifflin, 1938.

Zeitz, Joshua. *Building the Great Society: Inside Lyndon Johnson's White House*. New York: Viking, 2018.

Zelizer, Julian E. *The Fierce Urgency of Now: Lyndon Johnson, Congress, and the Battle for the Great Society*. New York: Penguin, 2015.

Index

Aspinall, Wayne (Rep D-CO): background, 26–27, 28–29; conservationists and, 43, 46; defeated, 179, 226; environmental impact statements and, 107; Green Years and, 246, 255, 259; Lyndon B. Johnson and, 250; legislation and, 52, 175, 200–201, 202, 203, 208, 228; mining and, 33, 246; national monuments and, 82–83; National Trails System and, 81; 1964 election and, 49; oil and gas leases and, 60; Public Land Law Commission and, 229, 230; Redwoods National Park and, 74–75, 77, 78; S. Udall and, 30, 39, 46–47, 73, 83; Wilderness Act of 1964 and, 28, 33, 34–35, 38–47, 48; wild rivers bills and, 66, 67–68, 69, 70, 71–72, 73. *See also* House Interior Committee

Atlantic Ocean, 157, 201

Atomic Energy Commission (AEC), 114, 120

Audubon Societies and magazine, 12, 106, 172, 173, 187, 251, 256

auto industry: Clean Air Act of 1970 and, 126–127, 129; court cases, 152; deadlines and, 154–155; Dingell and, 15, 174; emission standards and, 234; EPA and, 123–124; hydrocarbon and carbon monoxide standards and, 143–144; Japanese, 144; Muskie and, 126–127; regulation and, 88

automobiles, 22–23, 54, 85, 86, 87, 88, 198–199, 251. *See also* catalytic converters; Clean Air Coalition; emission and fuel standards; leaded gas; roads and highways

Baker, Howard (Sen R-TN): background, 125; bi-partisanship and, 5; on catalytic converters, 127; Dingell and, 258; Green Years and, 247–248; leaving Congress, 259; legislation and, 125–126, 136–137, 196, 234; Muskie and, 125–126, 129, 254, 259; Nixon and, 148; Reagan and, 248

Baucus, Max (Rep D-MT), 218, 232

beaches, 58, 160. *See also* oil spills

beauty: education and, 54; Lyndon B. Johnson and, 50–51, 54, 56, 57, 63, 80; Lady Bird Johnson and, 53–55, 248–249; legislation and, 55–57; National Trails System and, 80; strip mining and, 221; Yellowstone and, 19–20. *See also* multiple use; wild and scenic rivers

Beverage Container Reuse and Recycling Act of 1976, 199–200

Bible, Alan (Sen D-NV), 36, 37, 220

Biden, Joseph, 244

Biological Survey, 171, 172

bi-partisanship, non-partisanship, and compromise, 4–5, 14, 126, 254–259, 266–267, 268. *See also* Clean Air Act of 1970 *and other legislation*; Democratic control of congress; environmentalists; international cooperation; Johnson, Lyndon Baines *and other compromisers*

birds, x, 156, 168, 170–173, 175, 182, 183, 185, 186. *See also* Audubon Societies and magazine; oil spills; passenger pigeons

bison (buffalo), 169–170, 236

Blatnik, John (Rep D-MN), 91–92, 95, 147, 149, 150, 244, 258

Boggs, Hale (Rep D-LA), 60, 96

Brandeis, Louis (Supreme Court), 239

Brezina, Dennis W., 6–7, 8–9, 12, 131

Brower, David. *See* Sierra Club

Brown, George (Rep D-CA), 217, 218

Bureau of Land Management (BLM), 46, 82, 228, 230–232, 238. *See also* multiple use

Bureau of Reclamation (Reclamation Service), 26, 68, 103, 212

Bureau of Solid Waste Management, 120, 198

Burton, Philip (Rep D-CA), 74, 218, 235

Bush, George H. W. and his administration, 240–241, 265

Bush, George W. and his administration, 242–243, 248, 265, 268

businesses, commercial activity and private enterprise: climate change progress and, 244; coastal areas and, 160; Earth Day and, 11; environmentalists and, 266; Environmental Policy Institute and, 111; EPA and, 121; Ford and, 260; forests and, 211; Green Years and, 263–266; legislation and, 43, 45, 129; Muskie and, 86; national parks and, 22; North Cascades National Park and, 79; public lands and, 206; Republicans and, 261. *See also* development; economic factors; fish or commercial fisheries; industries; US Chamber of Commerce

Butz, Earl (Agriculture Secretary), 152, 223

Department of Environmental and Natural
Resources, 118, 119
Department of Health, Education, and
Welfare (HEW), 87, 88, 95, 96, 119–120,
188–189, 198
deserts and prairies, 227–233, 242
detergents, 8, 90, 93, 138, 242
development: Arctic National Wildlife
Refuge and, 244; court cases and,
115; eastern national forests and, 225;
endangered species and, 170; fish and
wildlife and, 174; legislation and, 49,
71–72, 115, 181–182, 202, 207, 223–224,
236; Muskie and, 86; National Park Service and, 25; Nixon administration and,
10; Pinchot on, 212; private lands and,
206; Republicans and, 262; wetlands
and, 160; wilderness and, 43–44. *See
also* businesses, commercial activity
and private enterprise; energy choices;
railroads; roads and highways
Dingell, John (Rep D-MI): background,
174; bi-partisanship and, 256–257, 258,
259; Carter and, 260; Endangered Species
Act of 1973 and, 180, 181; Green Years and,
15, 247, 258; legislation and, 107, 110, 161,
162, 179, 202, 215; water pollution and, 92;
wetlands and, 206; Wilderness Act of 1964
and, 39, 41–42, 44, 47
Dingell Jr., John (Rep D-MI), 174
Dole, Bob (Sen R-KS), 247
Domestic Affairs Council, 100, 111
Douglas, William O. (Supreme Court), 47,
85, 115–116, 117, 118, 139, 160, 177, 229, 253
Dowie, Mark, 10, 267, 268
drought of 1963–1967, 95
ducks, 170, 172
Dudley, Barbara (Greenpeace USA),
237–238, 253, 267, 269
dumps, junkyards, and scrap dealers, 57, 143,
199, 201, 206, 237
Dust Bowl of 1930s, 227

eagles, 173, 176, 183
Earth Day of 1970: described, 1–4; effects
of, 12–13, 259; environmentalism and,
15, 124; Nelson and, 5–9, 12, 15; parti-

sanship and, 9–11; roots of, 14–16; UAW
and, 8
East, the, 30, 61, 71, 213
Eastern Wilderness Act of 1975, 224–225
Eastland, James (Sen D-MS), 115
economic factors: abandoned cars and,
199; energy choices and, 153, 263; Ford
and Carter years and, 260; Green Years
and, 14–15; industry versus EPA on,
142; Jackson and, 245; legislation and,
18, 129, 143, 155, 181, 191, 192, 197, 203;
Nixon's political choices and, 143, 145;
primitive areas and, 43; Public Land
Law Commission and, 229; Reagan and,
239; Redwoods National Park and, 76;
Republicans and, 263; Ruckelshaus's
EPA and, 120; social attitudes and, 253;
technological innovation and, 268; toxins
and, 184–185; water and, 136, 145–146;
wilderness and, 18, 24. *See also* businesses,
commercial activity and private enterprise;
development; funding and revenues;
industries; jobs; multiple use; prices;
private lands and property owners
education and awareness: beauty and, 54;
climate change and, 265–266; habitat and
animals and, 177; Lyndon B. Johnson and,
17, 54; Lady Bird Johnson and, 55; legislation
and, 13, 46, 130–132; National Park Service
and, 22; Republicans and, 262, 263
Ehrlichman, John: CEQ and, 111, 113;
Clean Air Act of 1970 and, 126–127;
economics versus environment and, 146;
Haldeman and, 108–109; insecticides
and, 190; Jackson and, 207, 208; leaving
government, 144; legislation and, 146, 147,
207, 208, 209–210; Nixon and, 100–101,
102, 104, 105–106, 109, 111, 112, 122, 135,
141–142, 145, 210; pesticides and, 189;
quality of life reviews and, 145; Train and,
108, 111, 119, 127, 158; Watergate and, 5
Eisenhower, Dwight D. and his
administration, 26, 64, 65, 91–92, 214, 257
elites, 23–24, 26, 253
elk, 20, 21
emission and fuel standards, 13, 123–124, 127,
128, 144, 153, 155, 234, 243

endangered, protected, and threatened
species: defined, 182; Dingell, and
Williams on, 181; first list of, 173; Green
Years and, 183; hardship exemptions, 176,
177; history of, 170–173; legislation and,
4, 18, 47, 237; Nixon on, 177–178, 181.
See also extinction; fish or commercial
fisheries *and other species*; habitat; Land
and Water Conservation Fund Act of 1964
and other legislation; wildlife
Endangered American Wilderness Act, 235
Endangered Species Act of 1973, 13, 168–169,
172, 177–183, 242, 244, 257–258
Endangered Species Act of 1982, 238, 248
Endangered Species Conservation Act of
1969, 175–176, 177, 178
Endangered Species Preservation Act of
1966, 174–175, 178
energy choices: clean, 22, 244, 268; Clinton's
tax and, 241–242; coastal areas and,
159–160; economic growth and, 263; Ford
and, 260; jobs and, 268; legislation and,
154–155, 208, 225, 243; Nixon and, 145,
153–155, 260; Train on, 153; the West and,
214. *See also* climate change and global
warming; coal; dams; nuclear power; oil
and other fossil fuels; utilities
Environmental Action, 13, 124, 246
Environmental Defense Fund (EDF), 114,
115, 191
Environmental Financing Authority (EFA), 134
environmental impact statements: Alaska
pipeline and, 219, 230; Aspinall and, 107;
Caldwell and, 102; CEQ and, 101, 106,
109, 110, 142; Clean Water Act of 1972
and, 149; court cases and, 116–117, 149,
230; Dreyfus and, 103; effectiveness of,
118; environmentalists and, 108, 114, 142;
ignored, 108; Jackson and, 105, 106, 107,
142; loopholes and, 109; NEPA and, 4,
102–107; Nixon and, 110, 145; nuclear
power and, 145; Sierra Club and, 108. *See
also* National Environmental Policy Act
of 1970
environmentalists: Clean Air Act of 1970
and, 127–128
environmentalists and conservationists:
activism and, 12–13; Alaska National

Interest Lands Conservation Act and, 236;
Alaska oil and, 219; Appalachian Trail
and, 80; Aspinall and, 179; compromise
and, 236, 256, 266–267; corporations and,
266; dams and, 67, 68, 69; Earth Day
and, 3–4, 11, 15; economic growth and,
14–15; environmental impact statements
and, 108, 114, 142; Green Years and, 254,
255–256, 261; legislation and, 124, 127–128,
140, 196, 208, 215, 218, 230; Muskie's waste
water proposal and, 146; national parks
and, 75–76, 77, 79; New Deal, 59; 1972
election and, 152; Nixon and, 103–104,
110, 129, 152, 216; pesticides and, 189, 190;
Reagan and, 237–238, 261; Ruckelshaus
and, 121, 144; Saylor and, 246; timber and,
216, 223; water and, 135; Wild and Scenic
Rivers Act of 1968 and, 73; Wilderness Act
of 1964 and, 25, 27, 32–33, 41, 48, 223–224.
See also activism and advocacy; Douglas,
William O. *and other environmentalists*;
media and journalism; natural resources;
Sierra Club *and other groups*
Environmental Pesticides Control Act of
1972, 190–192. *See also* pesticides
Environmental Quality Council (EQC),
10–11, 105, 107
Environmental Quality Education Act of
1970, 130–131
EPA (Environmental Protection Agency):
air pollution and, 193, 241; CEQ and,
113, 119, 122; Clean Air Acts and, 126–127,
128, 129, 241, 265; costs and, 150; Dingell
and, 247; executive agencies and, 119–121,
145; funding of, 155; hazardous waste
and, 200, 237; leaded gas and, 123, 128,
193; legislation and, 137, 140, 146–147,
150, 159, 194, 195, 196, 197–198, 200, 203;
Muskie and, 120, 248; navigable waters
and, 143; Nixon and, 120, 121, 141, 145, 154,
155, 254; partisanship and, 242; pesticides
and, 122, 189, 190, 191–192; phosphates
and, 138–139; Reagan and, 237, 238, 239,
247; regulation and, 121–124; technology
installation and, 241; Train and, 260;
Trump and, 243–244. *See also* executive
agencies; Ruckelshaus, William; Train,
Russell; Water Quality Inventory

inflation, 260

Inhofe, James (Sen R-OK), 243

insecticides. *See* pesticides

Interior Department: agencies reorganization and, 118, 119, 120; Agriculture Department and, 76, 78, 188; coastal regions and, 156–157; Commerce Department and, 201–203; economic criteria and, 229; Endangered Species Preservation Act of 1969 and, 174–175; environmental impact statements and, 102–103; fish and wildlife and parks and, 178; forests and, 210, 211, 212; Lyndon B. Johnson and, 82, 83, 250; legislation and, 150, 157, 159, 162, 163, 180, 224; oil and, 108; pesticides and, 189; poachers and, 171; poisoning ban and, 177; predator control and, 176; Proctor & Gamble and, 138; Sagebrush Rebellion and, 238; strip mining and, 221–222; Train and, 156–157; Transportation Department and, 102–103; wastewater and, 134; wildlife and, 173. *See also* Fish and Wildlife Service; National Park Service; Pacific Southeast Water Plan of 1963; Udall, Stewart

Interior Secretaries, 22, 24, 27, 59, 220; international conference on species and, 175; legislation and, 32, 37–38, 73, 133, 161, 220, 230, 231–232; mining and, 231; wildlife preservation and, 173–175. *See also* Gorsuch, Anne; Hickel, Wally; Interior Department; Watt, James

Interior Subcommittee on Irrigation and Reclamation, 27

internal combustion engine, 124, 127

Internal Revenue Service (IRS), 115

international cooperation, 138, 160, 163, 179, 201, 240, 241, 243, 269

international fisheries, 165–168

international trade, 170, 174, 175, 179

interstate commerce, 197, 206–207

irrigation, 20, 28, 29, 31, 211

Izaak Walton League, 26–27, 28, 216, 226, 246, 267

Jackson, Henry "Scoop" (Sen D-WA): Alaska bills and, 220, 236; Aspinall and, 70; background, 66–67; billboard removal and, 57; bi-partisanship and, 5, 259; Church and, 15, 67; coastal plans and, 159; Columbia River plan and, 69; Crafts and, 82–83; Cross Florida Barge Canal and, 112; Earth Day and, 11–12; Eastern Wilderness Areas Act and, 226; environmental impact statements and, 105, 106, 107, 142; Environmental Policy Institute and, 111; EPA and, 120; executive agencies conflict and, 102–103; Federal Land Policy and Management Act of 1976 and, 232; Green Years and, 245–246, 255, 259; Lyndon B. Johnson and, 47, 59, 66; Land Use Policy Act and, 205, 207, 208–209; legislation and, 80, 102–103, 117, 105, 107, 110, 215, 259, 309; on Magnuson, 247; Muskie and, 107; Nixon and, 109–110, 112, 209, 253; North Cascades National Park and, 78, 79–80; Redwoods National Park and, 75, 76, 77; Senate Interior Committee and, 245; Sierra Club and, 75, 246; M. Udall and, 236; Vietnam War view and, 148; wilderness bills and, 36, 39, 44–45, 47, 67, 224–225; wild rivers bills and, 66, 259

Japan, 161, 166, 177, 215, 248

Japanese auto industry, 144

jobs, 10, 103, 142, 150, 217, 222–223, 260, 263, 268

Johnson, Lady Bird, 53–55, 57, 58, 63, 74, 82, 94, 164, 248–249

Johnson, Lyndon Baines and his administration: background, 54–55; ceremony and history and, 47; coastal areas and, 157; compromise and, 58–59, 267; on Eisenhower, 92; "Great Society" speech and, 17, 41, 251, 256; Green Years and, 4, 15, 62–63, 249, 250–252; J. F. Kennedy and, 6, 41, 164; legacy of, 61, 82–84, 98; 1964 election and, 49, 50–51; Nixon and, 134, 164, 252; poverty and, 17, 41; T. Roosevelt and, 41, 251; the South and, 16; on technology's garbage, 88, 198. *See also* air; Aspinall, Wayne *and other legislators*; beauty *and other values*; Endangered Species Preservation Act of 1966 *and other legislation*; national parks; Vietnam War; wastewater

Michigan, 11, 12, 121, 143. *See also* auto industry; Conyers, John; Dingell, John; Dingell Jr., John

mining: acid drainage and, 98; Aspinall and, 33, 70, 246; Baring on, 43; BLM and, 228; clear-cutting/habitat and, 220–221; conservatives and, 233; Eastern Wilderness Areas Act and, 225; history of legislation and, 220–222; Interior Secretaries and, 231; National land-use policy and, 205; NEPA and, 117; Public Land Law Commission and, 229; rural lawmakers and, 255; wastes and, 221; Watt and, 237; the West and, 16, 214; Wilderness Act of 1964 and, 25, 28, 36, 40, 42, 43, 46, 65; wilderness and, 32; wild rivers bills and, 72–73; Yellowstone and, 19. *See also* multiple use; strip mining

Mississippi River, 187

Missouri, 1–2, 3, 64, 172

Mitchell, George (Sen D-ME), 240

Mitchell, John, 121

Montana, 114, 237. *See also* Baucus, Max; Melcher, John; Metcalf, Lee

Morton, Rogers (Interior Secretary), 176, 208, 220

Moss, Frank (Sen D-UT), 32–33, 75, 232

Motor Vehicle Air Pollution Control Act of 1965, 88

Muir, John, x, 20, 22, 213

Muir Woods National Monument, 74

multiple use: Aspinall and, 33, 34–35; BLM and, 228, 229–232; CEQ and, 113; compromise and, 267; economic uses versus, 229; established/previous uses and, 28, 223–224; Forest Service and, 214; legislation and, 25–26, 28, 215, 223, 228; North Cascades National Park and, 78; Roadless Area Review and Evaluation and, 223. *See also* timber, logging, and timber companies *and other uses*

Muskie, Edmund (Sen D-ME): agencies reorganization and, 119; air and, 85, 86, 94, 126–128; air pollution and, 89; auto industry and, 126–127; background, 86–87, 93; Baker and, 125, 126, 254, 259; bi-partisanship and, 254, 257; Boggs and, 96; Clean Air Acts and, 129, 151, 234, 248, 259; Clean Water Act of 1972 and, 147, 151, 248, 259; consensus and, 146; detailed statutes and, 128–129; Earth Day and, 2–3; EPA and, 120, 248; Green Years and, 248, 257; international fisheries and, 165–166; Jackson and, 107; leaving senate, 258; legislation and, 155, 199, 215; Nixon and, 104, 124–125, 128, 135, 145–146, 147, 148, 151, 199, 203–204, 253, 254; S. Udall and, 64; water and, 93–95, 97, 107, 135–136, 145–146; Water Quality Improvement Act of 1970 and, 137. *See also* Senate Subcommittee on Air and Water Pollution

Nader, Ralph, 124, 164

NASA, 120, 241

National Academy of Sciences, 128, 148

National Air Pollution Control Administration, 120

National Association of Audubon Societies, 172

National Association of Manufacturers, 53, 147

National Education Association, 131

National Environmental Policy Act (NEPA) of 1970: bi-partisanship and, 257–258; CEQ and, 152–153; courts and, 114–118, 153; Dingell and, 174, 257; Jackson and, 259; negotiated and passed, 101–111; Nixon and, 109, 142, 154, 252; presidents and, 113; Water Quality Improvement Act of 1970 and, 149. *See also* CEQ; environmental impact statements; Jackson, Henry "Scoop"

national forests: eastern, 223–226; funding for, 31, 212; history of, 210–215; land area of, 215; multiple use and, 26; North Cascades National Park and, 78; number of visitors to, 25; roads and, 22–23; F. D. Roosevelt and, 214; Wilderness Act of 1964 and, 28, 48

National Forest Wild Areas Act, 224

national historic parks, 84

National Historic Preservation Act of 1965, 58

National Industrial Pollution Control Council, 138

National Land Use Policy bill (1970), 207–210

national monuments, 20, 21, 27, 31, 37–38, 82, 83, 131, 236, 256–257. *See also*

Senate Commerce Committee, 159, 164, 178, 187, 190, 191, 195, 246, 259. *See also* Magnuson, Warren

Senate Interior Committee: Alaska Native Claims Settlement Act of 1971 and, 220; coastal regions and, 157, 159–160; Eastern Wilderness Areas Act and, 225; Grand Canyon dams bill and, 70; Land Use Policy Act and, 209; National Environmental Policy Act of 1970 and, 103, 106; National Trails System and, 81; public lands commission and, 39, 43; Redwoods National Park and, 75; Wilderness Act of 1964 and, 224. *See also* Jackson, Henry "Scoop"

Senate Public Works Committee, 56, 89, 94–95, 135, 136–137, 146, 153

Senate Select Committee on National Water Resources, 64, 92

Senate Subcommittee on Air and Water Pollution, 87, 94–95, 125–127, 135–137, 156, 255. *See also* Muskie, Edmund

Senate Subcommittee on Irrigation and Reclamation, 31

Senate Subcommittee on the Environment, 178, 190–191

Sequoia National Park, 20, 115, 116

sewage. *See* wastewater

Sheridan, Philip, 169, 170

ships, 98, 116, 133, 201. *See also* fish or commercial fisheries

Sierra Club: Alaska Native Claims Settlement Act of 1971 and, 220; on bi-partisanship, 257; bi-partisanship and, 254; citizen suits and, 191; on climate change, 269; dams and, 68–69; economic factors and, 14–15; Endangered Species Act of 1973 and, 182; environmental impact statements and, 108; Green Years and, 16, 255–256; Jackson and Saylor and, 246; jobs and, 263; Lyndon B. Johnson and, 251; Land Use Policy Act and, 208; Leopold and, 32; Muir and, 20, 22, 213; multiple use and, 229; Nixon and, 253; on ozone layer, 240; primitive areas and, 25; on public opinion, 268; Redwood National Park and, 74–75, 77–78; on Republicans/Democrats, 262; road

forward and, 266; on roadless acreage, 238; Ruckelshaus and, 144; timber bill and, 215; wilderness bills and, 27, 28, 34, 48, 224–225

Sierra Club Legal Defense Fund, 114, 115, 116, 118, 216, 217, 223

Silent Spring (Carson), 16, 186–187, 188, 254

Simpson, Alan (Sen R-WY), 238, 258

ski resorts, 43, 115, 116

smokestacks, 127, 155

soil, 2, 134, 214, 218, 227–228, 237. *See also* erosion

solid waste, 8, 11, 152, 198–201, 204. *See also* automobiles; dumps, junkyards, and scrap dealers; recycling

Solid Waste Disposal Act of 1965, 198, 251

solitude, 19, 45

Soviet Union (Russia), 141, 143, 164, 165–166, 245

standard of living, 33

Stans, Maurice (Commerce Secretary), 127, 129, 143

state parks, 5–6, 30, 61, 74, 76, 77

states: air pollution and, 87, 88, 89; Aspinall and, 246; billboard removal and, 57; Boggs and Saylor on, 60; Clean Air Act of 1970 and, 128; climate change progress and, 244; Coastal Zone Management Act of 1972 and, 158–159; drinking water and, 193; Earth Day and, 3; elections and, 13, 152, 158–159; Endangered Species Act of 1973 and, 179; federal control and, 60, 193–194; fire control program and, 213; funding for recreation facilities and, 53, 61; insecticides and, 190; Interior Committees and, 157; Land Use Policy Act and, 207–208, 209, 210; MMPA and, 162; NEPA and, 117; Nixon and, 130, 151; oceans and, 157; permits and, 146–147; political change and, x; public lands and, 244; Refuse Act Permit Program and, 140; rivers and, 65; T. Roosevelt's conference and, 212; Safe Drinking Water Act of 1974 and, 194; solid waste planning costs and, 199; wastewater and, 90, 91, 98, 135, 145; water pollution and, 92, 97; water quality standards and, 136; wild animals and, 171; wilderness and, 20. *See also* Alaska; California *and other states*

steel industry, 57, 198–199
Steiger, Sam (Rep R-AZ), 72, 209, 230, 231
Stevens, Ted (Sen R-AK), 165, 178, 179
strip mining, 13, 54, 114, 221–223, 229, 235
sulfur, sulfuric acid, and sulfur oxides, 11, 96, 113, 153–154, 155, 240–241
Superfund, 200, 236–237, 238
supersonic transport planes, 11, 245
Supreme Court: Arizona water case and, 67; auto companies and, 144; federal oversight and, 239; Fifth Amendment to Constitution and, 239; on global warming, 243; Grand Canyon and, 21; impoundments and, 151; industrial waste and, 139; Muskie and, 248; "one man, one vote" decision of, 255; oysters and, 171; wildlife and, 172. *See also* Douglas, William O. *and other justices*
surgeon general, 138
swimming, 136, 137–138, 149. *See also* beaches; lakes

Taft, Howard and his administration, 213
Talmadge, Herman (Sen D-GA), 224, 225
taxes: cigarette, 5–6; Clean Water Act of 1972 and, 151; energy and, 241–242; fishing and, 173; Nixon and, 150; property owners and, 206; recycling and, 199; Republican donors and, 265; Superfund and, 236; timberlands and, 213; wetlands and, 160
Taylor, Roy (Rep D-NC), 60, 79
technology, 16, 125, 126–127, 143, 146, 148, 198, 200, 253, 268. *See also* Office of Science and Technology
television, 10, 95, 126, 176, 187, 193, 265, 269
Tennessee, 182. *See also* Baker, Howard
Texas, 60, 210. *See also* Poage, William
thermal pollution, 98, 133
throwaway containers, 11, 185, 199–200
Thurmond, Strom (Sen R-SC), 166, 196
timber, logging, and timber companies: Adirondack Park and, 20; Aspinall and, 34–35; Baring and, 43; clear-cutting and, 216, 217, 218, 220–221; conservatives and, 233; deforestation and, 210; drop in harvests and, 218–219; Forest Service and, 214, 215–216, 217, 223; legislation and, 72–73, 117, 215–216, 217–219; manufacturers of, 53, 143,

216, 247; national forests and, 215; National land-use policy and, 205; Nixon and, 216; primitive areas and, 23, 215–216; public opinion and, 65; Reagan and, 238; recreation and, 216; Redwoods National Park and, 74, 77; roadless areas and, 223; user fees and, 212; water quality standards and, 136; the West and, 214; Wilderness Act of 1964 and, 25, 28, 32, 46, 215; wilderness and, 20; wildlife and, 216. *See also* multiple use; non-point source pollution
tobacco industry, 264, 266
Tongass National Forest, 236
tourism, 22–23, 73, 93
toxic pollutants, 4, 86, 113, 117, 149, 151, 184–204, 243. *See also* chemicals; mercury
Toxic Substances Control Act of 1976 (TOSCA), 195–198
Train, Russell: agencies reorganization and, 119; on air and water standards, 113; Carter and, 260; on catalytic converters, 153; CEQ and, 110, 113–114; chemicals and, 195; Clean Air Act of 1970 and, 154; coastal regions and, 157; costs and, 114, 145; Ehrlichman and, 108, 111, 119, 127, 158, 210; energy choices and, 153; environmental impact statements and, 108, 142; at EPA, 122, 153, 154–155; on executive agencies, 110–111; Ford and, 222, 260; Green Years and, 244; Hickel and, 109; industry and, 143; Interior Department and, 156–157; Lyndon B. Johnson and, 101; Kerry and, 242; legislation and, 106, 113–114, 137, 146, 190, 194, 198, 210, 222–223; multiple use and, 229; national land-use policy and, 207; Nixon and, 111, 112, 128, 129, 145, 151, 153, 154, 155, 252; oil spills and, 108; pesticides and, 192; Poage and, 176; predator control and, 176; on Reagan, 238; Ruckelshaus and, 121, 122; Sierra Club and, 108; United States-Canada Working Group and, 138; Water Quality Improvement Act of 1970 and, 137–138. *See also* CEQ
Truman, Harry and his administration, 31, 163–164, 257, 268
Trump, Donald, 115, 118, 155, 243–244, 247, 263, 268

trust in government, 14, 242–243, 257, 263
Tunny, John (Sen D-CA), 135–136, 195

Udall, Morris (Rep D-AZ; House Interior
Committee chair), 15, 30, 71, 77, 162, 209,
220, 223, 236
Udall, Stewart (Rep D-AZ; Interior
Secretary): agency reorganization and, 118;
Alaska Native Claims Settlement Act of
1971 and, 220; Aspinall and, 30, 39, 46–47,
73; background, 29–30; BLM and, 228; on
Cleveland's forest policy, 211; dams and,
30, 64, 68, 69–70; on environmentalists,
124; environmentalists and, 68; forests
and, 28, 29, 210–213; Green Years and,
4, 244–245, 257; habitat and, 174, 177;
Hayden and, 68; Interior Department
and, 61; Lyndon B. Johnson and, 40–41,
51, 59, 62, 63, 65, 82–83, 84, 250–251, 252;
J. F. Kennedy and, 29–30, 34, 35–36; land
acquisitions and, 59–60, 75; on legislative
momentum, 53–54; marine mammals
and, 161; mining and, 221; national
parks and, 76, 77; national parks and
monuments and, 74, 79, 82–83; offshore
drillings and, 104; open space and, 206;
outdoor recreation and, 5–6; pesticides
and, 187–189; predators and, 173; *The
Quiet Crisis and the Next Generation*, 20,
40, 64–65; Reagan and, 239; on shoreline
recreation, 58; URRRC report and, 33–34;
wastewater and, 98; the West and, 70, 255;
on wilderness, 40; Wilderness Act of 1964
and, 20, 25–26, 28, 30, 35–36, 44, 46–47,
49; wild rivers bills and, 72, 73
unions, 3, 7–8, 9, 56, 94, 196, 223, 246. *See
also* National Education Association
United Nations, 3, 165, 166–167, 201
US Army, 173. *See also* Army Corps of
Engineers
US Chamber of Commerce, 96, 98, 142
used cars, 128
utilities, 11, 194, 240–241. *See also* energy
choices

Vietnam War: Agent Orange and,
190; Aiken and, 225; Church and,
245; disenfranchisement and, 255;
environmental regulation and, 148;
Jackson and, 66; Lyndon B. Johnson and,
15, 41, 50, 62, 66, 84; Nelson and, 6, 7,
246; Nixon and, 100, 142; preservation
and recreation spending and, 52; water
pollution costs compared, 3
Voyageurs National Park, 131

Washington, DC, 3, 10, 55
Washington Post, 42, 46, 60, 117, 195, 200
Washington state, 2, 3, 7, 12, 20, 34, 78–79,
116, 122, 159, 165. *See also* Jackson, Henry
"Scoop"; North Cascades National Park;
Pacific Northwest
wastewater (agricultural, industrial, and
sewage): Carter and, 235; costs and,
92, 96–97, 98, 136, 145–146, 150, 155;
economics versus environment and, 146;
Eisenhower and, 91–92; EPA and, 121;
funding and, 90, 91–92, 94, 95, 96–97,
98, 134, 135, 145–146, 155, 235; history of,
89–93, 204; industry and, 91, 95; Lyndon
B. Johnson and, 17, 54, 58, 59, 70, 92–98,
250, 251; land purchases and, 59; League
of Women voters and, 254; legislation
and, 4, 18, 107, 133, 235; mining and, 221;
Muskie and, 93–95, 107, 135–136, 145–146;
national study of, 70; Nixon and, 106,
112, 113, 133–140, 145–158; public lands
and, 211; Reagan and, 97, 239; recreation
and, 7–8; standards for, 137, 149, 174,
194; studies and, 133. *See also* Clean Water
Act of 1972 *and other legislation*; fish or
commercial fisheries; irrigation; Nelson,
Gaylord *and other legislators*; non-point
source pollution; oceans, seas, and marine
policy; oil spills; rivers and streams
Watergate, 4, 5, 15, 16, 152–153, 154, 155,
209–210, 225, 247
Water Pollution Control Acts, 90–92, 93,
96, 128–129
Water Quality Acts, 95–96, 111, 133–139,
149
Water Quality Inventory (2000), 155
Watt, James (Interior Secretary), 237, 246
Weaver, Jim (Rep D-OR), ix, 217, 218
Weeks Act of 1911, 75, 213, 214
Weeks-McLean Act of 1913, 172